The Political Economy of Greek Growth up to 2030

Series Editor
Panagiotis E. Petrakis
Department of Economics
National and Kapodistrian University of Athens
Athens, Greece

This book series analyzes the medium to long-term prospects of Greece's political economy by studying concepts such as sustainability, sustainable governance and political functioning, economic inclusivity, cultural behaviors, and economic dynamic growth through an evolutionary approach. This series also publishes policy-oriented books outlining steps for increased economic growth and a sustainable future for the Greek economy. This series stands out in that the books depict the conditions that must prevail for the Greek economy to escape the economic stagnation that has lingered from persistent economic recession.

Using Greece as a lens to discuss pressing questions, this series will be of interest to economists interested in Eurozone policies, economic growth, evolutionary economics, and more.

More information about this series at
http://www.palgrave.com/gp/series/16496

Panagiotis E. Petrakis

The New Political Economy of Greece up to 2030

palgrave
macmillan

Panagiotis E. Petrakis
Department of Economics
National and Kapodistrian University of Athens
Athens, Greece

ISSN 2662-7248 ISSN 2662-7256 (electronic)
The Political Economy of Greek Growth up to 2030
ISBN 978-3-030-47074-6 ISBN 978-3-030-47075-3 (eBook)
https://doi.org/10.1007/978-3-030-47075-3

This Palgrave Macmillan imprint is published by the registered company Springer Nature Switzerland AG
The registered company address is: Gewerbestrasse 11, 6330 Cham, Switzerland

Preface

The series of books with the general title of *The Political Economy of Greek Growth up to 2030* analyze the medium- to long-term prospects of the Greek reality—including the Covid-19 pandemic—in view of the political economy. They combine the notions of sustainability, sustainable governance and political operation, the inclusivity of the economic system, and cultural behavior, with the requirements of economic dynamic growth. The concurrent influence from those five areas, through suitable structural reforms, is a necessary prerequisite to change the production prototype of the Greek economy, which will ensure a medium- and long-term economic development and growth. This viewpoint has an evolutionary foundation. The view supported is that conditions can be created for the Greek economy, after the 2008 depression, to avoid losing another decade due to Covid-19 and to create the necessary conditions for a great growth transformation up to 2030.

The target of this book series, presented in successive volumes, is to assess the current situation of the Greek economy and detect future potential for development and growth, particularly on a medium- to long-term horizon. It represents the next step in a series of books, *The Greek Economy and the Crisis, Challenges and Responses*, P. E. Petrakis (2011), New York and Heidelberg, Springer; and *A New Growth Model for the Greek Economy: Requirements for the Long-Term Sustainability*, P. E. Petrakis (2016), New York, Palgrave Macmillan. These books marked the conditions in which the Greek economy entered Great Depression

(2008–2018) and put forth initial thoughts on exiting the crisis. In this current book series, conditions for the exit of the economy from the crisis are analyzed, along with its entry into a new period of development and growth.

In this first book of the series, *The Political Economy of the Greek Growth up to 2030*, the possible application of development theory and politics in the Greek economy is examined. This sets the theoretical framework for an empirical analysis that follows. It will be shown that after Covid-19, a rare window of opportunity for economic growth can be created due to Europe's approach of dealing with the 2020 financial crisis (monetary and fiscal easing) and the disciplined way in which the pandemic was successfully addressed in Greece, a rare opportunity in the 200 years of the modern Greek state's existence. This window of opportunity is based on four pillars: social discipline and safe progress (as a result of a successful epidemiological policy), economic policy reform, fiscal and monetary easing and strengthening, and prior (before Covid-19) fiscal discipline and the recovery of reliability of the economy's administration.

The following books deal successively with economic growth including the Covid-19 crisis and focus on how a lost decade can be avoided by emphasizing on structural reforms and fiscal management, cultural background related to the way individuals and society make their decisions .The analyses and the resulting projections run through to 2030.

The second book in the series, under the title *The Evolution of the Greek Economy: Past Challenges and Future Approaches* addresses successively the issues of what we call "normality" in the Greek economy by the beginning of 2020 when the COVID-19 great recession occurred and how to exceed this "normality," which has now incorporated two major recessions: those of 2010 and 2020. The emphasis is on structural reforms and fiscal management, on the cultural background on how people and society make their decisions. Attention is also paid to analysing the productive organization of the economy on the basis of its technological structure and the use of input-output tables, the role of power centers, power pooling, and oligopolistic organization of the economy, etc. The analyses, as well as the accompanying projections, extend up to 2030.

In the third book of the series, under the title *Policies for a Stronger Greek Economy: Actions for the Next Decade*, the conditions for the implementation of policies (fiscal, monetary, but mainly reforms) that are necessary for the Greek economy to enter -after the Covid-19 crisis- in a decade of economic growth are presented. To do this, as has been pointed out in the previous two volumes, policies must be developed in six areas: Policies for immediate action, mainly monetary and fiscal policies aimed at meeting the production gap in the short and medium term. In the medium and the long term, policies are developed on five issues: sustainability policies, sustainable governance policies, enhanced inclusivity policies, pro-growth social behavior policies, and policies for dynamic economic growth with medium- and long-term horizon. Moreover, a simulation of the policy implementation is provided, as well as a risk assessment and a scenario analysis presenting five different scenarios for the Greek economy (normal, optimal, European growth I, European growth II, and downside), as well as the possibility for the Greek economy to join a third wave of growth after 2021 and by 2030.

Athens, Greece　　　　Panagiotis E. Petrakis

Acknowledgments This book was based on the scientific contribution of my research team consisting of Dr. K. I. Kafka, Dr. P. C. Kostis, and Researcher D. G. Valsamis, with the valuable cooperation of Mr. G. Vasilis, Mr. M. Skotoris, and Mr. M. Chatzigakis. The language editing was done by Mr. S. Bouras. My key collaborator, Ms. E. Giouli, as well as the other colleagues in my office, offered me the opportunity to complete my research. The National and Kapodistrian University of Athens offered its support. My family offered me her patience.

Introduction

From 1830 until today, the Greek economy has experienced two significant waves of growth. In order for a period to be labeled as growth wave, two conditions have to be met: the occurrence of high growth, along with access to international capital markets. The first was between 1902 and 1914, the period which had described as "unseen prosperity" and the second, that had a much larger duration, was during the 1970s through to 2007. The second one was supported by broadening consumption spending and the expansion of the construction activity. Both waves were cut off by a large crisis that brought on a sharp drop in growth and then access to international capital markets was lost. The second wave even experienced two overlapping crises, as after the first one in 2008–2020 followed that of Covid-19 (2020).

The goal of this current book series is to look into whether, after the end of the second crisis of the twenty-first century, Covid-19, the Greek economy is headed into a third long wave of growth in the medium to long term that will be supported by a model of efficiency/demand and the conditions under which this could arise.

At the core of the analysis is the finding that the very large and non-reversible global evolutions that include certain characteristics, such as technological progress, longer life expectancy, and climate change, are expected to affect a series of productive areas—for instance the pharmaceuticals industry, agriculture, transport, recreation—which the Greek economy has an important presence in. The difference with previous cycles of global development is that in the past there was no room for the features of the Greek economy to unfold, as expansion came on the back of industrialization, and later information technology—both structural characteristics that are foreign to the abilities and the pattern of Greek productive system. Adversely, today's era involves the decapitalization of the productive process (tangibles versus intangibles) and the servitization of economies, creating more favorable conditions of adjustment and development of international changes, despite the consequences of Covid-19 crisis and the fact that basic developmental disadvantages continue to exist in Greek economy.

The Covid-19 crisis is being treated by this study as exogenous, related to the economy, a phenomenon that has increased the systemic risk with fast-deep-medium-term lasting economic downsizing effects, eventually having fading and negative consequences. Its basic character is consistent mainly as an accelerator and amplifier of lasting long-term socioeconomic tendencies, with a relatively limited game changer character in same resheets of socio and economic life. In the same time, the successful mitigate of the first phase of outbreak unleashed and created a new condition mainly in the trust of general public in institutions and government, which is a basic catalyst for a medium- and long-term growth.

Additionally, Greece's geographic position is and will be of crucial importance, outlining the border points separating Western Europe from eastern regions of the world that reach until China (Belt and Road Initiative) and Northern Africa. This creates development potential, given the upcoming development of Eastern European countries and the Balkans, along with the developing African continent and developed Middle East. Unfortunately, these regions are politically and economically unstable and, at the same time, create conditions that raise the economy's systemic risk, despite opening the door to opportunities that may play a decisive role in the future.

It can be noted then, that the Greek economy has a particular position (with positive and negative risks) among these emerging economic changes. From one point of view, development opportunities are given, while at the same time, serious risks will arise, since these crucial segments of the economy can suffer, if proper adjustments are not made. Given these conditions, some additional information must be taken into account that will give a positive direction to future development. The first is that the Greek economy came out of a long period of economic discipline—that came with a serious social cost—providing a balance in fiscal policy and trade payments, in addition to the reorganization of the production process. This gives it the opportunity to address the Covid-19 crisis from a more favorable position, taking into account the successful management of the first phase of the crisis (early 2020). The second relates to geostrategic shifts in the Eastern Mediterranean region that rests on three continents, in parallel with interest for hydrocarbon reserves and the transport of energy resources toward the European market. This is in contrast with energy supply routes entering through Europe's northern borders. At this point, we must add that the risk of uncertainty brought about by choices from global superpowers, such as a drop in interest in the broader region by the United States (due to its growing energy independence), and the increase in Russian interest in its bid to influence southern energy channels feeding the European economy. The third relates to Greek culture which is based on humanism. If combined with the upcoming technological revolution, this can give the Greek economy a unique rebranding opportunity in the international economy. Finally, the fourth point relates to exceptional ties between the Greek economy and the so-called blue economy (shipping, sea sports, and tourism) due to its relationship with the historically privileged sea element and Mediterranean Sea. The Covid crisis will delay globalization but will not eventually reverse it. By the end of the current decade it is very probable that it will be intensified again under China's influence.

But there are also negative factors in the medium- to long-term road ahead. Among them we must include delays in adopting technology, the lack of highly trained workers, and a socioeconomic mix that provides strong cultural resistance amidst a complex institutional and social framework and the geostrategic risks.

If the Greek economy manages to show a stronger growth rate than the Eurozone (decoupling), then it will have achieved three goals: to close part or all of the gap created by the country's big crises (2008, 2020), in comparison with prosperity levels enjoyed by Greeks ahead of the crisis; to approach the development levels of Eurozone partners (convergence), reigniting interest shown by Greeks in European affairs; and to turn into a focal point (as a good example) for foreign capital in comparison with its partners, a fact that would allow for the faster achievement of the above two goals.

In this process of (again) convergence likely to be activated, the fact that the Greek economy is starting from such a low point will help. The final results that will appear on long-term Greek growth depend on the impact from all of the above factors, in combination with political developments and the role played by political powers.

This current series of books aims to contribute toward the implementation of policies that could lead to a path of expansion.

The broader economic environment in the Eurozone—which Greece is a part of—is exceptionally well-organized, especially after (May 2020) the great European response to Covid-19, securing a stable general operating framework. Therefore, it is particularly likely that the Greek economy will head eventually toward a third wave of growth. However, we believe that there are two more scenarios that may arise ahead, in addition to the good one. The first one involves the continued dominance of populism in the Greek political scene, which will lead to an excessively large role played by the political system. The political element does not necessarily secure the efficient distribution of resources in the economy. This might not be enough to prompt an anti-systemic diversion, but this does not mean that the resources will be distributed in the most efficient and fair manner.

The peculiar populism that appears to filter through a significant part of the Greek political system has its roots in the autocratic regime of the seven years dictatorship government (1967–1974), which used it in its attempt to keep a political grip on the community. The regime's fall from power was combined with overriding views in the democratic political system that pledged an equivalent center-left employee policy to improve economic prosperity levels. This came with an economic policy based on promises, though in a different political direction. Meanwhile, there were very high capital inflows during this period that indeed helped raise the level of the people's prosperity, albeit without the introduction of a sustainable production model. This was maintained until the euro prosperity period (2000–2008), where the same results were recorded, i.e., an inflow of cheap capital led to growing volumes in non-market sectors (constructions), pushing public debt higher.

As a result, the political background of populism was maintained until our time, regardless of the fact that economic policy has been rationalized out of necessity due to the existence of Memorandums (2010–2018) and the needs of the Covid-19 crisis. The difference is that during 1974–2008, populism was fed by continual promises for improvement to living standards, on the back of favorable conditions (European funding and cheap euros), whereas after 2008 until today, it was based on the denial of domestic loan obligations that largely consist of the need for capital outflows and strict fiscal rules of management.

The second scenario involves the possibility of continued political turmoil, with the winners and losers being unclear. This situation will undermine whatever momentum the economy acquires. If we add to this progress the ambiguity from Europe's political elite on the prospects of the European project and an international environment of turmoil that puts upward pressure on military spending, then it is possible that its future prospects may be harmed.

In conclusion, the fact that there is a potential window of opportunity does not mean that the Greek economy will use it, as domestic restraints (in contrast with the domestic promotional factors of economic theory) and/or unexpected events may prevent this from happening.

The writer is neither optimistic, nor pessimistic. Pragmatism, however, leads to the acceptance that there are basic reasons to hope that the positive prospects are an important opportunity and that we must work to achieve it The second wave of growth took 35 years to peak and we cannot know how much time the third one will require, that will be the fruit of a double depression.

Social energy therefore must be channeled toward shaping the content of the development framework. Policy will ensure that it will give what is needed to make it a hopeful platform of prosperity, particularly for younger generations, by activating the positive catalysts it contains.

For Greece, however, to follow this third wave of growth, it will need to broaden and locate, promote, and cultivate the basic elements of the Greek social and production model, its administration method, development characteristics, and available resources, in line with respective characteristics seen in the international environment. These are traits that can promote or hold back the Greek economy. Finally, it is necessary to understand basic consistent parameters of social behavior. Under this prism, suitable policies must be adopted that will strengthen the positive scenarios, weakening the negative ones. This exercise is one of the basic issues of these books.

This first volume consists of three parts. The first part includes four chapters. The first chapter has an introductory and methodological nature. The second is concerned with the intertemporal issue of connecting theory and policy and the effects of this connection for economic development and growth. The third is concerned with the position of the Greek economy as a member of the Eurozone. The fourth chapter describes how integrated development and growth of the Greek economy are understood, according to perceptions presented in all of the books in the series *The Political Economy of Greek Growth up to 2030*. The second part of the volume includes a brief presentation of the Greek economy in the world (in the fifth chapter) and outlines inevitable future trends in the Greek and global economy at three levels: large macrosocial trends (Chapter 6), large macroeconomic trends (Chapter 7), and political mega trends (Chapter 8). Amidst all these long-term prospects, Greece's relative position is outlined with mostly qualitative comments, taking into account the recessionary effects of the Covid-19 crisis. The third part of the first volume relates to primary sources of growth, policies, and development policies in an era of low growth, inflation, and unemployment. The ninth chapter relates to sources of growth, the tenth with the endogenous growth logic, the eleventh with macroeconomic policies in the new era, and the twelfth with economic policy in times of low growth, inflation, and employment in the Greek economy. Finally, the thirteenth chapter refers to the vulnerability of the Greek economy and the recovery requirements of the Covid-19.

Contents

Abbreviations

AADE	Independent Authority for Public Revenue
AD	Aggregate Demand
AGS	Annual Growth Survey
AI	Artificial Intelligence
AMR	Alert Mechanism Report
APP	Asset Purchase Program
BN	Billions
BoG	Bank of Greece
BP	Base Points
BRICS	Brazil, Russia, India, China and South Africa
CEPR	Centre for Economic Policy Research
CHES	Chapel Hill Expert Survey
CO2	Carbon Dioxide
CRII	Corona Response Investment Initiative
CSPP	Corporate Sector Purchase Program
DEKO	Public Enterprises and Organizations
EAP	Economic Adjustment Program
EBRD	European Bank for Reconstruction and Development
ECB	European Central Bank
ECCL	Enhanced Conditions Credit Line
ECI	Economic Complexity Index
ECOFIN	Economic and Financial Affairs Council
EFSF	European Financial Stability Facility
EIF	European Investment Fund
EIP	Excessive Imbalance Procedure
ELSTAT	Hellenic Statistical Authority Hellenic Statistical Authority

EMU	Economic and Monetary Union
ES	European Semester
ESA	European System of Account
ESEE	Hellenic Confederation of Commerce and Entrepreneurship
ESM	European Stability Mechanism
GDP	Gross Domestic Product
GFNs	Gross Financial Needs
GHG	Greenhouse Gas
GSEVEE	Hellenic Confederation of Professionals, Craftsmen and Merchants
HCAP	The Hellenic Corporation of Assets and Participations
HCPI	Harmonized Consumer Price Index
HDI	Human Development Index
HFA	Household Financial Assets
HFSF	Hellenic Financial Stability Fund
HH	Herfindahl-Hirschman
ICT	Information and Communications Technology
IFRS	International Financial Reporting Standard
IMF	International Monetary Fund
IOBE	Foundation for Economic and Industrial Research
IoT	Internet of Things
IRR	Internal Rate of Return
IT	Information Technology
JER	Joint Employment Report
JVR	Job Vacancy Rate
KEPE	Centre of Planning and Economic Research
LCR	Liquidity Coverage Ratio
LTRO	Long-Term Refinancing Operations
MFF	Multiannual Financial Framework
MoU	Memorandum of Understanding
MPK	Marginal Product of Capital
MRO	Main Refinancing Operations
NAIRU	Non-Accelerating Inflation Rate of Unemployment
NATO	North Atlantic Treaty Organization
NBER	National Bureau of Economic Research
NIIP	Net International Investment Position
NKUA	National and Kapodistrian University of Athens
OCA	Optimal Currency Area
OECD	Organisation for Economic Co-operation and Development
OKA	Social Security Organization
OMT	Outright Money Transactions
OTA	Local Government Organization
P2R	Pillar 2 Requirement

PELTROs	Pandemic Emergency Longer-Term Refinancing Operations
PEPP	Pandemic Emergency Purchase Program
PFY	Primary Health Care
PIAAC	Programme for the International Assessment of Adult Competencies
PPP	Purchasing Power Parity
PSI	Private Sector Investment
QE	Quantitative Easing
R&D	Research and Development
RBC	Real Business-Cycle
RCP	Representative Concentration Pathway
REACT-EU	Recovery Assistance for Cohesion and the Territories of Europe
RMB	Renminbi
SBA	Stand-By Agreement
SDGs	Sustainable Development Goals
SETE	Greek Tourism Confederation
SEV	Hellenic Federation of Enterprises
SMEs	Small and Medium-Sized Enterprises
SOFI	State of the Future Index
SRES	Special Report on Emissions Scenarios
SSM	Single Supervisory Mechanism
SURE	Support to Mitigate Unemployment Risks in an Emergency
TAP	Timbro Authoritarian Populism Index
TARGET2	Trans-European Automated Real-time Gross Settlement Express Transfer System
TEE-TCG	Technical Chamber of Greece
TFP	Total Factor Productivity
TLTRO	Targeted Longer-Term Refinancing Operations
UGS	Union of Greek Shipowners
UN	United Nations
USD	US Dollars
VIX	Volatility Index
WEF	World Economic Forum
WTO	World Trade Organization

List of Figures

List of Tables

PART I

The Theoretical Principles of Integrated Growth and Development of the Greek Economy

CHAPTER 1

Introductory Chapter

1.1 Introduction

The introductory chapter aims at making this book easier to read, by explaining the rules of the game in a way that facilitates the grasping of ideas often useful in following a book like this with concepts, hypotheses and assumptions. It also aims at specifying the standing point from which the author deals with basic conceptual issues. This way, the opportunity arises for readers to utilize their own views in evaluating points of discussion.

This chapter lists methodological principles (Sect. 1.2), basic theoretical assumptions (Sect. 1.3), and the fundamental analytical approach (Sect. 1.4) on which the book is based on. Additionally, the influence of prevailing ideology in basic aspects of development and growth is highlighted (Sect. 1.5), as well as the role of forecasts in shaping and predicting economic reality (Sect. 1.6).

1.2 The Methodological Principles

Development is when the effectiveness of the social and financial system improves and, subsequently, the quality of life gets better. It is about a broader, qualitative concept, which does not focus on gross domestic product (GDP) expansion, but rather on the improvement to prosperity. When the potential of an economy grows beyond the point marked by the

P. E. Petrakis, *The New Political Economy of Greece up to 2030*, The Political Economy of Greek Growth up to 2030, https://doi.org/10.1007/978-3-030-47075-3_1

full employment of its productive contributors, we assume that growth conditions of its productive capacity are formed. We can, however, also have growth of the productive capacity when there is a productivity gap, namely, when productive contributors are not fully employed.

In this book, the terms "development" and "growth" are used interchangeably. Development is a broad concept and refers to the increasing change of key factors and resources relating to a country's expansion, such as human capital in qualitative dimensions (education, health, training, etc.), the state of its productive capacity, the quality of institutions, the way wealth is distributed in the economy, and the general well-being of citizens. Growth refers solely to the incremental change of production, namely GDP, a quantitative variable.

It is, therefore, obvious that the authors need to adopt a perception of economic shifts based on the principles of understanding human actions as an influence of change. In these books from the series *The Political Economy of the Greek Growth up to 2030*, the people of the Greek economy are treated as entities. Not only are they distinguished by their income and wealth, but also by their personality, which includes their mental makeup and physical health. Consequently, the discussion is broadened in order to include, not only quantitative reports of wealth and income, but also ones stemming from the quality of life. The broader human limits examined include dimensions, such as security and uncertainty for the future, which in the twenty-first century amount to basic components forming the quality of life.

1.3 Basic Assumptions

When readers get a book like this in their hands, they may ignore some of the critical assumptions the author uses. On the other hand, the author uses methodological tools that are responsible for the final result of the written work, such as ideological reference points, methodological and philosophical principles, without revealing them. They may do this out of ignorance. Often, however, the principles of their work are not clear even to the writers themselves. They may let personal ideological views and assumptions interfere with their conclusions, in a way which is not clear as to which part of the conclusion is a result of the methodological and philosophical hypotheses used, and which part of the conclusion is the product of rational analysis that is based on the cause and effect principle.[1] It should also be noted, that the problem is bigger when the analysis is of a normative nature (what needs to be done) rather than when it is of a positivistic nature (what is about to happen).

Introductory comments on the basic principles adopted are therefore a valuable aid to readers, helping them discern the quality of the conclusions, without being influenced by the writer's ideological and cognitive departure points.

Usually, a writer's basic assumptions are limited. We have highlighted the four most important ones that need clarification.

The first assumption is that the book is based on a classical approach of political economy analysis, as opposed to a one-dimensional economic analysis (as far as the discussion of Greek social transformation is concerned). Political economy is a general and comprehensive perception of the study that covers key aspects of social phenomena: the economy, society, politics, administration, social psychology, possibly anthropology, biology, game theory, etc. As we will see later on, this is essential if we are to formulate integrated and effective development and growth policies.

The second assumption is that we have accepted the idea that current reality is the evolutionary result of a long historical process shaping financial, institutional, and cultural outcomes. This constitutes the financial, social, political, and cultural environment that makes up Greece's reality. The assumption of evolutionary change—as opposed to the timeless depiction of reality—features the birth and existence of a series of determinants which are embedded in today's financial reality. This finding helps us a great deal in eliminating the illusion of easy change taking place at a political, economic and social level. At the same time, it highlights the complexity of effects normally brought about by policies. Thus, we know from the outset that economic policies focusing on some of reality's dimensions have limited effectiveness.[2] Lastly, the evolutionary assumption introduces the element of time, a fact that influences characteristics of the theory and policies being used, as well as the depth of the analyses being called for.

The third assumption concerns the acceptance and prioritization of positivism versus normativism. The former accepts a theoretical suggestion as being true only when it is proven, directly or indirectly, through empirically verifiable conclusions.

The fourth assumption concerns human action, namely the theoretical background of human behavior and, particularly, the distinction between rational and natural human behavior. Rational behavior, mostly in relation to maximizing welfare, is a system of human thinking that has dominated mainly post-war economic thought, even though its origins can be dated back to classical economists. This school of thought is at odds with what we could define as natural human behavior. Located between the two extremes, in terms of economic activity, there are different types of human behavior, such as bounded rationality, the timeless-dynamic decision-making process, expected utility logic, and, finally, the generalized Darwinism and evolutionary perception of human behavior. Each of these systems brings to the surface certain aspects of human behavior lead by the role of uncertainty. As we will see later on, this book adopts the general theoretical principle of methodological pluralism. Therefore, the book is close to the logic of accepting human behavior in a broader sense, which of course includes rationality as an individual theoretical concept.

This principle is more relevant in the case of the Greek economy since, as it will be determined, the Greek economy exhibits systematic characteristics of social behavior that need particular study. It is very difficult to support that these are signs of collective rational behavior.

1.4 Fundamental Analysis Principles

The criteria by which interpretation theory can be adopted, when observing economic phenomenon, can either be empirical or logical.

Empirical criteria can be of two kinds: (a) testing the assimilations of a theory for the sake of controllability and realism and (b) comparing the prediction of a theory to reality.

Logical criteria has to do with whether the adopted theory is characterized by: (a) productivity and suggestiveness; (b) cohesion and consistency of the internal structure; (c) simplicity (specifying that simple and economically correct theories are preferred) or elegance (focusing on beauty, the aesthetic appeal of a theoretical structure); (d) generality (argues that a theory incorporating an existing and well-documented body of knowledge into a simple, unified framework has to be judged as superior) or scalability (a theory is preferred, if it allows for expansion through abductions in other research fields); and e) operationality.

When deciding which theory will be used in order to analyze a case, it is first necessary to determine the criteria that this decision will be based on. Hoping that we can choose a theory that is absolutely objective is, of course, exceedingly ambitious. The possibility of using pure theory for the interpretation of economic phenomena becomes even harder, especially when analyzing complex socioeconomic formations, such as the Greek one.

After identifying criteria by which we accept a hypothesis, theory or law, the next question is to determine the extent to which we are going to be monists, eclectics, or pluralists. Here there are two extremes: on the one hand, we have those who believe that we should be defined only by one methodological approach (monists) and, on the other hand, we have the pluralists, who believe in utilizing different methodological approaches. But the real question is to determine the extent that we need to (and can) be methodological pluralists.

In a contemporary changing world where uncertainty prevails, a complex view of the existing reality is essential, in order to support a complete growth theory. For the purpose of locating, for example, the sources of growth (as they emerge through models and theories) and the development of implementation policies, a pluralistic approach is needed to provide for the required multidimensional analysis.

Pluralism gives us the ability to focus on the applied methodology, benefiting from tools provided by science philosophers, which appear to be skillfully created and suitable for this cause (Hausman, 1981).

The pluralistic approach frees us from the need to rely exclusively on the neoclassical model of economic thought, which, despite its organized mathematical formulation and its internal consistency, touches only on certain aspects of reality and may have partial spatial (perhaps in some developed economies) and temporal (e.g., short-term analysis) implementation. The same concern extends to newer versions of neoclassical theory, to monetarism, to neoclassical macroeconomics, etc., which also maintain the same assumptions at the core of neoclassical theory.

The expertise of the researcher is to shed light on the problem that needs to be analyzed, comprehend its theoretical documentation very well, and study the relationship between theory and reality. Rodrik (2015) argues that criticisms of economics are misleading when they claim that science suffers, because economists have not yet reached a consensus on what are correct models and theories. It is preferable to devote our energy to making a wise choice of the framework to be applied. After all, the important thing is not what economists do, but what they do not or refuse to do (Hausman, 1992).

Conclusively, the persuasiveness and beauty of economic thought should be sought in the completeness of citing causal connections with interdisciplinary freedom and interaction that is lacking in theoretical dogmatism of methodology.

1.5 Ideology, Bias, and Growth

Big recessions have a catalyst effect on the global economy and society on a series of areas, in terms of:

- changing the relative position of individual economies regarding the international division of projects and the power to determine the conditions for future development;
- lost products and income, particularly in comparison with the alternative course of the economy, had the crisis not taken place;
- employment, the diminishing value of human capital and requirements for the restoration of skills;
- shaping conditions to produce innovation; and
- quality of life and social cohesion, including the way that income and wealth are distributed.

However, as history has shown, the intensity of each economic crisis gave birth to a fundamental question in relation to the political and economic system's ability to foresee, therefore protect and efficiently avoid future crises. Answers were sought after in human nature, economic theory, and politics, as well as in ideology, thereby outlining the role of ideas and cultural background as determining factors of economic policy and growth in the midst of the crisis.

The role of ideas is important in understanding how the political economy of human well-being is organized. In reality, the basic components of each problem, optimization, preferences, limitations, and choice variable are supported by an underlying total of ideas (Rodrik, 2013).

We can see, among other things, four areas where the method shaping the ideology influences crucial parts of development and growth. These are debt, external balances, culture, and the shaping of expectations. We chose these four areas, despite the fact that we could have added more, as they are important in terms of the role played in economic evolution and because, as determined later, they are of exceptional importance—particularly for the Greek economy. Thus, the issue of public debt, especially as a percentage of GDP, is known to be of exceptional importance. The issue of external balances has played—and will play—a very big role in limiting evolution, while the cultural background of Greek society determines human attitudes. Finally, the way business and economic expectations are formed play a leading role in any growth process.

The ideological dimension connecting growth and debt is perhaps one of the most controversial issues. When Reinhart and Rogoff (2010) published their work on this, they probably did not expect to influence the whole world with their basic proposal: that there is a critical relationship between debt and GDP growth. At the time, this finding was of crucial importance to the European Union, since the European Union and the Eurozone, appeared to have reached some critical debt thresholds after the 2008 crisis. If, therefore, Reinhart and Rogoff's (2010) views were correct, then European authorities would inevitably have to take action on debt reduction When the Covid-19 crisis emerged as a Great Lockdown of economies, almost no one thought of reacting (as in 2008) to that the required budgetary and liquidity needs which were necessary to maintain productive structures would certainly increase the debt-to-GDP ratio of economies at a global level. On the contrary, there were prevailing views, which always existed, but were at a disadvantage, which would justify these positions. (monetization of debt, helicopter money). However, economic reality, once again, formed an ideological and theoretical background for economic policies, reversing the relevant ideological and theoretical priorities.

In relation to this issue, when it comes to exercising economic policy, the importance of external economic imbalances is quite different in terms of analysis and impact. Throughout the 2000s, and even before, external imbalances were highlighted. But they were not a major source of concern, especially within the Eurozone (as it was treated as a single entity) even though there was no external clearing mechanism, like in the United States that relied on central bank gold reserves in each state. On the other hand, Target2 Eurosystem offered an opportunity for capital flows to move between Eurozone member states. The Great Recession of 2008, however, brought to light a crucial concept: the net international investment position (NIIP), i.e., how much does a country owe the rest of the world or how much the rest of the world owes that country. This proved to be a key criterion in regulating and defining policies pursued, indicating that Europe is made up of countries that enter the bloc based on their strengths.

It is commonly accepted that cultural background is an area that produces powerful forces shaping economic and social priorities. It seems to affect the conditions in which a crisis arises, the way it unfolds, and the way it is exited. In particular, it affects the way social learning is shaped and, by extension, collective behavior.

Typical of this are thoughts on the nature of animal spirits as generative causes of sudden changes in collective economic behavior (Akerlof & Shiller, 2009; Dow & Dow, 2011). At a macroeconomic level, research has also focused on the long-term barriers to growth related to cultural factors (Spolaore & Wacziarg, 2012). Social research now examines the conditions of human survival during the course of a crisis, as well as the way it affects the way children are brought up (Cipriani, Hawton, Stockton. & Geddes, 2013) and how their attitudes are shaped. It is now certain that this has exceptionally long-term effects, especially on younger ages, with critical consequences on key financial functions, such as savings behavior, risk aversion, and more.

The formation of expectations is one of the most basic cultural elements of economic behavior. If society believes that the country will go bankrupt, then a huge effort is needed to avoid this. If the less privileged are the majority, they will view their economic future with pessimism. Therefore, a model of liberal democracy prevails where the present value of living conditions is small, and consequently, investing in knowledge and looking for work, are of no importance. In this case, the number of long-term unemployed workers increases, as do structural obstacles, harming momentum connected to the prospect of exiting the crisis.

The way in which expectations are formed is one of the most important issues in the organization of economic theory itself, affecting the way reality is interpreted and predicted, while also having an impact on the prospects for an exit to the crisis.

1.6 Forecasts and Future Scenarios

Forecasts are of key use, enabling economic and social policy objectives to be set and then implemented. They also (a) help to increase the predictability of the economy by increasing transparency and the value of effort made, (b) set goals, thereby facilitating the mobilization of resources needed to achieve them, and (c) create the conditions needed to secure a collective effort and help with the adoption of goals by society.

Forecasts, however, are the product of specific theoretical models under specific operating assumptions and do not cover other theories. For example, in an economy where under consumption and underinvestment make it difficult to grow due to the high private debt repayments (balance sheet recession), it is difficult to come out with forecasts, as these conditions are very difficult to enter into a model. Additionally, there are no direct opportunities to model institutional improvements, only indirect ones. Furthermore, secondary forecasts are rare, e.g., to transfer tax liabilities to subsequent years or the holding of repeated elections, which can, however, play a decisive role in the outcome. Also, the models used often do not include internal compatibility checks (e.g., to check whether the financing of planned investments is secured, etc.). In general, forecasts are based on knowledge and facts known to date, focusing on key data, especially if extended over long periods of time. Essentially though, events being characterized as "black swans", such as Covid-19, can be very difficult to be modeled. In fact, when this is attempted, the absence of historical experience makes the task of prediction very difficult.

Finally, projections play a role in shaping the future as main players take a position on the forecast in a positive or negative stance. This often leads to projections contributing to the outcome predicted.

Predictability has one more dimension that should be emphasized: it creates expectations. But when expectations relate to a whole society, they direct actions accordingly. The questioning of expectations demands rational thinking and important knowledge that is not commonly available on a large scale. Consequently, the systematic denial of expectations has broader structural effects on social cohesion and the activation of social creativity.

For these reasons, putting together estimates and forecasts on the course of an economy, including Greece's, is of crucial importance as it directly relates to the adoption of evolution and development policies and the prosperity of its people.

But if today we are in a position to make predictions about the Greek economy, or any other economy, even under normal circumstances, then what is the point of exercising policy that will pursue specific goals?

The answer can be found at two levels. The first one is that there must be normal conditions, something which is not a given since there is no autopilot for producing expected results, but effort is required. The second is that, in these conditions, it is very likely that there will be an issue of beating the trend. This involves the economy going beyond the projected trend of normal conditions.

An accurate prediction of the future is impossible because of the inability to include and assess all the factors that shape developments. One method that allows for the observation of these factors over a period of time is trend analysis. However, the method that will be followed for the Greek economy is the development and analysis of scenarios (scenario analysis), which allows for estimations under the consideration of different possibilities. This is a more in-depth assessment of the course of the Greek economy, with its results depending on the versions considered. More detailed explanations will be used to illustrate important trends in the Greek economy when the aim is to derive more specific results.

This book, as well as the other ones to follow, shapes the environment on formulating forecast scenarios and developments in the Greek economy up until 2030. However, the main target is not to create a detailed forecast through to 2030 but to describe main trends within the framework which the Greek economy will grow. Forecasts for the Greek economy "suffered" greatly during the decade of the great crisis (2008–2018) and in the short term from Covid-19 crisis. So much so that it is considered that systematic lack of satisfactory forecasts from highly credible entities—such as the IMF, the ECB, and the EC, with various reasons, e.g., using a wrong multiplier—played a big role in making the crises longer and deeper. Since we are trying to prepare reliable forecasts on the Greek economy (see the first volume of the book series), it is certain that satisfactory forecasts will play a significant role in creating conditions allowing for sound economic policies that will lead to long-term recovery of the Greek economy.

Notes

1. Of course, in addition to ignorance, this may be done on purpose but this is of no concern to us here.
2. The observation goes beyond talk of the economical dimension of the first-and-second best theory on policy selection and refers to the interaction between different parts of economic behavior (economy, politics, society, and psychology, etc.).

References

Akerlof, G. A., & Shiller, R. J. (2009). *Animal Spirits: How Human Psychology Drives the Economy and Why It Matters for Global Capitalism*. Princeton: Princeton University Press.

Cipriani, A., Hawton, K., Stockton, S., & Geddes, J. R. (2013). Lithium in the Prevention of Suicide in Mood Disorders: Updated Systematic Review and Meta-Analysis. *British Medical Journal*, *346*(f3646).

Dow, A., & Dow, S. C. (2011). Animal Spirits Revisited. *Capitalism and Society*, *6*(2), 1–23. https://doi.org/10.2202/1932-0213.1087.

Hausman, D. M. (1981). *Capital, Profits and Prices: An Essay in the Philosophy of Economics*. New York: Columbia University Press.

Hausman, D. M. (1992). *The Inexact and Separate Science of Economics*. New York: Cambridge University Press.

Reinhart, C. M., & Rogoff, K. S. (2010). Growth in a Time of Debt. *American Economic Review*, *100*(2), 573–578. https://doi.org/10.1257/aer.100.2.573.

Rodrik, D. (2013). *When Ideas Trump Interests: Preferences, World Views, and Policy Innovations* (NBER Working Paper No. 19631). https://doi.org/10.3386/w19631.

Rodrik, D. (2015). *Economics Rules: The Rights and Wrongs of The Dismal Science*. New York: W. W. Norton.

Spolaore, E., & Wacziarg, R. (2012). *How Deep Are the Roots of Economic Development?* (NBER Working Paper No. 18130). https://doi.org/10.3386/w18130.

CHAPTER 2

Theory and Policy

2.1 Introduction

In economics, like in other related social sciences, there is a fundamental two-way relationship between real phenomena and the way they are theoretically described. Prevailing conditions in an economy determine the framework within which a policy is designed and implemented. Thus, the most appropriate development policy depends on the real context in which it is to be implemented. This chapter analyzes concerns surrounding the relationship between theory and politics and the role of institutions and culture in the development process.

More specifically, Sect. 2.2 presents the relationship between economic analysis and policy-making and Sect. 2.3 looks at specific context versus generality in the theory of welfare economics. Section 2.4 highlights the relationship between policy and governance, with an emphasis on the role of institutions and cultural background in targeting and achieving policy plans. Additionally, the role of pressure groups and the elite is emphasized here, along with the importance of multi-level governance and the relationship between democracy and populism with growth. Finally, Sect. 2.5 analyzes the relationship between policy, reforms, and growth, with particular reference to reforms implemented in the Greek economy from 2010–2018 and their results.

P. E. Petrakis, *The New Political Economy of Greece up to 2030*,
The Political Economy of Greek Growth up to 2030,
https://doi.org/10.1007/978-3-030-47075-3_2

2.2 Economic Theory and Policy

One of the biggest concerns of the political system, and the way it operates, is its responsibility in selecting and implementing an appropriate economic model. It is well known that in Greece up until 2010, the country's economic model was characterized by high consumer demand and public sector expansion. Obviously, the electorate influences key choices made by political leadership, but the crucial question is how the latter interpret these choices and insert them into economic policies.

The relationship between economic theory and policy formation is characterized by complexity and different parts mutually affecting each other. This is due to the fact that the economic sphere interacts with institutions, social and political behaviors, and ideologies.

Humans-economists and their ideas, which are translated into proposals and policies, play a key role in this two-way relationship between economic theory and policy. Economic ideas, however, often overlap with political ones, and this poses the risk that they will serve the needs of specific political positions and interests.

Although politics precede the economy, as crucial decisions are made at the political level, public policies seem to be more defined by economics and less by political variables. Despite this, there are examples in communities, such as in the United States in recent decades and UK, where political partisanship seems to be a determining factor in shaping public policies and, in particular, economic policy. These factors appear to arise from interacting ideas, interests, political preferences, and the institutional and socioeconomic dimension.

2.3 The Specific Framework Versus Generality in the Theory of Welfare Economics

When conditions of perfect competition exist and markets provide for all goods, a point is reached where no one in society can improve their position (welfare) without harming another person's (Pareto Optimal). This situation reflects the first fundamental theorem of welfare economics, which implies that competition promotes the efficient allocation of resources. Consequently, according to the second fundamental theorem of welfare economics, if we as a society are not satisfied with the wealth distribution that arises through competitive equilibrium, then the redistribution of individuals' initial wealth—not by any means interference with the price system—leads to a more desirable Pareto Optimal equality point. The two theorems form a clear policy framework that is dominated by markets and competition as a first best condition. A deviation from the ideal situation may be due to various factors, such as externalities, public goods, etc.

The power of the market, i.e., the ability of firms to overcome competition by setting prices (rather than being price takers), is an immediate market failure, which may be due to distortions or imperfections, such as barriers to entry. In Greece, the oligopolistic concentration[1] of economically important sectors has played a major role in shaping the institutional environment and the way the Greek economy operates, harming the rules of competition. In the Greek economy between the years 2008–2016, the majority of sectors, according to the Herfindahl–Hirschman[2] (HH) Oligopoly Concentration Index (Fig. 2.1), showed a broader downward trend in oligopoly concentration. A high concentration (2016) occurs in the tobacco industry and its products, metallurgy, oil and gas bottling sectors, as well as in the leather furniture and books/newspaper/magazine markets. The highest concentration can be seen in air transport (HH = 7041), a category which exhibits significant volatility in the period.

Additionally, policies that do not promote (or act as an obstacle to) competition in product markets are more common in Greece, than in other Organisation for Economic Co-operation and Development (OECD) countries, in areas where competition is sustainable. The market regulatory environment in the Greek economy is presented in Fig. 2.2 and shows signs of improvement, despite worsening conditions of competitiveness, in comparison with the OECD countries (average).

Real-life constraints shape second best (or higher order) conditions, geared to a specific real-world policy framework. Interpreting and understanding existing conditions are necessary to properly formulate economic policy, as there are few situations where general economic policy rules always apply.

Ng (1977) developed the third best theory by considering that the likely problems created by the "indefinite formulation of general policy rules" (associated with second best theories) as driving any economy with specific geographic and time-specific features to a certain development policy. Its effectiveness, however, depends on the degree of information required and the costs (administrative costs) required to implement it. Thus, when conditions of "informational poverty" apply, the third best

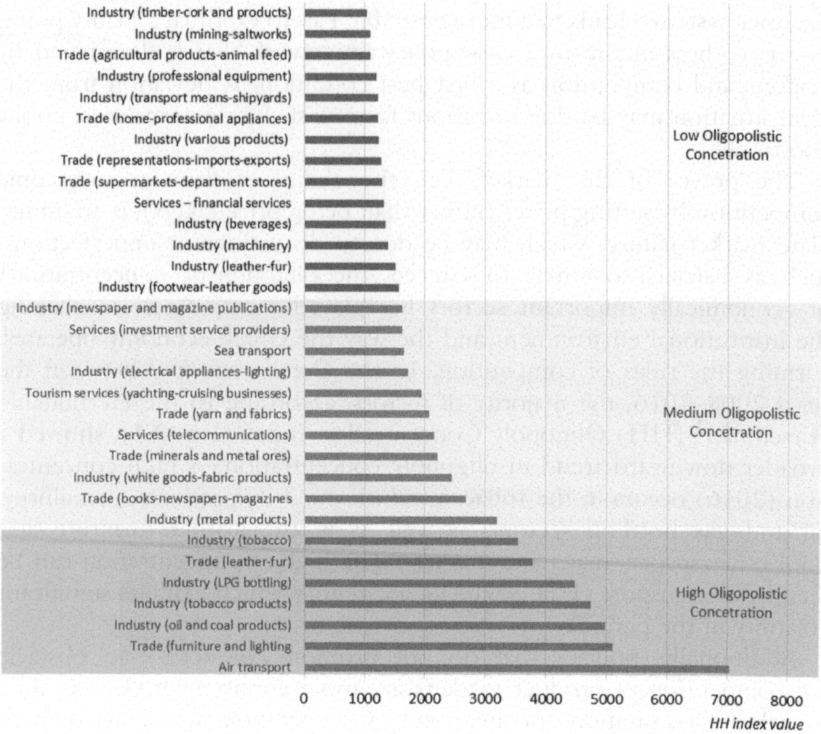

Fig. 2.1 The oligopolistic concentration index for sectors of the Greek economy (*Note* Sectors not referred to do not show an oligopolistic concentration. *Source* ICAP Group [2019] and author's own manipulations and creation)

theory is equivalent to the first best theory in terms of effectiveness. In this case, fulfilling the first best conditions is the best policy available. As a result, we must deviate from the first best conditions, only when there is a strong reason to do this.

It is therefore important to have a solid picture of the prevailing institutional framework, within which we will analyze development and growth problems, so that proposed policy solutions can be implemented.

An example of the demands required by this type of organizing, versus general demands, relate to the institutional and cultural context. Each society is characterized by a specific institutional background and set of cultural values that sometimes promote, but also impede, economic

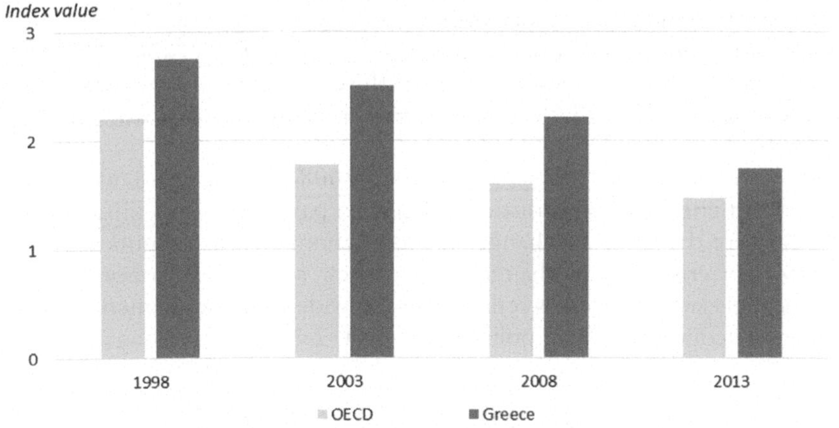

Fig. 2.2 Product Market Regulation Index in distinctive periods Greece and OECD countries (average) (*Note* A higher price indicates tighter regulation in products market. *Source* OECD [2020a] and author's own creation)

growth. Perhaps one of the most difficult tasks of the policy-maker is to identify special key features within the productive framework with an emphasis on the institutional and cultural level.

In the case of Greece—as analyzed in *The Evolution of the Greek Economy: Past Challenges and Future Approaches* (Petrakis & Kostis, in press), as well as in *Greek Culture after the Financial Crisis: An Economic Analysis* (Petrakis, Kafka, Kostis. & Valsamis, in press)—an idiosyncratic cultural background seems to have emerged. Specifically, it is supported that a distortion of the relative price (capital/labor) ratio in Greece favors capital which contributes to a continuous short supply of labor, appropriation of rules and high impact from the elite, high transaction costs, and the existence of oligopolies. At the same time, the cultural background is characterized by a non-diversification of investment behavior, risk aversion, in-group collectivism (family ties), high time discount preference, lack of trust and the generation of loss aversion attitudes.

Since idiosyncratic institutions and preferences prevail in the Greek economy, there are barriers produced that hinder innovation outcomes. Growth policy concerns should be devoted to how we can approach a growth performance pattern with endogenous ability to sources of growth. As a result, efforts must be turned to planning and implementing pro-growth structural changes with regard to institutions and preferences, while taking into account their coevolution process. Otherwise, the Greek economy has to rely on importing growth (e.g., capital inflows, incoming innovation), in a bid to create a pro-growth prototype that will promote growth.

In Greece, in the first crisis decade (2008–2018), there were seen significant changes at an institutional and, in particular, at a cultural level, which were the result of changes brought about by the bailouts after the 2010 debt crisis. These changes created new social and economic standards. This latter process is reflected in the widespread implementation of effective economic reform policies (see Sect. 2.5).

2.4 Political Systems and Shaping Economic Policy

Economic development and growth touches on the link between politics and political institutions in general via governance. Political institutions are believed to reflect individual preferences by helping harmonize conflicting interests and, at the same time, change balances in society. This leads to the continued coexistence of social tension and balances.

Political institutions include governing decision-making and control processes (governments, administrations, etc.) through the election and appointment of delegates, who have a significant impact on the way the social decision-making system is organized. They also create the right conditions to reduce pressure coming from different interest groups, which pose an obstacle to the well-being of the economy and income distribution and, thus, to economic development itself. An important role is also played by the effectiveness and the way which public administration is run. Organization and development levels of political institutions provide actors with different incentives, distributing the social product multiple times for the benefit of specific groups. Consequently, the way an economy operates is closely linked to the quality of governance.

In the case of the Greek economy, the level of governance and particularly the effectiveness of governments, as calculated by the World Bank's World Governance Indicator, is presented in Fig. 2.3, in comparison with the corresponding averages of euro area countries.

Government efficiency has significantly decreased over the years in Greece when compared with eurozone countries (average) in a gap that has been steadily increasing since 2004. The global financial crisis of 2008

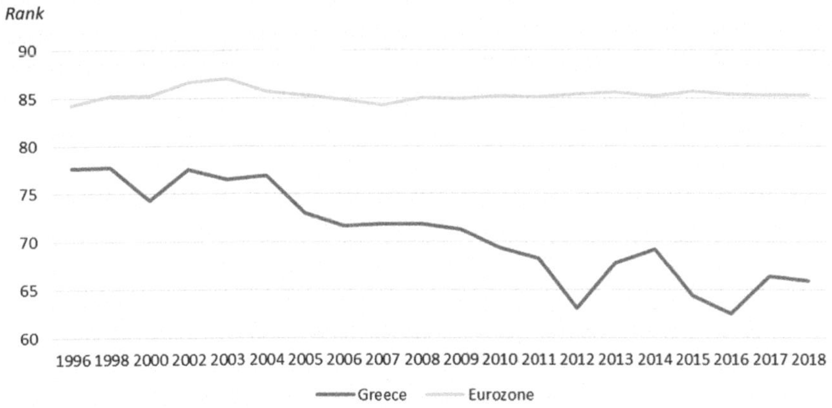

Fig. 2.3 Government effectiveness in Greece and Eurozone (1996–2018) (*Note* Percentile rank among all countries ranges from 0 [lowest] to 100 [highest] rank. *Source* The World Bank [2019] and author's own creation)

exacerbated this gap as government effectiveness remained stable in euro zone countries, while in Greece it declined significantly.

The picture changed significantly during the 2020 Covid-19 pandemic crisis when the Greek administration reacted exceptionally well to the exogenous virus phenomenon (Fig. 2.4).

Essentially, a culture of successful efficiency and discipline in society was formed, which is the positive result of the second great depression that can serve as a guide for the implementation of extensive structural programs in the medium to long-term.

2.4.1 Pressure Groups, Elite, and Multi-Level Governance

Multi-level governance is a term used to describe how power is shared and decisions are made. Power can be distributed vertically, across many levels of government, and horizontally, across many semi- and non-governmental organizations and bodies (Cairney, 2019), providing a useful transition from policy change to implementation.

This analysis is useful in helping identify political decisions and the way responsibility is shared, as governance in countries is spread across multiple levels (local, regional, etc.) while states themselves are part of broader supranational organizations. An overview of the complexity of

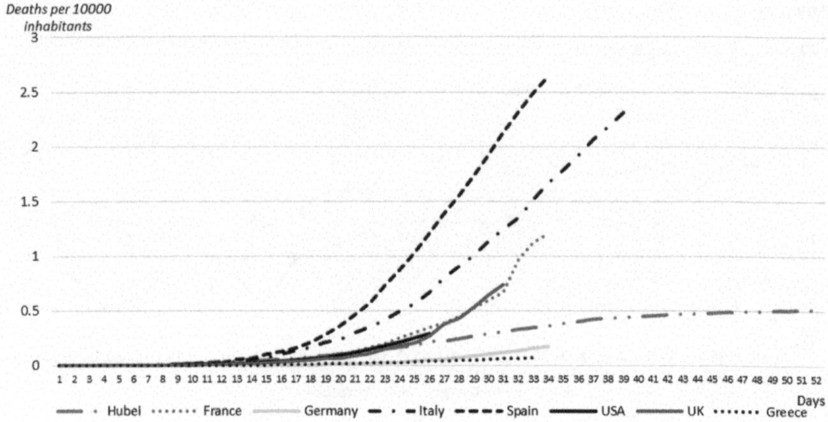

Fig. 2.4 Covid-19 death index in basic economies (*Note* Day 1 of the crisis is the day with the occurrence of 100 cases per 60 million population [for Greece day 1 is when 18 cases occurred, i.e. March 5, 2020, for Hubei is January 18 and for Italy is the 22nd February]. *Source* Our World in Data [2020] and author's own calculations and creation)

the Greek economy's important decision-making centers, and therefore its spending decisions (in comparison with the country's gross domestic product [GDP]), is given in Fig. 2.5.

In the vertical dimension, the development of local skills and introduction of incentives to boost the effectiveness of subnational levels of governance are critical to improving the quality and coherence of public policy. Decision-making is separated into top-down transitions, from national to lower levels, and bottom-up transitions, when local issues are bumped up to higher levels (Cerna, 2013). In the top-down approach, policy-makers are central actors, and the analysis focuses on central manipulative factors and on clear policies that need to be followed (Cerna, 2013; Matland, 1995). Adversely, the bottom-up approach emphasizes local-level policy and decision-making and networking techniques that identify local, regional, and national dimensions in the planning, funding, and execution of relevant governmental and non-governmental programs. This process offers a mechanism for transferring decisions from local actors to policy-makers.

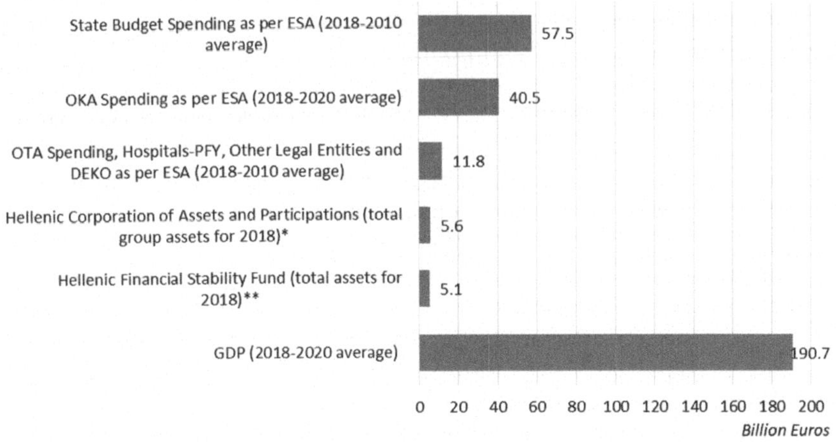

Fig. 2.5 Important spending and decision-making centers relative to GDP (bn euros) (*Note* ESA = European System of Accounts, DEKO = Public Enterprises and Organizations, OKA = Social Security Organization, OTA = Local Government Organization, and PFY = Primary Health Care. The Hellenic Financial Stability Fund [HFSF] is a special purpose legal entity operating under private law based in Athens that was created in 2010 to help stabilize the Greek banking sector amidst the Greek sovereign debt crisis. The fund was provided with 50 bn euros by the European Financial Stability Fund [EFSF] to recapitalize Greece's banks. The Hellenic Corporation of Assets and Participations [HCAP] has been responsible for the single management of a significant part of the Greek State's assets since it was set up in 2016. Its portfolio includes public enterprises active in key sectors of the national economy, as well as a significant amount of the Greek state's private real estate assets, able to create the right conditions for the achievements of local or broader economies of scale targeted at general development. *Source* *Hellenic Corporation of Assets and Participations [HCAP, 2019], **Hellenic Financial Stability Fund [HFSF, 2019], Ministry of Finance [2019] and author's own creation)

Pressure groups are generally, small or large, social groups with common characteristics and goals. In economic science, the term "interest groups," in the broad sense, refers to any non-governmental social group seeking to influence executive and legislative powers by securing the most favorable decision or solution for its members. Interest groups appear in different facets of society, in various forms and sizes. They display different levels of strength and serving an array of interests, while influencing many areas, such as the economy and politics.

The elite usually refer to a small group in society, that are close to influential decision-making centers, which they seek to exploit in order to acquire and maintain a large portion of economic and political power. The high positions they usually hold in businesses and organizations allow them to swing government decisions to their favor.

As far as Greece is concerned, there is evidence that the elite and pressure groups push for their own interests at the cost of the economy. By definition, these pressure groups, Greece's economic elite and multilevel governance, operate in a way that creates "winners" and "losers," resulting in gaps and accelerations in the process of economic growth. The Greek economy, however, has a similar presence of the elite as elsewhere in the (average of) Eurozone, as shown in Fig. 2.6.

However, it should be pointed out that this got worse for the Greek economy during the 2007–2018 period. The index value from 1.6 in 2007 rose to 4.1 in 2018. This is indicative of the fact that, in the midst

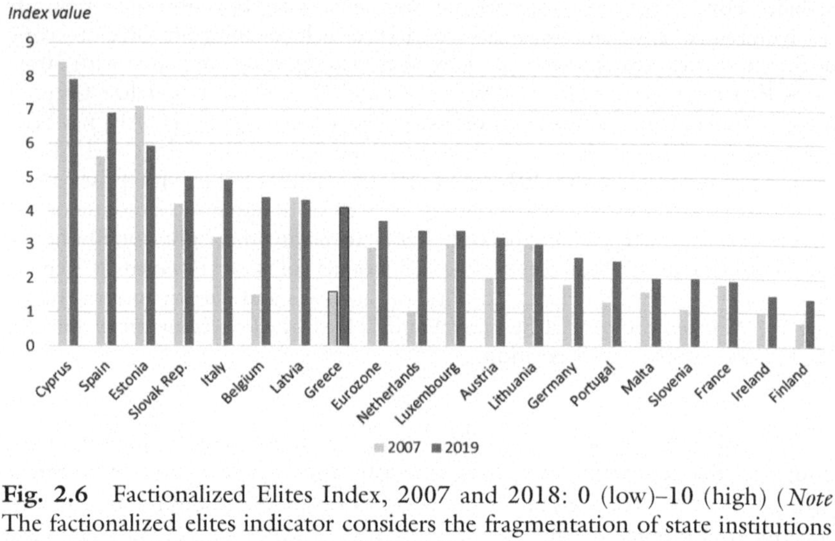

Fig. 2.6 Factionalized Elites Index, 2007 and 2018: 0 (low)–10 (high) (*Note* The factionalized elites indicator considers the fragmentation of state institutions along ethnic, class, clan, racial or religious lines, as well as and brinksmanship and gridlock between ruling elites. The higher the value, the more fragmented are the institutions in the country. *Source* The Fund for Peace [2020] and author's own creation)

of the first crisis of 2010, the elite in the Greek economy gained power in order to defend their interests and protect their economic position.

Another indication of the unequal distribution of power in the Greek economy is the fact that a small part of the population gathers large economic power and, most likely, influences significantly government policies and decisions. When looking at the number of annual tax returns for the 2018 economic year and different income levels (Independent Authority for Public Revenue [AADE], 2019), it turns out that total income from 4438 tax statements (with annual income of more than 200,000 euros) equals that declared in 2,124,033 tax returns (of those who reported income from 0 to 3333 euros). In terms of (disposable) income distribution based on the Gini coefficient (see Chapter 4, Fig. 4.4), there was more inequality in Greece (32.3) than the Eurozone (30.6) and the European Union (EU) (30.9) in 2018 (Statistical Office of the European Communities, 2019a).

Greek society is essentially organized based on Western standards that heavily feature interest groups at all levels—economic, social, political, and cultural. These groups are organized and systematically pressure for decisions that each one desires.

It should also be noted, that it is impossible to record and refer to each interest group active in Greek society, due to the large numbers and their lack of broader presence. Therefore, the first problem relates to a lack of information on pressure groups and, secondly, the problem concerns groups which do not self-identify with their cause, meaning that we do not precisely know who forms the group, its source and final goals.

One of the most important institutional pressure groups in any society is the clergy. Representatives of the clergy are justifiably regarded as playing a crucial role in domestic and foreign policy-making. In addition to dealing with religious matters, the clergy extends its powers to managing its economic and political interests. Due to its position in Greek society, as well as the traditionally strong religious consciousness of the Greek people, it has gained enormous power as a social institution, composing of 118 bishops, 9568 parish priests, and 266 employees (Mitralexis, 2016). This power is commonly accepted by the majority of the Greek people. Fifty five percent of Greeks are religious, in the sense that religion is considered important in their lives, and almost all of them are Christian Orthodox (Pew Research, 2018). This makes the group's claims more acceptable, and legitimate, to the people. This became particularly evident during the second crisis, that of Covid-19, when the state with great difficulty banned all religious gatherings in a population where the majority is religious.

Another very important institutional pressure group, whose interests are strongly represented, is that of the military. Soldiers are divided into more than one group based on the branch they serve, their specialties, etc. Greece's land troops, naval, and aviation forces number 141,450 people (Aristotelous, 2017). Funds intended to equip the armed forces are perhaps the most important issue for this interest group. In addition to the issue of armaments, which is a concern for this pressure group, they have other political, economic, and social interests. Greece's total defense spending is important, standing at more than 4 billion euros (North Atlantic Treaty Organization [NATO], 2019).

One more important pressure group is the academic community. University professors assumed a particular type of power with the founding of the first universities in Western Europe. In the Greek educational system, teaching staff at higher education institutions amounted to 13,923 at the end of the 2016–2017 academic year (Hellenic Statistical Authority Hellenic Statistical Authority [ELSTAT], 2019). The two most important issues for academics are academic freedom and self-governance. It is worth noting that the control they have over entrants into their profession gives them extra power and authority that cannot be overlooked.

An important pressure group is made up of judges and lawyers. Statutory hierarchy and the autonomous and independent functioning of the judiciary give justice officials special powers, either institutionalized or informal, which they can use to protect their rights or to promote change regarding the functioning of the body or their positions. The large number of lawyers—21,196 people registered with the Greek Bar Association (Council of Bars and Law Societies of Europe [CCBE], 2018)—push hard to keep the legal system complex, theoretically ensuring that lawyer's income streams will remain open. That is why justice moves at a very slow rate in Greek society, as shown in Fig. 2.7.

It is a fact that the continued inability to deliver justice quickly and effectively, in particular to enforce the legal consequences of breach of contractual obligations, burdens the business climate by discouraging the much-needed investment. Despite improvements to the clearance rate of first instance cases (cases closed versus new ones arising over a year) seen in Greece in recent years, the increase in time needed to rule on a first instance court matter during the crisis, as well as the accumulation of

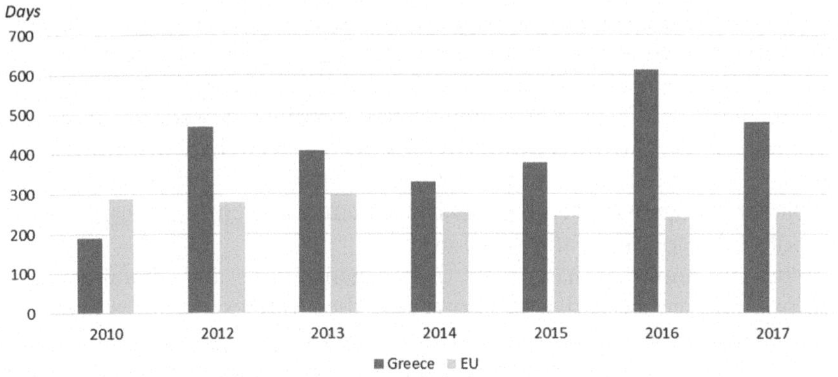

Fig. 2.7 Disposition time (in days) for first instance civil and commercial litigious cases (*Note* The indicator compares the total number of pending cases at the end of the observed period with the number of resolved cases during the same period and converts this ratio into a number of days. This indicator measures the theoretical time necessary for a pending case to be solved in court in the light of the current pace of work of the courts in that country. Disposition Time is obtained by dividing the number of pending cases at the end of the observed period by the number of resolved cases within the same period multiplied by 365 [days in a year]. However, it needs to be mentioned that this indicator is not an estimate of the average time needed to process a case but a theoretical average of duration of a case within a specific system. *Source* European Commission [2018] and author's own creation)

pending cases–300,476 in the fourth quarter of 2019 (Hellenic Ministry of Justice, 2020)–act as deterrents to development. This is because an efficient and independent judiciary is a condition to building confidence and contributes to an efficient allocation of funds in the economy, through rapid and guaranteed implementation of the law, therefore demonstrating the link between improving court efficiency and the development of an economy.

Furthermore, there are a number of professional organizations in Greek society that can be divided into basic categories such as employers' associations, the self-employed, labor unions, farmers, pensioners, the unemployed, and other pressure groups.

The recognition of the important role played by employers' associations (such as the Hellenic Federation of Enterprises [SEV], the Hellenic Confederation of Professionals, Craftsmen and Merchants

[GSEVEE], the Hellenic Confederation of Commerce and Entrepreneurship [ESEE], the Greek Tourism Confederation [SETE], the Union of Greek Shipowners [UGS], as well as 59 chambers of commerce) in public debate, with the institutional upgrade that ratifies it, reflects its essential political weight. In addition to a de jure power that surrounds their public actions, they also have a strong de facto power. The strength of employer groups has been particularly evident in recent decades, boosted by political, economic, and social events.

The self-employed have their own organizations and chambers that are primarily concerned with protecting their interests and, as a result, exert pressure on the state to both maintain their rights and to acquire new ones, while giving them the ability to broaden their influence in the community and affect the country's economic activity. Due to the relatively high rate of self employed in the broader labor market (Chapter 5, Sect. 5.3), their role is extremely important in shaping social dynamics. Typical cases in Greek society are engineers, who are registered with the Technical Chamber of Greece [TEE-TCG], lawyers who are represented by local law groups, doctors who are represented mainly by medical associations, and the sector of road transport.

As employer associations gradually increase their bargaining power in the political system distributing economic resources, labor unions have found themselves on the opposite path. Their relatively strong position in the 1970s and 1980s gradually declined as of the 1990s. The reasons for this weakening position, which are undoubtedly numerous, are due to the historical evolution of the workers' trade union movement, as well as the particularities shown by the domestic business structure. Private and public sector employers' associations in Greece cannot have the same social weight as their peers in most European countries where the number of salaried employees is higher than the self-employed. The falling trend showing the rate at which Greek workers participate in unions can be seen in Fig. 2.8.

An indication of the peculiarities that affect the way that labor interests are organized domestically is the fact that, on occasions, professional groups played a leading role in labor battles even though they may not be considered to be purely a worker's group. The leading position held by tobacco workers, who pre-war constituted the vanguard of the labor movement, was superseded post-war by builders and then by bank employees after the fall of Greece's military junta (Mavrogordatos, 1988).

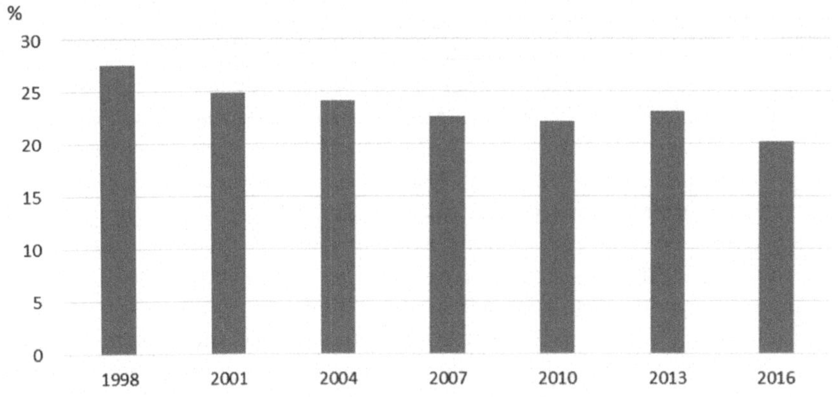

Fig. 2.8 Trade Union Density in Greece (*Source* OECD [2020b] and author's own creation)

This is not, however, the main reason for the gradual social weakening of labor unions in Greece. This development was mainly shaped by three factors, among others. Firstly, the asphyxiating relationship between the state and parties reflected by their direct economic reliance on the state and their own sharp interparty divisions and frictions. Secondly, differences separating the representation of public and private sector employee interests, in combination with an inability to represent significant parts of wage labor-both for institutional reasons and for causes related to changes in the domestic structure of production. Thirdly, growing dissatisfaction in public opinion with the role of labor unions, in light of the above, combined in the 1990s and on with a state policy which preferred consensus to conflict—in line with European policies—and focused on different aspects of production (flexibility, productivity, etc.) rather than distribution.

Regarding the agriculture sector, there are more than 1.1 million farmers in Greece (European Commission, 2019a) who actively protest, strike and seek claims, particularly in rural areas where sustainability and development is mostly based on agricultural professions.

Pensioners are a special case of pressure group, in that the pressure they can exert is limited, even though they constitute a significant part of the total population in Greece—more than 2.6 million people (see Chapter 5, Table 5.5). They are either people who have ceased working and maintain their own professional identity, or other categories of people, who receive a pension due to a parent, spouse or health problems that prevent them from working. The first category of pensioners has greater scope to apply pressure as, due to their profession, they may be associated with that professional body and receive support from fellow workers-colleagues, with the latter being interested in defending the interests of the group which they will later on join. In the second category, the scope to apply pressure is very limited as it is difficult to seek demands and gather supporters for their claims, since pensioners in this category do not have any clear and specific characteristics which can be identified with by any social group that can then support them.

But, in reality, because the pension system supports the broader socioeconomic fabric, the state has a very cautious attitude toward retirees and, as a result, they have not been severely hurt during the first crisis of 2010. During the second crisis, that of Covid-19, particular sensitivity has been successfully shown in preventing the virus from spreading to geriatric institutions as it did in other European countries. This observation may also be based on family's role, which prefers to support the elderly—and possibly benefit from pension payments—rather than place them in nursing homes.

As a pressure group, the unemployed do not differ from pensioners, in terms of their structural characteristics. They do not essentially belong to a particular group that is inherently motivated to support them. Like pensioners, they cannot use the tool of strike action that is often used as a pressure mechanism in this direction as they belong to different groups without any common characteristics. Their power and cohesion are weakened due to a lack of motivation, and they are basically divided into two non-formal but essentially differentiated groups.

On the one hand, there are the unemployed who are actively looking for work and, on the other hand, there are those who settle with the unemployment benefit and an undeclared work position that is hard to find but often generously rewarded. Thus, the unemployed in Greece cannot easily seek and support claims as a group as they do not have common goals and demands. In Greece, the number of unemployed workers reached 915,000 people in 2018 (Statistical Office of the European Communities, 2019b), remaining high despite a decline in recent years.

Other organized pressure groups active in Greek society can be distinguished based on their specific social, demographic, ideological-political, religious, and other characteristics. Depending on their age and ideology, we distinguish youth wings of political parties that push for ideological policies in a specific direction, based on interests that concern people belonging to a particular age group. Based on gender, one could easily recognize feminist groups, or groups based on location, representing villages, cities, regions, or based on ideology, accession to political parties, etc. These groups, even though they are not well known to the general public, exert pressure on political authority and their actions cannot be ignored. Non-governmental organizations (with environmental, scientific, and ideological objectives) are a broader category of pressure groups and perhaps a more organized and socially acceptable institutionalized group with specific sensitivities.

As we have already pointed out, some of the most important sectors of economic production are highly oligopolistic. As a result, these oligopolistic structures gain significant strength and exert pressure on state policy and government. Prices dictated by oligopolies are higher than the marginal cost of producing goods and, consequently, reduce the consumer surplus, creating social costs. This leads to a drop in utility for consumers, while there is a drop in household wealth and maximum benefits are not achieved. The oligopolistic structure of the market and the subsequent creation of goodwill for the business' shareholders/owners results in a transfer of wealth at the cost of the consumer and, consequently, an upward redistribution of income.

2.4.2 Democracy and Growth

The link between democracy and economic growth has drawn the attention of prominent economists (Barro 1996, 1999; Lipset, 1959), based on the fact that democracy promotes higher standards of living, having a two-way relationship with a country's economic performance. Barro (1996) supports that the effects of democracy on economic growth, although favorable at an institutional level, are not significant. Adversely, growth, significantly improves the chances of political institutions becoming more democratic with time.

Democracy boosts future GDP by encouraging investment, improving education opportunities, promoting economic reforms, improving the provision of public goods, and reducing social unrest. Additionally, scores on the quality of governance are significantly higher in more democratic countries (Rivera-Batiz, 1999). In the same direction, Papaioannou and Siourounis (2008) show that countries under democratization have higher growth in the long run after going through a changing transitional period. Furthermore, Meltzer and Richard (1981) argue that democracy reduces the level of inequality and improves the redistribution, in agreement with Acemoglu and Robinson (2000). There are also indications that democracy influences the level of public spending (Lindert, 1994, 2004), tax revenues (Acemoglu, Naidu, Restrepo, & Robinson, 2013) and is associated with higher wages and a higher share of labor in national income (Rodrik, 1999).

Greece has historically experienced three democratic periods: The First Hellenic Republic, from 1822 until the establishment of the Otto kingdom in 1932; the Second Hellenic Republic, from 1924 to 1935; and the Third Hellenic Republic in the period after the fall of Greece's military junta (1974) through to today. The latter two have coincided with the country's increase in per capita income as shown in Fig. 2.9.

In regards to the quality of democracy in Greece, the Economist Intelligence Unit (EIU, 2020) has a democracy index for 167 countries, based on five categories of criteria: electoral process and pluralism; civil liberties, the functioning of government, political participation, and political culture. Based on each country's score in these five categories, it is then classified as being one of the following: "full democracy," "flawed

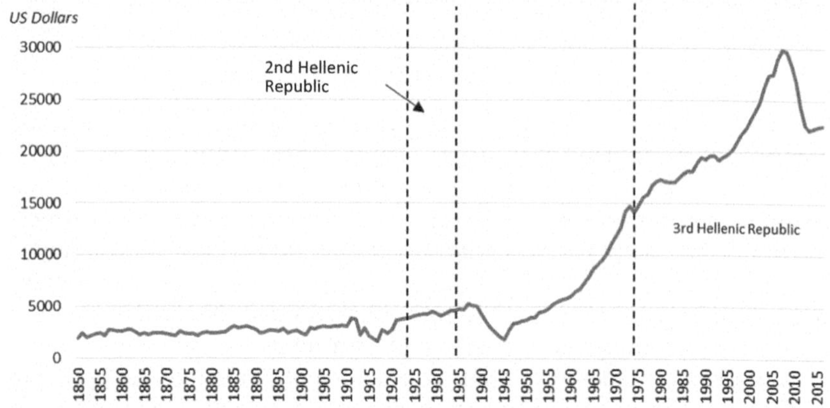

Fig. 2.9 The development of real GDP per capita in the Greek economy (1850–2016) and periods of democracy (*Note* Real GDP per capita in 2011US$, 2011 benchmark. *Source* Bolt, Inklaar, de Jong, and van Zanden [2018] and author's own manipulations and creation)

democracy," "hybrid regime," and "authoritarian regime." In this indicator, Greece (EIU, 2020) is characterized as a flawed democracy, with a score of 7.43 points, placing it in second last position (only above Slovakia) among Eurozone countries, while the corresponding average for Eurozone countries is 8.07 points in 2018.

Similarly, "Freedom in the World" (Freedom House, 2019) puts together a ranking of countries every year. In 2019 (reference period 2018) it covered 195 countries. The freedom index (a) is based on the premise that these standards apply to all countries and territories, irrespective of geographical location, ethnic or religious composition, or level of economic development; (b) operates on the assumption that freedom is best achieved in liberal democratic societies for all people; and (c) assesses the real-world rights and freedoms enjoyed by individuals rather than governments or government performance per se. Political rights and civil liberties can be affected by both state and nonstate actors, including insurgents and other armed groups.

For 2018, Greece received a top score[3] of 1 for political rights (Freedom House, 2019), above the Eurozone average, meaning that Greece enjoys a wider range of political rights, including free and fair elections. Candidates who are elected actually the rule, political parties are competitive, the opposition plays an important role and enjoy real power, and minority interests are well represented in politics and government. For civil liberties, Greece received a score of 2, falling below the Eurozone average, meaning that Greeks have slightly weaker civil liberties than Eurozone countries with a rating of 1 (because of factors such as limits on media independence, restrictions on trade union activities, and discrimination against minority groups and women.

Overall, Greece's Freedom rating based on the two indices (political rights, civil rights) is 1.5 which means it is considered a free economy, having a Freedom score 87 out of 100, but below the average in Eurozone countries (93) and the EU. This is in fact the lowest performance in the Eurozone, together with Lithuania.

Along with the average Freedom ranking, what is of importance in the Greek case is that there is an exceptionally low satisfaction of democracy (Fig. 2.10) with the difference, in comparison with the EU (average), picking up after the 2008 crisis.

It should also be noted that democracy satisfaction levels in Europe are not at high points, but the corresponding level for Greek society is really very low.

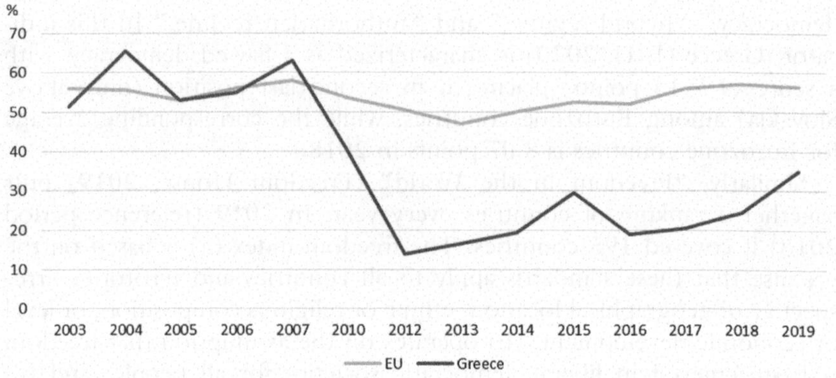

Fig. 2.10 Satisfaction with the way Democracy works in country level (*Note* There is no data for 2008, 2009, and 2011. *Source* European Commission [2019b] and author's own creation)

2.4.3 Populism and Growth

Populism is defined as the political stance that highlights the idea of the pure people versus the "corrupt elite." Thus, society is divided into two competing groups, with politics expressing the general will of the people (Mudde, 2004). Populism does not reject democratic values but liberal democracy, it advocates popular sovereignty and the principle of the majority, rejecting elitism[4] and pluralism[5] and minority rights.

The rise of populism is a response to the obvious failures of governments and states, but also to the development of globalization, which has disrupted balances in societies. However, waves of migration and the extended economic crisis suggest deeper causes lie behind its sharp rise. More particularly, austerity, insecurity (Insecurity Hypothesis), social transformations, and a change in values (Cultural Backlash Thesis)—which have been prevailing in societies recently—are changing the previously strong positions held by certain social groups and are a source of the populist wave (Inglehart & Norris, 2016). The question for the immediate future is whether or not Covid-19 will strengthen similar political currents. This, however, is being discussed below.

Conditions in the labor market or economic insecurity can partly explain the rise in populism. The economic causes behind the success of the phenomenon are complemented by the refugee and migrant crisis, a central issue for populist parties and voters. However, key questions are whether migration is motivated by economic incentives and what its economic consequences are.

In regard to the first question, immigration in the West is largely driven by economic issues, such as poverty, lack of employment opportunities, and wage differences. However, in regard to the second question, it appears that concerns among Western voters about immigration have nothing to do with its impact on economic well-being or insecurity (Margalit, 2019). Structural, long-term social changes can be seen as playing a central role in understanding the discomfort caused by the phenomenon. As generations change, those that were the previous ruling majority increasingly feeling that their social position is being eroded, opting for populist nostalgia in a "golden era" when traditional values, cultural homogeneity, and strong national identity prevailed.

According to Rodrik (2018), populism is characterized by views that represent and speak for the people and the unified popular interest, which is limited by democratic institutions and respect for the rule of law (political populism) and economic policies that are based on established policy rules and technocracy (economic populism). In the case of right-wing populism, the common popular will targets the enemies of the people, minority groups and immigrants, while the enemy in left-wing populism is the economic elite. But given that political populism is always dangerous and detrimental to public interest, an interesting issue is the examination of conditions under which populist economic proposals can benefit a society. In cases where the interests of many may no longer be served by liberal economic policies—such as (perhaps low) inflation targets set by central banks that are not coupled with employment/income goals, established international trade conditions which may harm labor in favor of capital, and the extreme liberalization of the economic system that brings higher risk and social costs after a financial crisis—economic populism could be justified and helps to prevent the dangerous possibility of political populism from arising (Rodrik, 2018).

After the 2008 global economic recession, populist trends have been gradually multiplying at a faster pace in the realm of politics, also extending to economic policy, bringing with them the foundation of a fiscal trend and greater interventionism and influence in monetary issues which come under the jurisdiction of central banks (see Chapter 8, Sect. 8.5). However, this trend has been hampered by the effects of Covid-19 crisis, which in some countries has elevated the role of institutions, international collective decision-making, organized society, and the role of experts—although in other countries it has had the opposite effect. The extent of this crisis has possibly marked serious political changes in these countries.

2.5 Reforms and Growth

The modern world and the economy are constantly changing and one factor behind the changes is the impact economic policies are having. These may cause small or medium-scale gradual changes or have the nature of more ambitious structural reforms programs.

Reforms are outlined by the following structural characteristics:

- They express a choice of values that represent a particular view of society.
- They have a distinct distributive impact between benefits and costs.
- They boost competition between groups which look to influence the above consequences.
- Their institutionalization or non-institutionalization is closely linked to political events or political crises.
- They can have a very significant impact on the political stability of a regime.

Political environments systematically differ when the period marking the outbreak of the crisis, is compared with the period prior to the crisis. The political repercussions of a financial crisis can be severe, even causing severe political failures. After a crisis, political functions may not be as effective as they were, as it is likely that the country failed to complete reforms exactly when they were needed. Evidence from the impact of banking crises in the last century shows them having a dramatic impact on the survival prospects of governments. Funke, Schularick, and Trebesch (2015) argue that financial crises are characterized and followed by political instability to a much greater extent than other types of economic crises The effects of pandemics are not the same, which in current and previous centuries caused deep but lasting downsizing depressions worldwide (Baldwin & di Mauro, 2020).

In Greece, the recent debt crisis and recession that followed led to a loss of confidence among Greek citizens in the country's political institutions (Fig. 2.11) and as a result they were discredited, a fact that made the

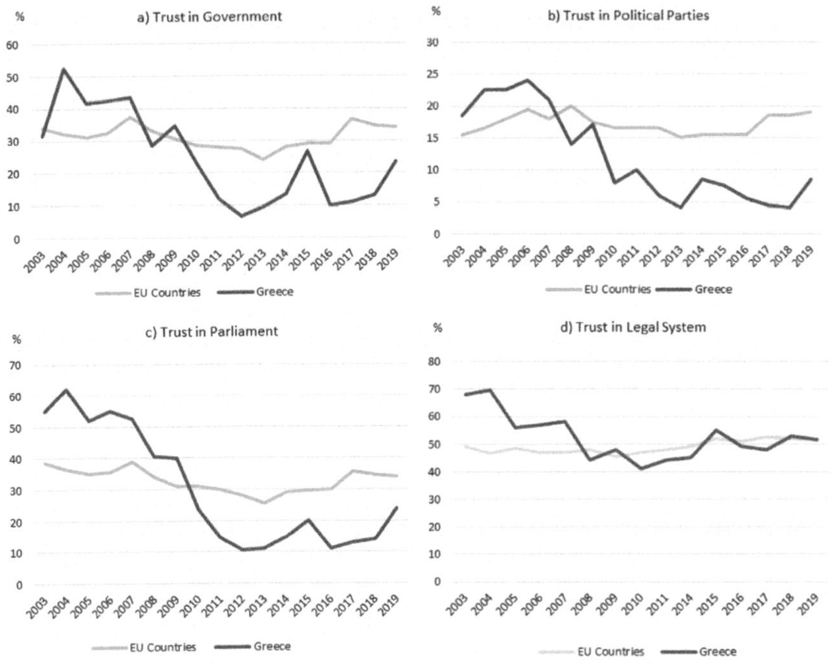

Fig. 2.11 The course of confidence in national political institutions in Greece and the EU (2003–2019) (*Note* There is no data for the "Trust in Legal System" in 2012 and 2013. *Source* European Commission [2019b] and author's own creation)

problem of effective crisis response even more difficult. On the contrary, the indications from Covid-19 so far are in the opposite direction, since 77.9% (MRB Hellas, 2020) of Greeks judge positively the measures taken by the government to deal with the pandemic and only 8.5% (!) answered negatively.

In fact, before 2010 the political institutions, the government, political parties, parliament, and the judicial system in Greece enjoyed a greater degree of confidence in comparison with EU countries (average). This later downward trend was temporarily halted in the 2015 elections, but the discrediting of political institutions and the system is a phenomenon in progress, despite the improving views of Greek society after the 2019 elections—a fact that is hampering the Greek economy's growth prospects.

There are clearly defined and outlined aims and tools by which the reforms policy in Greece will ultimately be pursued. But are the right conditions in place for growth and development policy to succeed in the Greek economy? Do Greek politicians have the ability and willingness to support it or do they settle with being reelected by adopting inferior policies that are popular and meet the needs of clientelism between politicians and voters? The agency problem is dominant between voters and politicians in Greek society and how does this affect the growth or development procedure? Does Greece's weak productive base and geographical location play a role in creating a more permanent tendency to adopting simplified political arguments? Are authorities responsible for achieving specific goals or is there a broader situation of misspending arising? These are catalytic questions that help determine the purpose, means and implementation of development policy in the broader sphere of the political process taking place in the Greek economy.

As of 2010, Greece has adopted a wide range of structural reforms to meet fiscal challenges, lower competitiveness, and productivity weaknesses. In evaluating the reforms processes (European Commission, 2019c) it has been noted that significant progress has been made in facilitating entrepreneurship, improving competition in transport and energy, and in the economic activities of the service sector, as well as the liberalizing of the product market in emerging sectors. Progress has also been made on privatization programs in various sectors, such as transport and energy, and the utilization of public assets. Privatization procedures are still taking place, though initial signs of their impact are deemed to be positive. The economic benefits of reforms are expected to become increasingly visible, along with the country's improved economic conditions, the development of new business activities, and the creation of new investments stemming from reforms. Despite this, the positive impact of reforms will only be felt when the Greek economy's key macroeconomic problems are resolved, such as that of effective demand.

The fact is, however, that relative performance indicators of government regulations are significantly lower than averages in the EU and OECD countries (Table 2.1), regardless of the country's reforms progress. The effectiveness of government regulation is based on three criteria: the (ex-ante) regulatory impact assessment, the degree of stakeholder engagement, and the regulatory planning and its ex-post evaluation. Regulatory impact assessment is a key tool for policy-makers in achieving economic policy goals, as it analyzes costs and benefits—based

Table 2.1 Regulatory Governance Index (2017)

	Regulatory impact assessment	*Stakeholder engagement*	*Ex post evaluation*
Greece	2.13	3.68	0.42
EU countries (average)	6.61	6.97	6.18
OECD countries (average)	4.28	4.31	3.45

Note The three criteria are broken down into two categories: (1) primary laws and (2) subordinate regulations. Each category is divided into four identical evaluation subcategories: (a) methodology (b) oversight and quality control (c) systemic adoption, and (d) transparency. Each subcategory has a maximum assessment of 1, each category has the best total score of 4 and therefore a maximum of 8 for each criterion
Source OECD (2019) and author's own creation

on substantiated policy proposals—as well as to whom they are directed, in order to avoid regulatory failures, while seeking the greatest possible benefit to society. Stakeholder engagement, which draws on empirical knowledge and stakeholder advice on problems related to policy issues, contributes to the regulation of needs among citizens, social groups, businesses, and society in general, improving in this manner the quality and transparency of regulatory planning. Stakeholder engagement also makes regulations more comprehensive and helps parties involved develop a sense of ownership of the regulations. This, in turn, enhances compliance with regulations, confidence in the government, and social cohesion. Ex-post evaluation also enhances confidence in the government by increasing regulatory transparency and accountability from regulatory authorities. Once a regulation is put into effect, governments can adequately evaluate the results, costs, benefits, and unintended consequences. Through feedback, this creates ideas on how to improve the design of regulations.

More specifically, Greece has shown small improvement in recent years (2014–2017), but still exhibits the largest weakness in ex-post evaluation of regulatory practices (OECD, 2019). It also seems to be in a better position, though still trailing performances in comparative countries, in ex-ante regulatory impact assessment and more so in stakeholder engagement in regulatory/reform processes.

It has been estimated that overall reforms in the Greek economy in the 2010–2014 period, in combination with those included in the Third Economic Adjustment Program, would contribute a total of 13.4% to the Greek economy's GDP over the course of a decade (OECD 2016). Out of this amount, 2.8% will come from improved employment and 10.6% from higher productivity brought about by the reforms. Also, from a different perspective, it appears that in the next decade, product market reforms will have contributed 7.8% to GDP, labor market reforms 3.3%, tax structure reforms 2.1%, and bankruptcy reforms that relate to the Third Program 0.2%.

We have no reason to believe that these estimates will change after the Covid-19 crisis. In fact, as seen during the progress of the book, the need for a reform program is more urgent with the aim of healing wounds caused by the crisis, with the main purpose of increasing the growth rate, so to faster reduce advancing debt as a percentage of GDP.

Reforms introduced as of 2010, combined with those included in the Third Economic Adjustment Program, as well as the new reform drive to be developed, are expected to significantly boost the economy's output in the next decade, offsetting to a large extent the potential loss of output due to the crisis. In fact, these estimates represent a minimum threshold in the sense that other critical reforms, such as those to the judiciary, bankruptcy rules, and modernization of public administration, have not been implemented.

As far the big impact from reforms on GDP for the whole of Eurozone seems to come, ceteris paribus, 5 years after they have been implemented (Anderson, Barkbu, Lusinyan, and Muir [2014]). This means that this year, and in the next few, significant benefits are expected to arise from total reforms carried out in the Greek economy in the last few years.

This, along with momentum from non-fiscal reforms to be implemented in the Greek economy between 2019 and 2021 is expected to provide a significant boost to output by 2030 and, therefore, achieve an anticipated outperformance of trends. Of course, it should be noted that non-budgetary reforms expected to take place from 2019 to 2021 are not seen as being as effective as those in 2010–2017 and, therefore, should be expected to have a less proportionate impact on GDP. This is due to the fact that, the more we approach the reform frontier, reforms become increasingly difficult providing fewer positive effects.

Notes

1. In order for an industry to be considered oligopolistic, it is not necessary for the number of companies operating in it to be small. A market is considered an oligopoly, even if it has a large number of participants, provided that only a few large companies produce a significant proportion of total output. This percentage is called the degree of concentration and indicates the degree of competitiveness in a sector of the economy. A low concentration of industry implies high competitiveness and means that the industry operates more competitively, rather than as an oligopoly. On the contrary, a high degree of concentration characterizes oligopolistic markets.
2. The Herfindahl–Hirschman (HH) index is often used in empirical research to measure the level of competition in an industry. It measures the degree of sales concentrated among businesses in a specific market. This index uses sales market shares held by businesses and is based on the sum of the squares of these figures. When the index is priced below 1000, it is considered to be a non-concentrated market, when it is priced between 1000 and 1500, there is a low market concentration, between 1500 and 2500, there is a medium market concentration and above 2500, it is considered to reflect a high degree of concentration.
3. A country or territory is assigned two ratings—one for political rights and one for civil liberties—based on its total scores for the political rights (0–40 points) and civil liberties (0–60 points) questions. Each rating of 1–7, with 1 representing the greatest degree of freedom and 7 the smallest degree of freedom, corresponds to a specific range of total scores. The average of a country or territory's political rights and civil liberties ratings is called the Freedom Rating, and it is this figure that determines the status of Free (1.0–2.5), Partly Free (3.0–5.0), or Not Free (5.5–7.0). The Freedom score is the total of the country's score on political and civil rights.
4. Elitism believes that the elite are pure and the people corrupt.
5. Pluralism offers a completely different cosmo-theory in comparison with elitism and populism, and considers that the community is divided into different groups with different interests, and is in favor of a policy that is based on consensus among all.

References

Acemoglu, D., Naidu, S., Restrepo, P., & Robinson, J. A. (2013). *Democracy, Redistribution and Inequality* (NBER Working Paper No. 19746).

Acemoglu, D., & Robinson, J. A. (2000). Why Did the West Extend the Franchise? *Quarterly Journal of Economics, 115*(4), 1167–1199.

Anderson, D., Barkbu, B., Lusinyan, L., & Muir, D. M. (2014). Assessing the Gains from Structural Reforms for Jobs and Growth. In M. Schindler, H. Berger, B. Bakker, & A. Spilimbergo (Eds.), *Excerpt: Jobs and Growth: Supporting the European Recovery* (pp. 125–150). Washington, DC: IMF. http://dx.doi.org/10.5089/9781484304464.071.

Aristotelous, A. (2017). The Military Forces of Greece and Turkey 2017/18. *Cyprus Center for Strategic Studies*. Retrieved from: http://strategy-cy.com/ccss/index.php/el/surveys-gr/item/349-oi-stratotikes-dynameis-elladas-tourkias-the-military-forces-of-greece-and-turkey-2017 (in Greek).

Baldwin, R. & di Mauro, B. W. (2020). Introduction. In R. Baldwin & B. W. di Mauro (Eds.), *Economics in the Time of Covid-19* (pp. 1–30). London: CEPR Press (a VoxEU.org eBook).

Barro, R. J. (1996). Democracy and Growth. *Journal of Economic Growth, 1*(1), 1–27.

Barro, R. J. (1999). Determinants of Democracy. *Journal of Political Economy, 107*(S6), 158–183. https://doi.org/10.1086/250107.

Bolt, J., Inklaar, R., de Jong, H., & van Zanden, J. L. (2018). *Maddison Project Database, Version 2018. Rebasing Maddison: New Income Comparisons and the Shape of Long-Run Economic Development* (Maddison Project Working Paper No. 10). Retrieved from: https://www.rug.nl/ggdc/historicaldevelopment/maddison/releases/maddison-project-database-2018.

Cairney, P. (2019). The UK Government's Imaginative Use of Evidence to Make Policy. *British Politics, 14*(1), 1–22. Retrieved from https://doi.org/10.1057/s41293-017-0068-2.

Cerna, L. (2013). *The Nature of Policy Change and Implementation: A Review of Different Theoretical Approaches* (OECD/CERI Paper).

Council of Bars and Law Societies of Europe. (2018). *Statistics from CCBE: Number of Lawyers in European Countries*. Retrieved from: https://www.ccbe.eu/actions/statistics/.

European Commission. (2018). *Study on the Functioning of Judicial Systems in the EU Member States: Facts and Figures from the CEPEJ Questionnaires 2010 to 2017*. Retrieved from: https://ec.europa.eu/info/publications/cepej-studies-2019_en.

European Commission. (2019a). *Greece: Agriculture Statistical Factsheet*. Retrieved from: https://ec.europa.eu/info/food-farming-fisheries/farming/facts-and-figures/markets/production_en.

European Commission. (2019b). *Public Opinion Survey*. Standard Eurobarometer: 59–92. Retrieved from: https://ec.europa.eu/commfrontoffice/publicopinion/index.cfm/Survey/index#p=1&instruments=STANDARD.

European Commission. (2019c). *Enhanced Surveillance Report - Greece* (European Economy Institutional Paper No. 116). Retrieved from: https://ec.europa.eu/info/sites/info/files/economy-finance/ip116_en.pdf.

Freedom House. (2019). *Freedom in the World* (online). Retrieved from: https://freedomhouse.org/.

Funke, M., Schularick, M., & Trebesch, S. (2015). *Going to Extremes: Politics After Financial Crises, 1870–2014* (CEPR Discussion Paper No. DP10884).

Hellenic Corporation of Assets and Participations. (2019). *Financial Results for Year 2018*. Retrieved from: http://www.hcap.gr/en/financial-results/.

Hellenic Financial Stability Fund. (2019). *Financial Information for year 2018*. Retrieved from: http://www.hfsf.gr/en/financialinformation.htm.

Hellenic Ministry of Justice. (2020). *Organization of Justice: Statistics by Degree of Jurisdiction 2019(Q3)*. Retrieved from: https://www.ministryofjustice.gr/?page_id=1603 (in Greek).

Hellenic Statistical Authority. (2019). *Survey on Tertiary Education (Universities): End of Academic Year 2016/2017* [Press Release]. Retrieved from: https://www.statistics.gr/documents/20181/471e01dd-9ae2-42d2-8f75-57a89ce6d2b8.

ICAP Group. (2019). *ICAP Data*. Retrieved from: https://www.icap.gr/Default.aspx?lang=2.

Independent Authority for Public Revenue. (2019). *Statistics-Indicators: Income, Annual Statistical Bulletins, Individuals Income (Tax Year 2017/Submissions 2018)*. Retrieved from: https://www.aade.gr/menoy/statistika-deiktes/eisodima/etisia-statistika-deltia (in Greek).

Inglehart, R., & Norris, P. (2016). Trump, Brexit, and the Rise of Populism: Economic Have-Nots and Cultural Backlash. *Social Science Research Network Electronic Journal*. https://doi.org/10.2139/ssrn.2818659.

Lindert, P. (1994). The Rise of Social Spending, 1880–1930. *Explorations in Economic History, 31*(1), 1–37.

Lindert, P. (2004). Social Spending and Economic Growth. *Challenge, 47*(4), 6–16. https://doi.org/10.1080/05775132.2004.11034254.

Lipset, S. M. (1959). Some Social Requisites of Democracy: Economic Development and Political Legitimacy. *American Political Science Review, 53*(1), 69–105. https://doi.org/10.2307/1951731.

Margalit, Y. (2019). Economic Insecurity and the Causes of Populism Reconsidered. *Journal of Economic Perspectives, 33*(4), 152–170.

Matland, R. E. (1995). Synthesizing the Implementation Literature: The Ambiguity-Conflict Model of Policy Implementation. *Journal of Public Administration Research and Theory, 5*(2), 145–174.

Mavrogordatos, G. T. (1988). *Between Pityokamptes and Prokroustes: Organised Interests in Contemporary Greece*. Athens: Odysseas.

Meltzer, A. H., & Richard, S. F. (1981). A Rational Theory of the Size of Government. *Journal of Political Economy, 89*(5), 914–927.

Ministry of Finance. (2019). *State Budget 2020: Presentation Budget Report*. Retrieved from: https://www.minfin.gr/web/guest/proupologismos/-/asset_publisher/qmvb5pyzdGAQ/content/kratikos-proupologismos-2020?inheritRedirect=false (in Greek).

Mitralexis, S. (2016). *Clergy Wages in Greece - and Their Correlation to Church Assets: Overview, Facts, and Prospects for Future Developments* (Jean Monnet Papers on Political Economy 17/2017). Retrieved from: https://jmonneteuldcs.wordpress.com/jean-monnet-papers/.

MRB Hellas. (2020). *Covid-19 Era: Research to Record Opinions, Concerns, and Expectations (Wave II)* (in Greek).

Mudde, C. (2004). The Populist Zeitgeist. *Government and Opposition, 39*(4), 541–563. https://doi.org/10.1111/j.1477-7053.2004.00135.x.

Ng, Y. K. (1977). Towards a Theory of Third-Best. *Public Finance, 32*(1), 1–15.

North Atlantic Treaty Organization. (2019). *Defence Expenditure of NATO Countries (2012–2019)*. NATO Public Diplomacy Division, Press Release [Communique PR/CP(2019)069]. Retrieved from: https://www.nato.int/nato_static_fl2014/assets/pdf/pdf_2019_06/20190625_PR2019-069-EN.pdf.

Organisation for Economic Co-operation and Development. (2016). *OECD Economic Surveys: Greece 2016*. Paris: OECD Publishing. Retrieved from: https://doi.org/10.1787/eco_surveys-grc-2016-en.

Organisation for Economic Co-operation and Development. (2019). *OECD Statistics: Government at a Glance, Regulatory Governance*. Retrieved from: https://stats.oecd.org/Index.aspx?QueryId=85336.

Organisation for Economic Co-operation and Development. (2020a). *OECD Product Market Regulation Statistics (Database): Economy-Wide Regulation*. Retrieved from: https://doi.org/10.1787/data-00593-en.

Organisation for Economic Co-operation and Development. (2020b). *OECD Statistics: Trade Unions and Collective Bargaining*. Retrieved from: https://stats.oecd.org/Index.aspx?DataSetCode=TUD.

Our World in Data. (2020). *Data on COVID-19 (Coronavirus)*. Retrieved from: https://github.com/owid/covid-19-data/tree/master/public/data.

Papaioannou, E., & Siourounis, G. (2008). Democratization and Growth. *Economic Journal, 118*(10), 1520–1551.

Petrakis, P. E., Kafka, K. I., Kostis, P. C., & Valsamis, D. G. (in press). *Greek Culture After the Financial Crisis: An Economic Analysis*. New York: Palgrave Macmillan.

Petrakis, P. E., & Kostis P. C. (in press). *The Evolution of the Greek Economy: Past Challenges and Future Approaches*. New York: Palgrave Macmillan.

Pew Research Centre. (2018). *Eastern and Western Europeans Differ on Importance of Religion, Views of Minorities, and Key Social Issues*. Retrieved from: https://www.pewforum.org/2018/10/29/eastern-and-western-europeans-differ-on-importance-of-religion-views-of-minorities-and-key-social-issues/.

Rivera-Batiz, F. L. (1999). Undocumented Workers in the Labor Market: An Analysis of the Earnings of Legal and Illegal Mexican Immigrants in the United States. *Journal of Population Economics, 12*(1), 91–116.

Rodrik, D. (1999). *The New Global Economy and the Developing Countries: Making Openness Work*. Washington, DC: The Johns Hopkins University Press.

Rodrik, D. (2018). Populism and the Economics of Globalization. *Journal of International Business Policy, 1*(1–2), 12–33.

Statistical Office of the European Communities. (2019a). *Eurostat: Gini Coefficient of Equivalised Disposable Income - EU-SILC Survey [ilc_di12]*.

Statistical Office of the European Communities. (2019b). *Eurostat: Unemployment by Sex and Age - Annual Average [une_rt_a]*.

The Economist Intelligence Unit. (2020). *Democracy Index 2019: A Year of Democratic Setbacks and Popular Protest*. Retrieved from: https://www.eiu.com/topic/democracy-index.

The Fund for Peace. (2020). Fragile States Index. Retrieved from: https://fragilestatesindex.org/excel/.

The World Bank. (2019). *Worldwide Governance Indicators*. Retrieved from: www.govindicators.org.

CHAPTER 3

The Greek Economy as a Eurozone Member

3.1 Introduction

Greece, as a Eurozone and European Union (EU) member, is subject to specific restrictions in regard to its economic policy. Institutions such as the European Stability Mechanism (ESM), European Central Bank (ECB), and European Commission play an important role. After 2010 and the entry of the economy into the so-called Memorandums (Adjustment Program), International Monetary Fund (IMF) entered the spotlight in May 2010 through the SBA (Stand-By Agreement). Gradually since 2012, however, the IMF's role began to weaken, even though it still carries out post-memorandum monitoring on the economy. These were suspended for 2020 on the occasion of the Covid-19 crisis.

EU established in October 2012 the ESM, the successor to the European Financial Stability Facility (EFSF)—a temporary funding instrument that was introduced in June 2010. Since then, ESM has been actively contributing to financial and macroeconomic stability in the Greek economy. It was the main financing mechanism for the 2012, 2015, and 2017 adjustment programs, preparing and monitoring domestic economic policy.

In August 2018, Greece officially exited its final adjustment program. The Greek economy has entered to a post-memorandum monitoring program—European Regulation 472/2013 (Council of the EU, 2013a)—that is imposed on any high debt country once it has completed

P. E. Petrakis, *The New Political Economy of Greece up to 2030*,
The Political Economy of Greek Growth up to 2030,
https://doi.org/10.1007/978-3-030-47075-3_3

an adjustment program in order to ensure a smooth transition to normality and secure the return to sustainable economic growth.

Initially, Sect. 3.2 deals with the effects of monetary integration in Europe, Sect. 3.3 presents the mechanism for economic policy-making in Eurozone, and then (Sect. 3.4) the existing economic policy framework for EU countries is analyzed, regarding nations that do not follow any adjustment programs. In Sect. 3.5 there is a reference to the preset economic policy framework of EU countries that are committed to fiscal adjustment programs. Section 3.6 provides some information on EU's changing position after the 2008 crisis, with a special reference to the Greek economy, and, finally, Sect. 3.7 introduces the effects of Covid-19 crisis on European economy.

3.2 A Common Currency Union

A monetary union of diversified economies improves trade and financial integration between members, having also redistributive effects. A common currency between strong and weak members has structural implications as, although wages and productivity adjust slowly, prices and flows—particularly capital flows—between economies adjust rapidly. The adjustment to the functioning and quality of institutions, however, is even slower. The key lies in bridging the gap between higher capital mobility and lower labor mobility, by collecting income based on the more mobile factor (income tax) and providing support to the less mobile factor (social security).

A discretionary program with broadened benefits aimed at reducing unemployment, funded mainly at a union level and supported by the borrowing capacity of each government, proves a powerful example of a timely and effective stabilization instrument (Nikolov & Pasimeni, 2019). The Eurozone creation provided economic and political incentives, favoring the strong economies (Perotti & Soons, 2020). The weaknesses of the regional economies were well known, while adjustment difficulties were underestimated. Core countries gained a comparative monetary advantage by benefiting from a depreciated currency that provided regional economies monetary and financing credibility. Cheaper lending to regional economies resulted in ballooning public and private debt—with most capital inflows being inefficiently used, leading to developments such as growth in non-marketable sectors—thereby further burdening their competitiveness.

Consequently, budgets worsened further at the outbreak of the crisis of 2008. Thus, large differences in the quality and functioning of national institutions and their inability to converge created deeper problems in the euro area, along with the lack of support for monetary integration through a common fiscal policy.

3.3 Mechanisms Forming Economic Policy in Eurozone

Since 2009, informally, and 2010, officially, the governments of Eurozone member states, ECB, and European Commission launched the beginning of a readjustment and redefinition period for objectives, ways to implement economic policy and Eurozone's general operating framework, in an effort to respond in a coordinated manner to the 2008 crisis.

This policy was mainly aimed at adopting a cooperative approach to restoring financial stability, protecting savings, securing a smooth and easy credit flow toward businesses and households, and gradually establishing a solid system of economic and political governance in EU. In particular, in 2010, European Commission and European Council adopted a total of six economic governance measures for EU, the Six-Pack, which reformed the existing Stability and Growth Pact established by the Maastricht Treaty. This new framework came into force in December 2011 and was set out by four fiscal policy regulations and two regulations on macroeconomic imbalances.

On the one hand, this improved the monitoring of state budgets and public finance in Eurozone, the coordination, acceleration, and clarification of the excessive deficit procedures being adopted, and the framework conditions within which the member states budgets should operate in. On the other hand, the prevention of macroeconomic imbalances in all EU countries was consolidated, as was the immediate response and regulation, via specific actions, of macroeconomic imbalances among euro area member states.

Furthermore, European Commission, in its effort to further broaden budgetary discipline, proposed in 2011 two regulations, the Two-Pack, which were launched in 2013 and imposed further coordination and budgetary surveillance among euro area member states, complementing the Stability and Growth Pact.

The first regulation related to systematic reviews and provisions from state budget plans, thereby ensuring the regulation of potentially high deficits of euro area member states, while the second focused on strengthening the broader financial monitoring of euro area member states faced with serious systemic threats due to their financial instability.

Finally, it is noted that all Eurozone member states must respect and stick to the first regulation, while the second regulation only comes into force when a member state is on an adjustment program, or is systematically monitored as part of the Excessive Imbalance Procedure (EIP).

The core objectives of this effort for reconstruction and creation helped introduce new structural coordination, monitoring, transparency, and prevention of macroeconomic imbalances among member states.

Such cases were: the European Semester (ES), the introduction of new mechanisms to ensure the financial and fiscal stability of crisis-hit member states; the ESM, the institutionalization of existing authorities that aim at protecting monetary and currency stability and supervising the financial system; and the Single Supervisory Mechanism (SSM). It should also be noted that as of 2008 the role of the IMF in shaping the economic policy of a subgroup of EU countries has been important (ES).

The ES is a structure established and launched in 2010 under the auspices of European Commission and aims to coordinate annual economic policies of Eurozone members, while also identifying and reporting economic challenges that may threaten EU.

In particular, it aims at ensuring fiscal discipline and stability, as well as avoiding excessively high public debt, unsound public finance, promoting structural reforms, proposing and implementing economic growth and development policies, and, finally, boosting investment by creating the conditions needed for a favorable and attractive investment environment. The diversity of tools and instruments used by the ES to achieve set objectives, on different countries and in general, will be analyzed in more detail below, in terms of how to implement economic policy on member states that are (or not) committed to a program.

Finally, it is worth noting that only member states that are not committed to other obligations and have an independent economic policy can be part of the ES, meaning that these countries have not agreed to an adjustment program. Those that are committed can join the ES once they have completed their program. Greece is an example which, although it did not participate in the ES from 2010 to 2018, joined it in November 2018 after completing in August 2018 its third adjustment program signed in 2017.

ECB is the central bank of euro currency and the core of Eurosystem which includes the nineteen central banks belonging to Eurozone member states. As it is being referred in the second paragraph of its charter, its fundamental task is to ensure price stability in Eurozone, while based on the charter's third paragraph, its basic duties are to implement monetary policy in Eurozone, conduct international exchange rate operations, hold and manage Eurosystem's foreign currency reserves, and manage a variety of financial market transactions through the TARGET2 payment system.

ECB's primary objective, in accordance with Article 127 of the Treaty for the functioning of EU (2012), is to maintain Eurozone price stability. This is in contrast with the United States, where Federal Reserve (Fed) has a dual role: to curb inflation and keep employment at desirable levels. In October 1998, ECB's board of directors ruled that, from a quantitative perspective, Eurozone price stability is defined as the annual increase of the Harmonized Consumer Price Index (HCPI) at a rate below, but close to 2%. The board added that this rate should be maintained over the medium term (ECB, 1998).

In short, the ECB, having a set of specialized tools, implements the necessary monetary policy to ensure price stability in Eurozone, thereby shaping conditions for monetary equilibrium.

The decision to set up the SSM was made at a Eurozone summit in June 2012 as an additional step to unifying the European banking system (*Council of the EU*, 2012). In September of the same year, it was formally listed and proposed as an institutional concept. The ECB accepted the proposal to oversee, via this mechanism, the financial system in general, though focusing primarily on banks operation. Therefore, the SSM, which was set up by the Council of the EU Regulation 1024/2013 (*Council of the EU*, 2013b) and came into operation in November 2014, is the legislative and institutional framework that provides a supranational authority—the ECB—with exclusive licensing powers on all banks active in EU, and has the ability to conduct precautionary reviews and supervision, directly, on large systemic banks and, indirectly, on smaller ones.

However, the institutional extension of SSM indicates that ECB undertakes the direct prudential supervision of 123 of the largest credit institutions (and their 1104 subsidiaries) that are based in Eurozone member states.

Credit institutions are required to meet demands on prudential requirements, while direct precautionary supervision of the remaining (approximately 3500) credit institutions continues to be exercised by national supervisory authorities, that can be either a central bank (in Greece it's the Bank of Greece) or an independent administrative authority (in some member states supervisory tasks have been delegated to both an independent administrative authority and a central bank), in accordance with ECB directions and guidelines. In the case of Greece, the four systemically significant credit institutions are directly supervised by ECB. Finally, only Eurozone member states are obliged to be part of SSM, while EU countries have the option to do so.

Since the crisis, the structure and function framework has gradually begun to adapt and evolve based on a new reality. This new reality was aimed at exercising economic policy in an EU that emerged fragmented, in terms of economic harmony and unity, mainly, between the north and south, that is, between mildly affected economies and those that had experienced a more severe crisis.

Specifically, the Greek economy in 2000–2019 had the lowest growth rate, the highest fiscal deficit, the highest debt-to-GDP ratio (2019) and an average inflation rate when compared to the other Eurozone countries (Table 3.1).

3.4 The Existing Economic Policy Framework of Countries Not Committed to an Adjustment Program

The economies that faced milder symptoms from the 2008 crisis, due to their high degree of resilience, were mainly the Northern European countries that certainly did not have to seek financial support to create safety mechanisms in their economies. Of course, Ireland was the exception as its economy was heavily exposed, forcing the country to resort to the IMF to avoid bankruptcy (bail-out) in 2010.

The explosion triggered by the crisis led to a shift in economic policy of the aforementioned economies and the entire EU. However, they focused on establishing both an a priori prevention and control line and a posteriori position completely guarding against any future disruptions that have now formed the process of implementing economic policy among EU member states, as we show immediately below.

Table 3.1 Basic national economic data for eurozone countries (2000–2019)

	GDP growth rate (2000–2019 average)	*Public deficit/surplus to GDP (2000–2019 average)**	*Debt to GDP (2019)**	*Inflation rate (2000-2019 average)***
Eurozone	1.4	−2.5	84.1	1.7
Belgium	1.7	−1.9	98.6	2.0
Germany	1.4	−1.1	59.8	1.5
Estonia	4.1	0.3	8.4	3.5
Ireland	5.0	−3.7	58.8	1.7
Greece	0.4	−6.3	176.6	2.0
Spain	1.8	−3.7	95.5	2.1
France	1.4	−3.6	98.1	1.6
Italy	0.4	−3.0	134.8	1.8
Cyprus	2.5	−2.7	95.5	1.8
Latvia	3.8	−2.3	36.9	3.6
Lithuania	4.1	−2.3	36.3	2.4
Luxembourg	3.1	1.7	22.1	2.3
Malta	3.8	−2.6	43.1	2.1
Netherlands	1.6	−1.4	48.6	1.9
Austria	1.6	−2.0	70.4	1.9
Portugal	0.9	−4.9	117.7	1.9
Slovenia	2.4	−3.2	66.1	3.1
Slovakia	3.8	−4.2	48.0	3.4
Finland	1.6	0.8	59.4	1.7

Source Statistical Office of the European Communities (2020a, 2020b*, 2020c**) and author's own calculations and creation

National governments that do not follow an economic adjustment program are coordinated and guided by the ES, as of 2010. ES ensures that these member states discuss economic and fiscal policy plans and targets with EU partners at specific times—in the first part of the year—so that in the second part of the year national governments have the ability to achieve set goals.

Interaction between European Commission and members that make up the ES, allows for more effective targeting and, as a result, achievement of common EU objectives.

These institutions analyze and examine the ability of governments to achieve set goals and secure the viability and compatibility of national policies (along with broader macroeconomic objectives targeting stabilization and structural reform) by intervening when necessary or by proposing alternative parameters and ways of implementing economic policy for the next twelve to eighteen months. If and when goals and incentives are successfully aligned, European Council comes forward to institutionalize proposals and mutually support them in order for them to be formally adopted.

However, it is national governments that make final decisions, adjusted to the given framework, on the way and means in which suitable policies for their economies are being formed.

It must also be stressed that European Commission monitors efforts by member states to establish and adhere to the ten-year Europe 2020 strategy, that it proposed in March 2010, in a bid to strengthen and stimulate employment, education, innovation, defend and protect the climate, and generally promote economic growth and development through the following five objectives (European Commission, 2010):

- Increase the employment rate from 69% of the population, aged between 20 to 64 in 2010, to at least 75% in 2020.
- Boost investment in Research & Development (R&D) to 3% of GDP by creating a favorable climate for private sector R&D investment and launching the European innovation cooperation program between EU and its member states.
- Converge with the "20/20/20" energy and climate goals calling for at least a 20% cut in greenhouse gas (GHG) emissions (from 1990 levels), a 20% increase in the share of renewable energy of final energy consumption, and a 20% increase in energy sufficiency.
- Limit the number of early school leavers from 15% in 2010 to 10% in 2020, and increase the proportion of the population, in the 30 to 34 years old age group, completing tertiary education from 31% to at least 40%.
- Reduce the number of Europeans living below the national poverty line by 25%, therefore removing 20 million people from poverty.

The aforementioned framework for the economic policy of EU member states, i.e., the ES, follows an exact and specific annual time schedule. ES's cycle begins in November of each year with the publication of the Annual Growth Survey (AGS), the Alert Mechanism Report (AMR) and the Joint Employment Report (JER) by European Commission, along with economic policy proposals for Eurozone member states.

In regard to public finance and national budgets, Eurozone member states are invited to submit draft state budgets for the following year to European Commission by the second week in October every year. Then, Commission examines the plans, based on the Stability and Growth Pact and each country's economic policy proposals, and expresses and publishes views and comments on each member state in November so that the proposed guidance can be included in the final version of budget.

Lastly, Eurozone finance ministers, those in charge of state budgets and the European Commissioner overseeing fiscal planning, hold special sessions to analyze European Commission's findings and to draw up EU's annual budget at the Economic and Financial Affairs Council (ECOFIN Council), thus winding up the yearly timetable cycle for the ES.

3.5 The Predetermined Economic Policy Framework of Countries Committed to an EU Adjustment Program

The 2008 global financial crisis unevenly shook balances within EU's broader economy. However, despite the fact that the northern EU economies managed to spot, and absorb, in time the large shock due to their structural integrity, a group of countries—economies on Europe's south—were caught off guard by the crisis.

This resulted in them failing to combat autonomously large-scale volatility affecting their economies, which was spread by the bursting of inflated financial market bubbles created within their financial systems.

As a result, these economies were forced to seek financial support and technical guidance from external bodies, such as EU and northern countries, as well as IMF. This safety feature provided by partners was not generously offered to southern EU countries, as it was accompanied by strict terms and conditions. However, it should be stressed that there was not much time for EU to process and study requests for support from hard hit economies. The shock to EU posed an existential threat, while a further delay in responding raised the risk of a total collapse.

The countries that faced the most critical economic issues are in descending order, based on budgetary needs and degree of uncertainty: Greece, Ireland, Cyprus, Portugal, Spain, Romania, Latvia, and Hungary. All eight of these countries are linked by the fact that they resorted to financial aid programs. The first four, in fact, signed macroeconomic adjustment lending agreements, while Spain signed a lending agreement indirectly recapitalizing its banks.

More analytically, the above countries signed an appropriately adjusted Memorandum of Understanding (MoU) that set out the terms and conditions on a broader set of economic policy mechanisms to be adopted by the country in order to receive the requested aid tranches during the agreed period. For the most part, the economic policy tools proposed were based on three pillars and aimed at eliminating structural imbalances.

The first pillar focused on fiscal consolidation policies, that is, measures to cut public spending, reduce public administration operating expenses, improve efficiency, stimulate public revenue through privatizations, or reform the tax system with a primary goal of increasing tax revenue. The second pillar included structural reform policies aimed at boosting productivity and improving markets technological efficiency and institutional structures, while removing obstacles to ensure efficient resource allocation and combating any deficiencies and structural rigidities in goods and services, labor, money, and capital markets. The third pillar included financial sector reforms, which mainly aimed at strengthening the banking system supervision, as well as recapitalizing banks.

In order to secure the right conditions that must be met by the borrowing countries, a monitoring process is conducted by Troika, that is by the technical representatives of European Commission, ECB, and IMF. In 2012, ESM also actively took part in this monitoring procedure.

These representatives hold extensive meetings with national officials responsible for the related issues to determine whether agreement terms are actually being respected, as only then are the program's payments disbursed. A MoU can only be successfully completed if all of the agreement's proposed criteria have been sufficiently met in the agreed time period and positively assessed by the technical experts.

Although terminating an adjustment program formally signals a return to normality and flexibility, regarding the economic policy framework, countries then enter a new period of enhanced post-memorandum supervision (Enhanced Surveillance of European Regulation 472/2013). This requires them to stick to new specific commitments and timetables, as there are also penalties in the event that agreed conditions are not met (Council of the EU, 2013a). In short, it is a process that seeks to ensure budgetary discipline and a continuation of the economy's institutional direction as outlined by the specific economic policy framework in the originally signed agreement, but focusing now on effective implementation of structural reforms after the successful completion of the MoU.

The "commitment" of an economic policy can be considered as being dependent on a country's level of public debt, that is, its debt-to-GDP ratio. Consequently, countries with high debt levels, both in absolute terms and, mainly, in relative terms (debt-to-GDP ratio), even after a MoU ends, may face future structural constraints on economic policy, given the debt repayment issue. Greece is a typical example of this.

3.6 EU Adjustment to the Facts After the 2008 Crisis

Greece's entry into Eurozone was a political decision, both on the part of European partners and Greece's political leaders, as well as Greek society, since it was a topic at the center of national elections in 2000. In economic terms, euro was adopted to contribute to economic integration, increase credibility and confidence in the Greek economy to investors, and allow for Greece's participation in European economic policy-making. As a result, Greece's accession to Economic and Monetary Union (EMU) was aimed at reducing the risk premium, which intended to reduce nominal and real interest rates and get rid of foreign exchange risk, while boosting domestic investment and stimulating faster long-term economic growth. In general, monetary integration costs, arising from the loss of independent monetary policy and the use of the exchange rate, were expected to be low for most new member states, as speculation on currency depreciation was seen as being eliminated.

The adoption of the single currency required certain economic and legal requirements (Maastricht criteria) to be met which were set out in the treaty (Maastricht Treaty) regarding the founding of EU. The goal of these criteria is to ensure that an economy that adopts euro is ready to operate within an EMU framework, which guarantees the broader smooth monetary union functioning.

Although Europe's political and economic integration was very ambitious and promising, the 2008 crisis showed that the single currency adoption was not a strong and effective shield against crises, given that many necessary conditions for an optimal currency area (OCA) (Mundell, 1961) were missing. The recent debt crisis and the divergence of performances among peripheral countries, as in the case of the Greek economy, versus Eurozone core countries have sharply raised concerns among citizens and governments.

The following figure is indicative of the drop in estimated confidence Greeks had in the institution of EU (Fig. 3.1) after crisis broke out, which prior to 2010 was higher than the average among EU countries. It is noteworthy, that after 2016 there is an upward trend on the relevant views held in Greek society. Covid-19 crisis may have created new conditions, as it was essentially the first time European institutions operated—probably in a timely manner—by agreeing on an initial intervention package (550 billion euros from the Eurogroup decision on April 9, 2020, about 750 billion euros via the ECB, and 750 billion euros from the Next Generation EU), even if this was considered incomplete. Objectively this affected the degree of public confidence in EU institutions and Eurozone.

The deep debt crisis that erupted in Greece in 2009 forced EU to change rules governing the institutionalization of the euro area, mainly regarding the non-activation of rescuing debt-ridden countries. As a result, however, the individual member states operation within the common monetary zone has been affected. At the same time, the currency's inability to be depreciated due to the EMU, in cases where a boost to competitiveness is needed, poses a serious lack of flexibility which lies at the root of the structure.

Participation in EMU and the fact that member states use the same currency (the euro), while not being its creators, create structural

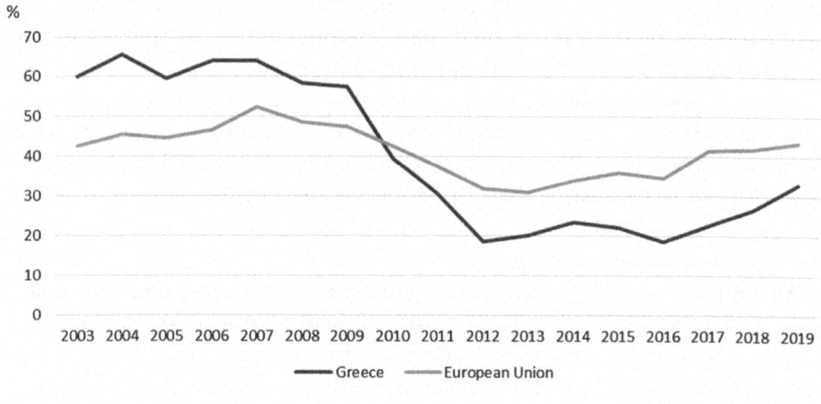

Fig. 3.1 Trust in the European Union (*Source* European Commission [2019] and author's own creation)

constraints. The countries that make up the union should have the ability to acquire, but not print, the euro they use. Failure to achieve this condition raises a serious bankruptcy risk. Instead, a state that creates its currency can calculate the taxes it wants to collect, print the money needed to accomplish its goal, and has an infinite ability to issue payment orders without fear of going bankrupt.

States that create their own currency keep control of it through fiscal and monetary policy. In a framework where the central bank does not add in any way fresh capital to the system, it has the ability through either system to impose an exchange of financial data, to intervene on individuals' preferences, without adding new financial elements. The entry and exit of financial elements into the system is fiscal policy's responsibility. Finally, tax payment removes capital, while deficits increase creates new capital.

Thus, despite monetary policy in Eurozone being of a central nature (one discount rate for all), fiscal policy is much more complex.

One of the system's major consequences is that, usually, euro countries tend to operate pro-cyclically—following the business cycle's flow. By contrast, in the United States there is a driving force, Fed, which adds new funding capital, and has the ability to operate counter-cyclically—go against business cycle's flow. So, in times of recession, the required budgetary discipline required for Eurozone countries often involves spending cuts at the worst point of the economic cycle. This procyclicality (Harrison, 2011) in managing financial crises can be devastating for economies.

But the 2008 crisis forced Eurozone and EU to take certain important initiatives. ECB, like Fed in the US, had to significantly raise funds available in the European economy through Quantitative Easing (QE) and the financing policies of national credit systems, causing even a limited risk transfer.

At the same time, the banking system monitoring has been restructured. ESM's capabilities have also been expanded, allowing it to be present in any new private or public debt crisis. But this tendency to return (at least part of the) power to national parliaments and the rise of Euroscepticism, that emerged as a result of crisis of 2008 and the refugee problem, is weighing on the European integration process.

3.7 The European Union and Covid-19 Crisis

This part aims to introduce the effects of Covid-19 crisis on European economy. To this end, the evolution of the economic crisis in European economy, economic policy requirements, and the specific policies developed by April 2020 are being examined.

Covid-19 pandemic pushed global economy and major economies into a deep recession in the first half of 2020. Initial estimates on economies' course have given way to worse estimates over time due to pandemic's spreading. Initially, forecasts for the whole of 2020 spoke of zero economic growth, amounting to the second weakest growth rate in fifty years.

However, forecasts then agreed on a large recession as multiple Covid-19 outbreaks caused shock, both in terms of supply and demand in global economy.

The lockdowns imposed by the economies helped to reduce the pandemic and protect human health, but at the cost of losing production. The mechanism for spreading the crisis in European economies, but also in global economy, in general, included the sharp tightening of financial conditions as well as liquidity restrictions for businesses.

However, before the pandemic being appeared in Europe, Eurozone had been showing some signs of concern since the beginning of 2020. Manufacturing activity has been in recession since the second half of 2018 with some signs of improvement, while services were resilient. The recovery of Eurozone, albeit at a slow pace, has been altered by Covid-19 pandemic, at a time when it could have benefitted from the trade agreement between China and United States.

China, where the pandemic began, was the first economy to return to normality, helping partially to resolve global supply chains and support global demand. Despite this, Eurozone was found recording large losses in the first half of 2020 and recovering in the second one.

Contributing to this was the gradual easing of social distancing measures, the resuming of discretionary spending as well as the fiscal and monetary economies' stimulation. The recovery was combined with how many small to medium-sized enterprises managed to survive the shock of the pandemic.

Partial or complete lockdowns in most European economies have caused major interventions in tourism, travel, and discretionary spending, leading to a reduction in household spending and exports in the short-term. The prevalence of high levels of uncertainty has led to reduction in business investments, reduction in demand and tightening of financial conditions.

States' intervention to avoid permanent damage to productive structures had to be immediate and decisive on the part of national governments, as EU announced on March 13, 2020. Given the limited size of the EU budget, the main fiscal response to the Coronavirus would come from Member States' national budgets. "Fresh" money could actually come from national governments with inevitable consequences for public finances' viability, especially when combined with GDP reduction. For this reason, European Commission proposed that the Council had to apply the full flexibility existing within EU fiscal framework to cater "unusual events outside the control of government," thus accommodating temporary deviations from the required fiscal adjustments.

In order to tackle the economic crisis caused by Covid-19, those in charge of implementing fiscal and monetary policy in Europe could not forget the lessons learned from the 2008 crisis. There could be no excuse for repeating mistakes made ten years before Covid-19 pandemic.

In March 2010, as investors abandoned Greek debt and Greek economy's ability to borrow again, European institutions were reluctant to use the mechanisms and resources at their disposal to the necessary extent or with a clear end goal (Honohan, 2020). Instead of maintaining an expansionary stance, fiscal policy was restrained prematurely, while monetary policy provided some sort of signal, and sometimes, even in the wrong direction.

The weakness of European institutions to act in a direct and effective way to reduce the debt crisis in Greece was apparent. This contributed to crisis' spread in other Eurozone countries with persistently negative effects on prosperity and political environment. It took more than two years for the situation to get under control and for economic activity to return to pre-crisis levels. The damage was greater in countries with macroeconomic imbalances as during growth periods they did not implement appropriate policies, however, the effects spread throughout the whole of Eurozone.

However, the nature of Covid-19 pandemic is different from the 2008 crisis in both its source and its geographical distribution. European economies were faced with a major external shock that raised hopes that there could be an effective collective response. Perhaps for Europe the time has come for a rapid and powerful policy implementation that would reduce the effects and secure the equal regionalization of the pandemic among all member states.

The implementation of direct economic policies was necessary as:

- They needed to limit the negative expectations of businesses and households before converting to self-fulfilling expectations. The increased expansion of the pandemic and the adoption of social distancing measures have led investors to take measures to mitigate their exposure. The fall in stock markets that followed and the increase in government borrowing costs could lead firms to overreaction.
- The impact of the recession on employees and small enterprises needed to be reduced. Major government interventions were needed to boost household incomes to ensure that employees and firms were not "punished" for their involvement in the collective action against the spread of the virus. In this regard, among other things, a safety net has been set up among various groups of the population who have been affected either by illness or losing their jobs. For small enterprises, moratoriums have been imposed on debt seizures with special guarantee programs and government collateral. At the same time, work was subsidized to ensure the non-bankruptcy of private companies and social collapse.

The need to implement the above measures was accompanied by an increase in public debt in many countries, while also being accompanied by an increase in borrowing costs. A typical example was Italy, where the market feared that the pressure on its public finances should weigh on the country without the intervention of its European partners. Under these circumstances, the activation of European mechanisms and especially ECB was a necessary condition. The activation of ECB to provide additional flexibility through QE helped stifle any unwarranted market pressures that threatened to disrupt financial markets.

The political answer, whether it is trying to cover problems from the supply or the demand side, focused on ensuring liquidity in the economy. Both monetary and fiscal policies were largely incapable of tackling the virus-induced disruption to supply, while preventing the desired results from lockdowns against the spreading of the virus. The boosting of businesses affected by the crisis and the provision of bank liquidity has been a key policy response to reduce possible future adverse effects. In this regard, it was necessary to provide as much liquidity as possible from central banks in order to limit contagion risks from money markets to real economy through the banking system (e.g., long-term refinancing operations [LTROs], QE).

EU was initially slow to come up with an organized and targeted response to Covid-19 crisis. But then the situation began to change, especially after Eurogroup decisions on April 9, 2020. As a result, Covid-19 crisis led to the need to develop mechanisms that would initially address liquidity issues in the economy by activating fiscal policy that increased fiscal deficits and debts, while also mobilized monetary policy to control states and firms cost of borrowing.

In essence, however, due to the required size approaching 1–2 trillion euros, there were inevitable consequences on the way the European structure has been organized through the cooperation of its two main branches: national governments and supranational institutions, namely ECB, ESM and European Bank for Reconstruction and Development (EBRD). Here we are interested in the supranational level of developments in which the main actions were the following:

3.7.1 Fiscal Measures

As March 23, 2020: Fiscal measures amounting to approximately 37 billion euros (0.3% of EU-27 GDP) include:

- The creation of the Corona Response Investment Initiative (CRII) in the EU budget to strengthen actions for investments in hospitals, small and medium-sized enterprises (SMEs), labor market, and affected areas.
- Enlargement of the EU Solidarity Fund to include the health crisis in its scope and resources mobilization up to 800 million euros in 2020 for EU's hardest-hit members.
- Redirecting 1 billion euros from EU budget as a guarantee to European Investment Fund (EIF) to motivate banks to provide liquidity to SMEs.
- Extension and freezing of borrowers' debt repayments that were negatively affected by the crisis.

European Commission has also activated the general escape clause in EU fiscal rules, which suspends the obligation of member states to make fiscal adjustments, allowing budget deficits to exceed 3% of GDP.

As of April 9, 2020: The latest additional package of measures amounting to 540 billion euros (4% of EU-27 GDP) includes:

- The possibility of ESM to provide Pandemic Crisis Support up to 2% of 2019 GDP for each Eurozone member state (up to 240 billion euros in total) to finance health spending.
- The provision of 25 billion euros in government guarantees to European Investment Bank to finance firms, mainly SMEs, with up to 200 billion euros.
- The creation of a temporary loan-based instrument (support to mitigate unemployment risks in an emergency [SURE]) of up to 100 billion euros to protect employees and jobs, backed by state guarantees from 27 EU member states.

3.7.2 *Currency and Macro-Financial Measures*

ECB has decided to provide monetary policy support through: (a) additional asset purchases of 120 billion euros until the end of 2020 under the existing asset purchase program (APP), and (b) the provision of temporary additional auctions for the liquidity facilitation of fixed interest rates and more favorable terms for existing targeted longer-term refinancing operations (TLTRO-III) between June 2020 and June 2021. Other measures include the 750-billion-euro pandemic emergency purchase program (PEPP), by the end of 2020, an expanded range of acceptable assets under the corporate sector purchase program (CSPP) and collateral easing for Eurosystem's refinancing operations (main refinancing operations [MROs], LTROs, TLTROs). Collateral standards were further eased in early April. These facilities include a permanent 20% reduction for non-tradable assets and temporary measures for the duration of PEPP (in order to reassess its effectiveness before the end of 2020), such as reduction to cuts by 20% in the expansion of Greek government bond eligibility as well as expanding the application of the so-called additional framework of credit receivables, so that they also include guaranteed public sector loans to SMEs, self-employed and households.

Bank Supervisory Board of ECB allowed major institutions to operate under the guidance of Pillar 2 Requirement (P2R), the regulatory framework to maintain capital and liquidity coverage ratio (LCR). Additionally, the new rules for capital composition on meeting the requirements of P2R were front loaded in regards to releasing additional capital. ECB considers that the appropriate release of the anti-cyclical capital stock by the national macro-prudential authorities will strengthen measures to alleviate capital. ECB's Banking Supervisory Board also decided to exercise—on a temporary basis—flexibility in categorizing claims and expectations to cover losses from non-performing loans covered by public guarantees and state moratoriums related to Covid-19. ECB also advised banks to avoid pro-cyclical assumptions in determining loss forecasts and to choose International Financial Reporting Standard (IFRS) 9 transition rules. More recently, ECB's Banking Supervisory Board asked banks not to pay dividends for the financial years 2019 and 2020, nor to repurchase shares during Covid-19 pandemic, but to use available capital to support households, small enterprises and corporate borrowers and/or to absorb losses from existing positions against these borrowers.

EU's proposal (end of April 2020) is to incorporate a 300-billion-euro recovery fund into its 2021–2027 budget and to borrow 320 billion euros from capital markets. In total, the fund will include 2 trillion euros for the economic recovery.

According to Commission's proposal, half of the funds to be raised will be given to countries in the form of loans, while the rest will remain in EU budget to cover annual interest payment of about 500 million euros. Apart from the temporary 300-billion-euro recovery fund in its new multi-year budget, European Commission's proposal provides for a 200-billion-euro recovery and sustainability fund, which will be reorganized by an old convergence tool.

It also predicts that 50 billion euros of cohesion funds will be used for another purpose and will be given up front in 2021 and 2022, as well as two 200-billion-euro funds to protect EU's internal markets.

National governments and ECB were at the forefront of the action. SURE mechanism and ESM's contribution, as mentioned above, are powerful tools to strengthen EU action. However, stronger involvement from the EU-27 is needed to ensure that they are able to fulfill their mission, to ensure necessary solidarity, and establish mechanisms for the post-crisis reconstruction of the entire European economy.

After several months of severe restrictions and lockdowns, corporate sector across Europe has been hit hard. Many companies faced the inability to service their debt, new operating regulations created new costs and investment needs to comply with new reality, while catering and tourism industry faced the biggest problems. The blow to airlines was similar.

However, individual state interventions raise concerns on two areas: firstly, there may be conditions for unfair competition in subsidized industries and businesses, and secondly, the amounts required will further weaken fiscally weak economies by threatening their fiscal sustainability.

As a result, it was suggested that it would be more productive to create a Recovery Fund (Bénassy-Quéré et al., 2020) to repair and rebuild European economy. The goal of such a recovery initiative is to consolidate corporate balance sheets, repair value chains and rebuild economy in a sustainable way by investing in public goods. Such an effort could be a mechanism for dealing with future pandemics and similar crises.

By examining these actions, it is clear that the course of European unification seems to be succeeding and is reminiscent of the process of United States unification, starting with A. Hamilton in 1790 and going through two world wars.

In these three cases, the federal composition of USA needed to be more active while developing a complex system of guarantees based on the redistribution of gold ownership by individual states in return for debt consolidation. This is how the common American structure was completed to a significant degree.

In essence, wars (and the threats to their existence) were the catalysts for the unification of the American structure. In Europe, it was not the enemy that led nation states to a common destination but it was the virus that would endanger Europe's administrative capabilities. Of course, in EU, the impact is a slow and evolving process, and it is clear that the mass production of bonds that easily and quickly consolidate national risks will still have to wait for some time yet. But in the past (in 2012) similar bonds had been issued by EFSF (54.2 billion euros for Greece, Ireland, and Portugal) to meet the needs of the debt crisis. These are loans granted under conditionality.

Adversely, ECB's PEPP provides about 820 billion euros that are symmetrically relevant to all European countries (even Greece that was not entitled to it) and consequently the most vulnerable, such as Italy, pulling the brake on Eurosceptics' analyses.

However, the similarities between the pressures on European structure are greater than those of United States in 1970 (Kirkegaard & Posen, 2018) and fewer than the 2008 crisis in the sense that virus effects have an almost symmetrical impact on all European economies, that is, they increase the overall systemic risk, without the policies of national governments being symmetrical, whether epidemiologically or economically. Of course, Covid-19 cannot be described as an endogenous problem of economic imbalance. Consequently, the arguments for moral hazard are much less powerful than those related to the heavily indebted economies of 2008. Of course, the economic impact is not exactly symmetrical, as for different reasons, different economies were affected by varying degrees. In general, however, European society has come to terms with a common enemy after 75 years.

Of course, Europe, unlike United States, does not have budgetary transfers mechanisms to support the less favored by the wealthier in the north. However, the holding bonds issued by ECB for the crisis for a very long time means that a supranational organization, or mechanism, will be created that could free ECB from possessing them.

However, it should be noted that the reaction of European states, mainly in the area of fiscal and health policies, was in the first place mainly characterized by a lack of coordination. Policies such as cross-border mobility and local lockdowns were also adopted in an uncoordinated manner, revealing a lack of predictability for the forthcoming phenomenon, despite there being sufficient information coming from China. This resulted in an extended period of social pain and its greater dispersion, and ultimately an increase in the cost of dealing with it. The lack of coordination even took on an aggressive dimension when large European countries seized medical supplies.

Perhaps the biggest risk facing the European structure is the debt problem that will be created in countries with high debt, with an emphasis, of course, on Italy, Spain, and Greece where debt can exceed 200% of GDP but without high risk of non-repayment. Here there is a risk of creating self-powered negative expectations on the cost of debt that will trigger spreads.

The European Commission on May 27, 2020 submitted its proposal for a recovery plan for EU member states. In particular, to ensure that recovery is sustainable, fair and without exclusions for all member states, it proposed the creation of a recovery tool, the "Next Generation EU" which is included in the EU's multiannual financial framework (MFF) 2021–2027.

Essentially, this is a temporary emergency tool created to dynamically start Europe's recovery and support sectors of the economy that need it most. Next Generation EU will have 750 billion euros in capital and, in combination with targeted EU budget support actions (MFF 2021–2027), offer an amount to the order of 1.85 trillion euros for the recovery of member states (European Commission 2020). Out of the 750 billion euros, 500 billion euros will be provided in the form of grants, while the remaining 250 billion euros will be in the form of loans for the recovery and promotion of strategic priorities. To raise funds, the Commission will issue 30-year bonds using its creditworthiness. Their repayment will begin in 2028.

The Next Generation EU program includes three pillars (Fig. 3.2).

The first pillar will finance national recovery plans by promoting investments and reforms:

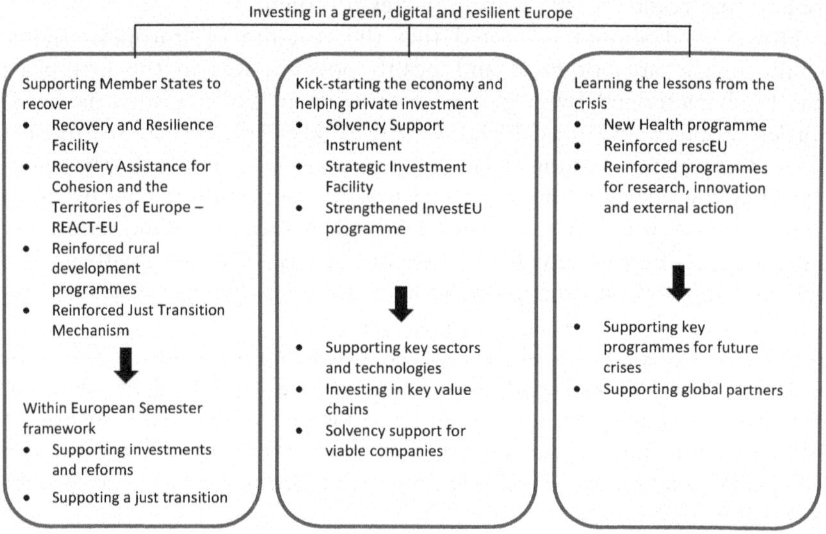

Fig. 3.2 The three pillars of Next Generation EU (*Source* European Commission [2020] and author's own creation)

- The 560-billion-euro Recovery and Resilience Facility to support investments and reforms.
- Strengthen existing cohesion policy programs with 55 billion euros from today through to 2022 under the new recovery assistance for cohesion and the territories of Europe (REACT-EU) initiative.
- Reinforcement of the Just Transition Fund up to 40 billion euros.
- Strengthening the European Agricultural Fund for Rural Development with 15 billion euros to support rural areas and promote Green Deal structural changes.

The second pillar refers to supporting healthy businesses through capital boosts, mobilizing private investment and strengthening the strategic autonomy of the European economy:

- 31 billion euros for the creation of the Solvency Support Instrument that will mobilize private resources aimed at urgently supporting sustainable European companies in the areas, regions, and countries most affected. It may be launched in 2020.
- Upgrading of InvestEU with 15.3 billion euros to mobilize private resources toward investment projects.
- Creation of the Strategic Investment Facility with funds of 15 billion euros integrated in InvestEU to create investments up to 150 billion euros.

The third pillar focuses on EU preventative and preparatory actions against future health crises:

- 9.4 billion euros for the new EU4Health program aimed at enhancing health security.
- 2 billion euros for the Union's Civil Protection Mechanism providing the EU with the ability to prepare for future crises.
- 13.5 billion euros for the Horizon Europe program, which will be boosted to fund vital research in health, resilience and the green and digital transition.
- 15.5 billion euros to finance partner countries, including humanitarian aid.

References

Bénassy-Quéré, A., Marimon, R., Martin, P., Pisani-Ferry, J., Reichlin, L., Schoenmaker, D., & di Mauro, B. W. (2020). Repair and reconstruct: A recovery initiative. *Vox CEPR Policy Portal*. Retrieved from: https://voxeu.org/article/repair-and-reconstruct-recovery-initiative.

Council of the European Union. (2012). *Euro summit documents 2010–2018: Euro area summit statement*, 29 June 2012. Retrieved from: https://www.consilium.europa.eu/media/21400/20120629-euro-area-summit-statement-en.pdf.

Council of the European Union. (2013a). Regulation (EU) No 472/2013 of the European Parliament and of the Council of 21 May 2013 on the Strengthening of Economic and Budgetary Surveillance of Member States in the Euro Area Experiencing or Threatened with Serious Difficulties with Respect to their Financial Stability. *Official Journal of the European Union, 52*(L 140), 1–10. https://doi.org/10.3000/19770677.l_2013.140.eng.

Council of the European Union. (2013b). Council Regulation (EU) No 1024/2013 of 15 October 2013 Conferring Specific Tasks on the European Central Bank Concerning Policies Relating to the Prudential Supervision of Credit Institutions. *Official Journal of the European Union, 56*(L 287), 63–89. https://doi.org/10.3000/19770677.l_2013.287.eng.

European Central Bank. (1998). *A stability-oriented monetary policy strategy for the ESCB* (Press Release). Retrieved from: https://www.ecb.europa.eu/press/pr/date/1998/html/pr981013_1.en.html.

European Commission. (2010). *EUROPE 2020: A strategy for smart, sustainable and inclusive growth* (Communication from the commission). Retrieved from: https://eur-lex.europa.eu/legal-content/en/ALL/?uri=CELEX%3A52010DC2020.

European Commission. (2019). *Public opinion survey*. Standard Eurobarometer: 59–92. Retrieved from: https://ec.europa.eu/commfrontoffice/publicopinion/index.cfm/Survey/index#p=1&instruments=STANDARD.

European Commission. (2020). *Communication from the Commission to the European Parliament, the Council, the European Economic and Social Committee and the Committee of the Regions* (COM/2020/442 final). Retrieved from: https://eur-lex.europa.eu/legal-content/EN/TXT/?uri=COM:2020:442:FIN.

European Union. (2012). Consolidated version of the treaty on European Union. *Official Journal of the European Union, 55*(C 326), 13–45. Retrieved from: https://eur-lex.europa.eu/LexUriServ/LexUriServ.do?uri=OJ:C:2012:326:FULL:EN:PDF.

Harrison, E. (2011). Pro-cyclical fiscal policy. *Naked Capitalism*. Retrieved from: https://www.nakedcapitalism.com/2011/07/pro-cyclical-fiscal-policy.html.

Honohan, P. (2020). Patrick Honohan: Coronavirus is no excuse for repeating errors of financial crisis. *The Irish Times*. Retrieved from: https://www.irishtimes.com/opinion/patrick-honohan-coronavirus-is-no-excuse-for-repeating-errors-of-financial-crisis-1.4205205.

Kirkegaard, J. F., & Posen, A. S. (2018). Realistic European integration in light of US economic history. In J. F. Kirkegaard & A. S. Posen (Eds.), *Lessons for EU integration from US history* (pp. 2–15). Washington: Peterson Institute.

Mundell, R. A. (1961). A theory of optimum currency areas. *American Economic Review, 51*(4), 657–665.

Nikolov, P., & Pasimeni, P. (2019). Fiscal stabilisation in monetary unions. *Vox CEPR Policy Portal*. Retrieved from: https://voxeu.org/article/fiscal-stabilisation-monetary-unions.

Perotti, E., & Soons, O. (2020). The Euro: A transfer union from the start. *Vox CEPR Policy Portal*. Retrieved from: https://voxeu.org/article/euro-transfer-union-start.

Statistical Office of the European Communities. (2020a). *Eurostat: GDP and main components (output, expenditure and income)* [nama_10_gdp].

Statistical Office of the European Communities. (2020b). *Eurostat: Government deficit/surplus, debt and associated data* [gov_10dd_edpt1].

Statistical Office of the European Communities. (2020c). *Eurostat: HICP (2015 = 100) - annual data (average index and rate of change)* [prc_hicp_aind].

CHAPTER 4

Political Economy of Integrated Growth and Development for the Greek Economy

4.1 Introduction

This chapter concentrates on presenting five factors which are essential for the Greek economic development and growth. The simultaneous focus on all five factors is a key parameter for future success. The chapter introduces the reader to the sense of the political economy of development and growth, used in the series of books analyzing the Greek economy (Sect. 4.2). Then it is presented the concept of sustainable development (Sect. 4.3), sustainable governance (Sect. 4.4), inclusive growth (Sect. 4.5), development-friendly social behavior (Sect. 4.6), and dynamic economic growth (Sect. 4.7), which relate to key conceptual categories of Greek development and growth. Finally, the importance of the integrated conception of development and growth for the Greek economy is analyzed (Sect. 4.8).

4.2 Revising What Is Relevant for Development and Growth

The first quarter of the twenty-first century is the era economic science is dealing with growth relied on an endogenous, micro-founded approach to development. Even when exogenous and systemic events of great intensity, such as Covid-19, arise, the interest of economic science focuses on how these events come into, endogenously, key features of the

P. E. Petrakis, *The New Political Economy of Greece up to 2030*,
The Political Economy of Greek Growth up to 2030,
https://doi.org/10.1007/978-3-030-47075-3_4

economic system. Thus, the prevailing theoretical view looks for growth key sources in knowledge and innovation, human behavior is based on individual rationality, while the concept of endogenous development has emerged, introducing at the same time elements, such as technological change and population growth rates.

A short time after the outbreak of the 2008 Great Recession, Robert Solow (2010) addressed the US Congress, in a speech titled "Building a Science of Real-World Economics," stating that modern macroeconomics has not just failed to solve present economic and financial problems, but was doomed to fail.

Perhaps this is why economic science, in its attempt to expand its potential, adjusted to include and investigate human behaviors, such as the role of psychological behavior among subjects in taking economic decisions. For example, there is talk that greed among managers in the financial sector caused the 2008 crisis. In trying to contribute toward interpreting the Great Recession, Akerlof and Shiller (2009) raised a crucial question directly linked to the psychological background, namely as, "how does human psychology lead the economy and why this is important."

In the book by Ignacio Palacios-Huerta, *Leading Economists Predict the Future*, which is dealing with what the future holds for us in 100 years by the perspective of ten renowned economists, Nobel laureate Alvin Roth (2014) notes that economics will continue to be (for 100 years) at the forefront of social sciences, partly because they will continue to incorporate ideas and data that were once regarded as vital part of sociology and political sciences, just as they have already begun to assimilate elements derived from psychology and biology.

The need for a general and comprehensive understanding of growth is summarized by:

- the prevailing global conditions for economies and societies organization (globalization, changes in the global projects allocation, etc.);
- the growing demand for the economic and social phenomena understanding, underpinning the improvement of our intellectual capacity; and
- the inability of linear and limited-scope analytical tools used to predict, interpret, and solve the major developmental problems of the early twenty-first century.

Moreover, social sciences, especially economics, in the great historical moments of their evolution, relied on borrowed concepts from related scientific areas for the analysis of ideas and behaviors (expectations, animal instincts, economic behavior, etc.). That is why the fields of psychology, social and behavior policy, anthropology, and biology are crucial and should be included in areas that cooperate in order to identify growth phenomena.

It is therefore ascertained that interdisciplinary research recognizing the diversity of interconnected forces operating at multiple levels is necessary. The disadvantage of a general and complete approach to growth, however, is that it creates a complex area of concerns, where causalities and effects are highly intertwined. On the one hand, theoretical thinking must respect the complex dimension of the—under study and research—issues, and, on the other hand, it must isolate the main causes producing basic results. In conclusion, the investigation of the analysis background and the cooperation of all branches of financial sciences comes with a price, given that it is very difficult for a scientist to gather the necessary knowledge to the extent needed to achieve the optimal synthesis.

Nevertheless, once we accept the need for a general and complete approach on growth, it makes sense to look for theoretical constructions which enable the description and interpretation of the general context of coexistence among different components and behaviors.

It is a fact that the neoclassical thought edifice contains theoretically sufficient references to the coexistence of all constituents related to the overall edifice. These are traits that govern human behavior, firms and industries, and, of course, the macroeconomic perception with the respective organization of development theory. We cannot, however, claim that there is a proposal for a complete organization, as alternative to neoclassical theory in a complete manner, till today. However, complex concepts can be developed and many of them could offer different perspectives. Some of them are extremely mature for an alternative understanding of development (such as the theory of evolution), but have limited analytical capabilities, despite offering a complete framework of general thought. Their choice and utilization will depend, among others, on whether the researcher will distance himself from the impressive way of constructing analytical tools and will be charmed by the real analytical ability their use offers.

Furthermore, there are three factors that weaken the position of neoclassical analysis in interpreting the contemporary developmental reality of the second decade in the twenty-first century. The first relates to the complexity, ambiguity, and uncertainty of the economic environment after the 2008 crisis, where established neoclassical and neo-Keynesian concepts that prevailed with considerable ease in the Great Moderation period (1980–2008). The second is located in the fact that in the diverse and specific, institutional and cultural, context of Southern Europe peripheral countries—and particularly for the Greek economy—it is difficult to apply assumptions about the absence of transaction costs or the maximization of their utility. Additionally, the over-exaggeration of the political factor and the broader receding of liberal democracy principles lead to the adoption, from a range of political forces, of economic policy actions that are very difficult to be incorporated into the logic of an established neoclassical framework. That is why it is imperative to recourse to a more complex development framework, such as the one used in this series of books.

A comprehensive and integrated approach to development and growth requires a thorough analysis of the growth economy over time. The growth process is highly interconnected with a number of factors, given that random and unforeseen changes and interactions take place. It is clear that there are systems, models, and long-term trends that are being applied and need to be highlighted. So, on the one hand, evolutionary dynamic trends must be highlighted, and on the other hand, micro-processes that identify paths linking equilibrium points within general trends should also be outlined.

4.3 Sustainable Development

Sustainable development is a holistic approach to human activity in relation to the environment, economy, and society (Fig. 4.1). This is how it views these three dimensions as being equal, as a single system, where one factor affects the other and they are all interconnected. In this context, the production and consumption structure are directly related to the quality of the environment and the availability of natural resources. The environment has a direct impact on the quality of life and society's level of health, and all these drastically determine in common the economy's productivity and development. Issues such as environmental protection and gender equality are being considered as "horizontal priorities," crossing fields such as labor, production, education, energy, water, infrastructure, etc.

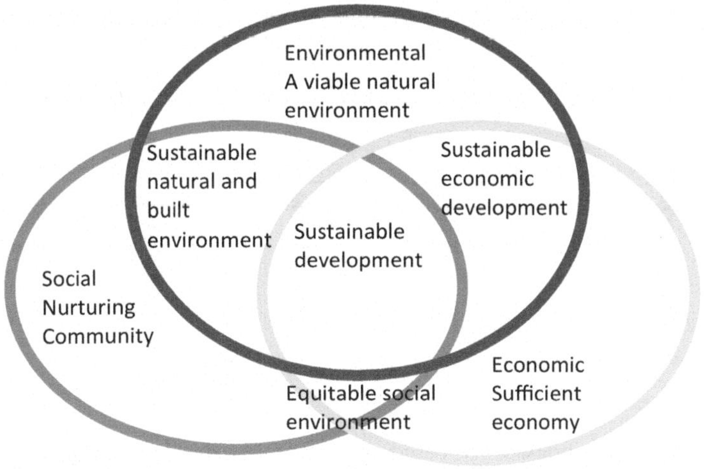

Fig. 4.1 Pillars of sustainable development and contact points (*Source* Author's own creation)

At the same time, sustainable development "leaves no one behind," that is to say, avoids exclusions and gives a high importance to reducing economic inequality in an effort to broaden the share of society enjoying the "fruits of development." It is also characteristic that structural goals are set in relation to institutions and governance. Covid-19 crisis has highlighted the fact that the concept of sustainable development contains elements affecting the economic system's efficiency. In reality, the crisis has highlighted the fact that human development factors, such as infrastructure in health systems (for example in Germany) that secure low rate of deaths per case, increase social cohesion and allow for a faster return to normality. This has obviously an impact on the medium to long-term growth rate of economy.

Figure 4.2 presents Greece's position, in comparison with Eurozone countries and the average of Organisation for Economic Co-operation and Development (OECD) and Eurozone countries for 2019, in relation to a global index based on the United Nation's 17 sustainable development goals (SDGs).

Achieving the SDGs will require deep transformations of education systems, health care, energy use, land use, urban planning, and deployment of information technologies. These transformations require strong

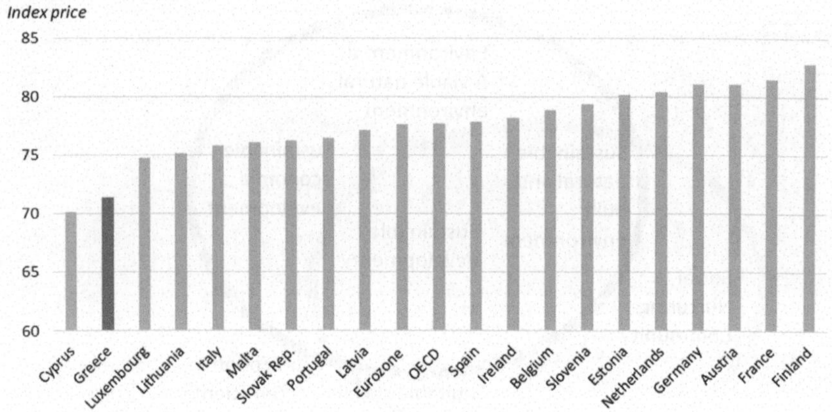

Fig. 4.2 Global index score based on sustainable development goals (2019) (*Source* Sachs, Schmidt-Traub, Kroll, Lafortune, and Fuller [2019] and author's own creation)

government leadership working in partnership with business and civil society. Integrating the SDGs by 2030 into national strategies, budgets, audits, procurement policies, regulatory and human resource management, and other dimensions of public policy poses major challenges for developed and developing countries alike.

Greece is in second last position among Eurozone countries—considerably below the Eurozone and OECD average—and, as a result, the improvement of public policies is needed in order to achieve all the SDGs within the next 10 to 20 years. Success will require massive innovation, learning, and sharing of best practices within and among countries.

4.4 Sustainable Governance

The sustainability and development of an economy depends on the structures that support it, setting the framework and goals. In other words, it depends on the political and economic institutions. The effectiveness and culture of these institutions determine to a large extent their resilience in adapting to new situations, as well as the resilience of the economy and the country. Essentially, sustainable development depends on sustainable governance.

According to the World Bank, governance consists of the traditions and institutions through which power is exercised in a country. This includes:

(a) the process by which governments are being selected, monitored, and replaced; (b) their ability to formulate and successfully implement sound policies; and (c) the level of respect from society and state for institutions, as well as their economic and social interactions. The better a country's governance is, the more effectively it can respond to internal and external challenges, absorb shocks, and adapt to new situations. Resilience is essentially the ability of states and societies to implement up to date reforms, trust institutions, and approach policy implementation with flexibility in all economic sectors, society, investment projects, education, trade, infrastructure, etc.

As far as institutions are concerned, it is important to note that governance takes precedence over the economy, as it has the final jurisdiction to the prioritization of social and economic issues, the decision-making process and the method chosen to implement these policies. Political institutions essentially shape and influence economic peers.

Coherent and long-term policy implementation is the transition vehicle to society and economy sustainability. This, however, does not take place automatically, as strong political will is required to support institutional structures and initiatives, representing a major challenge for governments. At the same time, long-term policies must be demanded by as many parts of society as possible and, as we shall see below, mainly from the middle-class.

Covid-19 crisis highlighted the value and importance of public administration efficiency in a number of areas:

- To what extent should life be offset by the rate of economic growth, since it was obvious that the first method of dealing with the pandemic, lockdowns, had a serious impact on economies? This is an issue that has two aspects difficult to be assessed: an epidemiological and an economic one. To the extent that there are structured administrative systems, there is an increased degree of confidence that decisions are more correct.
- What would be the optimal way out of lockdowns for economies and how could this be implemented effectively.Whether the measures, mainly of fiscal policy, decided upon could locate the recipients and beneficiaries and in what time period.

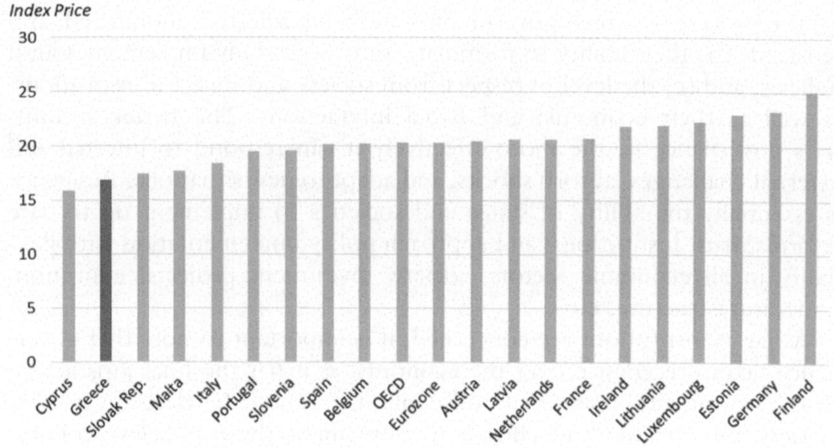

Fig. 4.3 Sustainable governance overall performance (2019) (*Note* The overall score [best value of 30] is added up based on the criteria, Policy Performance [economic, social and environmental policies], Quality of Democracy and Governance [executive capacity and executive accountability]. Each criterion is given an excellent score of 10. *Source* Sachs, Schmidt-Traub, Kroll, Lafortune, and Fuller [2019]; and Author's own calculations and creation)

The adoption, therefore, of policies that examine benefits for present and future generations, the successful implementation and evaluation of these policies, as well as the quality of democratic and institutional function supporting these government actions determine a country's performance on sustainable governance. By taking into account these three criteria, Greece's performance is presented in Fig. 4.3, in a comparison with Eurozone and OECD countries (average).

Greece is in second last position, scoring poorly on the governance index (5.4)—specifically on the government's executive capacity—and on the efficiency of economic, social and environmental policies implemented (4.6), but performing better on the quality of democracy (6.8), which is close to the average of Eurozone (7.1) and OECD (7.2) countries.

4.5 Inclusive Growth

Inclusive growth is a more restrictive concept than sustainable development and quite different from sustainable governance, as it examines social cohesion, focusing on issues of income and opportunity inequality and social mobility.

When we adopt inclusive growth, poverty and income inequality consist two of the most important monitoring indicators. These two factors affect access to opportunities and potential for social mobility with implications on social organization and status. In Greece, income inequality is consistently higher, as shown in Fig. 4.4(a, b), in comparison with Eurozone countries (average).

Individual advancement (social status) depends on policies that promote social mobility in countries, as the latter is capable of affecting education, career prospects, health quality, and, generally, opportunities and dimensions for individuals that shape their prosperity. Social mobility is directly linked to income mobility caused by changes in wealth and income and may involve upward or downward movements in social stratification. In Fig. 4.5(a) are being presented moves, over a period of four years (2011–2014), among people that belong to the middle-income quintile in Greece, in comparison with the OECD average and in Fig. 4.5(b), the rate of people remaining in the bottom income quintile for the same period.

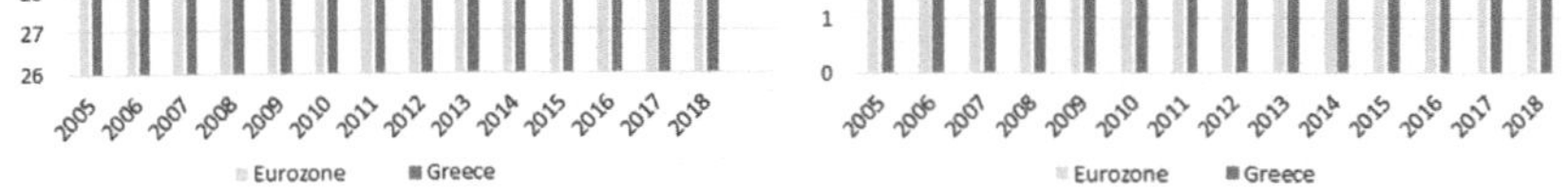

Fig. 4.4 Income inequality in Greece and Eurozone countries (average) (*Source* Statistical Office of the European Communities [2019a, 2019b*] and author's own creation)

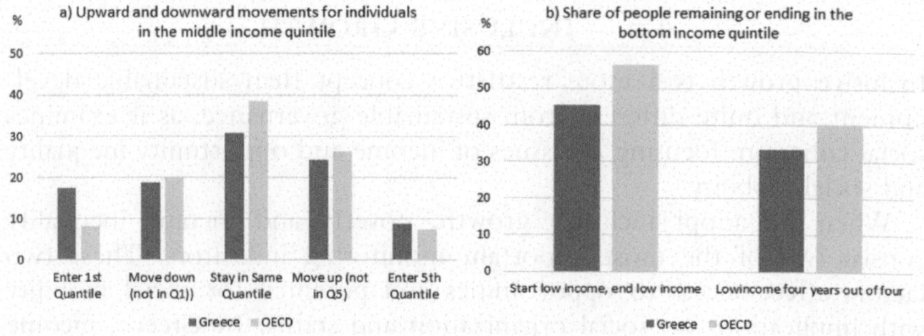

Fig. 4.5 Income mobility in Greece and the OECD countries (average) over a four-year period (2011–2014) (*Source* OECD [2018] and author's own creation)

To the extent that Covid-19 crisis affects unemployment, disposable income and the rate at which people are potentially impoverished, obviously worsens the relative problems.

Greece enjoys higher mobility in terms of movements among people in the middle-income quantile toward the lower and higher quantile, as well as a lower rate of people remaining in the lower quantile, compared with the OECD average for the four years in question.

At the same time, inequality and poverty affect prospects for social convergence between regions, generations, and families that belong to different socioeconomic groups. Inclusiveness to development is also related to increasing access to social goods through the implementation of appropriate policies. Figure 4.6(a) shows the people at risk of poverty and social exclusion in Greece compared to Eurozone average (after social transfers) and Fig. 4.6(b) the impact of social policy on reducing poverty, respectively.

Greece has a consistently higher proportion of people at risk of poverty and social exclusion throughout the whole period examined (2005–2018) than Eurozone average, which of course has been risen during the years of the recent crisis. At the same time, the effectiveness of social transfers in Greece, in reducing poverty, is significantly lower than the average among Eurozone countries, on a steady basis.

Generally, each country sets different priorities on increasing participation in development, directly depended on its social and economic structure and needs. Elsewhere, for example, there may be a serious shortage of complete education or population groups getting limited

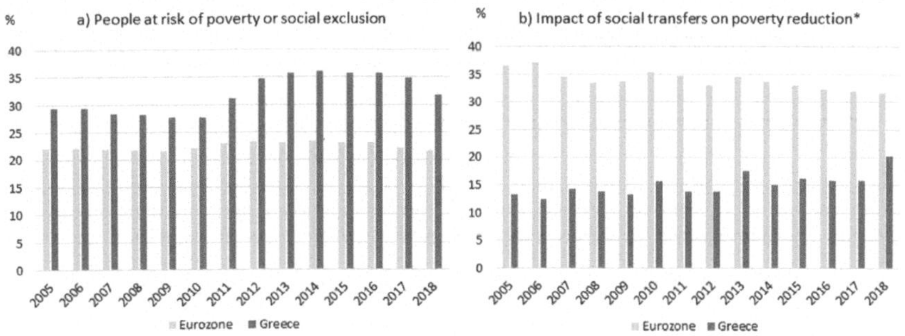

Fig. 4.6 People at risk of poverty and social exclusion and the impact of social transfers on poverty reduction in Greece and Eurozone countries (average): 2005–2018 (*Note* The poverty line relates to income below 60% of the average national income of households after social transfers. Impact [of social transfers] calculated comparing at-risk-of poverty rates before social transfers with those after transfers [pensions are not considered as social transfers in these calculations]. *Source* Statistical Office of the European Communities [2019c, 2019d*] and author's own creation)

access to education, low participation of women in the labor force, and high levels of economic inequality and poverty that hold back social mobility. Each case needs targeted action and for this reason, the definition of inclusive growth is not uniform, but differs depending on the spatial and temporal conditions that prevail each time.

In Greece, during the years 2010–2018, there is an increase in the percentage of young people (15–24 years) who were neither being employed, nor being educated (Fig. 4.7[a]). For the same period in the Greek economy, the employment gap between men and women tends to narrow down (Fig. 4.7[b]), despite the persistent gap with Eurozone (average).

Within the framework of European Union (EU), the "Europe 2020" strategy (European Commission, 2010) perceives inclusive growth as boosting an economy by increasing employment rates, aiming at the securing of economic, social and territorial cohesion. More particularly, it states that inclusive growth means empowering citizens through high levels of employment, labor markets modernization, as well as training and investing in skills, in addition to combating poverty and strengthening social protection systems. These elements help citizens prepare for and manage changes, by aiming to build a cohesive society.

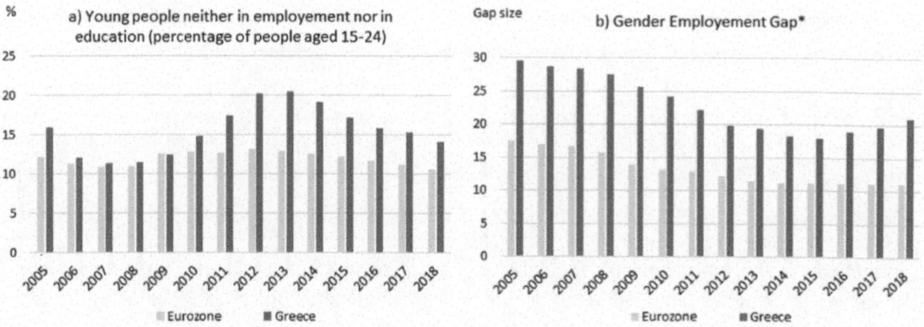

Fig. 4.7 Young people neither in employment nor in education and gender employment gap in Greece and Eurozone countries (average): 2005–2018 (*Note* Data are expressed as a percentage of the total population in the same age group. Gender Employment Gap is defined as the difference between the employment rates of men and women aged 20–64. The employment rate is calculated by dividing the number of persons aged 20–64 in employment by the total population of the same age group. *Source* Statistical Office of the European Communities [2019e, 2019f*] and author's own creation)

It is also important that benefits of economic development to be diffused, boosting social cohesion and providing access and opportunities for all the members of each society through each individual's life cycle.

4.6 Social Behavior Friendly Toward Development

The development of pro-growth behaviors is the second last place where the political economy of development and growth expands.

The exact impact that culture has on economic development is a subject that requires an interdisciplinary approach, employing scholars from both economic sciences (Schumpeter, 1934), psychology (McClelland, 1961), and sociology (Weber, 1958). Culture is made up of a total set of values and perceptions that prevail within a group of people. It consists of common values, demands, and expected behaviors.

The cultural traits of each culture have been gradually shaped, over time, by factors such as historical conditions, language, philosophy, and religion. The societies' cultural syndromes consist of a bonding between these distant factors and current reality. Culture may have specific and significant impact on economic development, by acting as either a stimulus or an obstacle.

One of the most important culture characteristics is its endurance over time, as it reflects the psychological and social stereotypes that have been formed over the centuries. These stereotypes generally show large resistance to change or redefinition. The long-term nature of the stereotypes that shape cultural background can be explained by one of two ways. The first relates to the exogenous nature of forces that have shaped them (environment, climate, etc.), while the second one presents a cultural background as an endogenous variable of human civilization.

In conclusion, the "portfolio" of cultures symptoms cultivated and reproduced within a society and the specific burden each of them carries is of crucial importance for economic growth, particularly in countries need to accelerate their normally sluggish economy, mainly due to their ability to change over the long-term.

Figure 4.8 presents the seven cultural dimensions of Shalom H. Schwartz for Greece and EU countries (average), after examining the problems faced by each society, along with preferences and values that could be developed to address these issues.

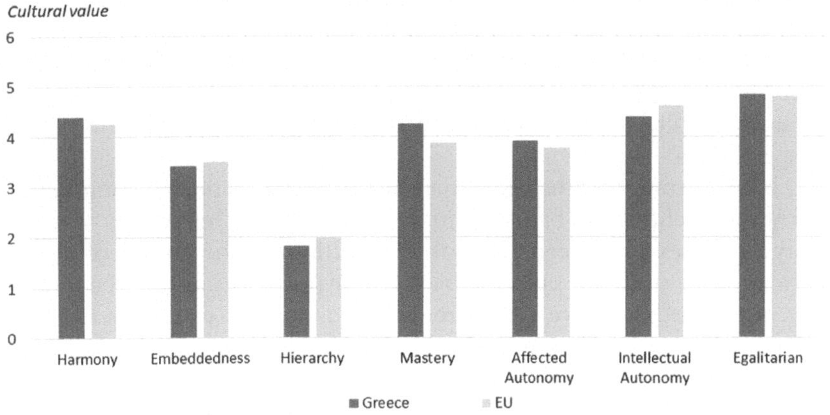

Fig. 4.8 The seven cultural dimensions (Schwartz) for Greece and EU countries (average) (*Note* Lithuania, Luxembourg, and Malta are not included. *Source* Schwartz [2006] and Author's own calculations and creation)

Differences appear in all of Greece's cultural dimensions when compared to (the average of) EU countries. In particular, Greek society places less emphasis on values, such as tradition and preservation of the current status quo, integration into collectiveness, and establishing common goals (embeddedness). At the same time, there is a smaller degree of broadmindedness, cultivation, and intellectual autonomy, while affective autonomy is being more emphasized. Greek society is also less characterized by a hierarchical culture, being less accepting of a hierarchical distribution of roles—and possibly the uneven distribution of power—and compliance with the obligations and rules associated with these roles. In regard to the extent that individuals act for the benefit of others, being concerned about the well-being of the total group (egalitarianism), Greek society identifies with the EU (average). Finally, Greek society is characterized by a relatively greater degree of acceptance of the social and natural environment (harmony) as well as a stronger desire and self-confidence in changing it, so as to achieve group or personal goals.

The question which arises is to what extent Covid-19 is changing and whether it will change certain attitudes in Greek society. We know that social behaviors under the conditions of shock are being affected, but it is very difficult to be sure how, especially when there is still no relevant research and studies. It would be of no surprise if the downsizing shock made Greeks more risk averse, while lockdowns are likely to reinforce group collectivism, by strengthening family structures. At the same time, successful management of the epidemiological crisis may strengthen the hierarchical culture and compliance with obligations and rules that these roles entail.

It is not certain that the egalitarian side of society is being strengthened or whether inclusivity is being promoted. But we must agree that the insecurity hypothesis has been strengthened, although the course of events is exogenous, and the cultural backlash hypothesis and the economic have not hypothesis have been strengthened to some extent, as incomes decline. As a result, opinions and preferences concerning a faster recovery of income will be strengthened.

We believe however, that despite the economic shock and, of course, the short to medium-term rise in uncertainty, Greek society, having experienced a climate of successful pandemic management, realizes that there can be effective collective behaviors. This was a general perception that prevailed in Greek society during the 2004 Olympic Games, a project that was admittedly very serious for the Greek economy.

A similar social mobilization could overturn the long-standing status quo and stance in the Greek economy—which have an anti-growth nature—and create supportive structures for a reform's effort. This, however, depends to a large extent on the political leadership.

A special volume is dedicated to social behaviors from the series of books *The Political Economy of the Greek Growth up to 2030* entitled *Greek Culture after the Financial Crisis: An Economic Analysis* (Petrakis, Kafka, Kostis & Valsamis, in press), where there will be a greater analysis of the effects of Covid-19.

4.7 Dynamic Growth and Convergence

Dynamic growth is the last and most basic area included in the political economy of development and growth. This sector has been affected most visibly by the outbreak of Covid-19 crisis, leading economy to another major recession in the last ten years. That is why its effects are studied in detail in the following chapters.

Economic growth is generally calculated as the annual increase rate in an economy's gross domestic product (GDP) and GDP per capita. It is usually expressed in fixed prices and not in current ones. When foreign exchange comparisons are being made, the use of purchasing power parity is necessary to avoid exchange rate problems.

Obviously, a similar definition of growth refers to an economy's level of materiality. It is normally expressed as the price—usually adjusted for inflation—of all finished goods and services produced in a country within a year. It is therefore an approximate measurement concerning living standards. This definition is of particular use when comparing economies.

A comprehensive concept of the political economy of growth and development provides crucial importance to dynamic growth for three reasons:

- Without dynamic growth there will be no means to organize policies to support sustainable growth, inclusive growth, sustainable governance, as well as pro-growth behaviors.The requirements needed to quantify the Greek economy's growth in coming years to overcome, ceteris paribus, the prescribed development conditions, are very important.
- The growth program needs to have endogenous features that secure a sustainable growth rate over time.

Figure 4.9 presents the Greek economy's GDP growth rate compared with the respective growth rates from EU (EU-28) and Eurozone countries (average).

Greece, following the severe recession experienced by the crisis from 2010 to 2017, appears to have now being recovered, approaching EU-28 and Eurozone countries (average). In 2019, specifically, GDP, for the third consecutive year, had a positive change, increasing by 1.9%. This performance is better than the average in Eurozone and EU countries. However, initial positive forecasts (European Commission, 2020) for the course of the Greek economy and in 2020 (a revised upward estimate for a GDP growth rate of 2.4%) were abruptly reversed after the outbreak of Covid-19 crisis.

Growth rates for European economies, but also worldwide, for 2020 are expected to fall steeply into negative territory. An accurate forecast for the course of Greek GDP in 2020 is impossible due to a lack of visibility during Covid-19 crisis, the management of the second phase of the crisis and the medium–long-term effects of the pandemic on the economy. Definitely, however, Covid-19 makes Greek economy more vulnerable than (most) EU economies in supply and demand disruption due to certain structural parameters, such as its degree of dependence on tourism

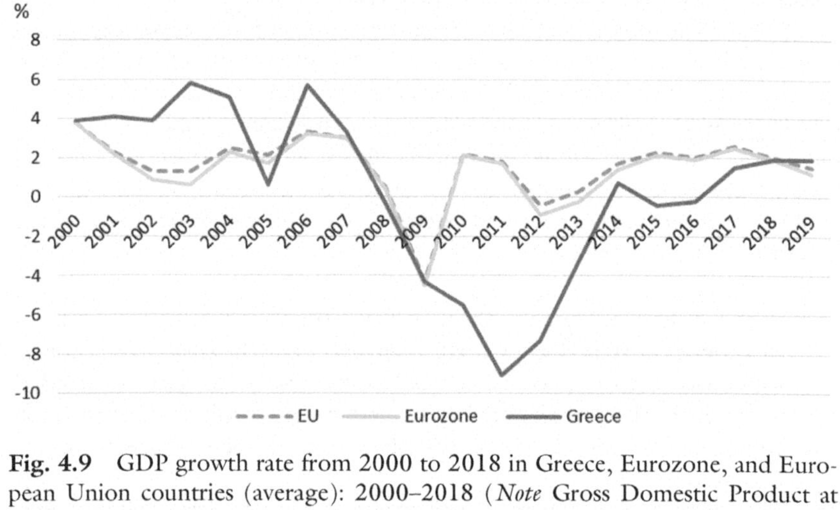

Fig. 4.9 GDP growth rate from 2000 to 2018 in Greece, Eurozone, and European Union countries (average): 2000–2018 (*Note* Gross Domestic Product at market prices. *Source* Statistical Office of the European Communities [2020] author's own creation)

and transport, the large share of very small enterprises and self-employed, and the low penetration of information and communication technologies.

4.8 The Importance of Integrated Perception of Development and Growth for the Greek Economy

A modern understanding of political economy and a comprehensive version of an analysis on the Greek economy's development and growth by 2030 should distinguish five different areas of policy analysis and application. These are: sustainable development, sustainable governance, inclusivity, pro-growth behavior, and dynamic development and growth. We should recall that economic analyses usually focus on the last point, highlighting mainly the financial dimensions of a project applying development and growth policy. Nonetheless, as it will be emphasized at the end of this chapter, a comprehensive presentation of this subject is not just a question of providing a complete analysis, but also a structural question of scientific efficiency.

A decision to activate development policy at the five distinct levels, starting from the broader and ending at dynamic growth, has the obvious aim of organizing an integrated concept of development and growth. However, the targeted integrated analysis has one and only purpose: to activate an endogenous mechanism of development and growth that will result from all of society's operational forces cooperation, ranging from the sustainable wider environment, to the provision of internal organization for social structure and the cultural background that governs human action.

It is not possible to believe that a program of economic development and growth can work effectively, if it has not secured the greatest alliance with social forces and their effective cooperation. Nor, can we believe that a program of intense growth that destroys the environment has no visible barrier to growth coming from the depletion of life's potential.

On the other hand, the fragmentation of objectives and the ways to achieve them, create an issue regarding the sharing of thoughts on applying development policies.

However, the complexity of today's reality demands, at least, the consideration of the most critical areas of development policy, regardless of priority decisions made on various sectors, as part of a broader analysis in the political economy of growth. So, from the whole portrayal of the growth process—as opposed to deeply analyzing only certain aspects of it—we choose the first option, namely the "big picture," emphasizing a number of key issues, such as investments, exports and balance of payments, production network structure, etc.

By referring to the understanding of the political economy of development and growth in the Greek economy, which we adopt in this series of books, two alternative scenarios for the future of the Greek economy by 2030 can be described. The first is based on the emerging trend, after the Covid-19 crisis. The second is based on an integrated concept of dynamic, inclusive growth with sustainable development, sustainable governance, and development-friendly social behavior. Thus, this second scenario describes an optimistic outlook for the Greek economy, which is worth being pursued by Greek society. The development and processing of these scenarios is dealt with in the second and third volumes of this book series.

References

Akerlof, G. A., & Shiller, R. J. (2009). *Animal spirits: How human psychology drives the economy, and why it matters for global capitalism*. Princeton: Princeton University Press.

European Commission. (2010). *Europe 2020: A strategy for smart, sustainable and inclusive growth. (Communication from the commission)*. Retrieved from: https://eur-lex.europa.eu/legal-content/en/ALL/?uri=CELEX%3A52010DC2020.

European Commission (2020). *Economic forecast by country: Greece*. Retrieved from: https://ec.europa.eu/info/business-economy-euro/economic-performance-and-forecasts/economic-performance-country/greece/economic-forecast-greece_en.

McClelland, D. C. (1961). *The achieving society*. Princeton: Van Nostrand.

Organisation for Economic Co-operation and Development. (2018). *A broken social elevator? How to promote social mobility*. Paris: OECD Publishing. Retrieved from: https://doi.org/10.1787/9789264301085-en.

Petrakis, P. E., Kafka, K. I., Kostis, P. C., & Valsamis, D. G. (in press). *Greek culture after the financial crisis: An economic analysis*. New York: Palgrave Macmillan.

Roth, A. E. (2014). In 100 years. In I. Palacios-Huerta (Ed.). *In 100 years. leading economists predict the future* (pp. 109–120). Cambridge: MIT Press.

Sachs, J., Schmidt-Traub, G., Kroll, C., Lafortune, G., & Fuller, G. (2019). *Sustainable development report 2019*. New York: Bertelsmann Stiftung and Sustainable Development Solutions Network (SDSN).

Schumpeter, J. A. (1934). *The theory of economic development*. Cambridge: Harvard University Press.

Schwartz, S. (2006). A Theory of Cultural Value Orientations. *Comparative Sociology, 5*(2–3), 137–182. https://doi.org/10.13140/RG.2.1.3313.3040.

Solow, R. (2010). *The prepared statement presented at the hearing before the Subcommittee on Investigations and Oversight Committee on Science and Technology House of Representatives: Building a science of economics for the real world*, Serial No. 111–106, 14–15. Retrieved from: https://www.govinfo.gov/content/pkg/CHRG-111hhrg57604/pdf/CHRG-111hhrg57604.pdf.

Statistical Office of the European Communities. (2019a).*Eurostat: Gini coefficient of equivalised disposable income - EU-SILC survey* [ilc_di12].

Statistical Office of the European Communities. (2019b). *Eurostat: Income quintile share ratio S80/S20 for disposable income by sex and age group—EU-SILC survey* [ilc_di11].

Statistical Office of the European Communities. (2019c). *Eurostat: People at risk of poverty or social exclusion* [SDG_01_10].

Statistical Office of the European Communities. (2019d). *Eurostat: Impact of social transfers (excluding pensions) on poverty reduction by sex* [tespm050].

Statistical Office of the European Communities. (2019e). *Eurostat: Young people neither in employment nor in education and training by sex* [TESEM150].

Statistical Office of the European Communities. (2019f). *Eurostat: Gender employment gap* [SDG_05_30].

Statistical Office of the European Communities. (2020). *Eurostat: GDP and main components (output, expenditure and income)* [nama_10_gdp].

Weber, M. (1958). *The Protestant ethic and the spirit of capitalism*. New York: Scribner.

PART II

The Inevitable Future Trends in the World Economy and the Position of the Greek Economy

CHAPTER 5

The Greek Economy in the World

5.1 Introduction

The study of alternative future scenarios for the Greek economy requires its position in the world to be outlined, something which is attempted to be clarified in this chapter. This can be done by tracking global and European economic forecasts for the period 2019–2030, reflecting the key features of the Greek economy in the international environment. In order, however, to provide a more complete picture, the analysis expands to the extent that socioeconomic conditions affect relative happiness level of Greek citizens, which consists of the ultimate goal regarding the efficiency of an economic system. This analysis takes into account the crisis of 2020 with Covid-19.

The chapter is structured as follows: Sect. 5.2 presents the key features of the major recession caused by Covid-19, at least as it was known until April 2020, Sect. 5.3 covers global and European economic developments expected by 2030, while the following section (Sect. 5.4) poses Greece in the international environment.

5.2 The World Depression of Covid-19

Covid-19 pandemic that erupted in early 2020 is the major recessionary fact of the early 2020s. The crisis highlighted humanity's weaknesses in handling events outside of the economy that have global and catastrophic

P. E. Petrakis, *The New Political Economy of Greece up to 2030*,
The Political Economy of Greek Growth up to 2030,
https://doi.org/10.1007/978-3-030-47075-3_5

consequences on basic economic behaviors such as consumption, productivity, linear production spreading to different parts of the world and confidence in financial systems' function.

Covid-19 crisis has the basic characteristic of, given its high uncertainty, causing a very large crisis in confidence—resulting in doubts about future incomes—and recessionary conditions, due to a reduction in overall consumption.

This first round of reactions took place in a very short period of time, having a global dimension (as was the speed at which the pandemic spread), resulting in the depth of the crisis being very large.

The difference between handling pandemics and handling climate change is important. The pandemic progresses very rapidly and a large share of the population is immediately sensitized. It has measurable results (number of cases and deaths), and mainly burdens public health systems, while climate change causes phenomena that have an independent existence, with consequences in various areas—such as tourism and construction—which are not directly related to climate change, resulting in a lack of mobilization by societies.

The world has dramatically changed with the evolution of Covid-19 (Fig. 5.1). Production losses associated with the measures taken to deal with the crisis outweigh losses arising from the 2008 crisis. Additionally, high levels of uncertainty have accumulated regarding the duration and intensity of the shock. Under these conditions, economic policy's priorities have changed and have differentiated from policies to strengthen overall demand that would apply, had we faced a downward phase in business cycle. Now the economy is facing structural supply problems that require special policies, given that horizontal demand-enhancing policies are incorrect, when the respective productive sectors are healthy.

In conclusion, the Great Lockdown (International Monetary Fund [IMF], 2020) will have a detrimental effect, causing an unprecedented recession in 2020, and this could be considered the first phase of the crisis, while the second phase raises issues of stabilization and recovery. This will lead to an increased recovery in 2021, but maintaining crisis damage in coming years. In this phase, high costs will be incurred to strengthen health systems and save social and productive networks, resulting in people living with much higher levels of budget deficits, debts, and inflated central bank balance sheets.

This way we will avoid causing a systemic crisis, mainly in financial system, taking advantage of opportunities arising from 2008 financial

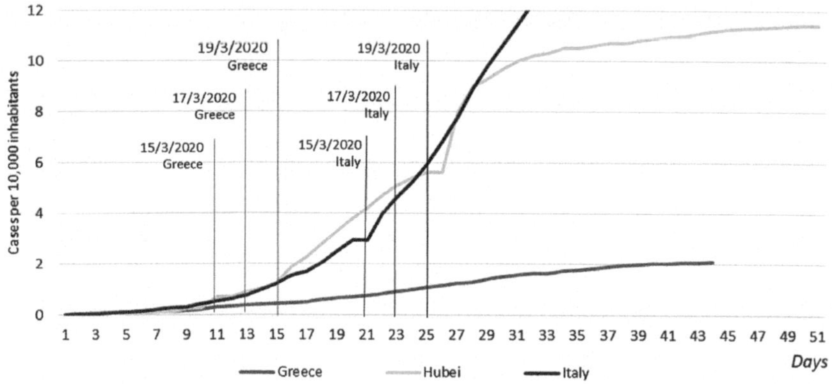

Fig. 5.1 Index of new events (diseased persons): Greece vs Italy vs Hubei (*Note* Day 1 of the crisis is the day with the occurrence of 100 cases per 60 million population [for Greece day 1 is when 18 cases occurred, i.e. March 5, 2020, for Hubei is January 18 and for Italy is the 22nd February]. *Source* Our World in Data [2020] and author's own calculations and creation)

crisis. At the same time, expectations will remain that are necessary to avoid starting the next day from a more difficult starting point.

5.3 Global and European Economic Developments: 2018–2030

Global development, after the deep recession due to Covid-19 of 2020, is expected to move positively in coming years through mild, cyclical-type, changes. Generally, however, the development outlook looks to be sluggish, while Eurozone indicates a weaker performance (Table 5.1). It should be noted that these trends preceded the Covid-19 crisis.

The Greek economy, after the rapid contraction of 2020, is expected to grow at a faster pace than the average of Eurozone economies (average) over the next decade. At the same time, however, the level of inflation rate in Greece (Table 5.2), located well below the (2%) European target, seems to be problematic, as it approaches it only during the second five-year period. Similar levels of inflation rate, at least over the next two years, can also be seen among other Eurozone countries.

After the recovery of 2020, relatively positive global developments mainly support consumer demand, in addition to the fact that a large

Table 5.1 Real Gross Domestic Product (GDP) growth: annual percentage change

	2019	*2020*	*2021*	*2022*	*2023*	*2024*	*2025–2030*
Greece	1.90	−5.94	6.52	4.46	2.65	2.27	1.73
Eurozone	1.23	−5.12	4.69	2.36	1.61	1.32	0.97
World	2.58	−3.50	6.44	3.76	3.00	2.92	2.66

Note Estimates have taken into account (April 2020) the effects of Covid-19
Source Oxford Economics (2020) and author's own calculations and creation

Table 5.2 Inflation rate, average consumer prices: annual percentage change

	2019	*2020*	*2021*	*2022*	*2023*	*2024*	*2025–2030*
Greece	0.25	−1.03	1.54	1.17	1.27	1.56	1.89
Eurozone	1.20	0.21	1.49	1.57	1.68	1.79	1.95

Note Countries with hyperinflation are not included. Estimates have taken into account (April 2020) the effects of Covid-19
Source Oxford Economics (2020) and author's own calculations and creation

part of the world is starting from lower development levels. The main central banks stance contributes to the maintenance of mild development trends. But the increase in uncertainty, associated with epidemiological phenomena and also with the field of politics, is creating recessionary forces.

The main sources of future crises in the medium-term appear to be partial or exogenous treatment of epidemiological phenomena, climate change, political uncertainty due to the trade war, central banks operations and their effects on global liquidity, low inflation and the appearance of asset bubbles, the maintenance of global economic imbalances, and a lacking arsenal of economic policy instruments—the depletion of monetary policy opportunities and lack of space to activate fiscal policy can be seen as the typical characteristics of the new era being emerged.

Generally, however, the likelihood of policy errors is increasing given that international conditions have entered an era in which is needed more careful treatment. At the same time, an environment is being created in which many economies are exposed to risks of political upheaval under the influence of exogenous effects, in regards to their economy, such as the large movements of refugees, political populism, and geostrategic energy developments.

European Union, and especially Eurozone, has entered a period of reorganizing its operational architecture. The transformation of the European Stability Mechanism (ESM) and reorganization of the fiscal policy framework, the progress on the European Banking Union's integration toward functioning on the pillars of the Single Resolution Mechanism (SRM)—with the Single Supervisory Mechanism already in place—and the European Deposit Insurance Scheme (EDIS), are of exceptional importance. The most critical part that would has been targeted by these reforms is related to the weakening of the so-called "doom loop," that is, the infectious link connecting state finances with troubled banks. So far, however, reforms implementation seems to enjoy positive, but extremely slow rates. Covid-19 took on the role of accelerator in the European Union, where in a very short period of time discussions started on even a partial direct debt expansion, multiple steps taken by ECB and the readiness of ESM and European Investment Bank, activation of European Planning and bonds issuance by European Commission for the benefit of those affected by Covid-19 crisis.

A significant finding from the work done by Reinhart and Rogoff (2008) was that periods of financial crisis are usually accompanied by about 6–8 years of low growth or economic stagnation. Their assessment seems to be confirmed, despite the fact that a new reality is appearing under the pressure of new facts. Thus, after the crisis with Covid-19, new facts on investment opportunities, the fourth industrial revolution, political shifts, and population changes are constantly repositioning the short and medium-term outlook on normality.

It is commonly accepted, moreover, that periods of widespread economic crisis are also accompanied by a rise in political populism that put forth a steady stance of doubting the importance and role of independent systems (legislative, administrative, justice, media) of mutual control and governance. Additionally, it is confirmed that political instability is more intense in periods succeeding financial crises, and the question that arises is whether Covid-19 will also lead to a financial crisis. More specifically, Funke, Schularick, and Trebesch (2015), comparing the political impact of "recessions after financial crisis" with the overall impact of "normal recessions" which are not linked to financial crisis, they conclude that financial crises stand out and are followed by political instability to a more intense extent, while compared with other types of economic crises.

This seems to be due to the fact that in financial crises: (a) endogenous problems arise due to the failure of applied policies, the increase in moral hazard, and the revealing of favoritism phenomena; and (b) financial sector bailouts usually result in even greater social dissatisfaction. However, a decade after the crisis started, most of social and economic variables are globally approaching historical averages.

As this book is being written, it is not yet clear to which extent the Covid-19 crisis will turn into a financial crisis, although there are indications that some areas of financial operations, such as the reduction of leveraging, will have negative effects.

At the end, therefore, of the second decade of the twenty-first century, existing conditions show that sources of economic turmoil have appeared, several of which have had an impact on the medium-term horizon. These conditions are: (a) movements of refugees and migrants and changes in age structure (i.e., predominance of elder people) that leads to shifts in economic and social behaviors (Chapter 6, Sect. 6.5), (b) technological changes (the 4th industrial revolution) combined with major changes in demand for work skills (Chapter 6, Sect. 6.6), (c) environmental risks and economies adjustments in terms of climate change (Chapter 6, Sect. 6.7), and (d) globalization and the transfer of weight among economic decision-making centers to the East (Chapter 6, Sect. 6.8).

In addition to these conditions, three separate phenomena are located within Western economies as a result of the cumulative effect of the above processes. These are: (e) increasing income and wealth inequalities and decreasing social mobility (Chapter 8, Sect. 8.2), (f) implications in the prosperity of the middle class and the empowerment of the individual with necessary skills (Chapter 8, Sect. 8.3), and (g) the most important changes in social behaviors (Chapter 8, Sect. 8.4).

Can these forces influence the economies' performance and the societies' structure in a way that in current situation the typical characteristics of the medium-term future will differ from those of the past?

This unusual mix of forces makes it very difficult to predict the future, which is making its mark as being more of a negative development than a positive one. Despite this, knowledge of possible negative developments often leads policy to take precautionary measures capable of mitigating the effects of these developments or even prevents them from occurring, while on other occasions, wrong policies can create fresh turmoil. Therefore, it is difficult to diagnose the ongoing developments accurately. A typical example is the Covid-19 crisis, which, as a "Black Swan," overturned the normality in 2020 and created a seriously negative starting point for the new decade.

5.4 The Greek Economy in the International Environment

A decade after the crisis (2008–2018), the challenge of the Greek economy is located in its essential recovery and strengthening, so that it can be fully integrated into the global economic stage. Tapping markets, borrowing at almost historically low interest rates, and the early partial repayment of its debts have contributed to this.

At the same time, it must address the challenges posed by Covid-19 crisis. The crisis affected the Greek economy via four channels:

- The supply of products and services through the disruption of production and supply lines (production-transport) as well as demand, due to increased consumer uncertainty.
- The negative animal spirit of investors causes reductions in the price of capital assets, resulting in business portfolios with excessive debt facing the possibility of not being able to meet their obligations. This leads to financial instability, limited credits, and turmoil in credit markets.
- The widespread diseases of employees and the obligatory restrictions on economic activity cause reductions in productivity which, in turn, cause a decrease in total demand due to negative expectations for future income. This triggers a negative spiral that leads to recession or at least economic stagnation.
- Losses on the side are arising, such as turmoil in oil markets with two major powers (Russia, Saudi Arabia) deciding that it was the right time to start a war on prices and oil supplies (at least this way, with such low oil prices, the tension in the SE Mediterranean went away!).

However, there are still several additional obstacles that must be overcome in order to reach normality, both internally and externally. The goal of sustainable development needs to be based, among others, on a healthy fiscal position, on the stability of the banking and political system, on building a favorable business climate, on efficient management of additional refugee flows, and on the equitable distribution of imminent benefits to Greek society.

These five factors, however, are also presented as being the most precarious in terms of the smooth operating of the Greek economy. Non-compliance with fiscal targets (which are under review due to Covid-19), the heavily burdened banking sector (whose condition is deteriorating in the short-term by Covid-19), non-sustainable governance, and increased refugee flows constitute—in order of importance—the highest risks to the undertaking of business activities. The regaining, therefore, of the Greek economy's credibility must be based on mitigating such concerns. This is the only way it can improve its performance and position in the international economic environment.

To form an image of Greece's relevant position some comparative data is required. In this chapter's analysis, Greece is compared with Portugal and Ireland, countries with similar recent problematic past in economic terms, but also with the experience of different crises management. Comparisons with these relatively "small" Eurozone countries is enlightening, given that Portugal in the years running up to the crisis lagged Greece in many indicators, but now is probably ahead. Ireland, on the other hand, is a country-reference point at an advanced level for many reasons, in relation to Greece.

The Greek economy is a relatively rich country that is comparable in terms of wealth to Portugal, but is considerably behind Ireland (Table 5.3). The elements that create its wealth are "Produced Capital"

Table 5.3 Key Greek figures in comparison with Portugal and Ireland

Economy	*Total wealth*	*Capital produced*	*Natural capital*	*Human capital*	*Net foreign assets*	*Population*
Greece	227,925	134,895	12,546	105,663	−25,179	10,892,413
Portugal	274,453	117,409	9189	172,163	−24,308	10,401,062
Ireland	627,256	189,309	15,912	473,656	−51,620	4,617,225

Note Estimates in the table (except population) are per capita figures—thousands of dollars ($) in exchange rates in 2014. Total wealth per capita is calculated as the sum of the estimate of each component of wealth: capital produced, natural capital, human capital, and net foreign assets. Net foreign assets are the sum of a country's foreign assets and liabilities, for example, foreign direct investment and foreign exchange reserves

Source Lange, Wodon, and Carey (2018) and author's own creation

and "Human Capital." The latter, however, creates the gap with the other two countries, despite common belief that Greece excels (in a general and indefinite manner) in human capital.

Extensive unemployment, low levels of education, and the structure (aging) of the working population (see Table 5.5) contribute to the gap in human capital. At the same time, there is a significant difference between Greece and Ireland, in terms of real disposable income and real GDP per capita (Table 5.4). The distance separating Greece from Ireland is large in both of these indicators, but approaches Portugal. In the meanwhile, the Greek economy's degree of globalization has increased significantly, especially after 1970, though it clearly lags behind these two countries.

In conclusion, the Greek economy is currently positioned between upper middle-income countries and high-income countries (Lange et al., 2018). The wealth it offers is significant, but the state of its citizens' welfare has deteriorated considerably since the 2010 crisis.

The structure of the Greek population, in relation to the labor market, includes certain important surprises. In order to be able to follow these structural features, it would be useful to focus on the entire population (2018), which does not include the old age bracket from birth to 14 years

Table 5.4 Basic Greek figures in comparison with Portugal and Ireland

Economy	*Real disposable income (thousands, €)*	*Real income per capital (thousands, $) PPP, 2017*	*Ranking on globalization index (KOF) 2019*[a]	*Shadow economy (% of GDP) 1991–2015 average*[b]	*General government debt (% of GDP) 2018*[c]
Greece	17.7	25	24	27.1	188.73
Portugal	23.5	26	15	21.9	145.3
Ireland	32.0	65	17	13.9	77.24

Note The KOF Globalization Index measures the economic, social and political dimensions of globalization on a scale of 1–100. The index examines 197 countries, with the score of 1 given to the most globalized and the remainder of the countries follows in the ranking in descending order. KOF GI Ranking 2019 is based on data for the year 2017. The size of the shadow economy for 2016, based on the publication of (Kelmanson, 2019), amounts to 30.2% for Greece as it reaches 24.5% for Portugal and 15.8% for Ireland. It must be mentioned that this is a different methodology from that used by Medina and Schneider (2018) in the above table

Source [a]Gygli, Haelg, Potrafke, and Sturm (2019), [b]Medina and Schneider (2018), [c]Organisation for Economic Co-operation and Development (OECD) (2018), Oxford Economics (2019) and author's calculations and creation

old. Thus, we find that only (!) 28.16% of the population is employed as dependent workers, compared with 41.5% in Portugal and 46.25% in Ireland, having a relative effect on productivity (Table 5.5). In contrast, 11.49% are self-employed, compared with 6.34% in Portugal and 6.71% in Ireland.

The unemployment rate is much higher in Greece and could rise even more—as is also the case in other comparative countries—if we include a form of joblessness made up of those who are involuntarily part-time, the "discouraged workers" and other potentially additional workforce. In 2018, the total of these three groups in the Greek economy numbered some 326,000 people.

Coronavirus crisis had a particular impact on the situation and the number of unemployed. It is estimated that in 2020 the number of unemployed will rise by 150,000 people, from levels seen at the end of 2019, mainly as a result of problems in the tourism sector, but also in the field of small and medium enterprises (SMEs). This effectively brings economy back one to two years, when it started to cover crisis gap from the first lost decade of 2010.

Among the self-employed are between 100,000 and 200,000 people who work for a company but are registered and able to issue invoices. They are salary workers who, in relation to the private sector, are declared as self-employed. Therefore, the total number of self-employed should be reduced by this figure, and then, in turn, be added to the total number of employees. In all categories of human resources, there are also a number of people working in the shadow economy. They are estimated to numerate at around 900,000–1,100,000 people. A person who works in the shadow economy may also belong to more than one group of workers at a time (employee, unemployed, retired, non-financially active, etc.).

Additionally, Tables 5.6 and 5.7 present income distribution among individuals and legal entities, respectively.

Most individuals' taxable income is being lying between 0 and 10,000€, while most legal entities declare losses.

Additionally, the largest group of taxpayers, reaching 35.41% is pensioners (!) immediately followed by employees (34.82%) (Independent Authority for Public Revenue [AADE], 2019). These two categories together account for 64.61% of tax revenues, while business activity employs 9.58% of taxpayers (including self-employed) and produces 22.41% of tax income.

Table 5.5 The labor structure of the Greek population (2018)

	Greece		*Portugal*		*Ireland*	
	People	*% of total population*	*People*	*% of total population*	*People*	*% of total population*
(1) Dependent workers	2,663,600	28.16	4,004,000	41.57	1,903,800	46.25
(2) Self-employed	1,087,400	11.49	611,000	6.34	276,200	6.71
(3) Total of workers	3,751,000	39.66	4,615,000	47.91	2,180,000	52.97
(3.1) Private Sector	3,028,080	32.01	3,931,050	40.81	1,881,800	45.72
(3.2) Public Sector	722,920	7.64	683,950	7.10	298,200	7.24
(3.3) Part-time employment and temporary contracts	628,000	6.64	1,251,000	12.98	613,000	14.89
(4) Unemployed	915,000	(19.3)	363,000	7	137,000	5.8
(4.1) Long term unemployed	644,000	(13.6)	160,000	3.1	50,000	2.1
(5) Labor Force (3 + 4)	4,666,000	49.33	4,978,000	51.68	2,317,000	56.29
(6) Pensioners	2,617,056	27.67	3,007,164	31.22	939,124	22.81
(7) Non financially active (not working and not looking for work—partly being educated)	2,173,800	22.98	1,646,700	17.09	859,400	20.88
(8) Total of people (5 + 6 + 7)	9,456,856		9,631,864		4,115,524	
(9) Total population	10,741,165		10,291,027		4,830,392	
(10) Population aged 0–14	1,546,667		1,423,896		1,006,448	

(continued)

Table 5.5 (continued)

		Greece		Portugal		Ireland	
		People	*% of total population*	*People*	*% of total population*	*People*	*% of total population*
(11) Completed tertiary education by age group	aged 25–34	42.8%		31.5%		56.2%	
	aged 35–44	34.2%		32%		53.8%	
	aged 45–54	29.2%		20.5%		42.9%	
	aged 55–64	21.9%		14.2%		31.2%	

Note Percentages in the second column are based on the total of the workforce, retirees (2016 data) and financially inactive people over the age of 15. Unemployment and long-term unemployment rates are exempt and calculated as a percentage of the workforce. Dependent employees are calculated after deducting the self-employed from the total number of employees. Self-employed and total of workers relate to people aged 14–64. Private sector employees result from removing public sector employees from total employed (assuming that the number of civil servants remains stable from 2015 to 2018). The data for public sector refer to the year 2015. The number of part-time employment and temporary contracts comes from adding up the corresponding categories for the 15–64 age group. Unemployment and long-term unemployment data are expressed as annual averages and relate to people aged 15–74. Workforce comes from adding those in employment (15–64 years old) with the unemployed (15–74 years old). The data for pensioners relate to 2016. Non-financially active individuals relate to people aged 14–64 (the data refer to 2018). The rest data (for categories 9, 10, and 11) refer to the year 2018

Source OECD (2017)[3.2], Statistical Office of the European Communities (2019a[2], 2019b[3], 2019c[4], 2019d[4.1], 2019e[6], 2019f[7], 2019g[9,10], 2019h[11]), and author's own calculations and creation

Table 5.6 Income distribution for individuals for 2017 tax year

Income bracket (€)	*Taxpayers (individuals)*	*Declared Income (€)*	*Total tax (€)*	*% of taxpayers*	*% of declared income*	*% of total tax*
0–10,000	3,752,187	13,026,187	415,559	58.9	17.7	5
10,000–30,000	2,126,164	36,280,687	3,292,898	33.4	49.3	39.5
Above 30,000	491,748	24,305,631	4,619,772	7.7	33	55.5
Total	6,370,099	73,612,504	8,328,229	100	100	100

Source Independent Authority for Public Revenue of the Hellenic Republic (AADE) (2019) and author's own creation

Table 5.7 Income distribution for legal entities for 2017 tax year

Brackets of Taxable profits (€)	*Total entities (firms)*	*Taxable profit (€)*	*Total tax (€))*	*% of total entities*	*% of total taxable profit*	*% of total tax*
Loss-making	99,991	0	0	39.21	0.00	0.00
Loss-making special cases	27	0	29,318,781	0.01	0.00	0.75
Zero	63,255	0	0	24.80	0.00	0.00
0–10,000	36,051	134,348,051	38,696,392	14.14	1.00	0.99
10,000–30,000	23,441	429,888,216	124,171,141	9.19	3.22	3.18
Above 30,000	32,253	12,804,505,631	3,706,922,679	12.65	95.78	95.07
Total	255,018	13,368,741,898	3,899,108,993	100	100	100

Source AADE (2019) and author's own creation

However, the largest tax burden is lifted by employees (41.95%) and then pensioners (22.66%), followed then by business activity (22.41%) (AADE, 2019).

Let's not forget that the shadow economy accounts for 27.1% of the economy (see Table 5.4), meaning that these percentages are subject to change if we include real data in total.

In regard to the structure of tax revenues, Greece appears much higher in the ranking (9th position), compared to Portugal (16th position) and mainly with Ireland (last place, EU-28), in terms of taxes as a percentage of GDP (Table 5.8). This gap is mainly due to the relative amount of indirect taxes paid, where Greece ranks in 4th position and Ireland is, again, in the best (last) position. There is also a significant difference in

Table 5.8 Income distribution for 2017 tax year (tax revenue as per type of tax and economic activity)

	Greece			*Portugal*			*Ireland*		
	%GDP	*Ranking*	*Revenues*	*%GDP*	*Ranking*	*Revenues*	*%GDP*	*Ranking*	*Revenues*
Type of tax									
Indirect taxes	17.3	4	31.1	15.1	9	29.4	8.5	28	25.1
Direct taxes	10.1	15	18.3	10.1	16	19.7	10.6	14	31.2
Social contributions	11.5	16	20.7	9.2	19	17.9	3.9	26	11.4
Total	38.9	9	70.1	34.4	16	67	23	28	67.8
Economic activity									
Consumption	14.6	3	26.3	12.7	11	24.8	7.6	28	22.4
Labor	16	17	28.8	14.5	18	28.1	9.9	28	29.1
Capital	8.4	9	15.1	7.2	14	14.1	1.3	18	3.7

Source European Commission (2019) and author's own creation

Note Ranking between European Union (28) countries. Revenues in billion of euros. Labor consists of payments from employees, employers, and those not employed. Capital broadly defined as including natural capital, intangible assets, and capital investments and savings. It is divided into subcategories: income from businesses, households, self-employed, and stock of capital

terms of taxes paid in different parts of economic activity. Greek economy's tax revenues are mainly being derived from consumption and capital, rather than labor. In fact, in the Greek economy, the tax contribution of consumption to state revenues is one of the largest among European Union (EU-28) countries—Greece ranks in 3rd position in the relevant ranking.

Greece, like Portugal but to a larger degree, has long been characterized as a consumer economy, with the total of private and public consumption in the Greek economy reaching 90.4% of GDP (stable prices 2010) for the period 2014–2018 (Fig. 5.2). Meanwhile, the corresponding rate in Ireland amounted to 47.6%!

During the Greek economy's adjustment to the bailout programs, the contribution of the external sector—due to the internal devaluation and increased competitiveness—was positive, but the investment sector was hit hard. In contrast, Ireland has been improved in both of these sectors.

Happiness among citizens can be used as the final and absolute indicator of efficiency in economic and social systems. One such indicator is the World Happiness Report, which is calculated for 153 countries and is based on six criteria that determine happiness levels (Helliwell, Layard, Sachs, & de Neve, 2020). The criteria look at GDP per capita,

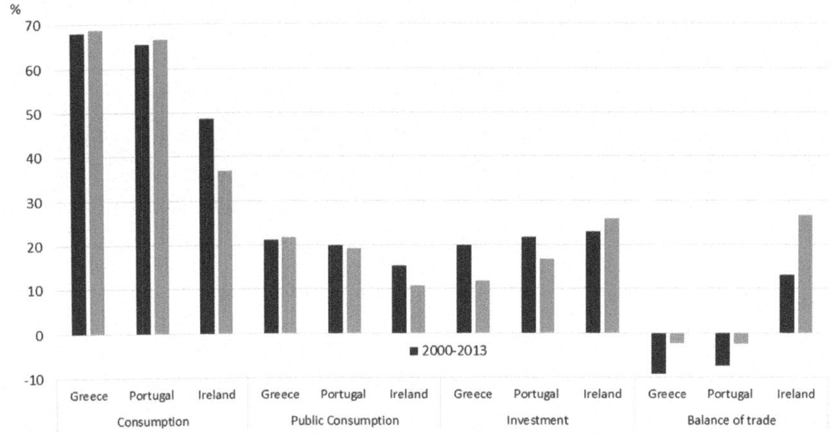

Fig. 5.2 Percentage contributed by the main components of GDP (averages for 2000–2013 and 2014–2018) (*Source* Oxford Economics [2019] and author's own calculations and creation)

life expectancy, social support, freedom of choice in personal life, levels of generosity but also corruption in society, and subjective feelings of euphoria/dissatisfaction experienced by the country's citizens.

Greece's economic and social system, due to the very large recession experienced, caused one of the greatest plunges in the happiness of Greek citizens (Fig. 5.3). Today, Greece is ranked in 77th position, Portugal in

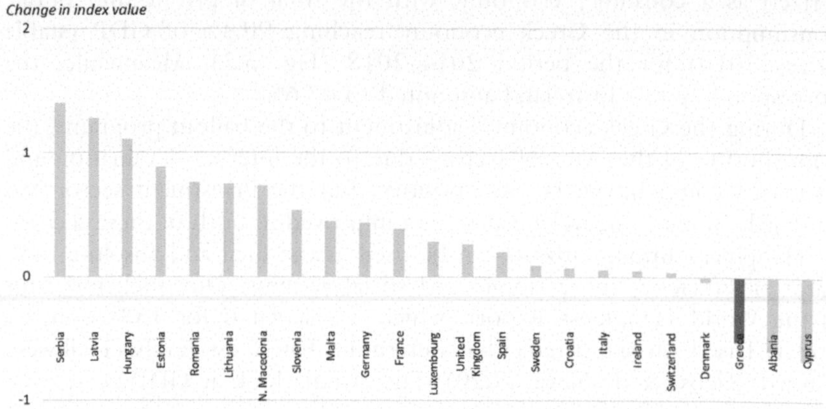

Fig. 5.3 Changing world happiness for European countries from the 2006–2008 to the 2017–2019 period (*Source* Helliwell et al. [2020] and author's own calculations and creation)

59th place, and Ireland is ranked in the 16th one. In comparison with Portugal, Greece appears to lag behind in social indicators (social support, freedom of choice), while compared with Ireland, it lags significantly in all indicators. It is noteworthy that Greece is ranked (Helliwell et al., 2020) in second-to-last position (only over Turkey) among OECD countries on the happiness index.

References

European Commission. (2019). *Taxation Trends in the European Union: 2019 Edition*. Luxembourg: Publications Office of the European Union European Commission.

Funke, M., Schularick, M., & Trebesch, C. (2015). *Going to Extremes: Politics After Financial Crises, 1870–2014* (CESifo Working Paper No. 5553).

Gygli, S., Haelg, F., Potrafke, N., & Sturm, J. E. (2019). The KOF Globalisation Index—Revisited. *Review of International Organizations*, *14*(3), 543–574. https://doi.org/10.1007/s11558-019-09344-2.

Helliwell, J., Layard, R., Sachs, J., & de Neve, J. E. (2020). *World Happiness Report 2020*. New York: Sustainable Development Solutions Network.

Independent Authority for Public Revenue. (2019). *Income from Individuals for the 2017 Tax Year (2018 Tax Declarations)*. Retrieved from: https://www.aade.gr/menoy/statistika-deiktes/eisodima/etisia-statistika-deltia (in Greek).

International Monetary Fund. (2020). *World Economic Outlook 2020: The Great Lockdown*. Washington: IMF.

Kelmanson, B. (2019). *Explaining the Shadow Economy in Europe: Size, Causes and Policy Options* (IMF Working Paper No. 19/278).

Lange, G. M., Wodon, Q., & Carey, K. (2018). *The Changing Wealth of Nations 2018*. Washington: The World Bank Publications.

Medina, L., & Schneider, F. (2018). *Shadow Economies Around the World: What Did We Learn Over the Last 20 Years?* (IMF Working Paper No. 18/17).

Organisation for Economic Co-operation and Development. (2017). *Government at a Glance 2017*. Paris: OECD Publishing.

Organisation for Economic Co-operation and Development. (2018). *OECD Statistics: General Government Debt*. Retrieved from: https://stats.oecd.org/Index.aspx?DataSetCode=GOV_DEBT.

Our World in Data. (2020). *Data on COVID-19 (coronavirus)*. Retrieved from: https://github.com/owid/covid-19-data/tree/master/public/data.

Oxford Economics. (2019). *Oxford's Global Macro Model*.

Oxford Economics. (2020). *Oxford's Global Macro Model*.

Reinhart, C., & Rogoff, K. (2008). This Time Is Different: A Panoramic View of Eight Centuries of Financial Crises. *Annals of Economics and Finance*, *15*(2), 1065–1188.

Statistical Office of the European Communities. (2019a). *Eurostat: Self-Employment by Sex, Age and Educational Attainment Level (1000) [lfsq_esgaed]*.

Statistical Office of the European Communities. (2019b). *Eurostat: Employment and Activity by Sex and Age—Annual Data [lfsi_emp_a]*.

Statistical Office of the European Communities. (2019c). *Eurostat: Unemployment by Sex and Age—Annual Average [une_rt_a]*.

Statistical Office of the European Communities. (2019d). *Eurostat: Long-Term Unemployment by Sex—Annual Average [une_ltu_a]*.

Statistical Office of the European Communities. (2019e). *Eurostat: Pensions Beneficiaries at 31st December [spr_pns_ben]*.

Statistical Office of the European Communities. (2019f). *Eurostat: Inactive Population by Sex, Age and Citizenship (1000) [lfsa_igan]*.

Statistical Office of the European Communities. (2019g). *Eurostat: Population on 1 January by Broad Age Group and Sex [demo_pjanbroad].*
Statistical Office of the European Communities. (2019h). *Eurostat: Population by Educational Attainment Level, Sex and Age (%)—Main Indicators [edat_lfse_03].*

CHAPTER 6

The Major Macrosocial Trends

6.1 Introduction

Major macrosocial trends include the forces that are expected to have an impact on shaping the elements of the social structure, while also changing the economic conditions and, thus, the population's level of prosperity. In order for an observed trend to be included in mega-trends, it needs to have an international dimension, sustainable effects, and significant consequences.

The chapter begins with the case of Covid-19, describing the way pandemic can affect global developments (Sect. 6.2) and then is structured as follows. The trends that will shape the future (Sect. 6.3) can be divided into three major categories: social, economic, and political. Those associated with wider social change include (a) high population aggregation trends (Sect. 6.4) refugee and migratory population movements, as well as changes in age structure (aging population), which bring about changes in economic and social behavior (Sect. 6.5); (b) technological changes (4th industrial revolution), which are being correlated with major changes in work skills' demand (Sect. 6.6); (c) environmental hazards and economies' adapting to deal with climate change (Sect. 6.7); and d) globalization and global structural changes (Sect. 6.8).

P. E. Petrakis, *The New Political Economy of Greece up to 2030*,
The Political Economy of Greek Growth up to 2030,
https://doi.org/10.1007/978-3-030-47075-3_6

6.2 How the Covid-19 Will Change the World

Covid-19 initially affected entire humanity in terms of health. However, its influence goes beyond an individual and collective level and affects the areas of geostrategy, dynamic growth, sustainable development, sustainable governance, inclusivity, and pro-growth (or antigrowth) behaviors.

The main feature of the crisis was that economic consequences were extremely rapid, particularly serious and, we estimate, of short to medium-term duration. However, crisis effects will spread to the medium-term through various channels (financial, behavioral, change of habits, etc.). History has shown that in general, crises of exogenous origin, natural disasters, pandemics, etc. have high negative effects, but the acute phase of their impact lasts for a few quarters, as opposed to financial crises. However, what we do not know is the extent that an exogenous crisis can turn into an endogenous one and whether pandemic waves can be more than one.

If, as we have already pointed out, the assumption for a short to medium-term duration does not apply, then we have a different example for which we are not prepared. But for now, let's accept that it does apply.

An important question is whether Covid-19, as an exogenous and not an endogenous disruptor in economic and social systems, will be a game changer or a great accelerator and amplifier. In other words, the question that arises is whether Covid-19 crisis will change the direction of already established key trends or whether existing trends and characteristics of economies will be strengthened in terms of their effectiveness, or whether both effects will coexist, and to what extent.

As for geostrategic changes that may be observed, the question that arises regards the specific weight held by the East in relation to the West. We have known that for the last two decades there has been a clear tendency to broaden the special weight of China, South Korea, and other Asian countries in global economic activity at the cost of United States and other Western economies.

However, crisis intensity in western economies and especially in the large economies of Italy, Spain, France, Great Britain, Germany, and USA, shows that these trends of international substitution may accelerate, leading world to higher tensions (Thucydides Trap) claiming hegemony. At the same time, because of issues related to the effectiveness of the pandemic's management, broader concerns are being raised about the real potential of the United States to understand its position and responsibilities in the world. In an article in the *Wall Street Journal*, Henry Kissinger (2020) noted that United States failure to support a role that would strengthen global community's resilience to the pandemic, as it did with the Southeast Asian tsunami, the outbreak of Ebola in East Africa and the global financial crisis of 2008, would strengthen global economy in the economic crisis and, thirdly, would preserve the principles of liberal world order, will have serious consequences for the future role of United States in the world.

Moreover, the institutions of many states will be deemed as inadequate, revealing inherent weaknesses and putting at risk state organizations that may need to be classified as failed states. The revival of the "city" with the protective walls at a time when progress depends on world trade and people's movement will remain an anachronism. Of course, these trends, to the extent defined by rational observations (e.g., the risk of developing poorly controlled offshore activities), have some basis. But the ideologicalization of new needs into broader social assumptions activates multiple and medium to long-term effects. On the contrary, a failure to respond to new conditions will be a source of potentially destructive forces. In any case, mankind's history shows that such events lead to greater intensity and not greater cooperation as they are considered to be more episodes of the "Thucydides Trap" for world domination than game changers that will lead to a new cooperation network. So, in the China–US trade war we can see a truce, but it will probably intensify after the crisis, rather fall in intensity, especially in the trade sector. The strengthening of Chinese power and the corresponding weakening of American power contribute toward this direction.

Any momentum in growth received a systemic exogenous shock from Covid-19 that created supply and demand problems, resulting in financial stability issues. At the same time, there were issues of shifts in expectations among individuals and entrepreneurs that were mainly responsible for the very large variation in economic activity.

This start will obviously bring about changes in the production model as several production activities will receive catastrophic blows (insurance systems, transport, tourism, etc.) while others will benefit accelerating their implementation (new remote technologies).

These productive changes will have a negative impact on middle-class, which has already been negatively affected during the Great Recession of 2008 and changes in technology, raising broader issues of income inequality, both within the economy itself and between various economies. The effects of Covid-19, as well as all pandemics and similar events, have a more negative effect on the younger, the poorer and males working in small and medium-sized enterprises (SMEs) (Bell, Bloom, Blundell, & Pistaferri, 2020) (either within the same economy or between economies). Of course, the richer an economy is, the stronger the recessionary shock it may receive, regardless of whether its recovery is then stronger. On the contrary, a weaker country faces the risk of becoming a failed state.

Covid-19 highlighted the issue of sustainable development in the sense that some key objectives set by the relevant framework such as issues of poverty (1st target), hunger (2nd target), health (3rd target), education (4th target) are being affected during the management of this crisis. This, in turn, has a serious impact on the extent of the economic shock caused by the crisis. Therefore, the extent to which a society has formally or essentially adopted broader growth and development definitions that ensure the maximization of the Human Development Index, rather than just the gross domestic product (GDP) growth rate, is of particular value. If it is later proven that countries with broader targeting performed better in dealing with the epidemiological problem (given, of course, their possible administrative adequacy at the time and subsequent epidemiological policy) then it is clear that the scope of developmental targeting will be of more importance, from here on.

It is clear that in the future, in order to avoid failures in dealing with such problems, three principles must be adopted: knowledge sharing, de-ideologicalization of economic intervention and a resilience agenda keeping. These principles do not refer to a debate on preferences between capitalism and socialism, but directly to the effects of global phenomena such as climate change, pandemics, and the aging of the population, which create new needs. These are the maintenance of international production lines and the development of international research and development capabilities in the fields of medicine and health.

At the beginning of Covid-19 pandemic, the prevailing view was that China's socio-political system had allowed a more effective policy in dealing with the phenomenon. But it soon became clear that efficiency was largely due to the experience of the Chinese authorities with the SARS ina 2004, while randomness (Chinese New Year) also played a negative triggering role.

Respectively, the same thing happened in Italy. To a large extent, the Italian drama was attributed to the open social system that did not allow for stricter management. However, it was found that coincidence (?) (football matches) played a significant negative role and the administrative inadequacy of its northern provinces played an important role. These observations were also confirmed by the fact that open societies, such as the Greek one, controlled the phenomenon much earlier and much more effectively.

Adversely, "herd immunity" policy choices that significantly influenced epidemiological policies in United Kingdom, and initially in United States, played a key role in negatively managing the crisis.

Behind the choice of the "herd immunity" policy, possibly stands the social and political model that promotes the role of the economy and the normal functioning of society at the expense of victims' number. However, it is clear that criterion of administrative competence as a criterion for leaders on how to handle the crisis plays a serious role in the quality of leadership in the future.

6.3 Trends Shaping the Future and Capitalism

Future-shaping trends related to wider social change include urbanization, demographic change, and population movements, the introduction of 4th industrial revolution technologies, climate change, and globalization in a multipolar world (as being analyzed in this chapter).

At economic level, we can distinguish six major trends that will characterize economic reality: debt development (public and private), the impact of financial instability on the credit system, productivity developments, global convergence (or divergence) of economies, developing uncertainty, and, finally, of industrial production organization changes and the role of technology.

In the political arena, large-scale developments are already bringing about significant changes and will continue to do so: wealth and income inequality along with limited social mobility, the strengthening of privacy protections and the role of the middle class in the West, as well as throughout the world, and great changes in collective social behaviors.

All of the above changes occur simultaneously at varying degrees of intensity resulting in the creation of nonlinear correlations and an alternative range of alternative future scenarios. At the same time, there are a number of other changes, of less importance, that make the plotting task extremely difficult.

As the transition from the present to the future is being evolved, some of the forces acting, play a leading role, and then give way to others. Therefore, when looking at specific issues and attempting projections, those forces that have the most serious impact on the development of the individual issues need to be identified in order to pinpoint sources of future developments.

From the basic description of the previous megatrends we find that the arrival of Covid-19 does not overturn the inclusion of any of the above major trends that are valid either way before Covid-19 crisis, nor does it add anything new.

It seems that crisis characterization as exogenous and systematic and as an accelerator and enhancer of existing trends retains its character. Covid-19 shortened the time by affecting the results of megatrends and in some cases, as we will see, strengthened their influence. But only in a few cases does it work as a game changer.

In other words, new attitudes about work life, travel, corporate, and government practices form a new reality, but they do not move the discussion to completely new areas.

Of course, the future, no matter how rationally approached, based on justified assumptions, is inherently uncertain. We can only approach it to the best of our ability, appreciating the alternate routes being appeared. One approach is the State of the Future Index (SOFI), which takes into account a set of critical parameters for the future, covering all human activities. These are divided into two major categories: "where we are winning" and "where we are losing." from the human perspective (Table 6.1).

Capitalism with its constituents (production, trade, consumption, investment, etc.) shapes and is shaped by future developments. The capitalism's universal adoption is based on the impressive change it has brought to the level of society's prosperity, but also rests on the assumption that tomorrow will be different and probably better than today. This belief is characteristic of the young—relative to the construction of the social nature of human beings—economic system as well as a hallmark of its modernity (Reeves, 2019).

The contradictions that distinguish economies are just as important. The dynamics of the system can and do unprecedentedly increase the living standards of individuals. At the same time these dynamics can cause

Table 6.1 State of the Future Index (SOFI)

Where are we winning	*Where are we losing*
GNI per capita	CO_2-equivalent mixing ratio
Poverty	Renewable internal freshwater resources
Foreign direct investment	Forest area
Freedom	Biocapacity per capita
Women in national parliaments	R&D expenditures
Share of high-skilled employment	Social unrest indicator
School enrollment	Unemployment
Literacy rate, adult total	Income inequality
Electricity from renewables	Terrorism incidents
Energy-efficiency	Number of wars and serious arm conflicts
Improved water sources	Corruption in the public sector
Physicians	
Health expenditure	
Prevalence of undernourishment	
Mortality rate, infant	
Life expectancy at birth	
Population growth	
Internet users	

Note The State of the Future Index (SOFI) is an outlook for the next decade, based on historical data on selected variables for the past 20 or more years, but also on judgements of the best and worst expected developments for each variable. It is constructed with key variables that are individually forecasted and that can aggregate to indicate the potential future trend. Created by "The Millennium Project" since 2000
Source Glenn and Florescu (2017) and author's own creation

great social inequalities and, in times of disorder, a sharp loss of prosperity leading to poverty in many strata of society. As a result, there are periods of trial and intense uncertainty.

Capitalism is the central issue to the ongoing debate on the markets' and state's role in growth, income distribution, the effectiveness of democracy, and its relationship to economic performance. Crony capitalism is defined as a system in which private business people and powerful political actors create close insider relationships to ensure economic benefits for themselves. Because of the permanent state's role in the economy, there will always be a potential for favoritism. In general, greater state involvement creates more opportunities for such abuse. But in the end, neither the market system nor the state capitalist system is immune to capitalism. Where regulations, taxes, and subsidies are designed to promote innovation, encourage competition, and ensure the dissemination of knowledge, market capitalism promotes prosperity. But where regulatory policy is excessive and competition is largely financed by strong special interests, market capitalism can also fail. If there is one key difference to bear in mind, it is that democratic processes continue to stand out as the most effective tool to remedy the problem (Dervis, 2019).

In its course, capitalism has been evolved by adapting to the new circumstances of each era. Thus, the mercantilist capitalism of the first industrial revolution was transformed into classic competitive capitalism, which due to the Great Depression of 1929 took a post-war Keynesian form. In the 1970s, due to the fatigue it showed, it is been evolved into what we have known, at least until recently, as globalized financial capitalism.

The question now is whether another major turning point in economic history, meaning the 2008 crisis, will be a factor in transforming the economic system. Signs of transformation are already evident, such as growing protectionism and national economies' isolationism. It is also important to explore the potentially transformative consequences at the social and political level that will follow the 4th industrial revolution.

The big question is whether capitalism, in the shape it will take in the years to come, will still have the force to increase the prosperity of current and future generations over time. This question is urgent, because in the Western world affected by the 2008 and Covid-19 crises, there is greater skepticism and lower expectations for the future among current generations (millennials) than previous ones, despite the fact that at many levels, such as education, there are much better conditions. It should be noted that, in an international Pew Research survey, 87% of Greeks believe that they will be worse off than 20 years ago. This figure is the highest among the survey countries (Stokes, 2018), followed by Italians (72%) and Spaniards (62%). The important thing is that pessimism about the future is extremely entrenched throughout the developed world, and these negative expectations are in evidence to a great degree even in countries such as France, Germany, United Kingdom, USA, and others.

6.4 Urbanization

One of the most important global macroeconomic trends is that of urbanization, fueled both by the general population growth and the movement of individuals to urban centers. Today (United Nations [UN], 2019a), more than 55% of the world's population lives in urban areas, with the rate expected to rise to 68% by 2050, while in 1950 the rate was 30%. The largest increases are expected on the Asian and African continents.

In Greece almost 9 out of 10 (87.7%) of residents are expected to live in urban areas by 2050 (UN, 2019a). During the second half of the twentieth century, the country experienced a gradual increase in its urban population, a trend that has continued to this day. A similar trend is observed in all European countries. Post-war urban concentration was accompanied by the contraction of the primary sector, while the secondary and subsequently the tertiary one has been developed, which greatly supported the economic growth. The slowdown observed in recent years and the projected decline in the urban population, in absolute terms, is partly due to the reversal of flows in residents' movements, with the main reason being the increase in migration due to the 2008 crisis and the overall population decline. The population in Greece is expected to decline significantly in the coming decades, while the rate of urbanization will continue to increase.

As urbanization grows, the demands for sustainable development and successful management of the phenomenon will increase. This is especially true in low and middle-income countries, where urban growth is expected to be higher. Success in management lies in addressing the imminent challenges at the economic, social, and environmental levels, identifying long-term population trends and preventing the adverse effects of overconcentration in urban centers, so that the potential benefits of the phenomenon can be maximized.

The sectors most likely to be affected are the building industry, due to high demand, energy and urban transport systems and technology, infrastructure, and the health system.

At the socioeconomic level, challenges will include increased spending to meet new needs, the employment restructuring due to urbanization, increased cost of living, social inequalities, and levels of absolute poverty and crime, which are expected to increase in inappropriately organized urban centers.

In addition, the increase in pollution from high population density and the higher risk of terrorist attacks and natural disasters are expected to affect the environment and political field, raising issues of prevention, organization, and security.

On the other hand, the benefits that can be gained from urbanization are market efficiency improvement through reduced transaction costs, increased production in the secondary and tertiary sectors with subsequent increased incomes due to increased productivity in the economy (especially in developing countries), improved quality of life, accelerated diffusion of information and knowledge as well as cultural and social upgrading.

6.5 Demographic Changes and Population Movements

For most of human history, people have tended to die young and poor. However, over the last 50 years the world has seen a great improvement in how long people live and how much money they can spend. As people live longer, there are more elderly people than in the past. The classic population pyramid (with many young and few elderly) now belongs to the past (Kharas & Fengler, 2019). The world today is steadily getting older and richer. Most countries are going through this transition with each taking a different path. However, all countries will face a new world in 2030. This predominantly richer and older world will have a population of 8.3 billion, about 700 million more people than today (2019). Going forward, the world will have fewer and fewer poor, about the same number of young and young adults, and many elder and wealthier people. Over the next decade it is projected that the world population above the age of 30 will increase by 800 million, while there will be 100 million fewer people under the age of 30. By 2030 there will be 1.8 billion more people with at least $11 daily purchasing power, while the number of poor and vulnerable with less than $11 a day will shrink by 1.1 billion (Kharas & Fengler, 2019).

The world population continues to grow till today, but the growth rate has been declining since the 1960s. Several factors contribute to this. As prosperity rises, there is a tendency for birth rates to go down. It may be an attempt to improve the prosperity of present generations, while at the same time diminished confidence in the future creates fear of taking responsibility for many children. The declining birth rate as an inherent process can have serious effects on economies' growth in the future.

It is well known that older people spend a larger share of their disposable income on services, so the relative size of the service sector increases as the population ages. The increase in the relative size of the service sector in many countries coincided with the increasing age of the population (Cravino, Levchenko, & Rojas, 2019).

These phenomena are expected to increasingly affect developing countries. Urbanization reinforces this effect, as well as restrictive fertility policies of countries such as China (restricting each family to one child until 2012).

The low birth rate of many developed countries, including Greece, means that the population is aging over time. Population aging is a demographic development that affects everyone, as it occurs in all regions and countries of the world, regardless of development levels. Indeed, it is evolving rapidly, especially in advanced countries—including those with large populations of young people (UN, 2020). Worldwide, the number of people over 65 is expected to more than double by 2050, from 703 million in 2020 to more than 1.5 billion, while the global population is expected to grow less than 2 billion in the same period.

According to UN (2020) estimates, in Greece more than one out of three (36.2%) will be over 65 by 2050, when the population is expected to have declined by more than one million. This percentage is well above the projected average of the corresponding age group in Europe (28.1%). Greece is already ranked among the top ten countries in the world with an aging population, with this position expected to worsen by 2050 (Table 6.2).

The aging of the population has an economic impact. The most important problem that arises is that the economy is underfunded by a reduction in the workforce and at the same time faces an increased burden on the state budget, due to greater spending on health care and pensions. It is also obvious that an aging population is more focused on the present and less concerned about future and long-term developments. As a consequence, the aging population is also expected to have a negative impact on entrepreneurship, as the proportion of young people, who tend to innovate and take risks, is being declined. In contrast, older people maintain a more conservative attitude toward risk (Levesque & Minniti, 2006), not having the ability to wait as long to make return on investments.

Table 6.2 The top ten countries or regions with the highest percentage of population over 60 in 1980, 2017, and 2050

	1980		*2017*		*2050*	
Rank	*Country/area*	*% aged 60 years or over*	*Country/area*	*% aged 60 years or over*	*Country/area*	*% aged 60 years or over*
1	Sweden	22	Japan	33.4	Japan	42.4
2	Norway	20.2	Italy	29.4	Spain	41.9
3	Channel Island	20.1	Germany	28	Portugal	41.7
4	United Kingdom	20	Portugal	27.9	Greece	41.6
5	Denmark	19.5	Finland	27.8	Republic of Korea	41.6
6	Germany	19.3	Bulgaria	27.7	China, Taiwan Province of China	41.3
7	Austria	19	Croatia	26.8	China, Hong Kong SAR	40.6
8	Belgium	18.4	Greece	26.5	Italy	40.3
9	Switzerland	18.2	Slovenia	26.3	Singapore	40.1
10	Luxembourg	17.8	Latvia	26.2	Poland	39.5

Note From 201 countries and regions with at least 90 thousand inhabitants
Source UN (2017) and author's own creation

Different age groups in a society may react in a different way to a monetary policy shock. These groups economic reaction differs in proportion to their employment and income levels, thus determining the effectiveness of monetary policy. Specifically (Leahy & Thapar, 2019), by broadly distinguishing three age groups (20–40, 40–65 and over 65), monetary policy is less effective the higher the proportion of young people (20–40), more effective the larger the middle-aged population (40–65 years) is, and finally, the population over 65 does not appear to have a significant impact on the monetary policy's effectiveness.

Today, a significant proportion of the population of the least developed countries is still young (44% under 25), testing these countries as they face the need for education and employment for these people (UN, 2019b). In underdeveloped countries the percentage of young people is even higher (59% under 25) while in most developed countries young people account for less than 1/3 (28%) of the total population.

Another major issue that is having global economic consequences is the movement of populations. The total number of people residing in a country other than their country of birth has increased (International Organization for Migration [ILO], 2019) from 84 million in 1970 to 271 million in 2019, with this population in Greece reaching 1.2 million in 2019.

Greek society has experienced post-war reverse trends in migration flows. In the 1950s and 1960s the net inflow of migrants (outflows minus the inflows of migrants) was negative, while the next three-and-half decades the net inflow was positive, culminating in the 1990s. More recently (since 2005) the picture has changed again, in spite of the refugee crisis and the waves of refugees the country received, due to Greeks seeking jobs abroad (Fig. 6.1).

Overall, global migration, despite its increase, especially in recent years, remains proportional to population growth since 1970—the rate of migration is estimated at 3.5% (2019) of the global population (ILO, 2019).

Economic crises and geopolitical instability are major causes of migration. Other more permanent sources of motivation for people to migrate are the economic development of the country of destination and its

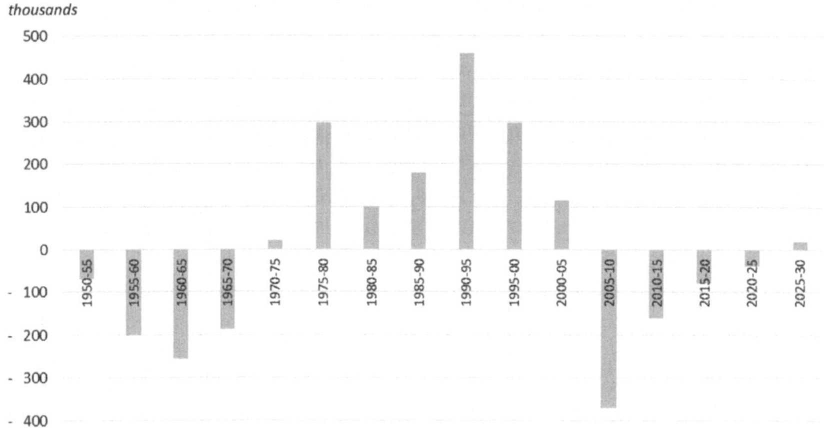

Fig. 6.1 The net number of migrants (thousands) in Greece (*Note* The number of immigrants minus the number of emigrants [five-year period average]. *Source* UN [2019c] and author's own creation)

distance from the country of origin, the existing migration networks, and demographic changes. These trends are exacerbated by media and social media that promulgate social standards of developed countries. In particular, declining birth-rates and the aging of the population in many developed countries are fueling demand for labor from abroad to support national economies.

When young people leave their country to seek work abroad, this means that the proportion of older people increases. Although some countries, anticipating remittances, encourage workers to emigrate, there are also concerns about losing human capital, which forms the base of developing society and economy (brain drain). The typical profile of someone who is likely to opt for emigration is that of a young man born, educated, and having social connections abroad.

Population movements are an integral part of human civilization and will continue to concern humanity. While many people express a desire to emigrate, few take steps to do so, and even fewer follow through.

6.6 Disruptive Technologies and the 4th Industrial Revolution

The world we live in is the result of a process of industrialization. The Industrial Revolution evolved in three phases (Petrakis, Valsamis, & Kafka, 2020). These phases were: (a) the steam engine and mechanical production of equipment (1760–1840), (b) the increasing division of labor, arrival of electricity and mass production (1870–1914), and (c) electronics, technology, information, communications, and automated production (1969–today), which have led to a sustainable increase in productivity. But in recent decades, the fact that most economies no longer rely on industry but have become service-based economies has brought about major changes.

In Greece, over the last two decades, the tertiary sector has been taking up an increasing share of total labor in the economy (72.5%, 2018), with the secondary sector declining significantly, especially in the years after 2008 (Hellenic Statistical Authority [ELSTAT], 2019). The primary sector employs a smaller but relatively stable proportion of workers. The share went down in the five years preceding the crisis, and has since remained at about 13% of total employment.

Technology developments, especially over the last century, are capable of changing the consumer model, create new needs, produce new goods and services, disrupt the status quo, and change the way people live, think, work, etc. This feature of new technologies has led to characterizing them as "disruptive technologies." The implications of technology development (Phillips, 2020) are:

- reduced demand for unskilled labor,
- lower prices for services,
- higher human capital returns on investment,
- the ability of small businesses to target larger markets,
- provision of digital services,
- improved business decisions, and
- a new global labor division.

To be characterized as "disruptive" a technology must represent a rapid rate of change in capabilities in price/performance ratio terms relative to substitutes and competitive products, or must accelerate the evolution of production or effect discontinuous capability improvements (Manyika et al., 2013). At the same time, however, in order for technology to be considered economically disruptive, it needs to have a significant impact on a significant number of businesses and organizations and to influence a large part of their productive functions, creating a massive economic impact.

Some of the disruptive technologies that have the potential to have significant economic and disruptive effects are mobile internet, automation of knowledge work, advanced robotics, autonomous and near-autonomous vehicles, next-generation genomics, 3D printing, advanced materials, advanced oil and gas exploration, and renewable energy, as well as information and communications technology and Big Data analysis.

At business level, a capable business leader must be able to predict and adapt to the coming changes, seeking the comparative advantage of new technologies. New business opportunities, potential new customers, new products, and investment opportunities are some of the potential benefits of new technologies. At the same time, the development of new technology causes significant changes in the workplace.

The disruption of productive functions is therefore closely linked to innovation. At national level, the Greek economy, in terms of innovation performance, ranks 41st out of 149 countries (Dutta, Lanvin, & Wunsch-Vincent, 2019), behind Bulgaria and followed by Vietnam. Compared to the countries of its income group, this performance is at the lower end, with the main barriers to innovation being identified in human capital, research, and in the institutional framework. Thus, due to poor performance in innovation, the impact of disruptive technologies on the productive structure of the Greek economy is expected to be relatively weak or delayed. This will lead to an overall lower level of economic competitiveness.

Businesses in information technology (IT) enjoy higher returns when they expand their range to more markets. Their average mark-up is higher, while their overall share of labor is lower. High productivity in products expand with innovation across more product lines, creating a temporary burst of growth. Because their profitability is difficult to match, less profitable businesses find it difficult to enter high-profit markets and therefore innovate less, resulting in declining profits. Mark-ups eventually fall for both high and low-productivity firms, as they are more likely to face high-productivity competitors. Ultimately, due to greater competition, innovation and development are eliminated. Thus, despite increasing returns, business incentives for innovation decline, reducing the long-term growth rate (Aghion, Bergeaud, Boppart, Klenow, & Li, 2019).

Although the growing strength of large firms in market power has so far had a fairly limited negative economic impact, it could have a larger impact on people's income and on development if not controlled. Policy makers around the world should ensure equal conditions between all businesses, including the new ones. This means reducing domestic barriers to market entry and barriers to trade and foreign direct investment—especially in the services sector. It also means enhancing certain features of the legal system and competition policies, such as the role of market examinations, reforming corporate taxes in order to tax excess market returns and ensuring that intellectual property rights protections encourage innovation.

6.7 Climate Change

Climate change, also, is one of the most important issues that will need to be addressed around the world both in the long and short-term, being one of the most important sources of uncertainty for economies, as it has a significant impact on economic output, while at the same time posing risks to humans and nature (Intergovernmental Panel on Climate Change

[IPCC], 2014). When comparing climate change phenomenon with that of Covid-19, we find that both phenomena have an exogenous character in terms of economic system and systematic but also uneven effects on it. However, while Covid-19—in terms of economic impact—has a short-term character, climate change has a medium to long-term character and at a first glance does not cause very deep damage, but at a local level.

That is why climate change is extremely dangerous for human society as its impact is gradual over time, resulting in the danger which it brings with not being perceived.

The main economic consequences of climate change worldwide are summarized in the following three observations: (a) the macroeconomic effects of temperature disturbances are unevenly distributed among countries; (b) high temperatures reduce per capita production in countries with high average temperatures, such as most low-income countries, where economic losses from rising temperatures are likely to be significant by 2100; and (c) countries with a well-developed and structured institutional framework are better able to address the changes brought about by climate change.

Global warming is expected to increase the incidence of natural disasters linked to climate change. This has serious socioeconomic consequences—8000 major climate disasters have been recorded between 1990 and 2014 (IPCC, 2014)—and raises ethical issues of intergenerational justice and solidarity among others.

Clearly, the problem of climate change cannot be geographically limited and indeed is not only a problem for the future, but is already manifesting today because of human activities—the main source of the phenomenon.

In the near future, the earth's climate is projected to change to a greater extent due to the high concentration of greenhouse gases in the atmosphere. The impacts of climate change are expected to vary by geographic area, but will have a significant impact on the entire planet.

The three major impacts of climate change are estimated to be: (a) geographical and crop yield changes, (b) reduction in water supplies for crops, and (c) land disappearance due to rising sea levels and increased ground salinity (Aydinalp & Cresser, 2008).

An increasing incidence of extreme weather events such as droughts, hurricanes, windstorms, and hailstorms will affect the development process (Alexandrov & Hoogenboom, 2000). At the same time, in many areas ice melting has a significant effect on the quality and quantity of water resources. Also, many terrestrial and marine species have changed behavior (geographic range, migration patterns, etc.), thus affecting the production chain.

Admittedly, the climate change evolution in the twenty-first century, with the main characteristics of rising temperatures and the retraction of ice from land and sea, will have a major impact on growth in some economies. Indeed, in 2018, William Nordhaus and Paul Romer won the Nobel Prize in Economics for being pioneers in adapting economic theory to integrate climate change and technological progress. Their research answers fundamental questions about how to promote long-term sustainable development and improve prosperity[1] in a wider context that incorporates climate change as an endogenous variable of the economic growth model.

The real problem for human kind posed by climate change is that the expected rise in ecological costs is in line with slower growth rates and the increasing effects of negative economies of scale. The predominant scenario (Bolt, Inklaar, de Jong, and van Zanden [2018]) for the next 40 years is that the world GDP growth rate will decline, while global warming will increase. In other words, it will become increasingly difficult to fund the fight against climate change.

Climate change may also affect the economies' growth through its impact on labor productivity. The study by Kahn et al. (2019) in a total of 174 countries for the period 1960–2014, showed that temperature deviations from historically adjusted values have a negative, but not significant, effect on the real GDP per capita growth rate. On the other hand, it is estimated that the continued increase in annual temperature without the application of preventive environmental policies, will be 0.04 °C until 2100, which could reduce world real GDP (per capita) by more than 7%. However, if the Paris Agreement on climate change were adopted, the annual temperature rise would slow to 0.01 °C, thereby reducing the loss of GDP to 1%.

In Greece, greenhouse gas (GHG) emission reductions in recent years and hence the country's relative improvement (Germanwatch, 2020) are due to the decline—caused by the decade-long recession—of national production, while the use of renewable energy remains low. In fact, the improvement in environment quality in Greece, but also in other countries where recessionary lockdowns were imposed was impressive.

Greece is committed to gradually reducing and permanently stopping (by 2030) the use of lignite, while increasing renewable energy sources and absorbing 3.5–4 billion euros of European funds to finance the transition. The fact, however, is that the country spends 1.3% (2018) of its GDP on environmental protection (in 2013 it was 1.7%), with this rate being the 2nd highest in the European Union (EU), where the average is at 0.8% (Statistical Office of the European Communities, 2019).

In EU, the Green Deal, which will constitute 25% of its 2021–2027 budget funding, using 7.5 billion euros from the Just Transition Fund (Giacomo, 2020), sets the conditions for decoupling the European prototype from the resource use of previous decades.

In conclusion, the serious problems posed by climate change are mainly two: the ever-increasing cost of dealing with its effects and the fact that it is exhausting the resources of future generations.

6.8 Multipolar World and Globalization

Globalization has the potential to determine the evolution and dynamics of the future by affecting multiple levels, such as culture, politics, economy, environment, and society. What concerns us here is the current economic dimension and the globalization's consequences as well as the consequences a globalized and multipolar world will have for the world economy and especially for business to take long-term decisions.

About two hundred years ago, Northwest Europe and later North America experienced rapid industrialization, turning the rest of the world into raw material suppliers for these new industrial centers. Subsequently, due to technological advances and new transport networks, transport and communication costs began to decrease and areas that were separated by long distances became more closely connected. At the same time, data processing, storage, and information retrieval costs have been reduced, creating the conditions for a new phase of globalization.

As transportation costs were reduced, the world's largest industrial centers were able to provide higher wages, which mitigated economic inequalities worldwide. At the same time, however, lower transport costs also allowed low-wage countries to compete with high-wage economies, especially those countries with a high population concentration. So, new centers of power began to be formed around the world.

However, trade has slowed down in recent years—even before the outbreak of the 2008 crisis—as the ratio of international trade to world GDP has declined sharply (Fig. 6.2). In fact, international trade took the biggest blow than anything else during Covid-19 crisis.

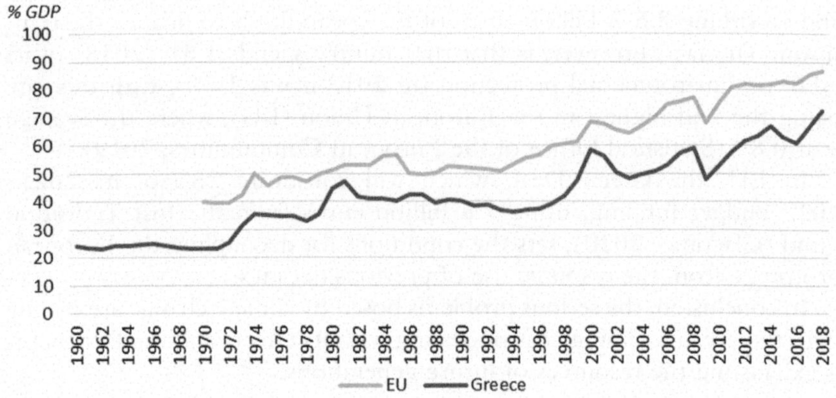

Fig. 6.2 Trade as percentage of GDP in EU and Greece (1960–2018) (*Note* Trade is the sum of exports and imports of goods and services measured as a share of gross domestic product. *Source* The World Bank [2019] and author's own creation)

With regard to Greece, the economic openness of the economy has generally been increasing since the 1960s, especially after its accession to Eurozone. Greece follows the course of European economies (EU average), but the distance has widened. In 2018, trade as a percentage of GDP in EU countries (on average) was 88%, while that of Greece was 72.5%.

The decline in trade contribution to economic growth affects, on the supply side, countries' productivity and their technological performance, as trade is a channel of technology transfer and confers comparative advantage. At the same time, on the demand side, net exports are a key sector of countries in financial crisis and, thus, if world trade slows down, it is more difficult for these countries to reduce external deficits and debt.

The relationship between technological shifts and commerce development is commonplace. When innovation is not favored and reduced returns prevail, lower tariffs only boost growth temporarily. However, trade liberalization increases productivity levels permanently (Hsieh, Hurst, Jones, & Klenow, 2019).

Under normal circumstances (in the absence of recession, economic crisis, general unrest, etc.), trade's growth rate is greater than that of production growth (Irwin, 2015). However, 2015 saw the largest slowdown in international trade since the onset of the financial crisis, which may be due both to structural factors and to the downturn in the business cycle (Cohen-Setton, 2015), as well as to increased protectionism and the trade and monetary wars of a global Thucydidean struggle for world domination.

According to Hoekman (2015), likely causes of the lasting decline in international trade are being found in that: (a) the production process is now geared toward products with lower income elasticity; (b) strong growth in trade was a transitional phenomenon, which ended because of the integration of countries such as China and the countries of Central and Eastern Europe into the world economy; (c) businesses have reached their limits in exploiting the production fragmentation in the global value chain of trade; and (d) domestic industries have been strengthened by government support, with the result that demand for product imports has dropped significantly.

Other factors responsible for the trade slowdown could be the presence of a high level of uncertainty—which creates difficulties in financing trade and in trust between trading partners—and the economic crisis. Furthermore, natural disasters, such as the earthquake in Japan and the floods in Thailand, which have led many industries to revise their policy of outsourcing their production to other countries (Crozet, Emlinger, & Jean, 2015), have the potential to damage world trade. Dadush (2015), on the other hand, demonstrates that the decline in investment (by consumers and businesses) can largely explain the slowdown in world trade.

At the same time, it is understood that events such as automation and the subsequent replacement of labor by machinery, technological advances, and a shift to new production methods, or even an increase in energy prices, could lead to some form of industry resurgence in developed countries and a corresponding drop in the share of trade.

The crisis of 2020, with the increase in uncertainty and transactions cost (increase in tariffs) that followed, but also the relative reduction in the cost of machinery in terms of labor (reduction in interest rates relative to wages), made the use of global supply chains more expensive, leading to a form of regeneration in manufacturing among developed economies (Kilic & Marin, 2020). In contrast to the 1990s and 2000s, a period of intense globalization during which the development of global value chains was a growth lever for global trade, many transnational companies are (re)turning their production to developed countries, relying to automation and investment in robots. At the cost of developing countries, this trend had begun in 2010 and is expected to intensify with declining global value chain activity due to Covid-19 crisis.

The competition for world domination, however, which now extends to more protagonists, brings to the fore the implications of a multipolar world, which also leads to an increase in global uncertainty.

The multipolar world unleashes a more serious source of uncertainty, that of geostrategic reordering. These rearrangements are accompanied by social, civil, or international conflicts. In conclusion, the birth and evolution of the multipolar world is accompanied by increased uncertainty in international political and economic relations.

The course of the globalized economy is marked by the end of monopolies and the dominance of a multipolar world, in terms of influence. The multipolar world first emerged with the industrialization of Japan, which was much poorer than Europe at the beginning of the twentieth century. Over the last three decades industrial production has been growing in East and South Asia, most recently in India. It is logical that as transport costs reduced, industrial production increasingly grew in places with high population concentration. And as the population is not concentrated in a single country, economic activity is expanding more widely internationally.

At the same time, in recent years there has been an unprecedented dramatic change in the composition of global GDP, with the result that global power centers are changing. The way in which wealth is created worldwide has changed significantly. Japan lost the ground it had won at the same speed it had gained it in previous decades. At the same time, China increased its share of world GDP, while the contribution of Western countries to world GDP fell sharply, more than the cumulative decline that had occurred over the past four decades (1960–2012) in United States and EU shares.

The change in shaping forces of global GDP has been accompanied by a change in the trends observed in global trade. Most of the change is due largely to the strengthening of the Chinese economy. From 2002 to 2011, China recorded an impressive average annual growth rate of trade, surpassing the UK, Japan, and Germany in terms of share in world trade, while the share of Organisation for Economic Co-operation and Development (OECD) countries as a whole declined.

Changes in the share of world trade held by states cause significant reshuffling in the international arena. In 2012, EU accounted for the largest share of world trade (about 1/3) and China had already surpassed the United States share (O'Neil & Terzi, 2014). In the future, EU is expected to lose its momentum, while China is projected to surpass the US trade share and to reach the total share of EU countries.

One of the possible effects of the formation of a multipolar world will be in the ability of sovereign currencies to act as reserves and as a means of stimulating world trade. It is evident that the world economic system is moving from a situation in which two currencies (dollar and euro) dominate to a situation of three currencies, with the addition of the Chinese renminbi.

In summary, the dollar bloc is expected (Tovar & Nor, 2018) to continue to account for the largest share of world GDP (40%), followed by the renminbi (RMB) bloc (30%) and the euro bloc (20%). The geographical area of the RMB bloc seems to be that of BRICS currencies. The British pound and the Japanese yen bloc have a much smaller share.

The effects of the dollar's dominance continue, making it easier for United States to finance its debt. How much other economies are willing to buy US debt depends on the stability of the global financial system. The reduction in US debt buying by large economies (China, Japan, and relatively smaller ones such as Russia, Turkey and India, which remains a strong buyer) is slow but steady, as the world shifts to a situation dominated by trade and monetary hostilities.

Greece ranks 24th out of 122 countries (Gygli, Haelg, Potrafke, & Sturm, 2019), related to its economy the globalization degree and has been ranked since 1990s higher than the high-income countries (Fig. 6.3). At the same time, however, the Greek economy appears to be less globalized than most other countries in Eurozone.

But apart from the general process of globalization and the exploration of dividing up projects, there are also specific issues that are distracting in this context. Perhaps the most important of these concern international capital movements.

The phenomenon of sudden stops (Merler & Pisani-Ferry, 2012) in international capital movements may be one of the major causes of global financial crises (Accominotti & Eichengreen, 2013). It is not always easy to interpret, because capital movements are usually treated as a symptom rather than as a cause of a crisis. But the 2008 Great

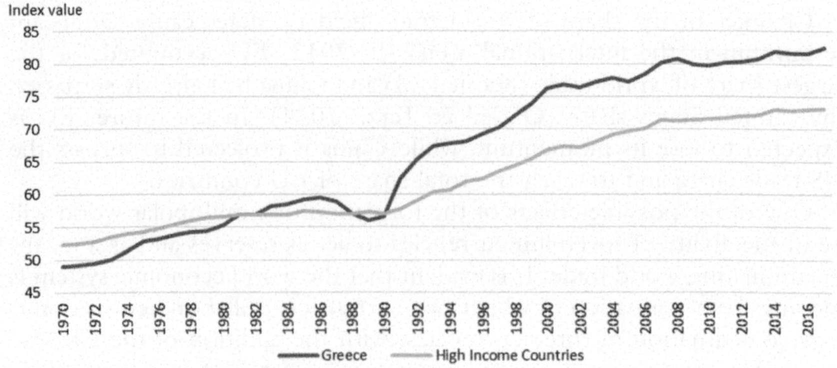

Fig. 6.3 Index of globalization of the economy (KOF) of Greece and the high-income countries (1970–2017) (*Source* Gygli et al. [2019] and author's own creation)

Recession showed that internationally coordinated actions to tackle recession, notably through international cooperation (G20), yielded some satisfactory results.

The experience of the 2008 crisis played an important role in Covid-19 crisis. So as soon as Covid-19 crisis hit hard, creating serious problems in global economy (at a faster rate than in 2008), supranational organizations (International Monetary Fund [IMF]) and large states (United States, China, etc.) developed large-scale policies aiming to address the problems that arose.

In addition, the future stage of growth will be shaped by the presence of international trade cooperation agreements in a world characterized by conditions of competitive advantage (trade policy) and the use of exchange rate policies. Trade liberalization policies, although strongly disputed in recent years, can create a non-zero-sum game in the growth of the economies of the countries involved. According to Hsieh et al. (2019) who studied the impact of reduced tariffs on growth in a two-country model, United States and the rest of OECD countries, find mutual benefit from the relaxation of tariff policy—with the more pronounced benefit for the OECD countries. Specifically, trade causes the economy to be restructured in the areas of labor, production, and the degree of businesses' export orientation. This accelerates creative destruction, transferring technology from the most to the least innovative countries, leading to the growth of economics. However, this process has long-term beneficial effects provided that technology originates from outside the economic system, that is, there is no decline in production of innovative ideas.

Furthermore, international supply chains have changed the structure of global growth, rendering many theoretical conceptions of competitive advantages, economies of scale, etc. unnecessary. Global structural changes are creating social and economic redistributions as they change the relative positions of political and economic power centers.

Consequently, the destruction of existing markets and the creation of new ones alter the relative position of individual economies and groups. This process requires a review of the individual development components. For example, an economy, whose exported products change their position in the international value-added chain and in the demand elasticity curve, will need to rethink its production model. Thus, the concept of future competitiveness comes to the fore.

International trade and globalization are perhaps the most representative examples where Covid-19 acts as an accelerator and enhancer of dominant trends and developments, as described above. So, what is now expected is a reduction in globalization in the decade 2020–2030. But then it will return again, accelerating after 2030 under the influence of rising China and India. Covid-19, after the 2008 crisis, makes the slowdown in trade and globalization in 2020 sharper.

Note

1. Paul Romer had shown how economic forces govern the willingness of companies to produce new ideas and innovations, laying the foundations for a new growth model, known as endogenous growth theory. William Nordhaus created a quantitative model that describes the interaction between economy and climate. Their findings significantly expanded economic analysis by building models that explain how the market economy interacts with nature and knowledge.

References

Accominotti, O., & Eichengreen, B. (2013). *The Mother of All Sudden Stops: Capital Flows and Reversals in Europe, 1919–32* (National Bureau of Economic Research Working Paper No. 19580).

Aghion, P., Bergeaud, A., Boppart, T., Klenow, P. J., & Li, H. (2019). *A Theory of Falling Growth and Rising Rents* (Federal Reserve Bank of San Francisco Working Paper 2019-11).

Alexandrov, V., & Hoogenboom, G. (2000). Vulnerability and Adaptation Assessments of Agriculturalcrops Under Climate Change in the Southeastern USA. *Theoretical and Applied Climatology, 67*(1–2), 45–63.

Aydinalp, C., & Cresser, M. (2008). The Effects of Global Climate Change on Agriculture. *American-Eurasian Journal of Agricultural and Environmental Sciences, 3*(5), 672–676.

Bell, B., Bloom, N., Blundell, J., & Pistaferri, L. (2020). Prepare for Large Wage Cuts if you are Younger and Work in a Small Firm. *Vox CEPR Policy Portal.* Retrieved from: https://voxeu.org/article/prepare-large-wage-cuts-if-you-are-younger-and-work-small-firm.

Bolt, J., Inklaar, R., de Jong, H., & van Zanden, J. L. (2018). *Maddison Project Database, Version 2018. Rebasing Maddison: New Income Comparisons and the Shape of Long-Run Economic Development* (Maddison Project Working Paper No. 10). Retrieved from: https://www.rug.nl/ggdc/historicaldevelopment/maddison/releases/maddison-project-database-2018b.

Cohen-Setton, J. (2015). Why Is Global Trade Slowing Down? *World Economic Forum.* Retrieved from: https://www.weforum.org/agenda/2015/09/why-is-global-trade-slowing-down/.

Cravino, J., Levchenko, A. A., & Rojas, M. (2019). P*opulation Aging and Structural Transformation* (Research Seminar in International Economics No. 674). Retrieved from: http://fordschool.umich.edu/rsie/workingpapers/wp.html.

Crozet, M. Emlinger, C., & Jean, S. (2015). On the Gravity of World Trade's Slowdown. In B. Hoekman (Ed.), *The Global Trade Slowdown: A New Normal?* (pp. 179–196). London: Centre for Economic Policy Research (CEPR) (A VoxEU.org eBook).

Dadush, U. (2015). *Should We Worry About the Great Trade Slowdown?* (OCP Policy Center Policy Brief PB-15/20).

Dervis, K. (2019). Cronies Everywhere. *Project Syndicate.* Retrieved from: https://www.project-syndicate.org/onpoint/cronies-everywhere-by-kemal-dervis-2019-12?barrier=accesspaylog.

Dutta, S., Lanvin, B., & Wunsch-Vincent, S. (2019). *The Global Innovation Index 2019: Creating Healthy Lives—The Future of Medical Innovation.* Ithaca, Fontainebleau, and Geneva: Cornell University, INSEAD, and WIPO.

Germanwatch. (2020). *Climate Change Performance Index (CCPI) 2020 Country Scoreboard: Greece.* Retrieved from: https://www.climate-change-performance-index.org/.

Giacomo, P. A. (2020). A Guide to the European Green Deal. *Continuum Economics*. Retrieved from: https://continuumeconomics.com/2020/01/29/eurozone/a-guide-to-the-european-green-deal.

Glenn, J. C., & Florescu, E. (2017). *State of the Future V. 19.0*. Washington: The Millennium Project. Retrieved from: http://www.millennium-project.org/publications-2-3/.

Gygli, S., Haelg, F., Potrafke, N., & Sturm, J. E. (2019). The KOF Globalisation Index—Revisited. *Review of International Organizations*, *14*(3), 543–574. https://doi.org/10.1007/s11558-019-09344-2.

Hellenic Statistical Authority. (2019). *Statistics: Population and Social Conditions, Labor Market, Labor Force Survey Yearly Time Series Since 1981/2018*. Retrieved from: https://www.statistics.gr/en/statistics/-/publication/SJO03/.

Hoekman, B. (2015). Trade and Growth—End of an Era? In B. Hoekman (Ed.), *The Global Trade Slowdown: A New Normal?* (pp. 3–20). London: Centre for Economic Policy Research (CEPR) (A VoxEU.org eBook).

Hsieh, C. T., Hurst, E., Jones, C. I., & Klenow, P. J. (2019). The Allocation of Talent and U.S. Economic Growth. *Econometrica*, *87*(5), 1439–1474.

Intergovernmental Panel on Climate Change. (2014). *Climate Change 2014: Synthesis Report. Contribution of Working Groups I, II and III to the Fifth Assessment Report of the Intergovernmental Panel on Climate Change*. Geneva: IPCC.

International Organization for Migration. (2019). *World Migration Report 2020*. New York: United Nations.

Irwin, D. (2015). *Free Trade Under Fire* (4th ed.). Princeton: Princeton University Press. https://doi.org/10.2307/j.ctt9qh0ch.

Kahn, M. E., Mohaddes, K., Ng, R. N. C., Pesaran, M. H., Raissi, M., & Yang, J. C. (2019). *Long-Term Macroeconomic Effects of Climate Change: A Cross-Country Analysis* (IMF Working Paper No. 19/215).

Kharas, H., & Fengler, F. (2019). Double Tipping Points in 2019: When the World Became Mostly Rich and Largely Old. *Brookings*. Retrieved from: https://www.brookings.edu/blog/future-development/2019/10/09/double-tipping-points-in-2019-when-the-world-became-mostly-rich-and-largely-old/.

Kilic, K. & Marin, D. (2020). How COVID-19 Is Transforming the World Economy. *Vox CEPR Policy Portal*. Retrieved from: https://voxeu.org/article/how-covid-19-transforming-world-economy.

Kissinger, H. A. (2020). The Coronavirus Pandemic Will Forever Alter the World Order. *The Wall Street Journal*. Retrieved from: https://www.wsj.com/articles/the-coronavirus-pandemic-will-forever-alter-the-world-order-11585953005.

Leahy J. V., & Thapar, A. (2019). *Demographic Effects on the Impact of Monetary Policy* (NBER Working Paper No. 26324).

Levesque, M., & Minniti, M. (2006). The Effect of Aging on Entrepreneurial Behavior. *Journal of Business Venturi, 21*(2), 177–194.

Manyika, J., Chui, M., Bughin, J., Dobbs, R., Bisson, P., & Marrs, A. (2013). Disruptive Technologies: Advances That Will Transform Life, Business, and the Global Economy. *McKinsey Global Institute*.

Merler, S., & Pisani-Ferry, J. (2012). Sudden Stops in the Euro Area. *Review of Economics and Institutions*, *3*(3), Article 5. https://doi.org/10.5202/rei.v3i3.97.

O'Neill, J., & Terzi, A. (2014). *Changing Trade Patterns, Unchanging European and Global Governance* (Bruegel Working Paper No. 817).

Oxford Economics. (2019). *Oxford's Global Macro Model*.

Petrakis, P. E., Valsamis, D. G., & Kafka K. I. (2020). *Economic Growth and Development Policy*. New York: Palgrave Macmillan.

Phillips, T. (2020). A Roadmap for Digital-Led Economic Development. *Vox CEPR Policy Portal*. Retrieved from: https://voxeu.org/article/roadmap-digital-led-economic-development.

Reeves, R. (2019). Capitalism Used to Promise a Better Future. Can It Still Do That? *The Guardian* (Broken Capitalism Series). Retrieved from https://www.theguardian.com/commentisfree/2019/may/22/capitalism-broken-better-future-can-it-do-that.

Statistical Office of the European Communities. (2019). *Eurostat: General Government Expenditure by Function (COFOG) [gov_10a_exp]*.

Stokes, B. (2018). A Decade After the Financial Crisis, Economic Confidence Rebounds in Many Countries. *Pew Research Center*. Retrieved from: https://www.pewresearch.org/global/2018/09/18/a-decade-after-the-financial-crisis-economic-confidence-rebounds-in-many-countries/.

The World Bank. (2019). *World Bank Data [NE.TRD.GNFS.ZS]*.

Tovar, C. E., & Nor, M. T. (2018). *Reserve Currency Blocs: A Changing International Monetary System?* (IMF Working Paper No. 18/20).

United Nations. (2017). *World Population Ageing 2017—Highlights* (Department of Economic and Social Affairs-Population [ST/ESA/SER.A/397]). New York: UN.

United Nations. (2019a). *World Urbanization Prospects: The 2018 Revision* (Department of Economic and Social Affairs-Population Division [ST/ESA/SER.A/420]). New York: UN.

United Nations. (2019b). *World Population Prospects 2019: Data Booklet* (Department of Economic and Social Affairs-Population Division [ST/ESA/SER.A/424]). Retrieved from: https://population.un.org/wpp/Publications/.

United Nations. (2019c). *World Population Prospects 2019: Migration Data* (Department of Economic and Social Affairs-Population Division [Online Edition. Rev. 1]). Retrieved from: https://population.un.org/wpp/Download/Standard/Population/.

United Nations. (2020). *World Population Ageing 2019* (Department of Economic and Social Affairs-Population Division [ST/ESA/SER.A/444]). New York: UN.

CHAPTER 7

The Major Macroeconomic Trends

7.1 Introduction

Major macroeconomic trends have a critical role in shaping the future. Issues such as growth sources, debt evolution, deep-rooted financial instability, declines in productivity, economic convergence, the high levels of uncertainty, and, finally, structural changes in production are the main macroeconomic trends that will decisively influence the future world. These trends pre-existed, but were reinforced by the Covid-19 crisis.

This chapter is laid out as follows: Sect. 7.2 analyzes the optimistic and pessimistic views on growth sources; in Sect. 7.3, global debt evolution is reviewed; and Sect. 7.4 considers the inherent instability of the financial system due to information asymmetry, as opposed to financial instability caused by human behavior. Section 7.5 examines productivity growth developments, followed by a review of the issue of economic convergence (Sect. 7.6). Section 7.7 focuses on the role of uncertainty and, finally, the last two sections of the chapter analyze the major changes in the production structure (Sect. 7.8) and the macroeconomic effects of Covid-19 (Sect. 7.9).

P. E. Petrakis, *The New Political Economy of Greece up to 2030*,
The Political Economy of Greek Growth up to 2030,
https://doi.org/10.1007/978-3-030-47075-3_7

7.2 The Optimistic and Pessimistic Views on Growth Sources

Optimists see the world with a positive outlook and view setbacks and failures as temporary and ephemeral, and mainly due to exogenous factors rather than personal failure. Pessimists see the situation as bad, and possibly getting worse, while expecting negative outcomes.

Optimists, also described as new technologists (Dervis, 2014), believe that the global economy is entering a fourth phase of the industrial revolution, which is expected to be characterized by "smart" machines that will replace low and medium-skilled work. In fact, based on a study by Manyika et al. (2017), "technological unemployment" is expected to reach 800 million jobs by the end of the decade. The optimists predict that new technologies will significantly boost productivity through their impact on energy efficiency, transport (e.g., autonomous vehicles), medicine, and mass production due to the adoption of 3D printing (Dervis, 2014).

Hand in hand with technological change goes the issue of the creation of oversized technology companies (Big Tech). As happens in the case of banks, size itself is not a problem, but their vast size makes regulatory management and policy-making very difficult. Therefore, Big Tech requires special treatment. Their complexity touches on a number of issues, such as the shift in investment from tangibles to non-tangibles, intellectual property, and brands, and the unequal wealth reallocation (with its consequent political impact, populism, etc.). The latter because of the standard financial practice of increasing shareholder wealth while at the same time stifling start-ups (due to the acquisition strategies of Big Tech) and, by extension, affecting employment.

Dervis (2014) distinguishes optimists and pessimists on the basis of their views on four different issues: (a) economic growth and the global economy; (b) income distribution, particularly in the case (Piketty, 2014) where capital becomes a substitute for work (exempted high-skilled work), taking into account that educational systems need time to foster new skill sets but with wage differentials increasing in the meantime; (c) the impact of further automation on employment, since people can thus be "released" from mundane jobs; and (d) climate change and possible constraints on natural resources, which may hinder long-term growth or may lead to a transition to green energy economies, reinforcing another technological revolution capable of increasing social prosperity.

Brynjolfsson and McAfee (2014) argue that the potential of new technologies is equivalent to the potential of past technologies and can transform the economy. Their optimism stems from their belief in the unlimited possibilities of innovation. More specifically, from the fact that even low-cost devices can now communicate with each other, that new technologies are able to respond to the amount of digital information being generated and that machines nowadays have high computing power.

Pessimists, on the other hand, predict that population growth will lead to increasing levels of malnutrition since resources will be insufficient to meet world's food needs and that rising demand will lead to the depletion of natural resources and the potential for conflict as states increasingly compete for scarce resources. They also believe that the over-intensive exploitation of the productive potential will lead to increased pollution and global warming. They worry that developed countries will continue to create problems in the global economy, such as threatening globalization by creating new obstacles for lagging industrialized countries, which also face Chinese competition and competition from other, more established exporting countries.

More generally, pessimists argue that the development of international trade is responsible for a number of problems, such as environmental decline and growing global inequality. They argue that increased trade leads to increased energy consumption with negative environmental consequences (e.g., carbon dioxide [CO_2] emissions from shipping). Finally, they believe that the benefits of increased international trade are not shared equally among countries, but increase the wealth of the strong economies at the expense of the weak.

A basic premise, commonplace among many pessimistic analysts, is their assessment of a slowdown in technological development, including the benefits of economic convergence for developing countries (Rodrik, 2013). Their main objection to the optimists is that the latter place too much faith in the market operation and its "ability" to correct problems.

Gordon (2012) notes that the US's rapid economic growth over the last 250 years, may represent a unique event in world history, which will not be repeated anytime soon. He agrees with Krugman (1990), who argues that slow growth during the period 1973–1990 was a harbinger of a new, more pessimistic future, and where the earlier high expectations of Americans will come down to earth. In addition, he emphasizes that US productivity has fallen significantly since 1970 and that economic growth will slow. In fact, he estimates that over the next decade growth rates will decrease significantly because the innovation impact has been smaller and more limited than previously, particularly since transport and energy technologies have changed little in the last half century. He argues that the high economic growth rates of the previous century were the product of the second industrial revolution (1870–1900), where the discovery and use of new technologies structurally altered economic activity and society (electricity, water, and sanitation, the internal combustion engine, radio and telephone, chemicals and oil, etc.). As such, the economic consequences of this earlier period were considerably more significant than those of the first industrial revolution—the era of the steam engine and railroads—but also more significant than those of the third industrial revolution—the information age and the internet.

Rodrik (2013) argues that growth will remain low at best. He believes that the global economy is entering a new phase in which future growth will not be the same as in recent decades, especially for East Asia countries where high growth rates will be difficult to be maintained. He believes that the distance between developed and developing economies is likely to decrease significantly relative to the levels of the last two decades, with developing countries continuing to grow faster than developed ones, but with economic convergence mainly be due to slower growth in developed countries.

Jones (2009) believes that the level of innovation will decline significantly in coming years since, as he argues, technological development is expected to significantly and continuously increase the stock of knowledge, resulting in reduced opportunities for innovation by future generations due to technological and cognitive constraints. And while this problem may be compensated for by greater investment in education, but to the detriment of experience, the resulting lack of on-the-job training may lead to reduced innovation at individual level as a greater reliance on teamwork will have a negative impact on economic growth. This is one of the reasons for the lack of growth in productivity witnessed in recent decades, despite an enormous growth in collective research. Jones (2009) stresses that such barriers to knowledge change the nature of innovation, leading to negative consequences for long-term economic growth.

A big question mark arising from the Covid-19 crisis is whether the Black Swan form of Covid-19 favored the camps of optimists or pessimists, regarding the economies' growth prospects.

At first glance, it favors the pessimistic analysis of data and that it causes a great recession without (pharmaceutical) innovation being able to deal with it effectively and in a timely manner, at least before it causes the great recession of 2020. Also, prosperity, wealth and income levels returned to levels seen in the past in almost all countries of the world. Analysis from pessimists, in regard to the evolution and role of international trade, have been strengthened, a fact which in some ways confirmed the correctness of views on its limitation.

At the same time, however, the Covid-19 crisis has shown that the use of technology in both education and work paves the way for their use and seek answers that make them more effective. The severity of the crisis is also certain to draw large sums of money to the pharmaceutical industry, which will give a new impetus—not just in the coronavirus era—to pharmaceutical innovation. In addition, it seems that social media networks are being required to include health data and social distancing policies. Finally, new data is being created for the development of supply chains. Based on all of the above, it seems that the Covid-19 crisis has indeed the nature to act as a catalyst and accelerator in the development of at least in some aspects of technology.

7.3 Debt's Evolution

The problem of over-indebtedness is both a fundamentally moral and real problem of intergenerational justice. High debt accumulation burdens deprive future generations of resources. Of course, this applies in cases where debt is channeled toward current consumption. If it is invested, the question then becomes one of investment returns. If investment return is lower than cost, this represents a preference for the present relative to the future, in which case the problem is essentially the same. Blanchard (2019) notes that, since 1980, US government bond yields have been falling steadily, they are now below the nominal rate of economic growth and are expected to remain at correspondingly low levels over the medium term. Asked about the impact of low interest rates on government debt policy, he notes that if the interest rate paid by the government is less than the growth rate, then the intertemporal budget constraint facing the government no longer binds. Thus, when borrowing costs remain below the gross domestic product (GDP) growth rate, debt (as a percentage of GDP) decreases through the debt rollover.

In the post-war period, global debt has been on an almost uninterrupted, upward course that continues to this day, with developed countries leading the trend in rising global debt/GDP ratios (Mbaye, Moreno-Badia, & Chae, 2018). Despite a significant increase in the share of developing countries' debt since the mid-2000s—with China contributing, after the 2008 financial crisis, to three-quarters of the increase in global private debt—the difference with developed countries remains large. At the same time, the share of debt issued by underdeveloped countries in terms of global GDP remains very low, below 1%.

Starting in 2000, private debt has been the main driver of this increase with an almost continuous upward trend until 2009, while from 2018 onwards, the trend in private debt appears to be more stable (Badia & Dudine, 2019). From 2004 to 2008, global public debt decreased (Badia & Dudine, 2019), but with the start of the recent global financial crisis, it rose again to an historic high in the 3rd quarter of 2016.

The amount of global debt is now more than three times the world's economic output and its evolution points toward an eventual rise in interest rates and a consequent slowdown in global output.

In the case of Greece, the evolution of public and private debt reflects two simultaneous but diverging trends due to the contraction in economic output over the last decade (Fig. 7.1). As a result of the crisis and Greece's economic adjustment programs, the ratio of public debt to GDP widened dramatically relative to private debt because the private sector was no longer able to "support" the public sector.

As a result, the debt/GDP ratio rose sharply during this period and continuing on an upward trend until today, but with the exception of 2012 (PSI). The European average increased much less in the years of the crisis, remaining below 90%.

It is clear that the Covid-19 crisis is increasing economies' debt. This increase is a key feature of the 2020 crisis. In fact, in the United States, the increase as a percentage of GDP will exceed the corresponding increase seen at the end of World War II. The question that arises is whether this defines a new debt crisis, like that seen in 2008. The same question, though more acute, relates to Eurozone, and countries that had been hit in 2008, such as Italy, Spain, and Greece.

A positive fact is that the deficiency environment that has been created helps keep the cost of borrowing low. The negative growth rate in 2020 may be lower than the cost of borrowing, but from 2021 onwards it will

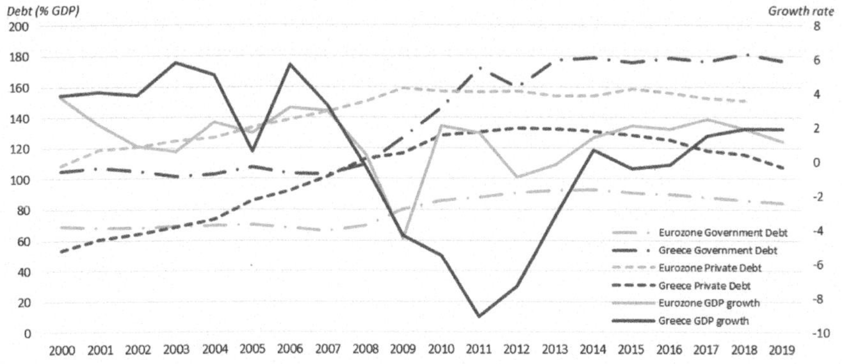

Fig. 7.1 Development of GDP growth, public* and private** debt (% GDP): Greece and the Eurozone (*Note* Eurozone's private, as well as public, debt is the average debt ratio for the euro area group countries, calculated by weighting each country's debt-to-GDP ratio by the share of that country's GDP in the group's aggregate GDP. *Source* Statistical Office of the European Communities [2019a, 2019b*, 2019c**] and author's own creation)

be reversed. Besides, decisions from credit rating agencies to downgrade ratings on government debt have to some extent been neutralized by the reactions of central banks (United States and Eurozone) that accept bonds with a low rating as collateral for liquidity. However, the future in this area has yet to appear.

7.4 The Inherent Financial Instability

Is the financial system "fragile by design" (Calomiris & Haber, 2014)? The instability of its design is linked to its operational foundations, where information asymmetry between buyers and sellers can lead to adverse selection practices, due to contracts imperfections and creation of moral hazard. Given these circumstances, significant changes to the financial system are now in process, focusing on financial intermediation and its direct impact on growth potential, and coming mainly from the adoption of new technologies (FinTech). It should be noted that, following the rapid growth of the financial sector in the 1970s and 1980s, the banking system's culpability in the Great Recession has come into focus, re-igniting the debate about the relationship between the financial system and growth.

It is important to understand the exact nature and extent of financial crises. It is also important to understand the role of asymmetric information in the repeated occurrence of extreme adverse developments in which the principal/agent relationship appears to be significantly responsible for the emergence of such crises.

The use of macroprudential regulation has evolved, with developed countries employing them more widely than emerging and low-income countries. A large and growing body of literature shows that many macroprudential policies seem to be effective and successful in ensuring overall financial stability (Cerutti, Claessens, & Laeven, 2018). However, we still do not know-how effective these policies will be over the long run since many have been implemented only very recently, and most countries have not yet weathered a full economic and financial cycle. Additional research and better data are needed to understand the interaction of macroprudential policies with other policies (e.g., capital controls), and to explore the best way to implement policies during the business cycle (rules versus discretion), their economic costs and how best to deal with the constraints of the political economy.

A well-functioning economy depends on the financial sector's ability to finance growth, providing the necessary capital to fill the gap between investment and return. Economic efficiency and growth depend not only on access to capital, but also on the very structure of the financial system. The financial system in the euro area (as in Japan) is geared toward traditional bank financing, as opposed to the structure of financing prevalent in United States, which is based on capital markets (Reid, Lakhani, & Templeman, 2019).

The Greek economy relies heavily on the mediating function of the banking system and much less on the market's "invisible hand." Indicative is Fig. 7.2, which shows Greek banking sector assets from 2000 to 2017 as a percentage of GDP compared to corresponding figures for United States and euro area economies. It should be noted that, since 2004, the Greek economy's dependence on its banking system has increased and that, since 2009, the role of bank financing in the Greek economy has been higher than the Eurozone average. The corresponding US dependence on the banking system is much lower throughout the period 2000–2017.

The functioning of a financial system and the growth potential of an economy are tightly linked. The relationship is characterized by a strong, reciprocal association, where the policies of banking institutions

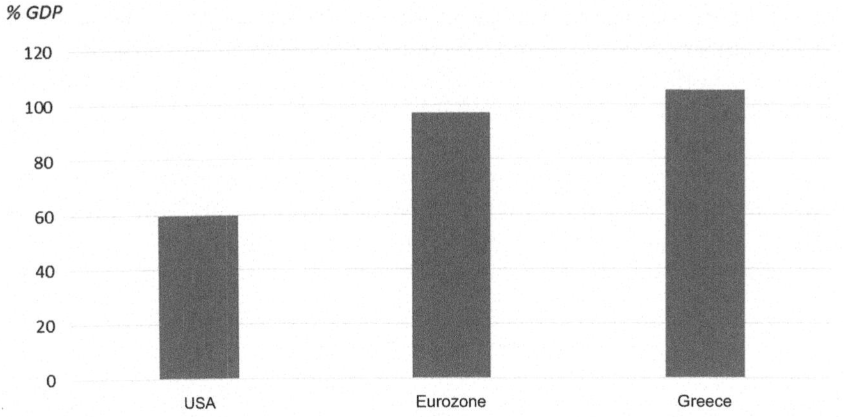

Fig. 7.2 Bank assets to GDP (*Source* International Monetary Fund [IMF] [2019a] and author's own creation)

and capital markets alternatively affect, and are influenced by, the growth rate of an economy.

Issues such as liquidity, leverage and risk-taking in an economy go hand in hand with the business cycle and serve as systemic, procyclical variables, leading to a high degree of volatility in the economic system. At the same time, however, the economic conditions affect the profitability of the financial system and, by extension, the funding policies of financial institutions.

The question that arises is whether this endogenous situation makes the financial system, and ultimately the capitalist system, fundamentally vulnerable to constant crises. Can macroprudential policies, to a greater or lesser degree, curb this problematic functioning of financial systems? And is it possible to eliminate the negative feedback loop that exists between public borrowing and banking systems through the continuous recycling of debt burdens? These are some of the questions where public policy can help shape the relationship between financial systems and economic growth.

This time, however, the crisis did not come from the financial system. Covid-19, having an exogenous origin—in terms of economic system—caused a negative shock in both supply and demand, resulting in expectations for a dramatic reduction in economic activity (as was the case). This caused recessionary expectations and then a recessionary reality.

This reality was reflected in expectations for business profits. Thus, stock market indices collapsed as did, of course, the values of all kinds of assets. But this is nothing more than a classic "Minsky Moment," which reveals the leverage exposure of over-indebted portfolios. Fortunately, liquidity injections, mainly of monetary and fiscal policy, have so far stopped the immediate transmission of the crisis within the banking system. However, it is a fact that non-performing loans will increase and the profits of banking institutions will shrink. Consequently, the transferring of the crisis' effects within the financial system will be, up to a point, inevitable.

7.5 Growth in Productivity

There is no question that the issue of productivity growth is a major subject in economic development, since it is closely linked to an improvement in standards of living. But while you would expect that in the modern age of technological progress and worker training, productivity would increase, this has not been proven. In recent decades there has been a worldwide decline in productivity growth. The recent crisis could be the main reason for this decline, but productivity growth has been slowing for decades across many developed economies (Organisation for Economic Co-operation and Development [OECD], 2019)—in recent years the decline in United States has also been significant. Figure 7.3 illustrates this declining trend.

The slowing rate of growth in productivity is a critical issue and poses one of the greatest threats to standards of living, economic prosperity, and development, whether it be in developing or developed economies. A crisis in productivity is being automatically translated into negative effects on wages and profits, limits to competitiveness and development, and a threat to jobs creation and global economic growth (van Ark et al., 2015). In fact, this issue, combined with the problem of aging populations, is one of particular concern to economists (Manyika et al., 2015).

In recent years, labor output has been marked by significant divergences. Productivity growth has varied among countries and, in some cases, has shown decreases (OECD, 2019). A typical case is the Greek economy (Fig. 7.3), which has experienced a significant decrease in labor productivity in recent years. Noteworthy is that Greece's level of productivity is among the lowest between OECD countries (OECD, 2019).

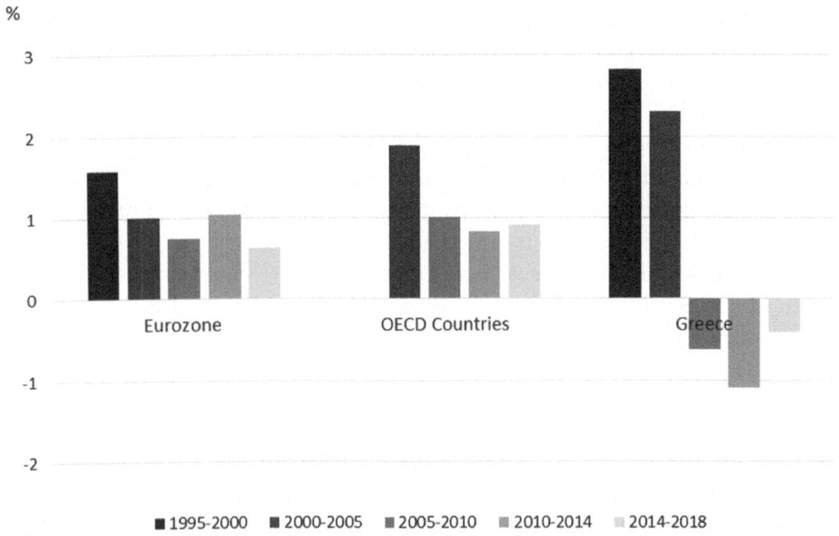

Fig. 7.3 Productivity growth (*Source* OECD [2019] and author's own manipulations and creation)

Van Ark et al. (2015) points out that, in order to maintain economic growth and living standards at the level it was in the 10 years before the crisis, the level of productivity needs to increase by 60% compared to that period.

In general, the problem globally seems related to the fact that firms have become less efficient at "transforming" work and capital into goods and services, while also confronting problems with policymakers. Also, it seems that slowing productivity growth is not just a result of the global financial crisis of 2008, which cut production and reduced investment, but also the result of structural issues facing economies worldwide (van Ark et al., 2015).

Nevertheless, the long-term trend of low growth rates is being accompanied, as one would expect, by low-productivity rates. Indeed, Gordon (2016) cites data from 1890 onwards that confirm this trend. He notes that during three broadly-defined periods for US economy (1890–1920, 1920–1970, and 1970–2014), the component explaining deviations in productivity growth rates appears to be total factor productivity (TFP).

From 1890–1920 to the period 1920–1970, TFP increased roughly fourfold (from a ratio of 0.45% in the first period, to about 1.9% in the second period), which was then followed by a significant decline to approximately 0.7% in the period 1970–2014. However, the contribution from human capital and capital deepening held steady, maintaining their respective shares over all three periods—the ratio for human capital is about 0.3% while for capital deepening it is about 0.7%. So, the interest remains on the persistent question: what is it that changes TFP?

In the case of the Greek economy, TFP has fluctuated widely in recent decades, declining sharply in the six years from 2008 to 2012, and possibly explaining the depth of Greece's recession (see Chapter 9, Sect. 9.3).

The escalation of the Covid-19 pandemic, through the lockdown of economies and the arising need for teleworking, directly and strongly affected economies' productivity levels. The change in the performance of remote workers depends, of course, on the nature of the profession itself. It is logical that, in professions that require physical presence, the exclusion of workers from the workplace nullifies productivity. However, continuing to work from home for professions where this is possible may involve maintaining employee performance, in some cases, or even increasing it. In general, however, teleworking in the midst of the coronary epidemiological crisis (Morikawa, 2020) seems to reduce productivity, as in many cases there is not the necessary technical infrastructure and familiarity to support employees from home, while at the same time the physical presence of employees and the sometime necessary access to an office environment cannot be completely replaced. Additionally, many employees do not have a properly designed workplace or favorable conditions to work remotely in the same efficient manner. In the future, the digital training of human capital and further advancement of technology in communications and information technology are expected to lead to more efficient forms of teleworking.

7.6 Convergences and Divergences in Economic Growth Rates

The concept of economic convergence is based on the assumption that income per capita in poorer economies tends to grow faster than in richer ones. The lower the level of real GDP per capita is, the higher the expected growth rate. Where economies have similar preferences and technology, they converge on the same steady-state, and if these conditions do not apply, they converge to different steady-states. The ideal outcome is for all economies to eventually converge in terms of income per capita.

There is broad consensus that data showing a convergence in incomes' per capita across countries does not exist. According to Johnson and Papageorgiou (2018) the process of development, and possibly convergence, is not a smooth one and is characterized by significant variations among countries. This should come as no surprise, since the concept of convergence is merely a theoretical construction that characterizes part of the broader dynamic development process. It appears, therefore, that recent optimism surrounding rapid and sustainable convergence is unfounded (Johnson & Papageorgiou, 2018). The conclusion is that apart from a few Asian countries that have managed to transform their economies, most of the economic successes in developing countries is related to improvements in efficiency, with only a temporary effect on growth rates.

Thus, it seems that acceleration in growth rates is influenced by a complex set of parameters, with only dependence on the past as a common starting point.

The evolution in Greek national income over the years is characteristic. Figure 7.4 shows the evolution of Greek GDP per capita in dollar terms from 1850 to 2016 (with 2011 as base year) and the country's four main economic crises (in 1893, 1932, 2008, and 2020).[1]

In general, we see almost no change in GDP per capita throughout the period before 1953. This begins to improve, almost exponentially, after 1953 and until the 2008 crisis, when it embarks on a sharp downward trajectory. Since 2012 we have seen signs of a slight recovery in income.

Over this period, the transformation of the Greek economy from a predominantly agricultural economy (in the nineteenth century) to a services-based one (in the twenty-first century) played an important role, along with the greater availability in financing (Thomadakis, 1981). Since the birth of the Greek state, however, economic growth has been accompanied by a series of national, social, and macroeconomic crises (Kalafatis, Demathas, & Petrakis, 2011). These have affected capital accumulation, labor development, and all the other factors of production and thereby influenced both the quantitative and qualitative characteristics of Greek economic growth, as well as attendant social attitudes and stereotypes in Greek society.

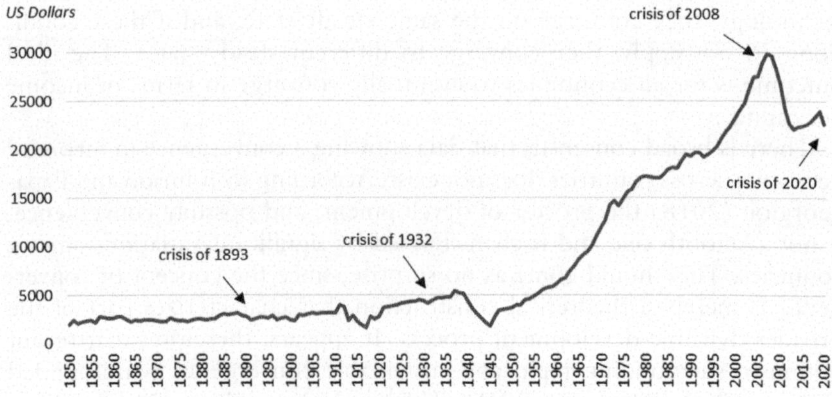

Fig. 7.4 The evolution of Real GDP per capita and economic crises in the Greek economy (1850–2020) (*Note* Real GDP per capita in 2011US$, 2011 benchmark. *Source* Bolt, Inklaar, de Jong, and van Zanden [2018], Oxford Economics [2020], and author's own creation)

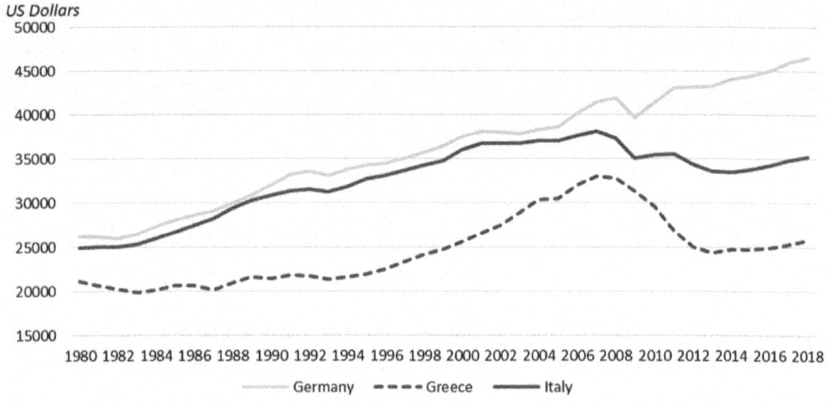

Fig. 7.5 GDP per capita in Greece, Italy, and Germany (1980–2018) (*Source* IMF [2019b] and author's own creation)

Greek income per capita in the 1980s was lower than in countries such as Germany and Italy, but not by a large amount. According to the theory of convergence, the Greek income per capita and these countries should have converged. Instead there was a divergence (Fig. 7.5) in income per capita, a trend that has become even more marked since the 1980s and which has clearly increased further since 2008, even though these countries were and continue to be important trading partners of Greece.

Rodrik (2011), with regard to economies' convergence, tried to explore whether the difference in growth between the developed and developing world can continue and, in particular, whether developing economies can continue the rapid growth they have experienced during the last decades of the twentieth century. He points out that growth in the developing world should depend not so much on the growth of the developed economies themselves, but on the difference in productivity levels between developed and developing countries, the so-called convergence gap, which remains quite large.

Throughout the second half of the twentieth century, there is a steady difference in growth rates between high income and other countries, with the exception of the 2000s when both middle and low-income countries recorded higher growth rates (Table 7.1). Thus, in conclusion, we observe that the gap has widened, in contrast with expectations of a convergence between rich and poorer economies based on the prospect of capital accumulation and transfer of technology and know-how.

Table 7.1 GDP per capita growth (%): average price per decade (1961–2018)

	1961–1969	*1970–1979*	*1980–1989*	*1990–1999*	*2000–2009*	*2010–2018*
High income	4.42	2.72	2.22	1.89	1.12	1.44
Upper middle income	3.54	3.89	1.47	1.41	4.99	4.11
Middle income	2.97	3.44	1.33	1.14	4.49	3.88
Low & middle income	1.54	3.35	1.26	1.02	4.33	3.72
Lower middle income	2.91	2.35	1.55	1.18	3.93	4.06
Low income			−0.12	−1.20	2.33	2.06
World	3.55	2.05	1.24	1.12	1.58	1.82

Source The World Bank (2019) and author's own calculations and creation

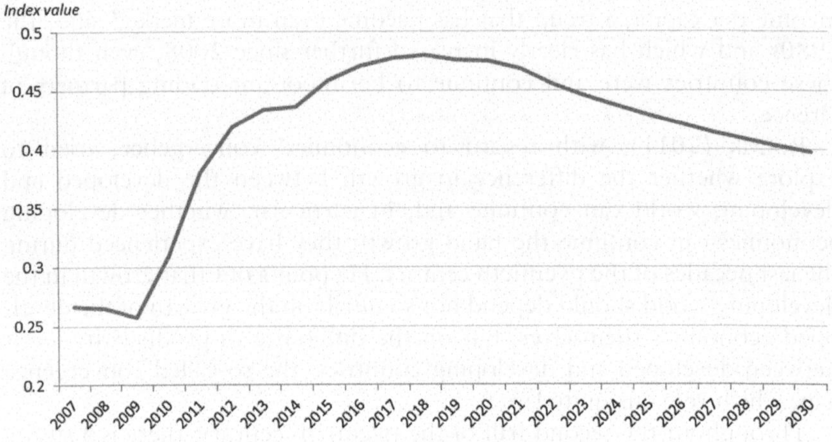

Fig. 7.6 Convergence of Greece with Eurozone countries (average) (*Note* When the index decreases, there is a convergence in economies. *Source* Oxford Economics [2020] and author's own calculations and creation)

Covid-19 shook economies' convergence process. Of course, due its systemic nature, it also has a recessionary impact on almost all economies. Based on the predictions that can be made, we find that at the Eurozone level the pandemic crisis will lead to the convergence of European economies (Fig. 7.6).

7.7 Uncertainty

Concern about the prevalence of high levels of uncertainty has intensified in recent years and is lying at the heart of economic thinking, particularly in the wake of the global financial crisis of 2008 and the debt crisis in the euro area countries.

The nature of uncertainty is due either to incomplete knowledge (subjective uncertainty), or to the variability of the system, i.e., the existence of continuous and volatile events (objective uncertainty) that can influence economic decision-making and business activity (van Asselt & Rotmans, 2002; Walker et al., 2003). Uncertainty due to incomplete knowledge can be differentiated through constant research, study, experience, and continuous evaluation and monitoring of the events and policies applied.

Research into the nature and consequences of uncertainty has grown over the last decade (perhaps in the past there was less research interest) and this may be one of the reasons why the subject has garnered more attention and gained in significance, although the topic is addressed in classical economic theory. Recent research findings examine uncertainty effects on economic activity, as uncertainty plays an important role in economic policy-making (Petrakis, Valsamis, & Kafka, 2020). The existence of uncertainty, therefore, does not favor long-term policy decisions. Decisions in periods of uncertainty are limited to a more short-term horizon at the expense of long-term planning.

Over the past three decades, uncertainty have increased significantly or has had an increased impact on the global economy (Fig. 7.7). In fact, rising uncertainty appears to be an ongoing trend, reaching—as shown in Fig. 7.7—at very high levels due to Covid-19.

The Greek economy is facing increasing levels of uncertainty. This directly affects business decisions on investment and job creation (Schaal, 2011), with an impact on employment and economic activity. As a classic Black Swan case, Covid-19 increased global uncertainty. With the

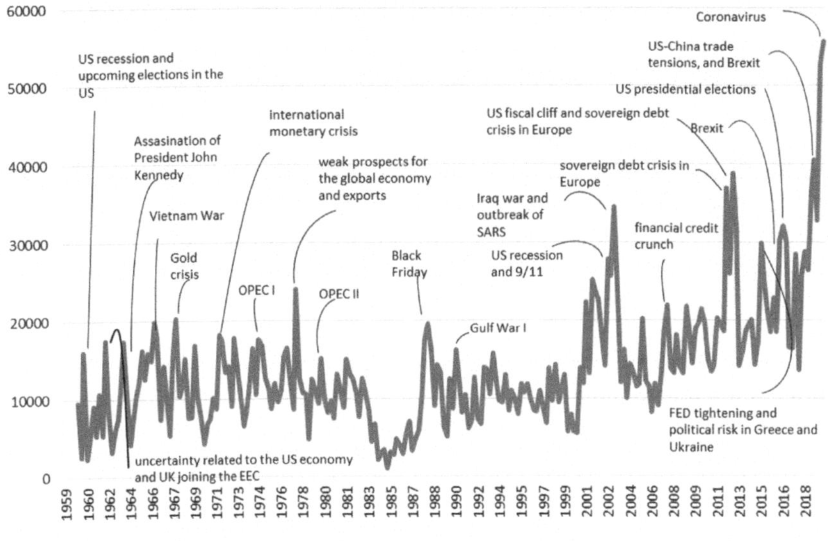

Fig. 7.7 World Uncertainty Index (*Source* Ahir, Bloom, and Furceri [2018] and author's own creation)

Table 7.2 The 5 most important risks for Greece

	Risk 1	*Risk 2*	*Risk 3*	*Risk 4*	*Risk 5*
Greece	Fiscal Crises	Failure of Financial Mechanism or Institution	Failure of National Governance	Large-Scale Involuntary Migration	Profound Social Instability

Source World Economic Forum (WEF) (2019) and author's own creation

outbreak of the Covid-19 pandemic, uncertainty in the Greek market—for the first time since July 2019—surpassed its historical (in the last two decades) average (Center of Planning and Economic Research [KEPE], 2020), demonstrating concerns raised by the epidemiological crisis.

It is difficult to describe all the possible random events that negatively affect the development of an economy. They appear haphazardly and involve risks that can be ascribed with a certain degree of predictability and danger. Such events are presented in Table 7.2 for the Greek economy, with fiscal derailment remaining the highest risk.

All of the events listed in the above table contain an element of randomness, but more importantly they include a risk element that can, however, be assessed and calculated. By contrast, there may be "black swan events" (Taleb, 2010) which have very significant effects, without being possible to accurately calculate the probability of their occurrence.

Among the random risks that Greece faces is the occurrence of major seismic events. Seismic events are inherently unpredictable, while the effects of strong earthquakes can have major financial consequences on society.

In fact, Greece is one of the most seismically active countries in the world with Fig. 7.8 showing the strongest seismic events in Greece since 1817. During these 202 years (from 1817 to 2019) 127 earthquakes of more than 4 on the Richter scale have been recorded, while 91 of them above 6 on the Richter scale.

A serendipitous approach to economic and social development is therefore also based on the existence of unforeseeable events, which may change the prevailing circumstances. Rasmus (2014), in fact, uses the term "serendipity economy" to describe an economic model that is emerging and unpredictable, and which is being evolved, not in a linear way, but rather through randomness and circumstance.

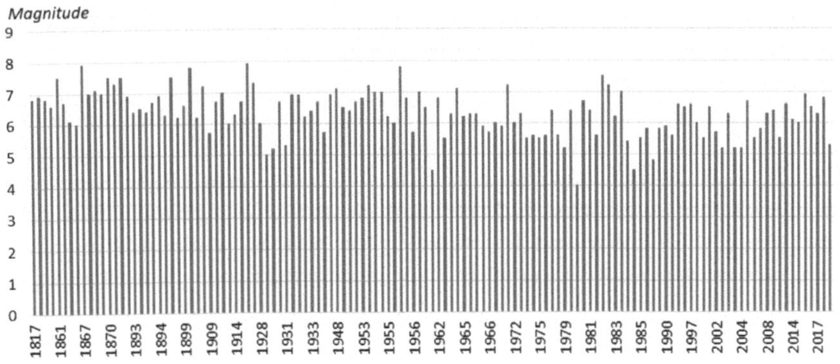

Fig. 7.8 Important seismic events in Greece (1817–2019) (*Note* Earthquakes of more than 4 on the Richter magnitude scale are taken into account. *Source* National Geophysical Data Center [2019] and author's own creation)

7.8 Structural Changes in Production

Major structural changes in production fall into two categories. The first relates to the geographical location of economic decision-making and production centers around the world (east/west, north/south).

The second relates to changes in technology, the rise of the services sector, the shift of investment from tangibles to non-tangibles, and the declining value of low and intermediate-skilled work and their replacement by digital processes.

In recent decades, the spread of digitization and the internet has radically reorganized the structure and functioning of economies and societies as a whole, altering production processes and outputs and, as a result, consumer attitudes and lifestyles. In the coming years, industrial trends and technological developments are expected to have similar effects. Also, trends such as aging populations are expected to have a significant impact on economies' structural transformation process (Cravino, Levchenko, & Rojas, 2019).

Structural changes in production can be evaluated based on three equally, of importance, elements: (a) technologies and trends which have the greatest impact on the organization, operation, and firms' viability in each sector, thereby revealing the outlook, concerns, and needed adjustments facing an industry; (b) the main types of firms investments, revealing their preferences and objectives and, ultimately, future industrial development; and (c) those factors which are seen as changing firms competitive landscape.

Thus, as regards the first point, almost all firms regard the Internet of Things (IoT) as the technological development that will have the greatest impact, both in the short and medium- to-long term (BMI Research, 2018), given its usefulness and the continuous rise in consumer demands. Improving the quality and functionality of devices, while also reducing costs across various economic and social activities, constitute the basic incentives driving this development, but also raising issues of security and privacy at the same time.

Automation & Robotics are also ranked among the technologies that are expected to lead to structural changes in production, mainly over the long-term in the fields of technology and communication, mining, construction, and manufacturing. Although a long-term proposition and only applicable in some industrial sectors, automation has nevertheless highlighted the debate over its impact on labor costs and employment, particularly among low-skilled workers.

Technologies and trends such as Artificial Intelligence (AI), Sharing Economy, 3D Printing, Blockchain adoption, and Space Economy are expected to have less of an impact.

By contrast, businesses are choosing to invest (BMI Research, 2018) in new energy-saving technologies (Energy Efficiency) and in the Personalization of Services. In doing so, they are conforming with the requirements of the age—greater efficiency in household energy consumption, rising costs to businesses for energy-related emissions, and protection of the environment—and seeking to diversify, providing higher value-added services and personalizing services to the consumer.

Those factors which businesses see as changing their competitive landscape are more enduring, with technological development and innovation in general seen as having the greatest impact (BMI Research, 2018). Changing consumer preferences and regulatory policies, such as the transition to low carbon economies, are seen as among the least influential factors.

In conclusion, two important phenomena have been identified: (a) increasing economic inequality and (b) economic and political power accumulation by monopolies and oligopolies, with the most visible concentration of such power being evident in the technology sector. While smaller, innovative companies espoused a free, open, and networked society, with easier access to information, cheaper products, and faster communication, the dominant influence exerted by the tech giants with the economic, cultural, and political power they wield and which they acquired with the advent of the digital age, creates a new environment (Wu, 2018). The relaxation of antitrust laws has led to the absolute dominance of a single search engine (Google), an e-commerce provider (Amazon), and a social media platform (Facebook). But if the fundamental laws of liberal democracy ensure that political power be restrained through checks and balances, then the same must apply to economic influence.

The important question that arises regarding the Covid-19 crisis is whether it can affect the Greek and, more broadly, the global production model.

We have repeatedly stated at this point that Covid-19 acts as an accelerator and amplifier of every trend observed in the economy. The isolation of people and economies' lockdown were a bulwark against virus transmission, but at the same time further highlighted the tendency and need to digitize, connect and automate economies by accelerating the technological megatrends of IoT, Automation & Robotics and AI. Productive and consumer structural changes, such as new methods of labor, production and distribution, electronic trade and e-markets, or new consumer habits are evolving processes.

It seems, however, that they were intensified by the epidemiological crisis of Covid-19. Although in some sectors, where high-capital investment is required (e.g., the automotive industry), the expected global recession of 2020 is likely to delay such changes. In the medium to long term, their further integration into industry is now imperative. This is because in the future the goal is to prevent and reduce costs from similar phenomenon to Covid-19 causing a break in supply chains and harming human resources. At the same time, a greater need for more "connected" economies increases the needs of cybersecurity. Finally, the side effects of reducing global greenhouse gas emissions, as an unintended consequence of the coronavirus, may increase the tendency to switch to low carbon economies.

7.9 Macroeconomic Consequences of Covid-19

The Covid-19 pandemic has created a new reality in the macroeconomic environment. Already, since the Great Recession of 2008, certain conditions have been created, which are summarized by the prevalence of low interest rates, low inflation, and low investment. The new situation created by Covid-19 includes all of the above. In essence, however, as we have already noted, the pandemic functioned as an accelerator and exacerbated existing problems.

In general, a pandemic outbreak has a number of expected negative consequences as it affects the economy as a whole. In particular, it reduces the supply of labor due to deaths and illnesses increases business costs, changes consumer habits, and the investment profile of countries, as investors reconsider their positions based on the reaction of government policies. At the same time, pandemics make economies more vulnerable to macroeconomic imbalances.

Covid-19 had a clear negative effect on the side of supply as factories and businesses closed and the operation of supply chains (OECD, 2020) were disrupted. The impact on demand is more difficult to measure, but it is crucial to identify them, because in terms of economic policy they are easier to deal with than supply deficiencies.

Changing consumer prices may indicate whether Covid-19 has had a major impact on demand. In particular, if the overall effects of supply dominate the effects of demand, we should see prices rise as activity decreases, in a kind of repetition of the 1970 stagflation.

In the period between February 20 and 28, 2020, markets were hit by the Covid-19 shock, and then the global economy was hit by other shocks (on February 28 the Fed chair said it would act appropriately, this was followed on March 3rd by an intermeeting, 50 b.p. rate cut, then followed the 3 March pledge by G7 ministers to "use all appropriate policy tools" to deal with the shock, the subsequent dispute between Saudi Arabia and Russia over oil, and the extension to the whole of Italy of emergency measures to contain Covid-19).

The Chicago Board Options Exchange's Volatility Index (VIX), as a measure of volatility in money markets, has more than doubled and global stock has lost about 10%. However, there is no sign of rising inflation in raw material prices. The impact of the Covid-19 shock was negative, particularly on energy and agricultural products.

Those developments show that the shock of the pandemic had significant effects on reducing demand. The total impact on demand from the shock is at least as significant as the total impact on supply and, therefore, policies that increase demand are justified.

However, the concern in such a situation, where there are disturbances in both supply and demand, is whether the Covid-19 pandemic can cause a demand-driven slump that will provide a boost to supply-demand loop and open the door to stagnation traps induced by any animal spirits (Fornaro & Wolf, 2020).

In a typical New Keynesian model (Gali, 2009), as in Keynesian economics, employment and product are determined by aggregate demand which in turn is determined by productivity growth. The reason for this is that faster productivity growth boosts agents' expectations of future income, inducing them to spend more in the present (Lorenzoni, 2009). This result creates a positive relationship between increased productivity and employment. However, the Covid-19 pandemic negatively affects expectations for future productivity growth resulting in a demand-driven recession (Fornaro & Wolf, 2020) with reduced employment and manufactured output.

In reality, however, the channel through which productivity growth passes are company investments which, in turn, depend on demand. When demand is high, the return on investment is high, and vice versa. Thus, there is a positive relationship between productivity growth and aggregate demand. Suppose the pandemic creates a negative shock. The initial shock to supply reduces demand but now lower demand pushes businesses to reduce investments, a fact which in turn creates a drop in productivity growth. In turn, lower productivity growth creates a further drop in demand, which again reduces productivity growth. So, a vicious circle is created, a supply-demand doom loop that strengthens the impact of the initial shock on employment and productivity growth.

However, in a period where we are at the zero-lower bound, the aggregate demand (AD) curve exhibits a kink. The horizontal part of the AD curve (Fornaro & Wolf, 2020) relates to a case where monetary policy is limited by zero interest rates and the economy faces liquidity traps. In this event, a negative productivity shock shifts the supply curve downward and creates two equilibrium points where the economy is in a liquidity trap and both growth and employment are depressed. This second equilibrium can then be thought of as a stagnation trap (Benigno & Fornaro, 2018). At which of the two equilibrium points the economy will be located at depends on the expectations of economic agents. Pessimistic animal spirits can push the economy into a stagnation trap.

In order to address the above disturbances in supply and demand, the reaction of fiscal and monetary policy was necessary. Thus, governments increased fiscal benefits and encouraged banks to lend to troubled businesses. This way, they tried to mitigate the loss of income to the present, creating future imbalances.

But what are the implications for inflation? In the short term, inflationary pressure created by this massive adverse supply shock is offset by falling prices in basic commodities and oil. But what will then happen as the lockdown gets lifted and recovery ensues, following a period of massive fiscal and monetary expansion (Baldwin & di Mauro, 2020)? As stated by Goodhart and Pradhan (2020), inflation is expected to increase by 5–10% in 2021.

Relative concerns had arisen after the Great Recession of 2008 and the implementation of quantitative easing (QE), with fears of rising inflation not being verified. However, according to Goodhart and Pradhan (2020), pandemic policies have directly increased the broader measures of money, in contrast to QE where interventions remained within the banking system. Also, the speed with which economies will recover will play an important role, as the stronger the recovery, the more implemented policies will seem procyclical. Finally, China's role in the global economy has changed, and with deflationary exports in the past, it is likely to develop into an element of inflationary pressure in the future.

Note

1. Omits reference to the crisis of 1843, which is not included in the data by Maddison.

References

Ahir, H., Bloom, N., & Furceri, D. (2018). *World Uncertainty Index*. Mimeo. Retrieved from: http://www.policyuncertainty.com/.

Badia, M. M., & Dudine, P. (2019). New Data on World Debt: A Dive into Country Numbers. *International Monetary Fund* (IMF Blog). Retrieved from: https://blogs.imf.org/2019/12/17/new-data-on-world-debt-a-dive-into-country-numbers/.

Baldwin, R., & di Mauro, B. W. (2020). Introduction. In R. Baldwin & B. W. di Mauro (Eds.), *Economics in the Time of COVID-19* (pp. 1–30). London: CEPR Press (a VoxEU.org eBook).

Benigno, G., & Fornaro, L. (2018). Stagnation Traps. *Review of Economic Studies, 85*(3), 1425–1470.

Blanchard, O. (2019). Public Debt and Low Interest Rates. *American Economic Review, 109*(4), 1197–1229.

BMI Research. (2018). *Towards 2050: Megatrends in Industry, Politics and the Global Economy*. London: Business Monitor International.

Bolt, J., Inklaar, R., de Jong, H., & van Zanden, J. L. (2018). *Maddison Project Database, Version 2018. Rebasing Maddison: New Income Comparisons and the Shape of Long-Run Economic Development* (Maddison Project Working Paper No. 10). Retrieved from: https://www.rug.nl/ggdc/historicaldevelopment/maddison/releases/maddison-project-database-20.

Brynjolfsson, E., & McAfee, A. (2014). *The Second Machine Age: Work, Progress, and Prosperity in a Time of Brilliant Technologies*. New York: W. W. Norton.

Calomiris, C. W., & Haber, S. H. (2014). *Fragile by Design: The Political Origins of Banking Crises and Scarce Credit*. Princeton: Princeton University Press.

Center of Planning and Economic Research. (2020). *KEPE Publishes the Composite Leading Indicator and the KEPE GRIV "Fear" Index (April 6, 2020)—March Estimations* (press release). Retrieved from: https://www.kepe.gr/index.php/en/2013-11-02-20-59-24.html.

Cerutti, E., Claessens, S., & Laeven, L. (2018). The Increasing Faith in Macroprudential Policies. *Vox CEPR Policy Portal*. Retrieved from: https://voxeu.org/article/increasing-faith-macroprudential-policies.

Cravino, J., Levchenko, A. A., & Rojas, M. (2019). *Population Aging and Structural Transformation* (NBER Working Paper No. 26327).

Dervis, K. (2014). The Future of Economic Progress. *Project Syndicate*. Retrieved from: https://www.project-syndicate.org/commentary/kemal-dervi–homes-in-on-the-key-questions-surrounding-the-nature-and-measurement-of-contemporary-growth?barrier=accesspaylog.

Fornaro, L., & Wolf, M. (2020). *Covid-19 Coronavirus and Macroeconomic Policy* (Centre for Economic Policy Research Discussion Paper No. 14529).

Gali, J. (2009). *Monetary Policy, Inflation, and the Business Cycle: An Introduction to the New Keynesian Framework*. Princeton: Princeton University Press.

Goodhart, C., & Pradhan, M. (2020). Future Imperfect After Coronavirus. *Vox CEPR Policy Portal*. Retrieved from: https://voxeu.org/article/future-imperfect-after-coronavirus.

Gordon, R. J. (2012). *Is U.S. Economic Growth Over? Faltering Innovation Confronts the Six Headwinds* (NBER Working Paper No. 18315).

Gordon, R. J. (2016). *The Rise and Fall of American Growth: The U.S. Standard of Living since the Civil War*. Princeton: Princeton University Press.

International Monetary Fund. (2019a). *IMF Data: Monetary and Financial Statistics (MFS)*.

International Monetary Fund. (2019b). *World Economic Outlook Database: October 2019 Edition*.

Johnson, P., & Papageorgiou, C. (2018). What Remains of Cross-Country Convergence? *Journal of Economic Literature, 58*(1), 129–175.

Jones, B. J. (2009). The Burden of Knowledge and the "Death of the Renaissance Man": Is Innovation Getting Harder? *The Review of Economic Studies, 76*(1), 283–317.

Kalafatis, T., Demathas, Z., & Petrakis, P. E. (2011). Economic Activity Cycles. In S. Asdrahas (Ed.), *Economic History of the Greek State: Establishment of a National Economy, Economic Functions and Performances, Evidence of Quantitative Analysis* (Vol. II). Athens: Piraeus Bank Group Cultural Foundation (in Greek).

Krugman, P. (1990). *The Age of Diminished Expectations: U.S. Economic Policy in the 1990s*. Cambridge: The MIT Press.

Lorenzoni, G. (2009). A Theory of Demand Shocks. *American Economic Review, 99*(5), 2050–2084.

Manyika, J., Lund, S., Chui, M., Bughin, J., Woetzel, J., Batra, P., … Sanghvi, S. (2017). Jobs Lost, Jobs Gained: What the Future of Work Will Mean for Jobs, Skills, and Wages. *McKinsey Global Institute*. Retrieved from: https://www.mckinsey.com/featured-insights/future-of-work/jobs-lost-jobs-gained-what-the-future-of-work-will-mean-for-jobs-skills-and-wages.

Manyika, J., Woetzel, J., Dobbs, R., Remes, J., Labaye, E., & Jordan, A. (2015). *Global Growth: Can Productivity Save the Day in an Aging World*. New York: McKinsey Global Institute.

Mbaye, S., Moreno-Badia, M., & Chae, K. (2018). *Global Debt Database: Methodology and Sources* (IMF Working Paper No. 18/111).

Morikawa, M. (2020). Covid-19, Teleworking, and Productivity. *Vox CEPR Policy Portal*. Retrieved from: https://voxeu.org/article/covid-19-teleworking-and-productivity.

National Geophysical Data Center. (2019). *World Data Service (NGDC/WDS): Significant Earthquake Database*. https://doi.org/10.7289/v5td9v7k.

Organisation for Economic Co-operation and Development. (2019). *OECD Compendium of Productivity Indicators 2019*. Paris: OECD Publishing. https://doi.org/10.1787/b2774f97-en.

Organisation for Economic Co-operation and Development. (2020). *OECD Economic Outlook: Interim Report March 2020*. Paris: OECD Publishing. https://doi.org/10.1787/7969896b-en.

Oxford Economics. (2020). *Oxford's Global Macro Model*.

Petrakis, P. E., Valsamis, D. G., & Kafka K. I. (2020). *Economic Growth and Development Policy*. New York: Palgrave Macmillan.

Piketty, T. (2014). *Capital in the Twenty-First Century*. Cambridge: The Belknap Press of Harvard University Press.

Rasmus, D. W. (2014). The Serendipity Economy. *Serious Insights*. Retrieved from: https://www.seriousinsights.net/welcome-to-the-serendipity-economy/.

Reid, J., Lakhani, J., & Templeman, L. (2019). How to Fix European Banking… and Why It Matters. *Deutsche Bank Thematic Research*. Retrieved from: https://www.dbresearch.com/PROD/RPS_EN-PROD/Thematic/THEMATIC.alias.

Rodrik, D. (2011). *The Future of Economic Convergence* (NBER Working Paper No. 17400).

Rodrik, D. (2013). *The Past, Present, and Future of Economic Growth* (Global Citizen Foundation Working Paper No. 1).

Schaal, E. (2011). *Uncertainty, Productivity and Unemployment in the Great Recession* (Society for Economic Dynamics Meeting Paper No. 1450).

Statistical Office of the European Communities. (2019a). *Eurostat: GDP and main components [nama_10_gdp]*.

Statistical Office of the European Communities. (2019b). *Eurostat: Private Sector Debt, Consolidated—% of GDP [tipspd20] and Author's Calculation*.

Statistical Office of the European Communities. (2019c). *Eurostat: Government Deficit/Surplus, Debt and Associated Data [gov_10dd_edpt1]*.

Taleb, N. N. (2010). *The Black Swan: The Impact of the Highly Improbable*. New York: Random House Trade Paperbacks.

The World Bank. (2019). *World Bank Data [NY.GDP.PCAP.KD.ZG]*.

Thomadakis, S. (1981). *Credit and Monetisation of the Economy, Discounting and the National Bank of Greece*. Athens: Cultural Foundation of the National Bank of Greece (in Greek).

van Ark, B., Ozyildirim, A., Bhide, P., Crofoot, E., Erumban, A., & Levanon, G. (2015, June). Prioritizing Productivity to Drive Growth, Profitability, and Competitiveness. *The Conference Board*. Retrieved from: https://www.conference-board.org/topics/productivity-competitiveness.

van Asselt, M. B. A., & Rotmans, J. (2002). Uncertainty in Integrated Assessment Modelling. *Climatic Change, 54*(1), 75–105.

Walker, W. E., Harremoës, P., Rotmans, J., van der Sluijs, J. P., van Asselt, M. B. A., Janssen, P. & von Krauss, M. P. K. (2003). Defining Uncertainty: A Conceptual Basis for Uncertainty Management in Model-Based Decision Support. *Integrated Assessment*, *4*(1), 5–17.

World Economic Forum. (2019). *Regional Risks for Doing Business 2019*. Geneva: WEF.

Wu, T. (2018). *The Curse of Bigness: Antitrust in the New Gilded Age*. New York: Columbia Global Reports.

CHAPTER 8

Political Megatrends

8.1 Introduction

The primacy of politics over economics demands the identification and observation of the most important political changes and trends, given that they directly affect decisions of economic development. There are three major issues that have prompted changes in the political maps of most countries, without these shifts always being clear.

The first issue refers to the income and wealth redistribution in favor of the rich, a fact which increases social inequalities (Sect. 8.2). The second one (Sect. 8.3) deals with the role of growth, privacy, and a move in the position held by the middle-class in society. It should be noted that these changes have a different direction in the Western world, when compared to the East.

The third issue (Sect. 8.4) concerns shifts in social behavior associated with complex and altering causes, such as the level and change of wealth and income, globalization, changes in age, and in general trends described in the previous two chapters. In the following section (Sect. 8.5), is analyzed the way in which political behavior evolves in modern changing societies.

It should be noted that all of the observed and existing above trends differentiated strongly by the Covid-19 crisis. Thus, the last part (Sect. 8.6) of the chapter focuses on the effects Covid-19 has on both political and cultural level.

P. E. Petrakis, *The New Political Economy of Greece up to 2030*,
The Political Economy of Greek Growth up to 2030,
https://doi.org/10.1007/978-3-030-47075-3_8

8.2 Inequality and Social Mobility

The theoretical foundation of bonding between economic and political institutions, income distribution, and resources produced in an economy is an issue that by definition seems self-evident, but in reality, is very difficult to demonstrate empirically. The issue of income and resource distribution is directly linked to the system of political institutions.

It is easy to understand that a political structure supports specific political forces, which then enjoy the benefits of their dominance (Alesina & Perotti, 1996). At the same time, it has been proven that the concept of democracy, as a political institution, is closely linked to income distribution (Acemoglu, Johnson, Robinson & Yared, 2008; Herwartz & Theilen, 2014; Perotti, 1996). This happens either directly, in a legal manner (e.g., income policy that is passed into law), or indirectly, via procedural interventions (e.g., ways of representation and strikes decision process).

On the other hand, at any reference to economic institutions, it makes easy to understand their role in the income and resources (tax system, insurance system, etc.) redistribution. And yet, it is not easy to extract empirically confirmed judgments, for example, on the way financial systems are being developed and on issues of wealth distribution.

It is clear, however, that systems based on bank-centric development are more likely to prefer a redistribution resource system in favor of financial capital. In contrast, systems that rely more on the direct markets functioning result in effects that favor shareholders wealth (Allen & Gale, 2000; Rajan & Zingales, 2001).

Revenue redistribution takes place through different mechanisms and is mainly influenced by fiscal policy. Attention must be drawn to identify policies that are most suitable in efficiently improving income distribution and to the politicians who support them (Frankel, 2014). Income redistribution mechanisms are divided into:

- transfer payments (unemployment benefits, disability benefits, social security programs, pensions);
- progressive taxation, through which higher levels of taxation are imposed on higher incomes; and
- public provision of social services, mainly in education and health.

Although taxes and social transfers have a direct impact on income distribution, the public provision of social services is an indirect redistribution method with a more long-term and qualitative character.

Income inequality has increased worldwide in recent years, mainly as a result of technological progress, globalization, and the liberalization of the labor market (Teulings, 2014). The increase in inequality was even greater due to the 2008 global financial crisis (Hellebrandt, 2014), while at the same time, the opposite does not seem to be the case, as we cannot blame inequality on the global crisis (Bordo & Meissner, 2012).

In reality, fiscal consolidation policies appear to have significant distributive effects, widening inequality, reducing the share of income from wages, and increasing long-term unemployment (Ball, Furceri, Leigh & Loungani, 2013).

Barry Eichengreen identified, in a 2016 speech in Lisbon on the issue of inequality (as cited in de Long, 2016), six similar historical phases in the last 250 years: (a) The increase in Britain's income inequality from 1750 to 1850, where profits from the British Industrial Revolution did not go to the poor but to the middle-class of the cities and the countryside. (b) From 1750 to 1975, income inequality spread worldwide as profits from industrial and post-industrial technologies were not equally shared to all. (c) From 1850 to 1914, living standards and labor productivity levels converged in the global North, as 50 million people left Europe to settle in places with abundant resources, transferring institutions, technologies, and capital. (d) From 1870 to 1914, domestic inequality increased in the global North, as entrepreneurship, industrialization, and financial manipulation channeled new profits mainly to the wealthy. (e) From 1930 to 1980, higher taxes on the wealthy helped to provide benefits and support public programs. (f) From 1980 till present, economic policy choices have again resulted in increasing inequality in favor of the global North. The arrival of Covid-19 crisis affects income and wealth inequality, exacerbating the phenomenon.

The degree of inequality in the case of the Greek economy compared to the Eurozone countries for the year 2018 is presented, through the Gini coefficient index, in Fig. 8.1.

In recent decades, growing global inequality is reflected in the significant cut in labor share seen in most countries (Karabarbounis & Neiman, 2014).

The decrease in labor share is combined with increased income inequalities for two reasons (Dao, Das, Koczan & Lian, 2017): (a) low skill

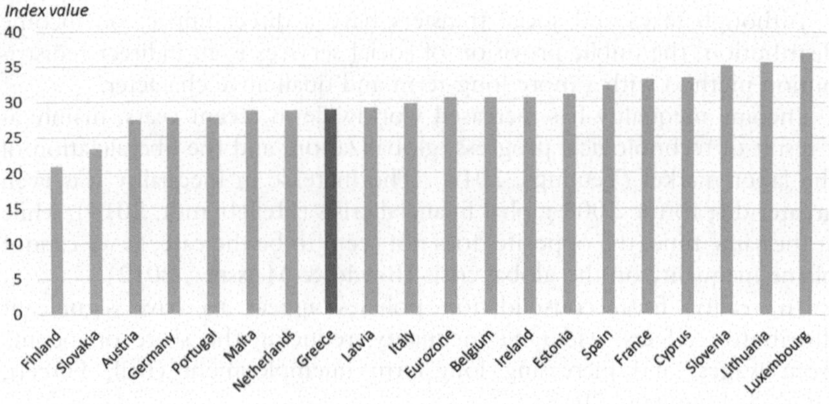

Fig. 8.1 Gini Index in Eurozone countries (2018) (*Source* Statistical Office of the European Communities [2019a] and author's own creation)

workers have been burdened with the drop in labor share, while there are indications of reductions in professions that require intermediate-level skills and income cuts to middle-skill workers in developed economies, (b) capital is mostly concentrated in high-income groups and, therefore, the income increase from capital tends to increase income inequality.

The decline in labor share taking place to a large extent in developed economies may be due to technological progress, which is accompanied by a sudden drop in the relative price of labor, in combination with the emergence of professions that do not involve repetitive routine tasks—something that seems to have a greater impact on gains for middle-skilled workers. In developing economies, the decline in labor share may be mainly due to the global integration process and, in particular, to the expansion of global value chains that contributed to higher capital intensity production.

Income inequality may be of concern to members of a particular society or between societies themselves. It is an issue with an ethical and economic dimension, having a philosophical basis which assumes that the earth's common, to all residents, resources are ultimately used for the production of income and wealth. As a result, the question which is raised concerns as to whether parts of wealth generated have been fairly distributed and how, and to what extent, is it fair to differentiate.

In addition to the ethical dimension, there is also a developmental issue, which is expressed by the question concerning the causal relationship between the income and wealth distribution and growth itself (Cingano, 2014). Despite the vast bibliography on the relationship between inequality and development, there are no clear indications at an empirical level as to whether inequalities' existence have a positive or negative effect—and to what extent—on growth rates.

At the same time, it is very likely that there are forces being developed in the political system fueled by the growing income and wealth redistribution, which may have the tendency to maintain and influence the distribution itself and, ultimately, the potential for economic growth.

However, this approach is only partially valid. While the rich are getting richer in developed economies, developing countries are growing faster than developed ones, thus reducing global inequality (Fig. 8.2). As a result, Gini coefficient is expected (Hellebrandt & Mauro, 2015) to decrease worldwide from 65 in 2013, to 61 in 2035—it stood at 69 in 2003—albeit it is not clear from the characteristics of the Covid-19 crisis whether this long-term trend will be prevented. And while income paid globally to higher echelons (90th percentile) in 2013 was 31 times higher than the lowest echelon (10th percentile), this ratio is expected

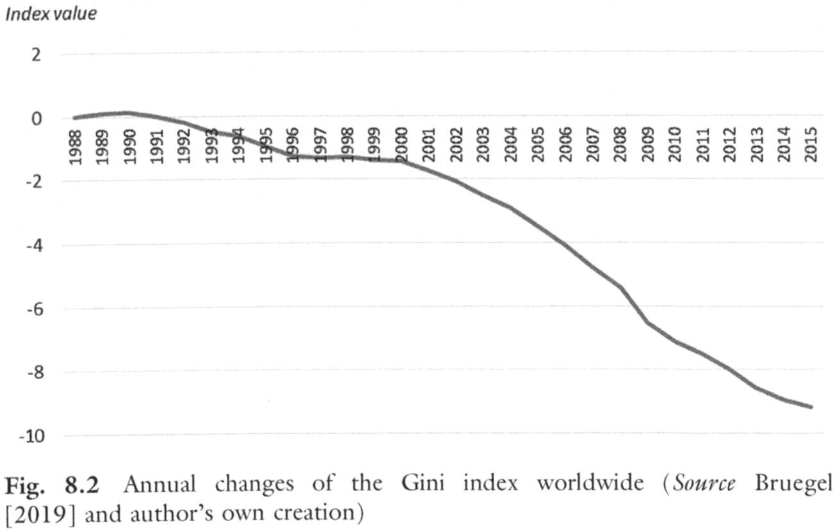

Fig. 8.2 Annual changes of the Gini index worldwide (*Source* Bruegel [2019] and author's own creation)

to decrease in 2035 to 24 times higher. Of course, this global improvement is expected on the condition that inequality within countries will not increase at an unprecedented rate.

In 2013, 40% of those at the lowest decile (decile 1) of the world's income distribution, were in Sub-Saharan Africa, more than 30% were located in India, 15% in China, and the rest largely in East and South Asia and the Pacific region. Almost 80% of the top decile (decile 10) was located in the advanced economies, with about 10% in China and the rest distributed mainly in the countries of Eastern Europe and Central Asia, Latin America, and the Caribbean as well as East Asia and the Pacific.

A reduction in income inequality is thus observed as: (a) the share of developing countries to high-income levels is being increased; (b) for developed European Union (EU) and Organisation for Economic Co-operation and Development (OECD) countries, Eastern European, Central Asian, Latin American and Caribbean countries, there is a shift in population numbers to lower income levels; and (c) for developing countries (mainly China, India and East Asian and Pacific countries) there is a shift in population levels toward middle and higher income levels. The only area where income inequality is expected to worsen is in Sub-Saharan Africa, where due to the low growth rate of its core economies, its share in low-income groups is expected to significantly increase in 2035.

In contrast, the development of income inequality within countries has varied, especially in some advanced economies, where low and middle incomes have been declining or stagnating, inequality has increased.

The unequal distribution of income is, of course, naturally linked to the unequal distribution of wealth. The unequal distribution of wealth (after taxes) is, on average, twice than that of income (Balestra & Tonkin, 2018). In OECD countries, the richest 10% of households own 52% of the total wealth, with their respective share of income distribution being at 24%. The countries with the highest wealth inequality are United States followed by Denmark and Netherlands, while those with the lowest are Slovakia and Japan. In Greece, 10% of the richest groups held 38.8% of total wealth in 2009, with this percent rising to 42.4% in 2014 (Balestra & Tonkin, 2018).

In regard to households with the lowest levels of wealth, this does not necessarily mean that they are poor in terms of income. Nor that they have no have assets, as in the cases of Netherlands, Denmark, Norway, and Ireland. Households are found to have low levels of wealth (in levels below 20%), combining high reserves of assets with high debt levels.

After the 2008 financial crisis, wealth inequality in United States and United Kingdom increased (Balestra & Tonkin, 2018), as falling prices and lower real estate returns, along with the rising prices of financial assets, benefited those with higher levels of wealth.

Rising inequality rates increase the risk of poverty in societies. In Greece, the percentage of people at risk of poverty (after social transfers[1]) increased, as expected, after 2008 by 3 points, but at a decreasing pace as of 2013. Specifically, in 2018,[2] was 18.5% (for per capita incomes below 4718 euros per year) and is estimated to relate to more than 760,000 households, or the equivalent of 1,954,400 people (Hellenic Statistical Authority [ELSTAT], 2019). The corresponding rate before social transfers and pensions reaches 50%.[3]

Figure 8.3 indicates the number of people at risk of poverty in Greece and the EU-28, presenting absolute numbers for the period 2003–2018.

In Greece, from 2009 to 2012, the number of people at risk of poverty increased significantly, while from 2013 to 2018 it fell considerably. In the EU-28, from 2006 and for about two years, the number of people at risk of poverty increased and kept increasing until 2018, excepted the years 2013 and 2017 (Fig. 8.3).

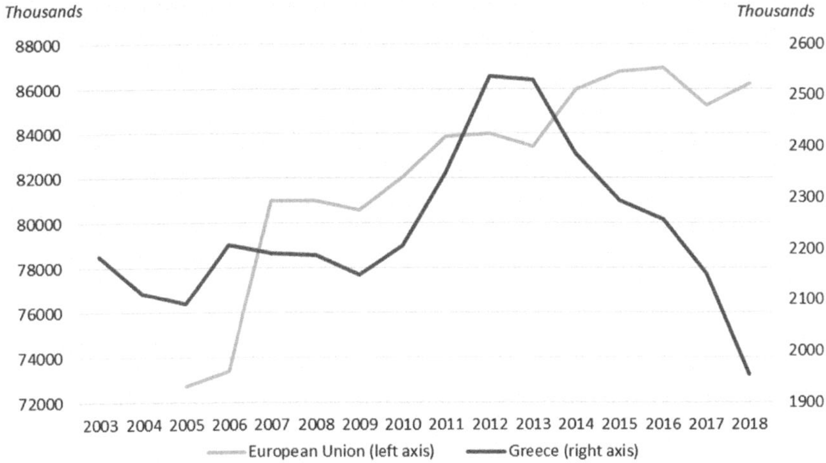

Fig. 8.3 People at risk of poverty in Greece and European Union: 2003–2018 (thousands) (*Source* Statistical Office of the European Communities [2019b] and author's own creation)

More than 1/3 of the world's population, with an income above the poverty line, is economically vulnerable, meaning that they are unable to cope financially with a sharp loss of income (Balestra & Tonkin, 2018). In Greece, this ratio exceeds 1/2, ranking among the highest among OECD countries.

With income inequality and wealth being one side of the coin, developments in social mobility are on the other side. Intergenerational mobility is socially important, both from a justice and an economic efficiency point of view.

Figure 8.4 presents the World Economic Forum's (WEF) Social Mobility Index.[4] The main conclusion of the report is that a person's opportunities in life remain linked to his or her socioeconomic status at birth, a fact that reinforces historical inequalities. This is a significant problem, not only for the individual, but also for society and the economy. Low social mobility combined with an inequality of opportunities creates obstacles to economic development.

The Nordic countries achieve the best results as they combine access, quality, and equality in education, offering job opportunities under good conditions, along with quality social protection systems without exclusions. Greece ranks in the last positions among high-income countries (and 48th among 83 economies in the world), beating only Saudi Arabia

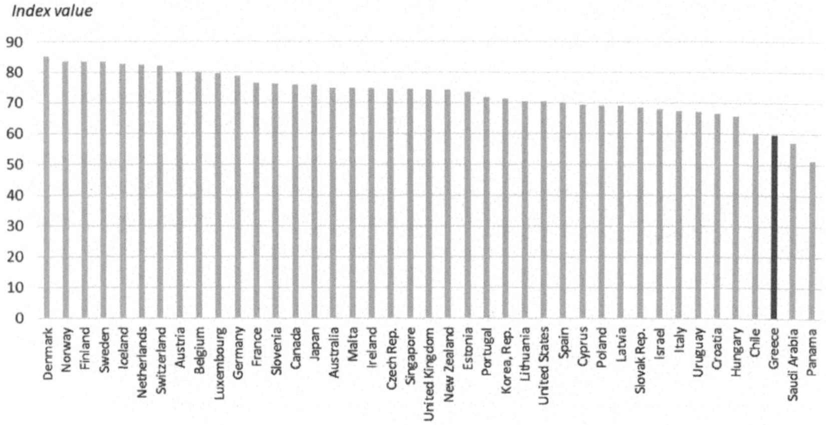

Fig. 8.4 Social Mobility Index for high-income countries (2020) (*Source* World Economic Forum [2020] and author's own creation)

and Panama. The above indicator reveals that there are few countries with the right conditions able to promote social mobility. Most countries have weaknesses in four areas that affect social mobility: fair wages, social protection, working conditions, and lifelong learning.

Perceptions of mobility vary widely between countries. In United States, if one works hard and "plays by the rules," one can expect to enjoy a living standard higher than that of their parents'. And it is precisely this promise of intergenerational mobility that has been evoked as justification (Jacobs & Hipple, 2018) for persistently high poverty rates and high economic inequalities in the largest market economy in the world. Despite widespread belief in upward mobility, improving economic opportunities in United States is clearly a challenge, more so than in other advanced economies. While relative mobility in the country has not deteriorated dramatically in recent decades, the combination of static relative mobility and a reduction in absolute mobility means that economic opportunities seem to be considerably less for young adults today than in previous generations.

A society with high mobility between generations is one where the well-being of an individual, in comparison to others of his generation, is less reliant on the socioeconomic status of his parents. Forty percent of Greeks believe that they lived better than their parents, while at the same time, the percentage of those who believe that their children will live better than them, falls by almost half (Narayan et al., 2018).

Undoubtedly, there are two basic reasons why higher mobility in a society should be the goal of public policy: justice and economic efficiency. When mobility is low, the chances of success are largely determined by birth, which runs counter to the basic concepts of justice in most societies. Low mobility also hinders the development and effective use of human resources and the efficient allocation of resources, as talented people from disadvantaged families are cut off from opportunities that ultimately benefit those born with greater privileges, and not those with the greatest potential. Limiting this inefficiency is beneficial for economic development. Given that the wasting of human resources is more likely to occur among low-income levels, policies that promote higher social mobility are likely to promote more inclusive development.

It can be seen that for large sections of the world's population born in 1980s, a person's education is still very closely linked to their parents' education (Narayan et al., 2018). Sub-Saharan Africa and South Asia stand out as the areas with the lowest levels of mobility. 13 of the 15 countries with the lowest mobility are either in Africa or South Asia. Adversely, the highest levels of mobility are in Western Europe, Canada, Australia, and Japan. On average, mobility is significantly lower in developing economies (with low and medium incomes) compared to high-income economies (Narayan et al., 2018). Among the developing economies, East Asia and the Pacific, the Middle East, and North Africa are areas with the highest average mobility relative to education, which remain well below averages in high-income economies.

Averages relative to social mobility are lower in developing economies, without any indication that the gap with developed ones is narrowing. Additionally, income mobility in many developing economies is much lower than their level of educational mobility would allow us to expect.

These findings support that improving intergenerational mobility requires policies to reduce opportunity inequality at all stages of life, promoting the development of human capital.

8.3 The Strengthening of Privacy, the Role of Individual Skills, and the Development of the Middle-Class

The role of the individual in the context of a changing environment is also changing. While there were previous discriminations that clashed with the "continuation of history," with the world being formed into the western and eastern (communist) bloc, the role of individuals was in a weaker position when compared to "collective societies." But that changed when the world "integrated" providing a new and much stronger position to individuality. In the current period, due to the global crisis, social needs are creating more pressures, leading the individual to face even more challenges globally.

The new individual is possessed by strength, skills, and abilities, in order to be able to meet the changing globalization conditions and also to make decisions and meet current and future goals. When the individual is in a position to adequately perceive the reality around him, then he can achieve what we call "individual empowerment." The stronger the individuals that make up a society, then the stronger a society is.

Thus, the concept of individual empowerment initially refers to a process of transforming the individual, during which the individual is being improved and takes control of his decisions. Then, regarding his empowerment process, he gains self-confidence which allows him to make decisions. It is an interactive process that takes place between the individual and his environment. The results of the process are being translated into skills, based on knowledge and abilities, with key characteristics being (Kieffer, 1984) the formation of political and social consciousness, the ability of co-operating, active participation, the ability to cope with failure, and the struggle for influence over the environment. The individual creates the suitable conditions to be in a position of choosing the most appropriate solution among various alternatives, having full knowledge of all available options. This significantly increases the range of possibilities to shape future situations.

The important role of an empowered individual can be made very clear through his performance in the workplace. No vision and no strategy can be achieved without capable and strong employees (Argyris, 1998). This is why top executives take the responsibility of trying to develop specialized employees. A common feature of countries where the problem of mismatched skills (i.e., the deviation of qualifications and skills in the workforce with labor market demands) is particularly evident, is the low level of public resources poured into the education and training of individuals.

The funding for education in Greece, as a percentage of Gross Domestic Product (GDP), is one of the lowest in EU (Fig. 8.5)—a ranking that has been consistent over time (Statistical Office of the European Communities, 2019c). This, in combination with the (often) inefficient use of resources, contributes to a reduction in the workforce quality and also negatively affects its ability to adapt to the labor market's changing needs.

When the individual is empowered, he develops the necessary skills and characteristics to adapt to new conditions.

The mismatch of skills negatively affects the competitiveness and growth of economies, increases unemployment, undermines social inclusion and bears significant economic and social costs. These developments increase levels of uncertainty.

Developing the skills of individuals is seen as being necessary in order to take advantage of opportunities that arise and address challenges posed by the ever-increasing demands of changing economies and new globalization technologies.

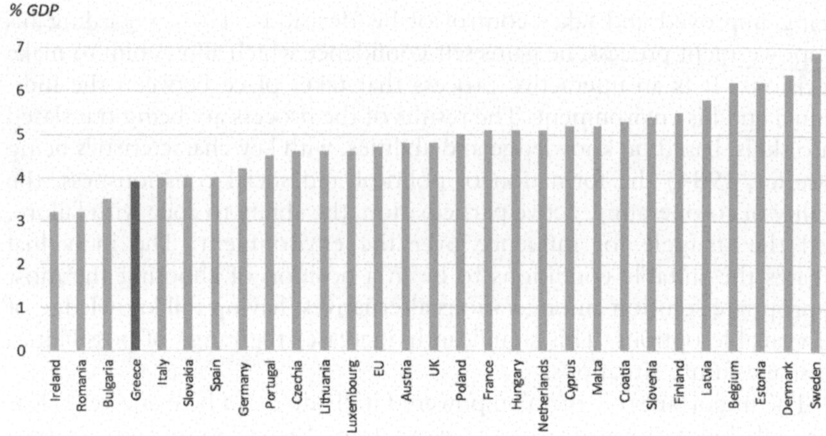

Fig. 8.5 General government spending on education as % GDP: EU countries (2017) (*Source* Statistical Office of the European Communities [2019c] and author's own creation)

Economic developments include concerns about the reality that is expected to emerge in the wake of the recent large global crisis. Having previously experienced the history of capitalism for centuries, a period of long-term recovery is what is expected, but this is not certain, neither is its pace, nor whether the recovery's share of benefits will be distributed equally among countries. The recovery will be determined by its driving forces and the extent to which it will be driven by the demand coming from the rise of the middle-class[5] in developing countries.

Figure 8.6 shows the declining role of consumer power among the middle-class in Europe and United States over time (until 2030) and its replacement by corresponding forces coming from (Kharas, 2010) China and India.

The shift in demand patterns will have multiple effects on the global organization of production and growth. The recovery created may be fueled by supply coming from either energy supply conditions, or the use of new technologies. It can also be strengthened by the supply that comes from reducing debt-to-GDP ratios and the correcting of macroeconomic imbalances.

In many countries, mainly developed (principally in United States and Europe), the role and importance of the middle-class has declined in recent years. Middle-class life is typically associated (beyond specific

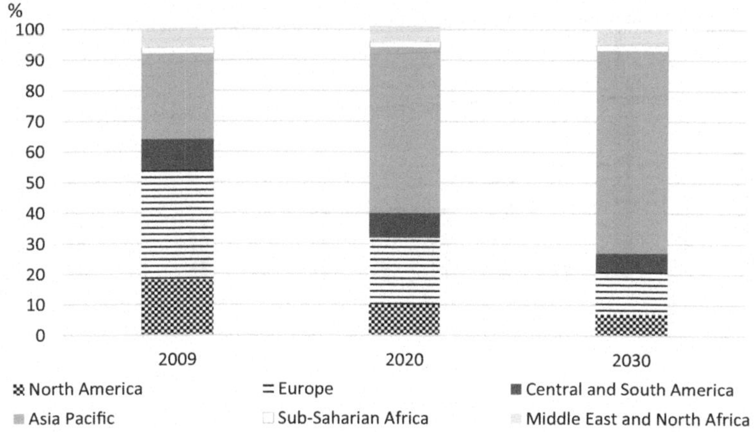

Fig. 8.6 Share of spending by the middle-class globally: 2009–2030 (percentage) (*Source* Kharas [2010] and author's own calculations)

income levels) with certain goods, services, and living conditions, such as decent housing, a good level of education and health, and a healthy environment.

In most societies, the middle-class consists of the majority of the population. Income and expenditure levels of the middle-class are relatively higher (as a percentage) than the size of its population in OECD countries (OECD, 2019), which shows its contribution to the economy of the countries. In Greece, spending by the middle-class accounts for 57% of total expenditure (OECD, 2019) and is directly proportionate with the size of the population and its income, but is lower than the OECD average. The contribution to expenditure from the lower class is 20%.

The change in income seen by the middle-class in Greece over the last two decades has been impressive, as was the case in Ireland and Spain, while in other countries it has been milder (Fig. 8.7). During the decade 1995–2005, the middle-class in Greece saw income being increased by more than 40% and expenditure by almost 55%. In contrast, over the next decade, its revenue fell by 45% and its expenditure dipped by 40%, in a trend showing how painful the crisis has been for the country's economy. However, a similar development is observed in Spain. In Ireland, in the decade 2005–2015, expenditure by the middle-class decreased by 27%, but at the same time its income continued on an upward trend (4.5%)!

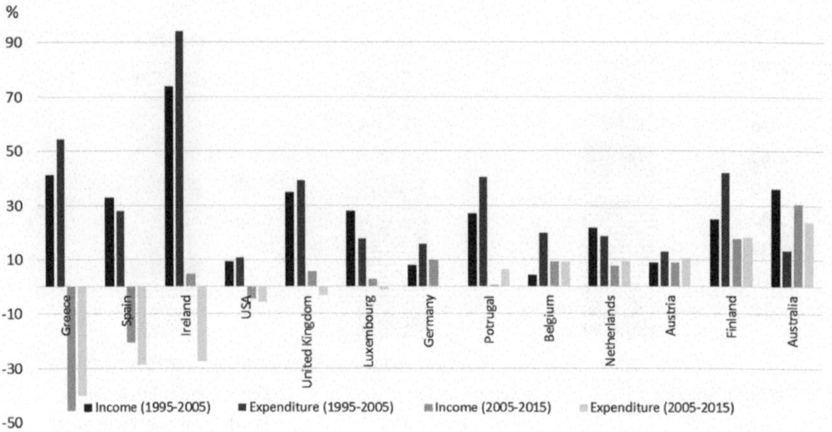

Fig. 8.7 Percentage change in income and expenditure of the middle-class during the period 1995–2015: Greece, EU countries, and USA (*Source* OECD [2019] and author's own creation)

Consequently, as the cost of living increases (costs increase faster than income) many middle-class Greek households have become financially vulnerable with some having excessive debt levels. Nearly 40% of middle-income households in 18 European OECD countries are economically vulnerable, with this figure reaching a maximum of 70% in the case of Greece (OECD, 2019). At the same time, 95% of Greek middle-income households say they are unable to meet expenses related to necessary goods (in OECD countries the average rate is 40%) and 50% say that they spend more than their income (in OECD countries the average rate is 20%).

With the sharp rise in unemployment, the Covid-19 crisis has again weakened the position of the middle class both in Greece and all over the world, since most of the unemployment came from its ranks.

A large and secure middle-class is the solid foundation on which an effective, democratic state is built and maintained, according to the ideas of the French Enlightenment. Its disappearance could play a major role in maintaining very low development levels, high corruption levels, and social tensions, mainly due to the weaker support for development institutions and the negative reign of pressure groups.

The reduction of the power held by the middle-class does not take place through a slow evolutionary process, but occurs abruptly, within a short period of time, mainly in times of economic recession. The factors that put pressure on it come on top of increased taxation, employment reduction, and the introduction of flexible forms of work.

At the same time, in developing countries, the middle-class is getting stronger. Three decades ago, these countries did not have a middle-class, as their societies were marked by high-income inequalities and the majority of people lived below the poverty line, while at the same time the upper classes enjoyed concentrated economic power. Economic growth in these countries after 1990s (with the most important examples being China, India, and Brazil) gave a significant boost to large masses of the poor populations, boosting their per capita income and strengthening the middle-class. In fact, this process continued in countries such as Kenya, Nigeria, Tanzania, etc.

8.4 The Cultural Evolution: The Search for Post-materialistic Society

Reflections from the cultural background are located in both economic and political institutions. Initially, the cultural background affects the quality and functioning of political institutions and this consists the first-round effects. Then, political institutions shape economic institutions, and this is the second-round affect, which in turn create structures and provide incentives for individuals to take action. The prevailing economic institutions ultimately determine the wealth distribution and the extent of economic growth. This amounts to the third round of effects.

The first and very critical level of influence, the interconnection between cultural background and political institutions, is located when different portfolios of cultural values and practices prevail in a society, developing different political institutions. Societies, for example, that place a big emphasis on the notion of collectivism naturally form participatory institutions at different levels of organization in society. If, on the other hand, the concept of results has a dominant position in a social-cultural organization, then society itself, especially in times of crisis, will more easily accept a solution of authoritarian rule.

Inglehart (1997) states that it is foolish to believe that culture is neutral. Every society legitimizes the establishment of a social order, in part because the ruling class seeks through culture to shape the values that will help perpetuate it (Inglehart, 1997). Alesina and Glaeser (2004) argue that in order to identify the forces that have shaped the current form of society, one must include in the analysis a review of historical events, while one must also identify what interests are being served by the dominant cultural background. At the same time, while referring to the Western world, what is needed, is to be focus on how Western political leaderships managed to direct the public into supporting their ideas and positions.

Politicized culture, as it is known, is an aspect of cultural background that has been deliberately created by political leaders to direct groups of people (de Jong, 2009). There are many examples where leaders, in their efforts to lead their country to economic growth, implemented development programs based on the values of other countries or religions (e.g., the case of Malaysia in the 1980s and 1990s). Subsequently, the cultural background may be used, as shown by examples, in order to promote the goals of political leadership.

A cultural background, dominated by features of collectiveness and denial to privacy, will tend to develop processes where the state will have a highly intervening nature. However, a cultural background dominated by collective-type characteristics and the promotion of privacy creates a very different environment, where the two types of political institutions coexist in a context that is more characteristic of Northern Europe. On the other hand, a cultural background dominated by uncertainty develops an environment that will tend to face high levels of uncertainty by creating a large number of complex laws and regulations—a characteristic of Europe's south. Adversely, a cultural background dominated by trust and certainty may organize the functioning of society by using simpler customary procedures. It is clear that a bulky and complex legal framework do not necessarily ensure its efficiency.

The cultural background, therefore, influences political institutions which then shape structures and motivations. However, apart from this indirect process, the individual elements of economic institutions are also directly affected by the cultural background. Economic institutions, finally, shape growth conditions and income and wealth distribution (third round effects). These variables, as well as the individual elements of economic institutions, are directly dependent on cultural values. The extent to which society's set goals are linked to the per capita product or income or happiness enjoyed by its members depends on the culture it offers. At the same time, income and wealth distribution may result from the functioning of economic institutions, but it is directly related with the values of society and, more specifically, with whether the desirable goal of the society is the greater or lesser redistribution. Finally, it should be noted that the growth rate and wealth and income distribution, in turn, affect political institutions.

To sum up, the cultural background influences the formation of political institutions and the policy pursued. However, at the same time, the political field influences the formation of the cultural background.

There is, of course, one more behavior very distinct in society. A distinction formed by the dipole of forces that influence political and social human behaviors: the problematic financial situation (economic have-not) and/or a riveting cultural behavior (cultural backlash). This distinction refers to the extent that citizens take into consideration and vote, based on their economic difficulties (real and/or comparative) or based on their reaction to evolutionary cultural change. It should be noted that these two hypotheses have been used to explain the rise of populist parties worldwide and consist of the most serious political platforms for the prevalence of populist political parties and the widespread repercussions of populism.

Cultural backlash behavior is reinforced by issues such as the impact of civil conflicts (Catalonia, Greece) while loss aversion behaviors are reinforced by a nostalgia for previous levels of prosperity and the safeguarding/confirmation that there will be positive economic developments (recovery), once combined with lower tax rates. Additionally, raising issues related to corruption stems from the cultural characteristics of lacking of trust and loss aversion.

Suspicions that cultural backlash behavior will prevail are strengthened by the fact that in advanced Western societies there is now a perception, in society and in politics, that the economic situation is not the primary issue concerning citizens (Fig. 8.8).

The onset of the European economic crisis has changed attitudes since 2010. In 2010, the biggest problem in European society reflected in key indicators was unemployment and the economic situation, but these indicators later declined.

What do these findings mean? The world—first United States, then Europe and then Greece—is leaning toward a post-materialistic era, where economic issues play a minor role. This will be completed after the improvement of economic conditions, due to the lessening of consequences from the 2010 crisis. That is why political conflicts expected to

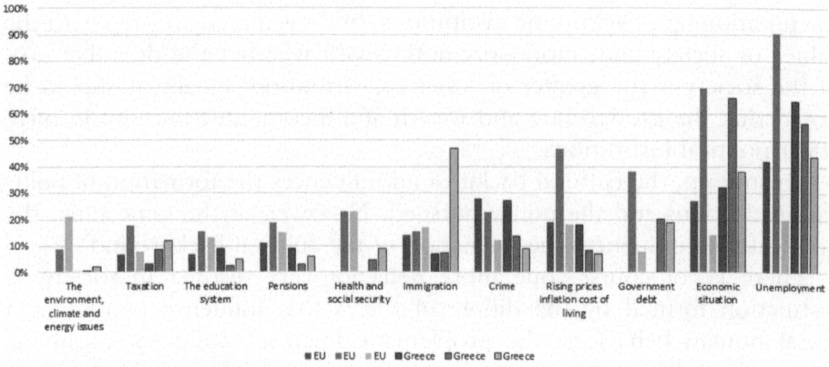

Fig. 8.8 Most important issues for EU countries and Greece (2003, 2012, and 2019) (*Source* European Commission [2019] and author's own creation)

be in this field are the loss of a position in the society, refugees, terrorism, etc. In Greece, however, economic issues continue to be a priority for citizens, though there is declining tendency.

Covid-19 crisis is too great to expect that it will not affect people's social behavior and priorities, job choices and lifestyle. Of course, at this point it is too early to estimate how this will be eventuated. But it is very logical that, in the short term, issues such as health, unemployment and economic conditions will be of much greater importance.

In conclusion, we believe that the post-materialistic period of reflection will give way to a period of economic uncertainty, where basic behavioral hypotheses—such as insecurity hypothesis, cultural backlash hypothesis (see next section) and economic have not hypothesis—will gain new power, each perhaps for different reasons.

8.5 The Evolution of Political Behavior

Growth does not mean that every aspect of life is continually improving. This would not be evolution. This would be a miracle (Pinker, 2018). The belief or perception, however, that things are much worse than they really are, is widespread, having a significant harmful effect on societies. If we assume that disaster can strike us at any time, we will in all likelihood invest mainly in security and not sufficiently in education or other aspects of prosperity. The political consequences are also damaging, as citizens turn to demagogic views. At the same time, the opposite perception—that things are always and inevitably changing for the better—can also be counterproductive. In this case, why make any changes? A more constructive approach is the acknowledging that things are getting better, but that this progress is neither automatic nor optimal (Fengler, 2019).

But, why are we, ultimately, so pessimistic? Firstly, our brains work in such a way, making us exceptionally responsive to risks. As a result, people pay much more attention to the negative, rather than the positive news. Secondly, negative news is "more significant," as it is more dramatic, sudden, and spectacular. Thirdly, this "partiality of negativity" is further reinforced in the era of social media. In the past, traditional institutions, authorities, and bodies (such as the church, political parties, trade unions, etc.) defused extreme positions. Today, these traditional methods of mediation have largely collapsed and the new ways of interacting put people directly in contact with each other.

The next day of the economic crisis of 2008 and Covid-19 as well as the consequent slowdown of the world economy seem to be creating additional problems for the political system (Fig. 8.9). This situation is

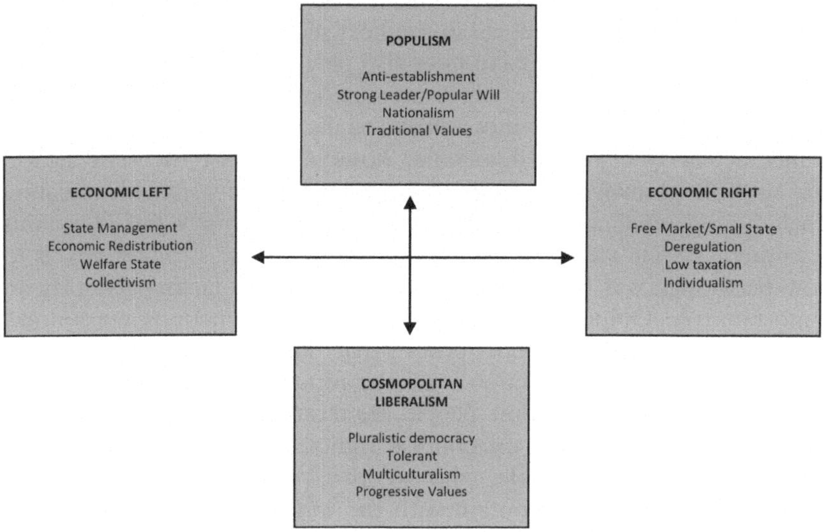

Fig. 8.9 Political competition in Western societies (*Source* Author's own creation)

getting worse due to the intensifying pressure put on the low and middle-classes, as a result of the crisis and income reclassification caused by globalization in United States and EU in recent years. In fact, the Covid-19 crisis somehow "confirmed" these views. In Europe, the average share of populist parties in national elections and European Parliament elections has been doubled since 1960s, rising from about 5.1 to 13.2%, at the expense of centrist parties (Doring & Manow, 2016).

Social anger at the political elite, economic dissatisfaction, and anxiety about rapid social changes have fueled political unrest in many parts of the world in recent years. Leaders, parties, and movements, both on the right and on the left of the political spectrum, have, in some cases, challenged the fundamental rules and institutions of liberal democracy. Discontent with democracy is linked to economic disappointment, the status of individual rights, as well as perceptions that political elites are corrupt and uninterested in citizens (Wike, Silver & Castillo, 2019).

Additionally, in Europe, results show that dissatisfaction with the way democracy is operating is linked to EU citizens' views on the EU, views on whether immigrants are adopting national customs, as well as also linked to attitudes toward populist parties. These emerging trends have had mixed (negative and positive) effects from the Covid-19 crisis, so we explore this issue in more detail in the next section.

Views on economic opportunities also play a role. Those who believe that their country is a place where most people are not able to improve their living standards are more likely to be dissatisfied with the way democracy works. Personal income, however, is not the only factor, and multi-level analysis suggests that, in general, demographic variables (including gender, age, and education) are not closely linked to this discontent. While views on economic conditions are strongly linked to how performance is being perceived, non-economic factors also play an important role. Opinions on how well a democracy functions in a country are related to whether citizens believe that their fundamental rights are being respected. Dissatisfaction with the function of democracy is also linked to perceptions on how people are treated by a country's judicial system. Apart from views on political rights, the stance toward politicians is important, as people, who say, that politicians in their country are corrupt, are more discontent with the way democracy is working in their country.

On a long-term basis, the rise of populism coincided mainly with the electoral decline of the center-left and social democracy, and, in some cases, with the rise of the center-right. The center-left's decline is linked to the reduction in the middle-class' social power, due to technological changes, the reduction of labor value share in products produced after the fall of the Berlin Wall, as well as the representation problems posed by the liberal democracy, mainly due to technology changes and the consequent spreading of social media, that influenced sources of information and the decision-making process.

The financial consequences of populism in the current phase of the global economy are quite controversial, given deflation, low interest rates, insufficient effective demand, weak economic growth, and the dominance of uncertainty in international trade. More specifically, although increased fiscal expansion seems to be gradually fighting off deflationary conditions—stimulating active demand and, consequently, fueling economic growth—the growing influence of populist governments on central banks remains relatively unspecified in economic terms. In general, however, it seems to be hurting the expectations of actors, given that uncertainty surrounding the central bank's decision-making process runs counter to their rational predictions, possibly cultivating a pessimistic environment of economic activity. In addition to these two dimensions of economic policy, populism seems to be also disrupting a third dimension, that of structural reform, as it poses an indisputably large threat to the background of political and economic institutions. It may also have a catalytic effect on free international trade, as when populism is accompanied by nationalism, then mercantilist conditions seem to be emerged, leading to practices of protectionism and limited economic extroversion.

Furthermore, the possibility of a global recession, which seems quite likely, given the current characteristics of the world economy, makes populist-driven policies more attractive, than if the global economy was at a different stage of the economic cycle. In particular, these policies are distinguished by monetary expansion, with the ultimate goal being the stimulation of inflation—low interest rates and increased money supply—and by fiscal expansion aimed at strengthening sluggish demand by boosting deficits and public debt and, in general, by nationalist-oriented policies strengthening the primary sector. Given the above, there is a general tendency of populism to invoke the national feeling, to use the expansive monetary and fiscal policy at the cost of future generations and for the benefit of the present generation, while maintaining a controversial stance toward globalization.

Two fundamental factors favor the implementation of these policies: (a) the plethora of political forces that promote populism, which are gradually strengthening at parliamentary level, and/or winning national elections, gaining thus executive power and taken over the governance in their countries; and (b) the fact that current economic conditions provide the right backdrop for popular economic policies, which further reinforces their position, undermining other approaches to economic policy. Further structural trends that contribute to the revival of populism are:

- the gradual weakening of representative democratic governments, given that the principal-agent problem between voters and national governments seems to be intensifying, or a supranational government is in charge, such as in EU;
- the limited barriers to the political organization process, due to the power of social media that serve populism, by spreading it; and
- the sense of intense economic disappointment that has gradually been established since the Great Repression of 2008 and is reflected in low price levels, sluggish demand, weak growth, and increased income inequalities in developed economies.

Moreover, it seems that a plethora of developed economies (some of which are included in the G7), a product of time, have been caught up in the political trap of populism, while a large majority of populist political forces are increasing their power beyond expectations.

More worrying is the fact that, under the rule of populist regimes and with the spread of the notion that the current monetary policy framework is outdated and inefficient, the very existence of central banks and monetary policy has been severely doubted. In particular, the accusation that central banks are institutionally biased toward keeping inflation low is being supported by the persistent behavior of low prices and deflation.

The pursuit of influence on central banks and expansionary fiscal policy are common key features among populist governments. Based on these two characteristics, interventionist economic policy, the degree to which nationalist views prevail within the countries as well as attitudes toward immigration are listed in Table 8.1, which ranks 13 countries based on the degree of populism distinguishing each government, with Greece in a relatively high position.

Table 8.1 Ranking populist governments by policy priority

	Fiscal expansion	*Seek influence over Central Bank*	*Interventionist economic policies*	*Nationalist issues*	*Overall score (max = 2)*
Hungary	2	2	3	3	10
Turkey	1	3	3	2	9
Italy	3	2	2	2	9
US	3	1	2	2	8
India	1	3	1	2	7
Poland	2	0	3	2	7
Greece	1	1	3	0	5
Romania	2	1	2	0	5
Serbia	1	2	0	1	4
Mexico	1	0	2	1	5
Czch rep.	1	0	−1	2	2
Austria	1	−1	−1	2	1
Brazil	0	−2	−3	1	−4

Source Oxford Economics (2019) and author's own calculations.

The cultural backlash theory of Inglehart and Norris, which sees populism as being the result of rigidity in traditional social categories driven by social change, does not allow us to understand why so many voters have gone from an economic definition to a cultural definition of their identity. Political identity is a group stereotype. As neither "camp" exactly meets our expectations, we choose the one we are closest to and which is also the furthest from the ideas we reject (Pisany-Ferry, 2020). This identification, once implemented, colors our perceptions of reality. There are, however, different ways of defining ourselves politically: on an economic basis, based on work challenges, income distribution, and social mobility and, alternatively, in a cultural basis, in relation to levels of openness to minorities or attitudes toward migration. The coexistence of these two dimensions (and possibly more) can lead voters to move from one stereotype to another. This analysis makes it possible to understand how moderate-sized social developments can cause political restructuring. At any moment, economic and cultural preferences coexist and only a small change is required to change human actions.

After all, economic nationalism, which is defined as being the preference of policies to promote national economic interests to the detriment of foreign interests, has increased since the mid-2000s. This is a broad increase and includes markets of advanced and emerging economies, right and left-wing parties, as well as existing and new entrants. While parties labeled as being populist by political scientists tend to have far more nationalist proposals for economic policy, the shift in preferences toward economic nationalism is broadly visible. Clearly, these shifts are not universal. In advanced economies, the biggest changes are being related to limitations on migration and trade. In emerging economies, the biggest shifts in preferences were in connection to industrial policies that favored specific sectors and industrial concentration. Trade protectionism and skepticism toward multilateral organizations and agreements have increased in both advanced and emerging economies. Right-wing parties tend to be more nationalistic than left-wing parties in terms of imposing restrictions on migration and foreign direct investments and in being involved in confrontations, but there is no significant difference in terms of trade protectionism (de Bolle & Zettelmeyer, 2019).

A recent attempt to measure populism by free-market think tank Timbro, that calculated the Timbro Authoritarian Populism Index (TAP), from 1980 to 2020, for 33 European economies[6] (countries are included as soon as they are categorized as a "free" society by Freedom House).

Figure 8.10 shows the percentage of votes for populist political parties, highlighting the difference between Greece and the rest of Europe. It is

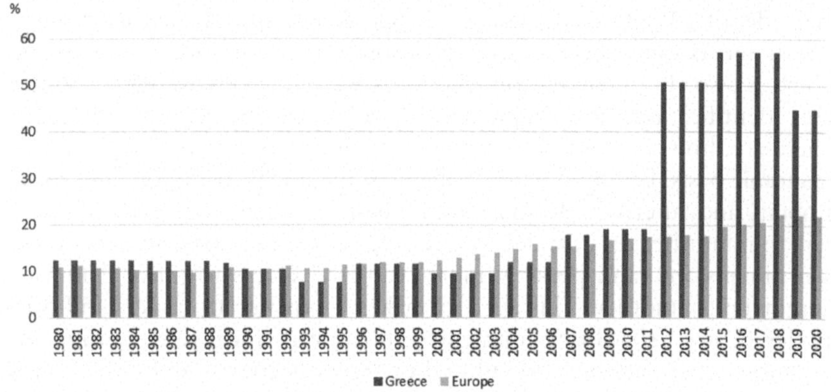

Fig. 8.10 Percentage of votes for populist political parties (*Source* Timbro [2020] and author's own creation)

clear from the chart that Greek voters support populist political parties, particularly from 2010 onwards.

It is worth pointing out that since 2018 it seems that the populist expressions of the electorate in Greece tend to be limited, especially after the July 2019 elections, when the SYRIZA government, which had ruled since 2015, was replaced by the New Democracy government.

In concluding, after the domination of capitalism at the end of the twentieth century, a typology of political systems emerged, which, as it turned out, has played a decisive role in economic decision-making.

It is therefore clear that this typology is influenced by global forces that shape the future and has its starting point in the disintegration of the archetypal political formations belonging to both the left and the right. We could argue that this distinction was strong up until the fall of the Berlin Wall (November 9, 1989) that led to the global domination of capitalism. Then, after a period of dominance of center-left and social democracy political forces in the West, the lack of division among political lines with the simultaneous dominance of capitalism began to favor the center-right in the West. At the same time, a different form of state and authoritarian capitalism emerged, mainly in China, the oil-producing countries and Russia.

The impact of the 2008 economic crisis, the decline in the special weight of the middle-class, the resumption of GDP growth but with increases to the difference between domestic and transnational income and changes to the cultural background (cultural backlash hypothesis), along with the rise of technology emphasizing on social networking and information platforms, is accompanied by the general decline of liberal democracy—separation of powers, political rights, etc.—and particularly the shrinking of the center-left and social democracy.

Their position has been taken by political expressions of a center-right nature, which are in line with the general prevalence of capitalism, which is the combined result of all the above.

In particular, in Greek society and beyond, after the turbulent period 2010–2018, there are factors of political change that are in line with international trends, with the main feature being the prevalence of center-right and populist views (Petrakis, Kafka, Kostis & Valsamis, in press) that refer to the cultural and political background of Greek society. To the extent, however, that political populism fails to deliver on its promises, the scales of political behavior will return to center-right and center-left approaches.

8.6 Political and Cultural Effects of Covid-19

The effect of the COVID-19 crisis on political systems, their functioning, and cultural attitudes are far-reaching and will evolve over coming years.

When the crisis was in its early stages, the question arose as to whether its outburst raised issues of the superiority of certain social systems in major crises over others (China vs Western liberal democracies). The impression is that the centralized character of the Chinese state allows for more effective responses to major crises, such as the pandemic. Obviously, this position has a high degree of truth to it, but it soon became clear that the experience of previous crises (SARS) that were similar played a major role in China. Moreover, many Western liberal democracies (Germany, Greece, etc.) have shown a satisfactory level of reaction.

Later, concerns turned to deeper political fields. That is, we wonder whether the liberalization of trust in market efficiency has been dealt a decisive blow since everyone's eyes turned to the "land of last resort" that was the state and central banks.

In this sense, the political forces in liberal democracies that gather around the political center should be strengthened, since traditionally this area has much better ties with the state's regulatory factors. In fact, it seemed that populist political regimes (Italy, the United States, Great Britain) showed characteristic inability in controlling the sanitary phenomena. However, non-populist regimes, such as France and Switzerland, were not able to efficiently react.

It is certain that a pandemic is within the logic of markets that are impossible to manage. Moreover, the theoretical infrastructure based on the market supremacy ideology allow for the existence of the regulatory factor of the state with the presence of Leviathan of Hobbes.

Therefore, the question "how much and where the state applies" is not freshly raised by Covid-19. It existed before and will continue to exist. However, what appears to be a new dimension is an emphasis on supporting public health systems. Let's not forget that deaths from Covid-19 are not caused by the virus itself but in combination with the absence of capable medical facilities.

So, what is it that separates the reactions of political systems to the crisis? It is too early to have similar answers and political science research will help us in the future.

However, it is now certain that the timely mobilization of experts and their good cooperation with politics is key to a satisfactory response.

The specialists include epidemiologists and doctors of all specialties, economists, communications specialists, etc. After all, it is a given that from the moment a crisis arrives, there is always an initial accumulation around the leadership and only later do political conflicts concerning the management of the crisis develop.

But the effects of the crisis are also fueling change in social behavior that is significant and noteworthy. We knew that this happens from all the great crises of the past (1929, 2008, etc.). Children that live in crisis conditions create more permanent attitudes and behaviors, especially during the shutdown of schools.

At the same time, it is certain that the increase in uncertainty levels has a profound effect on all aspects of economic activity with the main focus being on consumption, savings and investment.

But the question that remains is whether and to what extent confidence in the institutional framework in which the economy and society operate in is weakened, or strengthened.

If a society successfully copes with the crisis then it will emerge from it with a much better chance of implementing policies that have a social cost to the whole of society or to certain groups. This brings it closer to the possibility of implementing structural policies, a possibility that is usually seen among younger societies. If the need to tackle the pandemic also leads to very large horizontal programs improving overall demand, then again, conditions are in place for reform programs to be implemented, as it is well known that reform programs under austerity conditions have fewer chances of succeeding.

At the same time, societies that experience a successful management of such a crisis, with the help of the scientific community, seem to have increased confidence in the research and expertise of experts.

The opposite applies in societies that experience failed management of the crisis. They become much more vulnerable to the spread of random or malicious news, they create representations of injustice, racial and nationalist segregation, illusions of national isolation, etc.

In practice, this means that they support political forces that deny the cost of their proposals, particularly to future generations that are easy to ignore.

However, a crisis of this dimension may have a much deeper impact on society's attitudes that are summarized in the "insecurity hypothesis," Ingelhard's "backlash hypothesis" and the "economic not-have hypothesis."

We understand that in societies particularly hit by the 2008 crisis, had increased feelings of insecurity and led social behaviors to be driven by citizens' pressure to improve their finances, leaving behind their post-materialistic concerns.

The current crisis, with its deep-fast medium-lasting character, may not reach the point of being able to activate these behavioral issues on a more permanent basis, in contrast to the 2008 financial crisis which was deep, slow-moving and long-lasting.

But the health crisis of 2020 is likely to create wider economic turmoil by creating Covid-moment situations (according to the Minsky moment) accompanied by financial imbalances.

This is likely to activate classic behaviors of "insecurity hypothesis" and "note have hypothesis," if the economic crisis lasts much longer.

Additionally, if we live in a world where money has no cost (zero interest rates) then social demands are likely to lose their rationality and take on an anarchic formulation. However, this creates an environment that is much more difficult to control, making it more difficult to implement policies. At the same time, however, forces created by the behaviors keep people away from strongly anchored perceptions that are often likely to weigh on development.

However, cultural liquidity can have both positive and negative dimensions, so that some may act as a deterrent to economic development, while others promote it!

Notes

1. The risk of poverty after social transfers is defined as the percentage of people living in households whose total equivalent disposable income is less than 60% of the national median-equivalent disposable income.
2. With the year 2017 being the income reference period.
3. That is, not including social benefits and pensions.
4. The World Social Mobility Index compares 82 economies, and is designed to provide policy makers with a way to identify areas for improving social mobility and the promotion of respective opportunities in economies, regardless of their development.
5. The "middle-class" is defined as the share of the population whose disposable income ranges from 60 to 200% of the median disposable income. Those households with an income below this limit are considered to be "lower-class" and those who earn more than 200% of the median income belong to the "upper-class".

6. Non-democracies are excluded, since there is no real meaning in comparing countries where democratic rights systematically are being limited or violated to consolidated democracies. The same goes for semi-authoritarian countries with regular, but only somewhat, free elections: North Macedonia, Albania, Bosnia and Herzegovina and Moldova. Very few parties call themselves populist and even fewer brag about their authoritarian streak. It is also, given the scope of the material, not possible to scrutinize each and every party. Since the aim of the categorization is to reflect deeply held ideological views of the party, the index relies heavily on secondary sources. To the extent that it has been possible, it follows typical and existing categorizations. Thus, a number of different sources have been used: scholarly literature on the European party system focusing in general on populist parties, as well as particular parties; ideological labels from internet sources, and the expert study Chapel Hill Expert Survey (CHES), a quantitative summary of where parties belong on the left-to-right spectrum, combined with additional dimensions that serve to identify right-wing populists (but not left-wing populists) using, for instance, views on minority rights, immigration and multiculturalism. In general, it is not as difficult to categorize political parties as one might expect. Despite some disagreement on labels, there is a rather wide consensus among scholars on where parties fit in—when in doubt, Timbro has tried to judge the very core of a party's ideology using both secondary and primary sources (such as official party platforms). The division between "authoritarian" or "extreme" depends on the specific view on the concept of democracy. Only explicitly anti-democratic parties have been categorised as anti-democratic. Parties embracing nazism, fascism, communism, trotskyism and maoism have been regarded extreme. Parties classified as authoritarian are anti-liberal, but still democratic.

References

Acemoglu, D., Johnson, S., Robinson, S. J., & Yared, P. (2008). Income and Democracy. *American Economic Review, 98*(3), 808–842.

Alesina, A., & Glaeser, E. L. (2004). *Fighting Poverty in the US and Europe: A World of Difference*. Oxford: Oxford University Press.

Alesina, A., & Perotti, R. (1996). Income Distribution, Political Instability, and Investment. *European Economic Review, 40*(6), 1203–1228.

Allen, F., & Gale, D. (2000). Financial Contagion. *Journal of Political Economy, 108*(1), 1–33.

Argyris, C. (1998). Empowerment: The Emperor's New Clothes. *Harvard Business Review, 76*(3), 98–105.

Balestra, C., & Tonkin, R. (2018). *Inequalities in Household Wealth Across OECD Countries: Evidence from the OECD Wealth Distribution Database* (OECD Statistics Working Paper No. 2018/01).

Ball, L. M., Furceri, D., Leigh, D., & Loungani, P. (2013). *The Distributional Effects of Fiscal Consolidation* (IMF Working Paper No. 13/151).

Bordo, M. D., & Meissner, C. M. (2012). Does Inequality Lead to a Financial Crisis? *Journal of International Money and Finance, 31*(8), 2147–2161.

Bruegel. (2019). *Bruegel Datasets: Global and Regional Gini Coefficients*. Retrieved from https://www.bruegel.org/publications/datasets/global-and-regional-gini-coefficients/.

Cingano, F. (2014). *Trends in Income Inequality and Its Impact on Economic Growth* (OECD Social, Employment and Migration Working Paper No. 163).

Dao, M. C., Das, M., Koczan, Z., & Lian, W. (2017). *Why Is Labor Receiving a Smaller Share of Global Income? Theory and Empirical Evidence* (IMF Working Paper No. 17/169).

de Bolle, M., & Zettelmeyer, J. (2019). *Measuring the Rise of Economic Nationalism* (Peterson Institute for International Economics Working Paper 19–15).

de Jong, E. (2009). *Culture and Economics: On Values, Economics and International Business*. London and New York: Routledge.

de Long, J. B. (2016). A Brief History of (In)Equality. *Project Syndicate*. Retrieved from https://www.project-syndicate.org/commentary/history-income-distribution-by-j–bradford-delong-2016-07?barrier=accesspaylog.

Doring, H., & Philip, M. (2016). *Information on Parties, Elections, and Cabinets in Modern Democracies* (Development version). Parliaments and Governments Database (ParlGov). Retrieved from http://www.parlgov.org/.

European Commission. (2019). *Public Opinion Survey: Eurobarometer*. Retrieved from https://ec.europa.eu/commfrontoffice/publicopinion/index.cfm/Survey/index#p=1&yearFrom=1974&yearTo=2020.

Fengler, W. (2019). Why Are We so Pessimistic? *Brookings*. Retrieved from https://www.brookings.edu/blog/future-development/2019/06/13/why-are-we-so-pessimistic/.

Frankel, J. (2014). How to Address Inequality. *Vox CEPR Policy Portal*. Retrieved from https://voxeu.org/article/how-address-inequality.

Hellebrandt, T. (2014). *Income Inequality Developments in the Great Recession* (LIS Cross-national Data Center Working Paper No. 604).

Hellebrandt, T., & Mauro, P. (2015). *The Future of Worldwide Income Distribution* (Peterson Institute for International Economics Working Paper 15–7).

Hellenic Statistical Authority. (2019). *Risk of Poverty 2018—Survey on Income and Living Conditions* (Income reference period 2017) [Press release]. Retrieved from https://www.statistics.gr/documents/20181/13058a0c-e1cb-d2d7-dc94-f274dffb5d83.

Herwartz, H., & Theilen, B. (2014). On the Political and Fiscal Determinants of Income Redistribution under Federalism and Democracy: Evidence from Germany. *Public Choice, 159*(1), 121–139.

Inglehart, R. (1997). *Modernization and Post-modernization: Cultural, Economic, and Political Change in 43 Societies*. Princeton: Princeton University Press.

Jacobs, E., & Hipple, L. (2018). Are Today's Inequalities Limiting Tomorrow's Opportunities? A Review of the Social Sciences Literature on Economic Inequality and Intergenerational Mobility. *Washington Center for Equitable Growth*. Retrieved from https://equitablegrowth.org/research-paper/are-todays-inequalities-limiting-tomorrows-opportunities/.

Karabarbounis, L., & Neiman, B. (2014). The Global Decline of the Labor Share. *The Quarterly Journal of Economics, 129*(1), 61–103.

Kharas, H. (2010). *The Emerging Middle-Class in Developing Countries* (OECD Development Centre Working Paper No. 285).

Kieffer, C. H. (1984). Citizen Empowerment: A Developmental Perspective. *Prevention in Human Services, 3*(2–3), 9–36.

Narayan, A., van der Weide, R., Cojocaru, A., Lakner, C., Redaelli, S., Mahler, D. G., et al. (2018). *Fair Progress? Economic Mobility Across Generations Around the World*. Washington, DC: The World Bank.

Organisation for Economic Co-operation and Development. (2019). *Under Pressure: The squeezed Middle-Class*. Paris: OECD Publishing.

Oxford Economics. (2019). *Populist Risks Across Global Economies Swing both Ways*. Oxford Economics Research Briefings.

Perotti, R. (1996). Growth, Income Distribution, and Democracy: What the Data Say. *Journal of Economic Growth, 1*(2), 149–187.

Petrakis, P., Kafka, K., Kostis, P., & Valsamis, D. (in press). *Greek Culture after the Financial Crisis: An Economic Analysis*. New York: Palgrave Macmillan.

Pinker, S. (2018). *Enlightenment Now: The Case for Reason, Science, Humanism and Progress*. New York: Penguin.

Pisany-Ferry, J. (2020). Understanding Populism. *Bruegel*. Retrieved from www.bruegel.org/2020/01/understanding-populism/.

Rajan, R. G., & Zingales, L. (2001). The Influence of the Financial Revolution on the Nature of Firms. *American Economic Review, 91*(2), 206–211.

Statistical Office of the European Communities. (2019a). *Eurostat: Gini Coefficient of Equivalised Disposable Income—EU-SILC survey SILC* [ilc_di12].

Statistical Office of the European Communities. (2019b). *Eurostat: At-Risk-of-Poverty Rate by Poverty Threshold, Age and Sex—EU-SILC and ECHP surveys* [ilc_li02].

Statistical Office of the European Communities. (2019c). *Eurostat: General Government Expenditure by Function (COFOG)* [gov_10a_exp].

Teulings, C. (2014). Why Does Inequality Grow? Can We Do Something About It? *Vox CEPR Policy Portal*. Retrieved from https://voxeu.org/article/why-does-inequality-grow.

Timbro. (2020). *Timbro Authoritarian Populism Index: The Data*. Retrieved from https://populismindex.com/data/.

Wike, R., Silver, L., & Castillo, A. (2019). Many Across the Globe Are Dissatisfied with How Democracy Is Working. *Pew Research Center*. Retrieved from https://www.pewresearch.org/global/2019/04/29/many-across-the-globe-are-dissatisfied-with-how-democracy-is-working/.

World Economic Forum. (2020). *The Global Social Mobility Report 2020. Equality, Opportunity and a New Economic Imperative.* Geneva: WEF. Retrieved from http://www3.weforum.org/docs/Global_Social_Mobility_Report.pdf.

PART III

Sources of Growth and Development Policy in the Age of Global Low Growth and Low Inflation

CHAPTER 9

Sources of Growth and Development Policy in the Greek Economy

9.1 Introduction

What are the possible sources of growth in an economy and particularly in the Greek one? Where and how are conditions created to increase the potential of products produced?

This chapter identifies the sources of growth that can be applied to the Greek economy (Sect. 9.2). They are distinguished in fundamental or deep sources, which have a hereditary nature, where economic development policy cannot directly intervene effectively, and in appropriate/direct or proximate sources in development policy, as recognized in the relevant literature. In the third part (Sect. 9.3) the Solowian concept of growth is examined, with exogenous technological progress and in the fourth part (Sect. 9.4) the concept of balanced and unbalanced development is presented. Finally, in the fifth part (Sect. 9.5) the Lucas paradox is examined in the process of converging economies and international capital flows, in reference to the Greek economy.

9.2 The Sources of Growth and Development Policy

The process of economic growth is mainly influenced by fundamental, deep or primeval sources of growth such as institutions, cultural background, geographical location, as well as long-term human traits. It is

P. E. Petrakis, *The New Political Economy of Greece up to 2030*,
The Political Economy of Greek Growth up to 2030,
https://doi.org/10.1007/978-3-030-47075-3_9

also influenced by natural and human capital, by the growth rate of the population and the labor force, and by technology—elements subject to development policy. The latter factors play catalytic role in the creation of theoretical models, given that they can be quantified more easily and can, therefore, become a more direct and distinct tool in setting out development policy. Primary sources are more characterized by their quality background, structural complexity, and relative difficulty in being influenced.

In its attempt to explain how differences in technology, human and natural capital, and population or labor force differentiate per capita income between different countries, the theory of economic growth and development has raised the timeless question: since technology, natural and human capital, and workforce are key factors in diversifying nations wealth, then why don't some societies just improve their technology, invest in natural capital, accumulate human capital, and increase the size of labor force like other societies?

However, it is easy to see that if economic growth models were based solely on the differences between technology, human and natural capital, and labor, then their interpretive power would be limited, while there would also be very high residual made up of all the other unspecified growth factors. In concluding, in the background of factors where there are underlying short and medium-term development policy changes, fundamental sources play a primary and dominant role and are not sensitive subjects of development policy.

When an economy stands above the long-term equilibrium point (and therefore above its potential output) due to various short and medium-term disturbances that may have destabilized it, pressure is then exerted on prices, causing either inflation or deflation, depending on the nature of the disorder. That is why it is necessary to pursue macroeconomic stabilization policy. On the contrary, implementing expansionary fiscal (e.g., public infrastructure program) or monetary policy (e.g., a quantitative easing [QE] program) is an antidote when a negative productivity gap is identified, while implementing restrictive fiscal (e.g., reducing public spending and projects) or monetary policy (e.g., stopping QE program, increasing interest rates) is applied when there is a positive productivity gap, in order to achieve the gradual normalization of the business cycle and the immediate restoration of the economy to its potential output, i.e., its long-term equilibrium.

From one point of view, when an economy is above its potential output in the long-term, there is an ideal opportunity to activate a productive restructuring plan and make structural changes in order to shape a mechanism framework able to make it more resilient to business cycle fluctuations and downturns. Thus, conditions for the long-term dynamic economic development are set, so long-term problems can be solved with the gradual reconstruction and modernization of the cultural background, adding flexibility to its institutions.

However, measures to strengthen an economy's potential output take time to pay off. If an economy is expected to return to equilibrium with a zero productive gap in order to adopt a development program, then it will be too late, given that it is likely that inflationary pressure has begun, reversing long-term growth aspirations. Adversely, when development initiatives are taken on under conditions of a productivity gap, it is usually difficult for them to be socially accepted.

It is therefore understood that in the short and medium-term, economic policy of development and growth activates direct sources of growth, while in the long-run it could set more ambitious goals and activate fundamental sources. However, the most recent events, and particularly the Great Recession of 2008, have highlighted in all Western countries—especially in the Greek economy—the urgent need for simultaneous macroeconomic policy and structural changes, i.e. the adoption of a complex policy of parallel targets in the short and long-term. This is due to the fact that it was essential to close the productivity gap, while at the same time broaden the development potential of the economy.

In the Greek economy, there has been a coexistence of growth in the production gap and reduced potential output in recent years (see Chapter 12, Fig. 12.18).

9.3 Solowian Growth

The Solow model, also known as the Solow-Swan model (Solow, 1956; Swan, 1956), based on the neoclassical function of production, had a catalytic effect on the way economists had, up until then, approached economic growth and generally the macroeconomic field. The model reflects the net long-term impact that savings (= investments) have on quality of life (= per capita income).

The model concludes that an increased rate of savings boosts an economy's rate of capital accumulation and, consequently, an economy's growth rate as a means of dealing with decreasing returns to scale.[1]

There are five conditions under which an economy's law of declining returns could be activated:

- Provided that there is an excellent combination of production factors and one of them is kept constant, the increase in other factors promotes a total decrease in marginal returns.
- If one of the factors of production is in short supply, it is reasonable to assume that it is very difficult to proportionally monitor the change in the remainder production inputs.
- If there are no perfect substitutes for the production factors, then the exhaustion of some of them leads to their restricted use.
- Provided that a combination of productive inputs is excellent, in terms of production efficiency, any disturbance to fixed and variable inputs will lead to an output level inferior to the excellent one.
- If the size of all inputs constantly increases, even proportionally, then symptoms of ineffective management and, consequently, a progressive returns reduction, may occur.

When this law was introduced into the economic literature of the eighteenth century, the way it worked was fairly obvious. With the passing of time, however, the functioning of economies has become more composite, given that an economy is a complex system, resulting in the law of decreasing returns being gradually suspended due to a variety of factors that counterbalance each other. As we will see below, two concepts have played a catalytic role in tackling decreasing returns: human capital—that is, pure knowledge, technical knowledge, skills, and experiences—and innovation, that is, new ideas. However, before extensions to the theory of endogenous economic growth appeared, regarding human capital and innovation, there was an attempt made to answer the following question: how will emerging economies manage to bridge the gap with developed economies?

Both the neoclassical theory and inherent subterranean theories on the introduction of innovation provide an answer. According to the neoclassical theory (Solow, 1957), the main source of economic growth in the long-term is exogenous technological progress, while in the short-term it depends on capital reserves, population growth, and product distribution for alternative purposes (savings and consumption). Alternatively, subterranean theories focus on the role of productivity and innovation.

When it comes to applying development theory and growth in the Greek economy, the real question is, whether in the Greek case the traditional neoclassical interpretive models have a stronger application than the models of endogenous growth. Obviously, this depends on whether the production of technology is of exogenous origin and whether savings behavior is also of an exogenous nature. The question, of course, could be extended to other theoretical conceptions.

While the hypothesis of the exogenous determination of technology is plausible, in case of Greek economy (we will look at this in more detail below), "exogenous" savings are a less accepted concept. That is why we need to look at the real level of savings in the Greek economy. For the year 2018 (Foundation for Economic & Industrial Research [IOBE], 2019), 64.4% of household financial assets (HFA) in Greece were in cash and deposits, compared to just 31.1% in EU (average), with Greece in first position among 30 European countries based on the percentage of cash making up HFA (10.4%, compared to 2.4% in EU). Additionally, in comparison with other European countries, but even more so when compared with other Organisation for Economic Co-operation and Development (OECD) countries, capital markets are not sufficiently used in Greece. Specifically, in 2016, the value of capital market versus the value of private sector bank lending was at 18% in Greece, compared with an average of 72% in Eurozone, 135% in OECD, and 279% in United States (IOBE, 2019).

It should be noted that Greek households have traditionally invested a large part of their savings in real estate market and a very small part in capital market products. As a result, the amount of Greek investments in securities via institutional investors is one of the lowest in EU. In conclusion, domestic savings do not appear to always find their way into investments, as one in two units are either abroad or in cash (Table 9.1).

From the above it can be seen that the issue of savings in the Greek economy is highly dependent on external conditions, such as the external economic environment in relation to Greece's domestic political environment and political risk. There is possibly a more permanent stance among population that prefers to hold liquid cash, which could be the result of economic and political events.

Table 9.1 "Stagnant" cash in the Greek economy

	2018	*Notes*
Placed abroad (In deposits abroad)	57.5 bn (*33 bn*)	Were 88.4 bn in 2015
Deposits at Greek banks	132.7 bn	Were 237.8 bn in 2009
Cash	25.5 bn	
Total	215.7 bn	

Source Foundation for Economic & Industrial Research (2019) and author's own calculations

However, savings maintain a high degree of dependence on internal conditions and are linked to investments (Fig. 9.1) according to the specifications of the Solowian model. In the next volume of the series, a modeled exploration of the power of Solowian model is held, while here we are content with a descriptive presentation of certain trends in key variables.

Both the rate of investment and savings follow a long-term downward swing (Solowian forecast), which may initially indicate that the economy

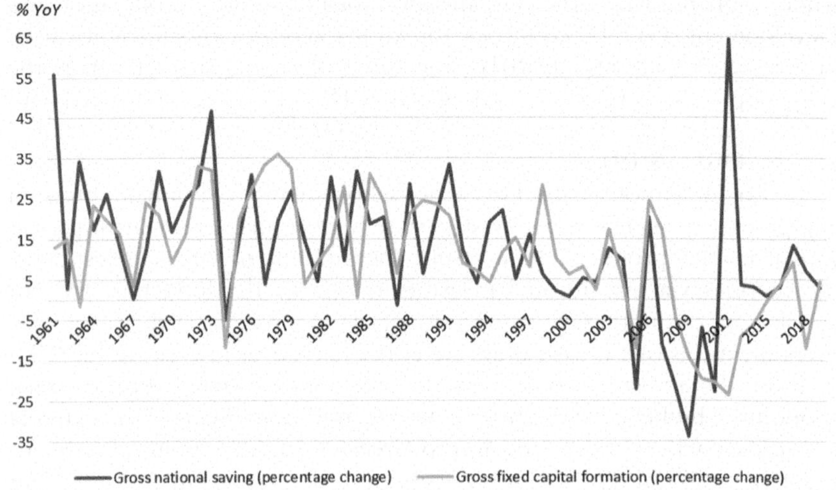

Fig. 9.1 Investments and savings in the Greek economy (*Source* European Commission [2019] and author's creation)

is seeing a more permanent trend of decreasing capital returns, which are clearly strengthened by sluggishness in investments. However, given that there have been periods of growth in the Greek economy, the downward trend looks to be linked to capital inflows from abroad, either in form of public and private debt, or, in form of direct investments (Fig. 9.2).

To calculate the contribution of natural and human capital—as integrated into total factor productivity (TFP)—and their share in gross domestic product (GDP) growth, we can use Growth Accounting, which is essentially based on Solowian growth logic. Growth Accounting provides an analysis of economic growth with input data (Barro, 1998a). This method can give us a good view of the decisive determinants of growth.

In particular, Growth Accounting leads to the calculation of the relevant share of formation costs of GDP, in regard to the main factors: labor, capital, and residual, which is the balance that is not interpreted by the contribution of production factors. These calculations are shown in Table 9.2 for a number of countries, but for reasons of simplicity are distinguished as capital and all other factors (human capital and residual) integrated into the TFP.

The contribution of TFP to the growth rate varies between countries. Countries such as Greece, Spain, Italy, but also Portugal during the period 1990–2017 experienced negative growth rates in TFP.[2] It can be seen that

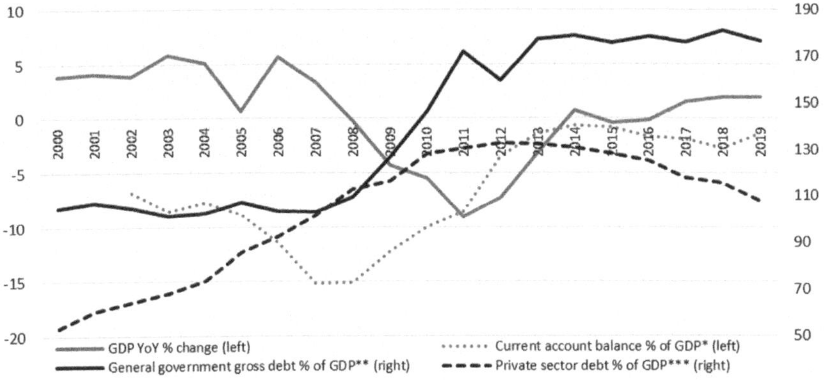

Fig. 9.2 Change in debt and current account balance as a percentage of GDP and growth GDP rate in the Greek economy (2000–2019) (*Source* Statistical Office of the European Communities [2020a, 2020b*, 2020c**, 2020d***] and author's creation)

Table 9.2 Growth accounting: 1990–2018

	Contribution of			*Share of*	
Country	*Growth rate*	*TFP growth*	*Capital deepening*	*TFP*	*Capital*
China	9.1	4.2	4.9	0.46	0.54
US	2.4	0.4	2.0	0.17	0.83
Spain	2.2	−0.3	2.5	0.1	0.9
UK	2	0.2	1.8	0.1	0.9
France	1.6	0.1	1.5	0.06	0.94
Germany	1.4	0.5	0.9	0.36	0.64
Portugal	1.5	−0.1	1.6	0.06	0.94
Japan	1.1	−0.7	1.8	0.28	0.72
Italy	0.8	−0.2	1.0	0.17	0.83
Greece	0.8	−0.2	1.0	0.17	0.83
Average	2.29	0.39	1.9	0.19	0.81

Source The Conference Board (2019) and author's own calculations

in all countries in Table 9.2, 17% of the average growth rate is due to TFP, while in Greece and Portugal the contribution of TFP is negative! That is, remaining growth factors, after the removal of the role of capital, have a negative effect on the formation of growth rate, a fact which suggests that labor rate and other factors (institutional environment, etc.) play a very small role.

9.4 Balanced and Unbalanced Growth in the Greek Economy

To achieve the results of balanced growth, as supported by Rosenstein-Rodan (1943), it is not necessary to mobilize the least productive sector and break up dualism. The mobilization of the production network through linkages toward the next and previous stages of Hirschman's productive activity (1958) could be enough. Thus, an automated growth process could be activated, which in reality would be the result of achieving economies of scale, market size, and linkages to subsequent and previous stages of productive activity, with ultimate goal of increasing productivity.

But Hirschman (1958) rejected the view of strategic investment coordination as an appropriate policy. Instead, he suggested the promotion of some key areas with strong links, even if they create disequilibrium. The resulting process would produce development. Hirschman gave rise to the theory of the operation of Leontief's (1953, 1966), input-output tables that describe an economy's linkages. But the issue raised by Hirschman was not so much about securing multi-component linkages in an economy. This is the descriptive result of his proposals. The crucial issue is the creation of new sources of growth that will result from the size of the market and the economics of growth. Essentially, market size creates external economies and economies of scale.

These external economies may relate to linkages with subsequent stages of productive activity or to linkages with previous stages of productive activity. The former case is linked to the ability of different productive sectors to improve the efficiency of industries using their products, while the latter can develop demand for intermediate products, so that suppliers enjoy the benefits of market size and economies of scale created. Essentially, these views make the issue of market structure the basic focal point.

In the past, the Greek economy has shown intense symptoms of unbalanced development, which has given some sectors of the economy the opportunity to develop and, in turn, push the economy to higher levels of economic activity. Perhaps the first such case could be "raisin development," where the agricultural economy (based on vineyards and raisin production) led Greek economy to a remarkable development, in the period around 1870–1890, the end of which started the raisin crisis (1893–1905).

In the second wave of growth (1960–2007) two areas of intense economic activity appeared, the tourism and construction sectors, with the main lever being construction activity. Their backward linkages were, and remain, strong. In the post-crisis period, the tourism sector seems to have been reactivated, in connection with issues such as aging, climate change, etc., which increase its product demand.

In these cases, the phenomenon of "unbalanced" growth occurs. If this is connected with the phenomenon of the observed reduction of complexity in the production process (see Chapter 10, Fig. 10.4), we are led to think that the emerging one-sided development rests on issues raised by Kuznets (1971) on the role of the complex portfolio of development dynamics.

Table 9.3 presents the sectors of the Greek economy of backwards and forwards linkages, according to the latest available tables of inputs and outputs of the Greek economy (2015).

In Table 9.3 it can be seen that there are sectors where the production improvement affects the previous (backward linkages) and the next stages (forward linkages) of the production process. The sectors with the highest backward linkages are: wood and of products of wood and cork, paper and paper products, food, beverages and tobacco products, constructions and construction works, furniture and other manufactured goods, basic pharmaceutical products and pharmaceutical preparations, electrical equipment, other non-metallic mineral products, basic metals, textiles, wearing apparel, leather and related products. Sectors with the highest forward linkages are: wood and of products of wood and cork, mining and quarrying, repair and installation services of machinery and equipment, printing and recording services, rubber and plastic products, paper and paper products, financial services, insurance and pension

Table 9.3 Top 10 industries: Backwards and forwards linkages in the Greek economy (2015)

Backward linkages		*Forward linkages*	
Wood and of products of wood and cork	1.3	Wood and of products of wood and cork	1.587
Paper and paper products	1.212	Mining and quarrying	1.571
Food, beverages, and tobacco products	1.17	Repair and installation services of machinery and equipment	1.464
Constructions and construction works	1.145	Printing and recording services	1.455
Furniture and other manufactured goods	1.12	Rubber and plastic products	1.367
Basic pharmaceutical products and pharmaceutical preparations	1.115	Paper and paper products	1.282
Electrical equipment	1.098	Financial services, insurance, and pension funding	1.278
Other non-metallic mineral products	1.09	Fabricated metal products, except machinery, and equipment	1.274
Basic metals	1.077	Other non-metallic mineral products	1.245
Textiles, wearing apparel, leather, and related products	1.055	Electricity, gas, steam, etc.	1.137

Source Papadakis & Markaki (2020), Statistical Office of the European Communities (2019) and author's creation

funding, fabricated metal products, except machinery and equipment, other non-metallic mineral products, electricity, gas, steam, etc.[3]

Market size was the central issue in Nurkse's (1953) theory. Large-scale investments in many sectors simultaneously promote complementarity of demand among sectors. Therefore, the market size expands, as does the willingness of the economy to invest. Market size is determined by a series of factors, among which productivity plays a dominant role. Low productivity reduces real purchasing power and so Keynesian perceptions on boosting active demand do not have a significant impact. On the contrary, improving productivity increases the flow of goods and services in an economy, increases consumption and, through a higher tendency to invest, the growth rate is increased.

Market Table 9.4 shows that, although the three economies (Greece, Ireland, Portugal) are similar in size, the differences between them in terms of output produced per working hour are particularly large. Ireland has almost three times higher output (per working hour) than the other two economies, while Portugal, which has a slightly larger market size than Greece, has similar productivity level with Greece.

It is, therefore, possible that four factors play a role in the Greek economy:

- The medium size of the economy.
- The high participation in GDP of the public sector and companies controlled by the public sector (see Chapter 2, Fig. 2.5).
- The significant concentration of oligopolies (see Chapter 2, Fig. 2.1), which we already know is linked to declining investment activity (Philippon, 2019). The existence of oligopolies leads to limited investment, as large companies in oligopolistic sectors do not need to make large-scale investment decisions, absorbing (with

Table 9.4 Market size and level of productivity (2018)

	Market Size (Gross National Income in bn euros)[*]	*Productivity level (GDP produced per labor hour)*
Greece	183.8	39.5
Ireland	254	104.1
Portugal	199.3	41.7

Source OECD (2020), Statistical Office of the European Communities (2020c)[*] and author's creation

financial transactions) smaller companies, and, thus, strengthening their position in the industry and favoring further concentration. Increases in concentration are associated with a weak increase in productivity and with drops in investment rates (Philippon, 2019).
- The existence of a political environment characterized by interrelated ties with significant presence of organized interests of the elite and/or interest groups (see Chapter 2). This creates power centers that contribute to the formation or strengthening of a pre-existing regulatory environment (see Chapter 2, Table 2.1), targeting rent seeking that hinders the development and growth processes.

The issue raised is whether if, and to what extent, are conditions created and maintained that weigh on economic development and growth when these four factors of the Greek economy interact.

9.5 The Paradox of Lucas and the Convergence of Prosperity in the Case of the Greek Economy

In contrast to what is proposed by neoclassical theory, Lucas (1990) observed that world resources do not flow from developed to less developed countries, but are mainly invested in the richest countries. This discrepancy between theory and practice is what is called the Lucas Paradox. The Lucas Paradox aims to explain why capital flows are not directed from developed countries to developing ones, despite the fact that developing countries have lower capital levels per worker. Possible explanations include the differences between countries in technology, production factors, government policies, and institutional structure. Other possible reasons are the international capital markets imperfections (with an emphasis on the failure of countries), asymmetric information, and high uncertainty, associated with high expected returns. The result of the Lucas Paradox is that emerging economies do not easily converge with developed ones.

More recently, Rodrik (2011) discusses whether developing economies can continue the rapid growth experienced in the final decades of the twentieth century, noting that growth in the developing world should depend, not so much on growth of developed economies themselves, but on the difference in productivity levels separating the two groups of countries. This is the so-called "convergence gap," which remains quite large.

The return on capital is a basic reference point in the Lucas Paradox (1990), explaining why capital is not directed from rich countries to low-income countries.

Figure 9.3 shows the course of capital returns[4] from 1950 to 2017, in specific countries. The two decades that followed World War II have been characterized by high-capital returns, in combination with the need to rebuild countries. However, we see reduction in return of capital over time, which is attributed to capital accumulation versus the production of fewer business profits.

In the case of the Greek economy in particular—compared to other countries (Fig. 9.3)—it appears that the rate of capital returns does not ensure an equivalent inflow of capital (foreign direct investment [FDI]) from abroad (Fig. 9.4), confirming the Lucas Paradox. Of course, a scientifically based conclusion demands a look through a more complex economic model. However, by examining the relationship between the real internal rate of return and foreign direct investment, net inflows (% of GDP), for the period 1970–2017, it can be seen that the correlation

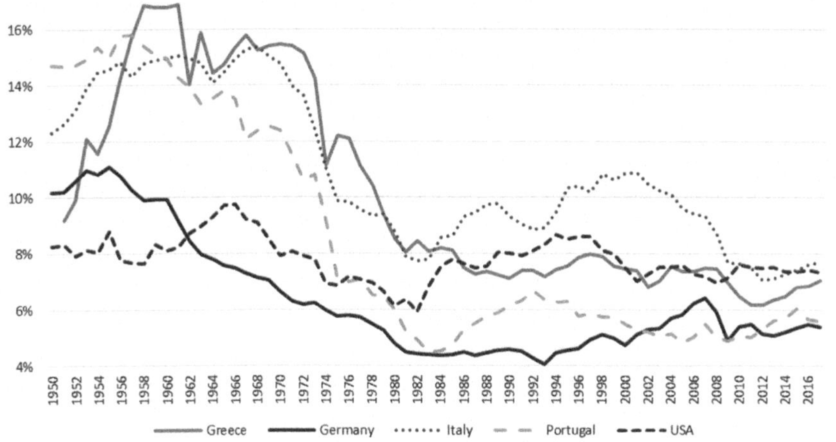

Fig. 9.3 Rate of return on capital (1950–2017) (*Note* Rate of return on capital is based on the variable "real internal rate of return on capital" [IRR]. *Source* Feenstra, Inklaa, and Timmer [2015] and author's creation)

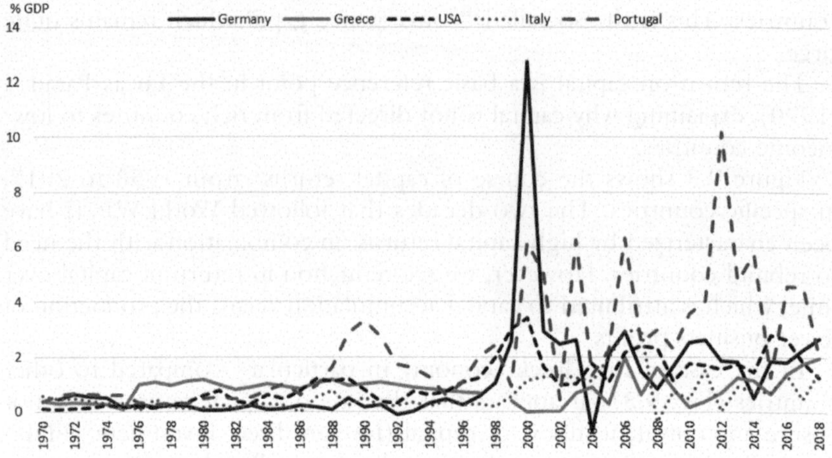

Fig. 9.4 Foreign Direct Investments (% GDP) (*Source* The World Bank [2019] and author's creation)

coefficient in the case of Greece is negative (−0.31). The same negative relationship is observed in the case of Portugal (−0.33), while for Germany, Italy, and the United States there is no correlation recorded.

These findings show that the issue of capital inflows is a very complex matter and it is logical to link it with issues such as the institutional framework of the economy, the political risk, and in general the systemic risk that may ultimately alter the picture of economic performance.

The Lucas Paradox has direct consequences on the converging process of economies. The idea of convergence is the assumption that poorer economies' per capita income tends to increase at a faster rate than that seen in richer ones (Barro & Sala-I-Martin, 1992). The lower real GDP per capita is, the higher the expected growth rate (Barro, 1998b).

When economies have similar preferences and technology, they converge at the same constant equilibrium, while if these conditions do not apply, they converge at different levels of constant equilibrium. The result of such a process is that all economies eventually converge in terms of per capita GDP. However, it is a fact that developing countries have the potential to grow faster than developed countries, as diminishing returns in the former are not so strong, while at the same time, they can replicate production methods and technologies used in developed countries to converge with them (Barro, 1998b).

Figure 9.5 gives the point where the convergence rate approaches

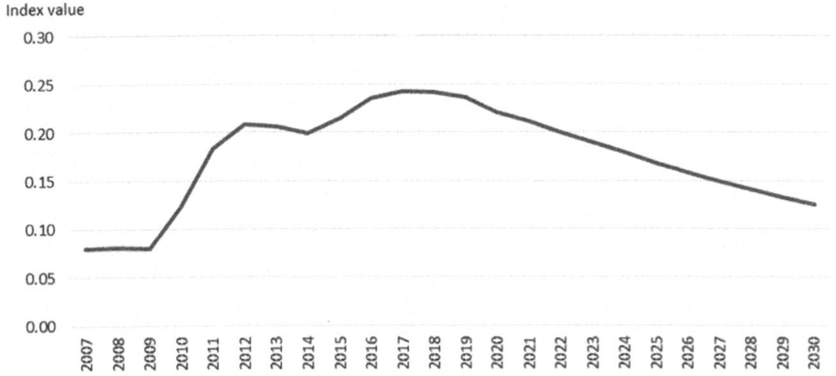

Fig. 9.5 The Greek-European Welfare Gap: The deviation of per capita GDP (*Note* When the index decreases, there is convergence among economies. The index is calculated as the quotient of the standard deviation for the average real GDP per capita [in PPP, USD] for Greece and the average of Cyprus, Spain, Italy, and Portugal. The methodology is based on Barro and Sala-I-Martin [1992]. *Source* Oxford Economics [2020] and author's own calculations)

between the economies of Cyprus, Spain, Italy, and Portugal.

When the index presented in Fig. 9.5 reaches a zero value, then Greece and the European economies have converged completely. Thus, it seems that while until 2009 the convergence rate with Cyprus, Spain, Italy, and Portugal was quite satisfactory, after 2010 a significant deviation was observed, showing a declining trend as of 2017.

Notes

1. The law of decreasing returns to scale stipulates that an increase in an inflow, with other inflows stable and given the technology, leads to an increase in output produced, however, from one point onwards, the output will continue to increase at a decreasing rate.

2. Growth Accounting's findings spark debate on some issues, especially on how capital is measured. Hsiech (2002) argues that there is an overestimation of capital accumulation in the data, as technological advances are often incorporated into new capital goods, making it difficult to separate the effect of capital accumulation from the effect of innovation (Aghion & Howitt, 2017).
3. Part of the results of the Papadakis and Markaki (2020) analysis which is expected to be included in the book, *Interconnections in the Greek Economy* (Manuscript in Preparation).
4. The real internal rate of return (IRR) on capital allows for monitoring of the developing return on capital over time and comparability between countries. To calculate the variable, the Jorgenson and Nishimizu (1978) method is applied, which is a more accurate measure of the return to capital than the often-used marginal product of capital (MPK) because it accounts for differences in the composition of the capital stock. The required rate of return on capital is chosen to exhaust the income left after subtracting labor income from GDP. This gives an IRR on capital which sets "pure profits" at zero and is therefore consistent with the issue of perfect competition.

References

Aghion, P., & Howitt, P. (2017). Some Thoughts on Capital Accumulation, Innovation, and Growth. *Annals of Economics and Statistics, 125*(126), 57–78. https://doi.org/10.15609/annaeconstat2009.125-126.0057.

Barro, R. J. (1998a). *Notes on Growth Accounting* (NBER Working Paper No. 6654).

Barro, R. J. (1998b). *Determinants of Economic growth: A Cross-Country Empirical Study*. Cambridge: MIT Press.

Barro, R. J., & Sala-I-Martin, X. (1992). Convergence. *The Journal of Political Economy, 100*(2), 223–251.

European Commission. (2019). *AMECO Database* [online]. Retrieved from https://ec.europa.eu/economy_finance/ameco/user/serie/SelectSerie.cfm.

Feenstra, R. C., Inklaa, R., & Timmer, M. P. (2015). The Next Generation of the Penn World Table. *American Economic Review, 105*(10), 3150–3182. Retrieved from www.ggdc.net/pwt.

Hsieh, C. T. (2002). What Explains the Industrial Revolution in East Asia? Evidence from the Factor Markets. *American Economic Review, 92*(3), 502–526.

Hirschman, A. O. (1958). *The Strategy of Economic Development*. New Haven: Yale University Press.

Jorgenson, D. W., & Nishimizu, M. (1978). U.S. and Japanese Economic Growth, 1952–1974: An International Comparison. *Economic Journal, 88*(352), 707–726.

Kuznets, S. (1971). *Economic Growth of Nations: Total Output and Production Structure*. Cambridge: Harvard University Press.

Foundation for Economic & Industrial Research. (2019). Boosting Savings and Growth through the Capital Markets. *IOBE Research Activities* (12 November 2019). Retrieved from http://iobe.gr/research_dtl_en.asp?RID=189.

Leontief, W. W. (1953). *Studies in the Structure of the American Economy: Theoretical and Empirical Explorations in Input-Output Analysis*. New York: Oxford University Press.

Leontief, W. W. (1966). *Input-Output Economics*. New York: Oxford University Press.

Lucas, R. Jr. (1990.) Why Doesn't Capital Flow from Rich to Poor Countries? *American Economic Review, 80*(2), 92–96.

Nurkse, R. (1953). *Problems of Capital Formation in Underdeveloped Countries*. Oxford: Oxford University Press.

Organisation for Economic Co-operation and Development. (2020). *Productivity Statistics: Level of GDP per Capita and Productivity*. Retrieved from https://stats.oecd.org/Index.aspx?DataSetCode=PDB_LV.

Oxford Economics. (2020). *Oxford Economics Global Macro Model*.

Papadakis, S, & Markaki, M. (2020). Input-Output Analysis for the Greek Economy. In P. E. Petrakis (Ed.), *Interconnections in the Greek Economy*. Manuscript in Preparation.

Petrakis, P. E. (in press). *Interconnections in the Greek Economy*. New York: Palgrave Macmillan.

Philippon, T. (2019). The Economics and Politics of Market Concentration. *NBER Reporter 2019*(4), 10–12. Retrieved from https://www.nber.org/reporter/2019number4/philippon.html.

Rodrik, D. (2011). *The Future of Economic Convergence* (NBER Working Paper No. 17400).

Rosenstein-Rodan, P. N. (1943). Problems of Industrialization of Eastern and South-Eastern Europe. *The Economic Journal, 53*(210/211), 202–211.

Solow, R. (1956). A Contribution to the Theory of Economic Growth. *The Quarterly Journal of Economics, 70*(1), 65–94.

Solow, R. (1957). Technical Change and the Aggregate Production Function. *The Review of Economics and Statistics, 39*(3), 312–320.

Statistical Office of the European Communities. (2019). *Eurostat: Supply, Use and Input-output Tables* [naio_10].

Statistical Office of the European Communities. (2020a). *Eurostat: GDP and Main Components (Output, Expenditure and Income)* [nama_10_gdp].

Statistical Office of the European Communities. (2020b). *Eurostat: Current Account Balance—Annual Data* [TIPSBP20].
Statistical Office of the European Communities. (2020c). *Eurostat: General Government Gross Debt* [SDG_17_40].
Statistical Office of the European Communities. (2020d). *Eurostat: Private Sector Debt, Consolidated—% of GDP* [TIPSPD20].
Statistical Office of the European Communities. (2020e). *Eurostat: Gross National Income (at Market Prices)* [teina080].
Swan, T. W. (1956). Economic Growth and Capital Accumulation. *The Economic Record, 32*(2), 334–361.
The Conference Board. (2019, April). *The Conference Board Total Economy Database.*
The World Bank. (2019). *The World Bank Data* [BX.KLT.DINV.WD.GD.ZS].

CHAPTER 10

The Endogenous Logic of Growth in the Greek Economy

10.1 Introduction

From around the early 1970s to the mid-1980s, growth and development research focused on short-term fluctuations that incorporated rational expectations into the real business cycle theory. This macroeconomic view centered on the mechanism of business cycles and the anti-cyclical effects of monetary and fiscal policy. As of the mid-1980s, a new researches' wave returned to the determining factors of long-term economic growth.

At the time, it was clear that exogenous economic growth models could no longer explain per capita growth in a state of equilibrium. The assumption that technology in economy is exogenously defined was a structural weakness of exogenous growth models, given that, in reality, new technology produced is the result of decisions from economic actors. Therefore, theory and growth models must justify how to respond to decisions and choice incentives in completing technology investments.

Essentially, technological change, and especially the need to interpret and rationalize it, was the litmus test for the further development of growth theory. All the attention of growth analysis was focused on offsetting declining capital returns.

Neoclassical economic theory had already begun in 1980 searching for a theoretical infrastructure that would make the rate of technological progress dependent on the model's other variables (thus founding the "New Growth Theory") at the core of which were models of endogenous

P. E. Petrakis, *The New Political Economy of Greece up to 2030*,
The Political Economy of Greek Growth up to 2030,
https://doi.org/10.1007/978-3-030-47075-3_10

growth. In short, it located an endogenous process that takes place during the production procedure. Thus, the models of endogenous growth were formulated.

The aim of the chapter is to investigate the conditions for the application of endogenous thinking in the Greek economy. Section 10.2 presents the theoretical background of endogenous models and then refers to the endogenous elements of the Greek economy.

Section 10.3 introduces the concept of productivity and its evolution in all three forms, namely, labor productivity, capital productivity, and total productivity (Total Factor Productivity [TFP]) in reference to the Greek economy. Finally, Sect. 10.4 presents Romer's (1986) concept of complexity of the economy and the "product-variety model."

10.2 Endogeneity and the Greek Economy

The first model of endogenous growth, the AK model (Arrow, 1962), is the simplest model of endogenous growth and is the first theoretical attempt to make neoclassical models of economic growth endogenous. This is how the chronic condition of declining returns to scale had been combated and technology was unlocked, which is the driving force behind increasing returns to scale.

According to this model, technology and technological progress are the product of the learning by doing process. More specifically, through this process, the marginal product of capital increases, which offsets the downward trend in marginal product (i.e., declining returns to scale), when technology is unchanged and provided exogenously. Moreover, when capital accumulation increases, the process of learning by doing broadens. Of course, it should be noted that this model is a precursor to modern models of endogenous growth that link human capital with the challenge of innovation and, consequently, to economic growth.

The process of learning by doing and generally technology assimilation requires workforce that is able to assimilate new technology. This depends on workforce's skills and abilities.

Research on adult skills, a product of the OECD's[1] Programme for the International Assessment of Adult Competencies (PIAAC), provides an overview of the competencies of Greek adults in three basic information processing skills: (a) their ability to understand and answer questions on written text (literacy); (b) their ability to use numerical and mathematical concepts (numeracy); and (c) their ability to solve problems in a technological environment (problem solving in technology-rich environments), i.e., the ability to access, interpret, and analyze information in a digital environment.

Figures 10.1 and 10.2 show Greeks' performance compared with the corresponding average of OECD countries, in regards to the above mentioned three basic information processing skills.

Regarding the performance of adults in their ability to answer questions on a written text (literacy proficiency), Greece achieved a score of 254 and ranks significantly below the average of OECD countries. Greece's score is below the OECD average of 266 points and is statistically comparable[2] to that of Slovenia (256 points), Israel (255 points), and Spain (252 points) (OECD, 2019a). In regards to the ability of adults to use numerical and mathematical concepts (numeracy proficiency), only 5.6% of Greek adults achieved a score of 4 or 5, versus the OECD average of 10.9%. The results show that 28.5% are at a very low level of use on mathematical and numerical concepts (level 1 and below 1), while at the same time, the corresponding OECD average is 23.5%. Finally, regarding the level of adults' ability to solve problems in technology-rich environments, Greek adults have one of the weakest performances in any level compared to the OECD countries (OECD, 2019a).

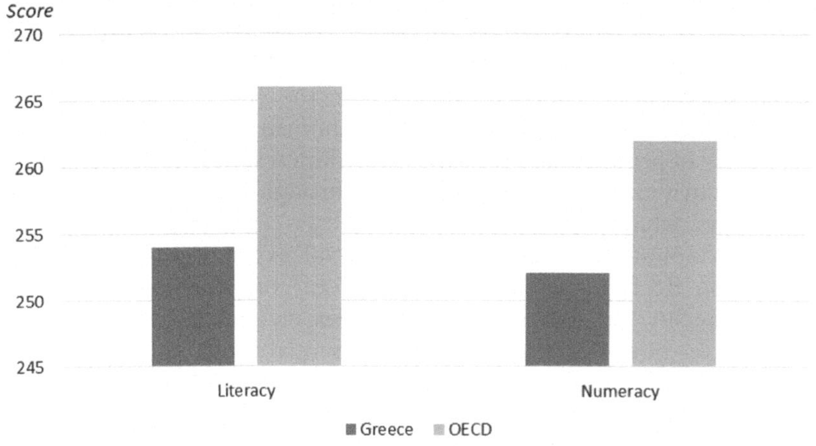

Fig. 10.1 Adult skills (literacy and numeracy) in Greece in relation to the average of OECD countries (2018) (*Note* Mean [literacy and numeracy] score in the Survey of Adult Skills [PIAAC]. *Source* OECD [2019a] and author's own creation)

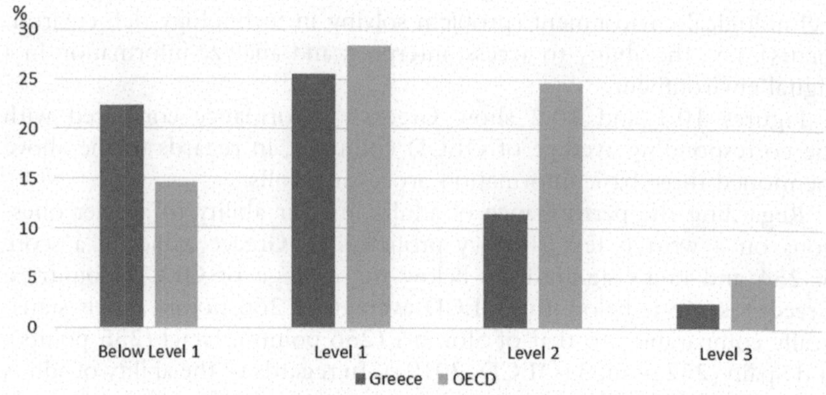

Fig. 10.2 Percentage of adults scoring at each proficiency level in problem solving in technology-rich environments (2018) (*Note* Not including the percentages of the categories, "No computer experience," "Opted out of computer-based assessment," "Failed information and communications technology [ICT] core," and "Missing." *Source* OECD [2019a] and author's own creation)

It is clear that the AK model is not complete, since its results, despite having a positive sign, are included in its basic assumption, i.e., the hypothesis of constant returns to capital. However, the more modern models as of 1980, try to justify the way in which constant returns to capital are reduced from five perspectives: the effect of knowledge on capital accumulation, the accumulation of human capital, the production of a variety of products and services, expanding research and development (R&D) activities, and improving quality through the process of creative destruction, which triggers innovation.

Gross domestic spending on R&D (total expenditure—current and capital—on R&D carried out by all resident companies, research institutes, university and government laboratories, etc., in a country) is a good indicator on how R&D forms a more essential input of an economy's output (Fig. 10.3).

It can be seen that Greek economy has been converging in recent years with the economies of Ireland and Portugal, in terms of expenditure on R&D, but despite this Greek production (Fig. 10.4) continues to mainly include low and medium-intensity technology activities, in comparison with other EU countries.

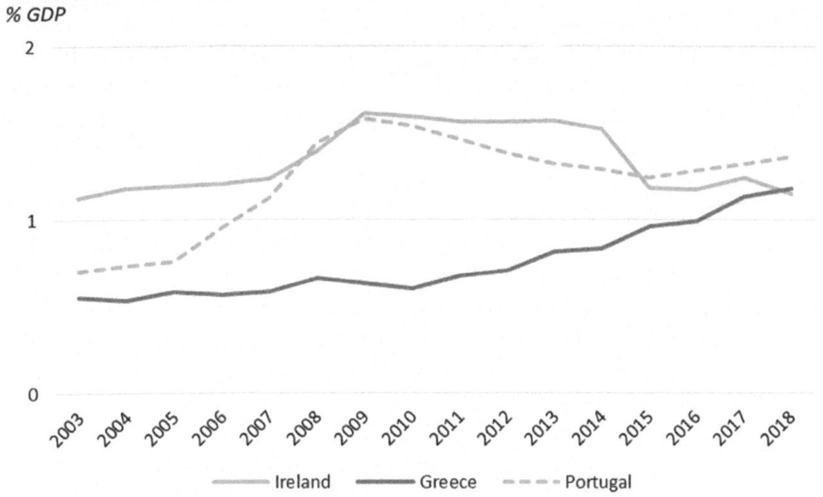

Fig. 10.3 Gross Domestic Spending on R&D (*Source* Statistical Office of the European Communities [2020a] and author's own creation)

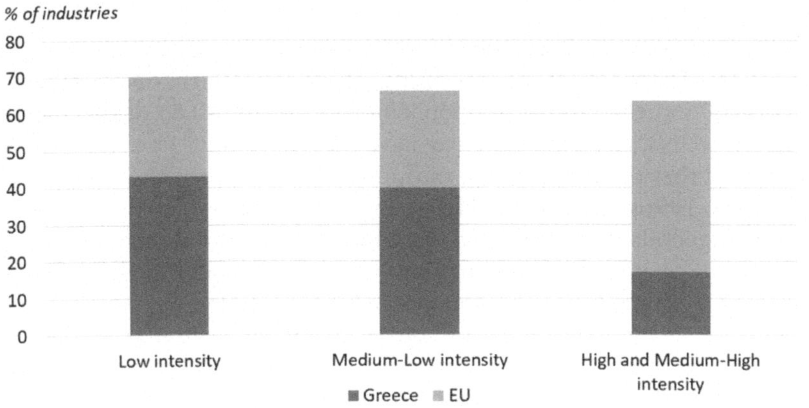

Fig. 10.4 Technological intensity of the manufacturing sector, in terms of gross value added (2013) (*Source* Dianeosis [2016] and author's own creation)

Lucas (1988) in his model focuses on the process of accumulating human capital through knowledge, as he points out that human capital stimulates the productivity of an economy and, consequently, increases output produced. That is, human capital contributes to the growth process through work within businesses, creating internal influence and, through its mass influence on all businesses, it also causes external influence. Lucas also believed that the process of accumulating human capital requires resources, which it takes from production. In general, however, many skills, abilities, experiences, and pure knowledge are acquired through work, that is, during production and not exclusively through education. The process of accumulating human capital is achieved through the compensatory dilemma of economic actors between work (learning by doing) or education.

Ultimately, the growth process faces declining returns to scale, as human capital, apart from endogenous growth, causes externalities (knowledge spillovers), as an employee's productivity may not only depend on his human capital, but also on the total human capital of the economy. Thus, the higher the rate of learning (that is, the rate of human capital accumulation), the higher the economy's growth rate of per capita output.

The human capital accumulation in the Greek economy in the last three decades has been steadily rising, if we look at the mean years of schooling and the human development index (Fig. 10.5) of the United Nations (UN). Despite this, we have already found (see Chapter 9, Sect. 9.3) that the contribution of human capital to growth is limited.

In the 1990s, Grossman, Helpman, Aghion, and Howitt developed the endogenous growth models based on innovation, as a result of the concept of creative disaster that Joseph Alois Schumpeter observed to be inherent in capitalism's economic system. These models attempt to incorporate the Schumpeter concept, internalizing innovation that emerges through the R&D process. They also focus on the type of innovation, the source of innovation, and the concept of creative destruction as a means of innovating. In particular, the innovations under consideration are divided into process innovations, that increase the productivity of production factors, product innovations, that introduce new products to the market, and organizational innovations, that stimulate the effectiveness of combined factors of production.

Additionally, innovation can be created by both public and private sectors, through investment in R&D, skills, and technical training. What

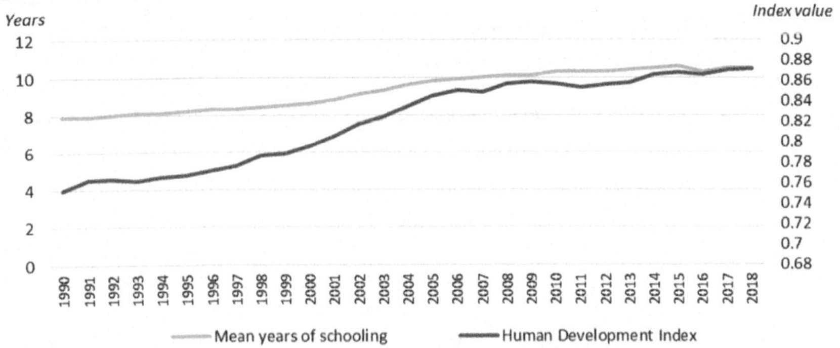

Fig. 10.5 Mean years of schooling and Human Development Index for the Greek economy (*Note* The variable mean years of schooling is calculated as the average number of years of education received by people aged 25 and older, converted from education attainment levels using official durations of each level. The Human Development Index [HDI] is a summary measure of average achievement in key dimensions of human development: a long and healthy life, being knowledgeable and have a decent standard of living. *Source* UN [2019] and author's own creation)

must also be added to the above is that, often, private sector in a free economy tends to invest less in R&D and workforce training due to financial market imperfections. In any case, the state is called upon to play the catalytic role of co-investor in human capital.

Table 10.1 presents the performance of Greece, Portugal, Ireland, and Germany for the period 2012–2014, regarding variables on their innovative performance, such as the number of scientific articles and citations and the amount of R&D investments. Table 10.1 shows an important

Table 10.1 Scientific and technical journal articles, citations, and gross domestic spending on R&D: 2010–2014 (average)

	Greece	*Portugal*	*Ireland*
Scientific and Technical Journal Articles**	11.885	13.960	7.273
Citations	276.901	311.307	231.090
Degree of Innovation (Gross Domestic Spending on R&D, % of GDP)*	0.78	1.33	1.55

Source SCImago (2019), Statistical Office of the European Communities (2020a)*, The World Bank (2019a)**, and author's own creation

point regarding the relationship between publications and the rate of innovation in the Greek economy. While the total number of Greek publications is higher than that of Ireland, and similar to that of Portugal, there is an oxymoron: the Greek economy's rate of innovation is proportionally lower, at just 0.78, compared to the other two countries. Essentially, the scientific work of universities and research centers does not turn into innovation, that is, the degree of integration is quite low.

The share of Greek publications in the total number of publications in EU countries for 2016 decreased slightly to 2.03, compared with 2.11 in 2014. However, there is an improvement in the share of citations to Greek publications among the total number of citations to EU publications, as from 2.29 in the five years 2010–2014, it reached 2.36 in the five years 2012–2016 (SCImago, 2019).

In the five years 2012–2016, Greek publications received an average of 7.13 citations per publication, exceeding respective averages in the EU (6.36) and the OECD (6.24). A corresponding increase, compared to the previous five years, is recorded in the relevant impact indicator of Greek publications, which is 1.12 in relation to the EU and 1.14 in relation to the OECD (SCImago, 2019).

These findings show that the domestic scientific system produces knowledge that cannot be integrated into domestic production (supply-side problem) or that the domestic production system does not seek the knowledge produced because it comes out with products that do not require similar knowledge (demand problem) or, finally, demand and supply knowledge systems do not communicate with each other due to institutional discrepancies (mismatches of demand and supply requirements) (Fig. 10.6).

One of the most serious reasons for the low integration of technology in the production of products is the small and medium size of Greek companies. Based on the number of employees, it appears that the vast majority of companies (97.4%) are considered to be of micro size (0–9 employees), when in the European Union the corresponding figure is 93% (European Commission 2019). At the same time, Greek small and medium-sized enterprises (SMEs) account for 63.5 percent of total value added, a rate higher than that of the EU average (56.4%) and an 87.9% share of employment, significantly higher than the corresponding percentage in the EU average (66.6%). Although there are conflicting views in literature on the contribution of small businesses to the development and growth of economies, the small size of businesses indicates a potentially negative endogenous development factor, with limited access

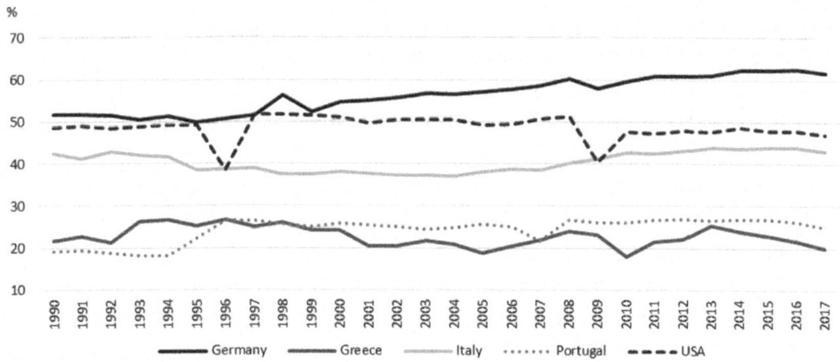

Fig. 10.6 Medium and high-tech industry (including construction): % manufacturing value added (*Note* The indicator is calculated as the share of the sum of the value added from medium and high-tech industry economic activities to manufacturing value added. *Source* The World Bank [2019b] and author's own creation)

to capital and having difficulties in putting it toward R&D investments and human capital.

10.3 Endogeneity and Productivity in the Greek Economy

The concept of productivity, the quantity of goods and services that can be produced per unit of inflow, entered the analysis of endogenous growth models based on knowledge and human capital accumulation. So, the more productivity increases, the more economic system's efficiency improves. In short, this is the "Holy Grail of economics" according to Krugman (1994), who states that: "Productivity is not everything, but in the long run it is almost everything" (p. 13). That is to say, the prosperity of societies is almost entirely based on the ability to increase production.

In reality, the evolution of productivity in all three forms—labor productivity, capital productivity, and TFP—reflects the extent to which the effects from the law of declining returns are addressed. Therefore, productivity helps to create a regulatory framework for the presentation of the productive capacity and efficiency of economies, while reflecting their competitiveness.

The evolution of productivity helps to determine the capacity of the production mechanism and, consequently, to determine the position of economies in the business cycle and to forecast economic growth, or to determine whether inflationary pressures will arise. In other words, an economy that is showing very little, or continually declining productivity, is likely to later exert inflationary pressures, due to the depletion of efficient input combinations.

While maintaining the level of analysis in Western societies, especially after the 2008 crisis, it can be seen that the decline in the effects of the crisis was accompanied by the phenomenon of declining productivity (total, labor, and capital) en masse, in almost the whole global economy, including developed and developing economies (Adler et al., 2017). Thus, an investigation began into whether the global financial crisis of 2008 may have intrinsically harmed the pace of technological progress, and consequently, endogenous logic.

Some views attempt to explain the aforementioned situation of growth and development process from the point of view of the financial system and the price mechanism. Initially, some turn their attention to the remnants of the financial crisis—such as credit constraints, and even to borrowers with high willingness to pay—saying that this limits the availability of short-term capital, increasing the internal capital cost of businesses (Aghion, Angeletos, Banerjee, & Manova, 2010). In short, natural capital and labor have higher short-term returns, when compared with investments in R&D, something which delays their realization.

Furthermore, it is noted that banks have become stricter in financing R&D investment due to the low value as collateral (Garcia-Macia, 2015), but it is also noted that low prevailing prices in recent years, which act as signposts of production and investment, discouraging or making it impossible to adopt new technology. This endogenously explains the low productivity observed (Anzoategui, Comin, Gertler & Martinez, 2019).

But how do we investigate the causes of slowdown in productivity arising from the 2008 crisis from the point of view of endogenous growth theory? On the one hand, there is the view that, if the crisis did hit productivity, then companies with the highest exposure to the financial crisis would have the incentive to invest less in intangible assets, such as new ideas, which, if only temporarily, adversely affects total factor productivity growth and leads to a permanently lower output level.

In addition, the arduous task of deleveraging business balance sheets has become problematic, as evidenced by the 2010 data, which confirms that policies rapidly contracting the financial sector, such as restrictions and upper limits on capital access of businesses, harm the ability to finance investments in research and development. As a result, the effects of the crisis are exacerbated, in contrast to consolidation policies and the restoring of functionality to commercial bank balance sheets. These desired consolidation policies re-enable commercial banks to provide an efficient role in lending companies with high returns on R&D investment plans, thus supporting productivity growth.

On the other hand, there is the view that the growth rate of developed economies is declining, not because people are running out of ideas, but because they are more expensive to come up with. In the economics of ideas, there is a principle that says the more we know, the more blurred and denser the exploration landscape becomes in the attempt to locate and discover something new.

Despite optimistic economists (see Chapter 7, Sect. 7.2.) hoping that the advent and dominance of the 4th Industrial Revolution (which already indicates the arrival of new technologies) will be marked by a series of endless underdeveloped "golden" opportunities (Brynjolfsson & McAffee, 2014), pessimists of growth highlight that the potential productivity growth has reached its limits, as the importance of the productivity growth process through innovation has now been extracted (Gordon, 2016).

In a recent empirical study conducted by Bloom, Jones, van Reenen, and Webb (2017), an attempt was made to prove that the theoretical discussion should not be about the amount of innovation on offer, but about the cost and, consequently, the willingness to pay for finding it. It is, thus, justified that, although the market of new ideas includes reserves of innovation, it is characterized by excessive demand, as new ideas are governed by scarcity. This fact raises sharply the cost of discovering, extracting, and acquiring ideas. The result is that, based on the law of demand, the level of research, development, and discovery of new ideas declines.

In short, low productivity is a consequence of the inability to offset declining research productivity, due to the slow increase in research effort. For this reason, if the primary goal of societies is to restore economic growth and development, they need to increase their spending on generating new ideas.

If the discussion of increased cost of generating new ideas and the inability of financial systems to manage technological requirements is transferred to the ecosystem of Greece, we realize that conditions to produce innovation—and even innovation that can be integrated into the production process—become more difficult.

Despite this, the Greek economy's TFP, has been continuously improving, mainly as the result of improvement in human capital resources in the past years and the implemantation of structural reforms in the previous decade, favoring the developmental logic of endogenous models (Fig. 10.7). It should be noted that these trends are common to countries comparable to Greece, such as Ireland and Portugal.

But while TFP increases, the same is not true for labor productivity, which puts downward pressure on TFP to the extent that it includes improvements to human capital quality. Figure 10.8 presents the evolution of labor productivity in the Greek economy, compared to Portugal and Ireland.

As seen for the Greek economy, after 1984, (the rate of change in) labor productivity decreases almost systematically, as in Portugal, while Ireland presents peculiar characteristics.

This permanent decrease in productivity connects us to one side of the Real Business Cycles Models' (Kydland & Prescott, 1977, 1982) interpretation, which refers to the prospect of perpetuating negative shocks in productivity and interprets, to a large extent, the relationship between

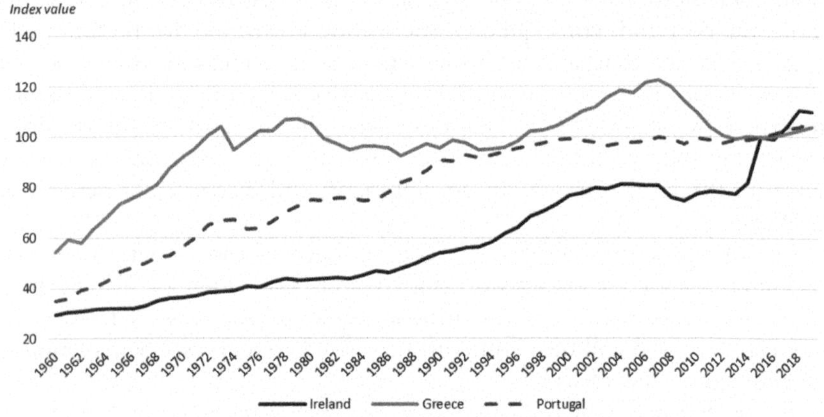

Fig. 10.7 Total Factor Productivity Index 1960–2019 (2010 = 100) (*Source* European Commission [2020] and author's own creation)

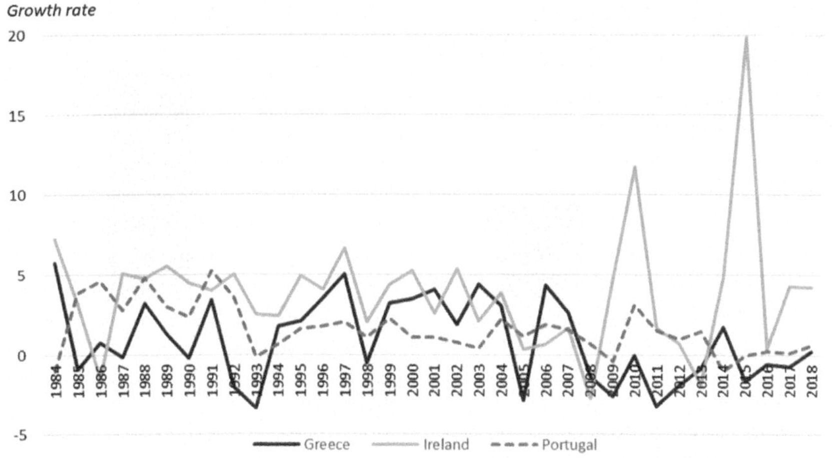

Fig. 10.8 Labor productivity growth (*Source* OECD [2019b] and author's own calculations)

declining productivity and recessions in the Greek economy, particularly after 2007.

The strict implementation of the adjustment program's internal devaluation was a major shock for the Greek economy after 2010, with the main focus being the implementation of structural reforms, which usually have a delayed response, in combination with the structural decline of the domestic production system in the global production network (technological changes) which are the result of broader productive changes.

A productivity shock is expected to reduce output produced, for a given level of labor and capital. Initially, this shock will have impact on the labor market. The demand for labor will shift to the left. This creates an oversupply of labor (unemployment) and, therefore, real wages fall and unemployment rises (see Fig. 10.9). This further reduces output produced. A drop in income in relation to wealth, which is not affected by these developments, creates a reduction in savings. Overall, then, after a real shock to productivity, real wages, employment, output, consumption, and investment decline.

When productivity shocks are permanent, this can lead to an even greater reduction in out-of-work incomes and increase in unemployment.

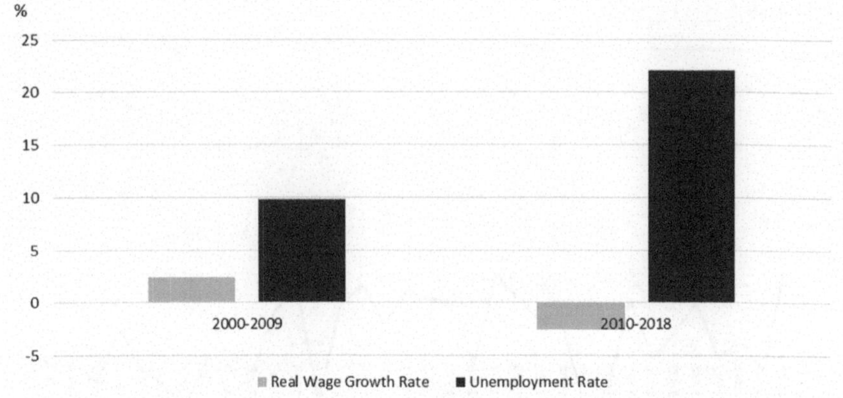

Fig. 10.9 Real wage growth rate and unemployment rate in the Greek economy (*Note* Periods average rates. Average annual wages 2018 constant prices *Source* OECD [2020], Statistical Office of the European Communities [2020b], and author's own creation)

This in turn will lead to a greater reduction in real wages. This permanent change in productivity may have no other effect on savings, but it will reduce investment level. Reducing investment will, in turn, lead to a reduction in capital stock, a development which deepens the recession.

The demand for labor is further reduced lowering more the level of real wages. But as capital stock decreases, the marginal product of capital increases. From one point onwards, the increase in the marginal product of capital increases investment and, therefore, interest rates and employment.

In the case of the Greek economy, the interpretive potential of the above framework is confirmed by the reduction of real wages (Fig. 10.9) and savings (see Chapter 9, Fig. 9.1), but it does not appear to be able to interpret the development of the recession and the low recovery that followed, as it appears that real business cycle (RBC) models' microfoundations were not activated, nor are they sufficient to bring the system into equilibrium.

This is probably due to the fact that even if behaviors are developed that are friendly to increasing labor supply, employment does not increase. The reason lies in the economy's limited potential to absorb the increase in labor supply (supply-side obstacles). Here, however, it should be recalled that this generation of models aims at interpreting business cycle fluctuations rather than interpreting structural recessions. Despite this, the concept of the permanent negative productivity shock is particularly interesting.

10.4 The Complexity of the Economy

More than three decades ago, Romer (1986) introduced the product-variety model, which supports that innovation increases productivity by creating new products, which are not necessarily improved. That is, it supports that through innovation the variety and range of products in the market is expanded, but their quality does not necessarily improve. Productivity across the economy rises, as capital stock can be spread across a variety of economic activities, each of which would be showing decreasing returns to scale. The model also introduces the impact of technology and knowledge on the process of proliferation of different products offered in the economy, while declining returns to scale are offset by either improving the variety of products, or by improving the quality of products that destroy and replace old ones over time.

Ultimately, the existence of innovative entrepreneurs investing in efficient research, the free movement of businesses in and out of the market, and the level of profits contribute essentially to improving innovation and increasing economy's products.

The Economic Complexity Index (ECI) can give us an approach to the concept of product variety used by Romer and is a key source in the process of economic growth. The ECI is a measure of the amount of capabilities and knowhow of a given country determined by the diversity, ubiquity, and complexity of the products it exports.

Figure 10.10 shows the complexity of the Greek economy. It is noteworthy that from 2008 onwards there is a sharp downward trend indicating an increase in the concentration of Greek productive capacity, which in turn reflects a shrinking portfolio of production activities in the Greek economy.

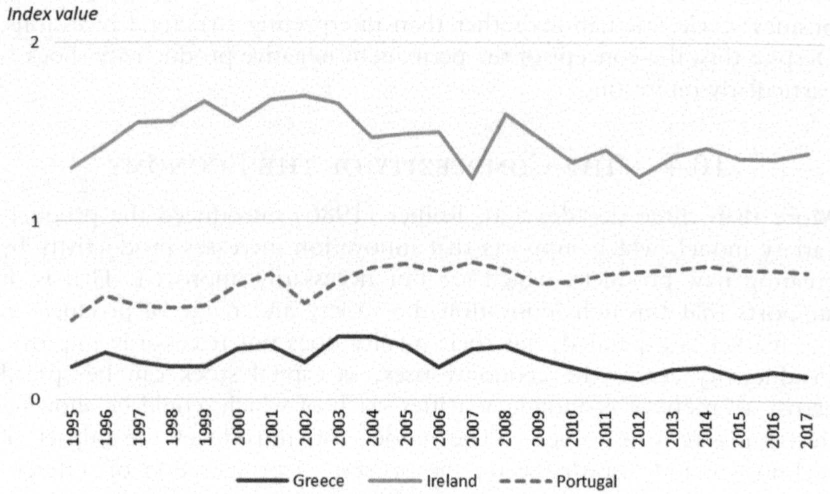

Fig. 10.10 The complexity of Greece, Ireland, and Portugal (*Source* The Growth Lab at Harvard University [2018] and author's own creation)

Notes

1. OECD stands for Organisation for Economic Co-operation and Development.
2. With countries whose average score does not significantly differ from the country they are compared to.

References

Adler, G., Duval, R. A., Furceri, D., Celik, S. K., Koloskova, K., & Poplawski-Ribeiro, M. (2017). *Gone with the Headwinds: Global Productivity* (IMF Staff Discussion Note No. 17/04).

Aghion, P., Angeletos, G. M., Banerjee, A., & Manova, K. (2010). Volatility and Growth: Credit Constraints and the Composition of Investment. *Journal of Monetary Economics, 57*(3), 246–265.

Anzoategui, D., Comin, D., Gertler, M., & Martinez, J. (2019). Endogenous Technology Adoption and R&D as Sources of Business Cycle Persistence. *American Economic Journal: Macroeconomics, 11*(3), 67–110.

Arrow, K. (1962). The Economic Implications of Learning by Doing. *Review of Economic Studies, 29*(3), 155–217.

Bloom, N., Jones, C., van Reenen, J., & Webb, M. (2017). Ideas Aren't Running Out, but They Are Getting More Expensive to Find. *VOX CEPR Policy Portal*. Retrieved from https://voxeu.org/article/ideas-aren-t-running-out-they-are-getting-more-expensive-find.

Brynjolfsson, E., & McAfee, A. (2014). *The Second Machine Age: Work, Progress, and Prosperity in a Time of Brilliant Technologies*. New York: W.W. Norton.

Dianeosis. (2016). *The Impact of Research on Greek Economic Growth (DiaNEOsis Study in Collaboration with the German Institute for Economic Research DIW Econ)*. Retrieved from https://www.dianeosis.org/en/2016/11/research-innovation-greece/.

European Commission. (2019). *SME Performance Review–SBA Fact Sheet: Greece*. Retrieved from https://ec.europa.eu/growth/smes/business-friendly-environment/performance-review_en#sba-fact-sheets.

European Commission. (2020). *AMECO Database* [online]. Retrieved from https://ec.europa.eu/economy_finance/ameco/user/serie/SelectSerie.cfm.

Garcia-Macia, D. (2015). *The Financing of Ideas and the Great Deviation*. Retrieved from https://ssrn.com/abstract=2758274.

Gordon, R. J. (2016). *The Rise and Fall of American Growth: The U.S. Standard of Living since the Civil War*. Princeton: Princeton University Press.

Krugman, P. R. (1994). *The Age of Diminished Expectations: U.S. Economic Policy in the 1990s* (3rd ed.). Cambridge: MIT Press.

Kydland, F., & Prescott, E. (1977). Rules Rather than Discretion: The Inconsistency of Optimal Plans. *Journal of Political Economy, 85*(3), 473–491.

Kydland, F., & Prescott, E. (1982). Time to Build and Aggregate Fluctuations. *Econometrica, 50*(6), 1345–1370.

Lucas, R., Jr. (1988). On the Mechanics of Economic Development. *Journal of Monetary Economics, 22*(1), 3–42.

Organisation for Economic Co-operation and Development. (2019). *Education GPS. Flagship Programmes: Survey of Adult Skills (PIAAC)*. Retrieved from http://gpseducation.oecd.org.

Organisation for Economic Co-operation and Development. (2019b). *Productivity Statistics: Labour productivity growth in the total economy*. Available at https://stats.oecd.org/Index.aspx?DataSetCode=PDB_LV.

Organisation for Economic Co-operation and Development. (2020). *OECD Stat: Labor-Earnings*. Retrieved from https://stats.oecd.org/Index.aspx?DataSetCode = AV_AN_WAGE#.

Romer, P. M. (1986). Increasing Returns and Long-Run Growth. *Journal of Political Economy, 94*(5), 1002–1037.

SCImago. (2019). *SJR—SCImago Journal & Country Rank [Portal]*. Retrieved from http://www.scimagojr.com.

Statistical Office of the European Communities. (2020a). *Eurostat: Gross Domestic Expenditure on Research and Development (R&D)* [TIPSST10].

Statistical Office of the European Communities. (2020b). *Eurostat: Unemployment by Sex and Age—Annual Data* [une_rt_a].

The Growth Lab at Harvard University. (2018). *Growth Projections and Complexity Rankings* (Harvard Dataverse). Retrieved from https://doi.org/10.7910/DVN/XTAQMC.

The World Bank. (2019a). *The World Bank Data* [ID: IP.JRN.ARTC.SC].

The World Bank. (2019b). *The World Bank Data* [NV.MNF.TECH.ZS.UN].

United Nations. (2019). *United Nations Development Programme-Human Development Reports: Data (1990--2018).* Retrieved from http://hdr.undp.org/en/data.

CHAPTER 11

Monetary, Fiscal, and Structural Policy in the European and Greek Economy

11.1 Introduction

The chapter deals with the possibilities of setting monetary, fiscal, and structural policy in an era of low growth and low inflation. Monetary, fiscal, and structural policies are three active policies that can be used when we aim to fill the output gap and increase the productive capacity of the economy. The evolution of the Covid-19 crisis has added to the picture of high unemployment and short-term output gap.

Of course, the Greek economy is a member of the Eurozone and, therefore, there is no potential to pursue independent economic monetary policy. However, observing the Eurozone contributes to reaching necessary conclusions for the Greek economy.

Fiscal policy has wider potential but also greater limitations versus monetary policy. For the next years after exiting fiscal adjustment programs, Greece will be subject to an enhanced surveillance procedure by EC, as the level of public debt owed to European institutions makes it necessary for the Greek economy to be supervised long-term. Adversely, structural policy has greater possibilities for implementation, especially after the 2010–2018 memorandum supervision period.

At the same time, the Covid-19 pandemic crisis is creating a new global economic policy environment, where the need to support economies is changing established monetary and fiscal policy rules.

P. E. Petrakis, *The New Political Economy of Greece up to 2030*,
The Political Economy of Greek Growth up to 2030,
https://doi.org/10.1007/978-3-030-47075-3_11

The chapter includes five sections. In Sect. 11.2, monetary policy is presented, and in Sect. 11.3, the implementation of fiscal policy conditions is created after the Great Recession of 2008. In Sect. 11.4, structural reforms are analyzed, beyond fiscal and monetary policy. In addition, in Sect. 11.5, reference is made to specific economic policies to address the issue of development and growth in combination with the needs to cover the output gap and, finally, in Sect. 11.6, the impact of Covid-19 on economic theory and politics is assessed.

11.2 Monetary Policy

During the Great Moderation (1980–2008), the world economy experienced particular stability. Low and stable inflation, steady growth in advanced economies, and the rapid development of emerging economies shaped the landscape.

The synchronization of central banks to exercise common monetary policy leads to inflationary stability and a reduction in fluctuations for output produced. During the Great Moderation (1980–2000), the models used to conduct monetary policy followed Taylor's rule and were based on the Central Bank's style model. According to Taylor's rule, interest rates adjust to changes in inflation and output. Low product and inflation volatility were largely due to the application of rules on interest rates (Taylor, 2013).

In a globalized environment, however, the size of cross-border impact from policy spillovers is geographically more extensive, in comparison with the 1980s. Additionally, the results of applied policies tend to spread more when periods of recession and intense uncertainty prevail, but ultimately with weak effects. As a result of the above two factors, the effectiveness of national policies is now less than it was in recent decades, while policies applied to wider transnational organizations play a major role. In addition, the implementation of demand reduction policies or the deleveraging of public and private sectors by members of a monetary union may serve as a stabilizing policy for the economy without, however, increasing its development prospects.

In general, the joint implementation of macroprudential policies is expected to lead to better results, compared to policies that are limited to each national economy (Constancio, 2014). Despite this, the benefits of policy coordination are not empirical highlighted (Obstfeld & Rogoff, 2002). Figure 11.1 shows the evolution and convergence of key interest rates from central banks as an effort to manage the 2008 crisis on the part of monetary policy.

Coordinating macroeconomic policies is not an easy task as a number of factors need to apply, given that at an institutional level every economy is distinguished by different organizational and administrative structures. At the same time, uncertainty and external shocks are conditions that cannot be predicted, making any attempt to carve out a common economic policy difficult.

The two guiding axes of monetary policy are quantitative easing (QE) and forward guidance. Although quantitative easing is popular, given its heavy and unusually extensive use on both sides of the Atlantic, it has undetermined, ambiguous, and highly controversial—according to the different schools of economic thought—effects on the real economy. On the one hand, there are economists (mostly central bankers who have

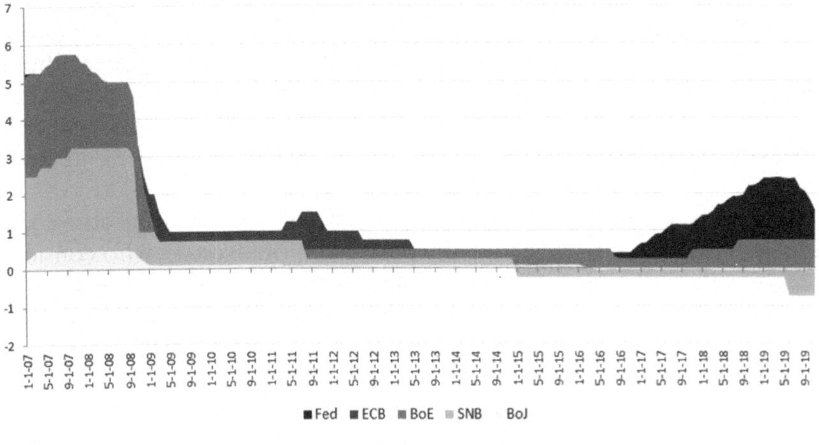

Fig. 11.1 Basic interest rates from central banks (*Source* Bank of England [2019], Bank of Japan [2019], Board of Governors of the Federal Reserve System [2019], European Central Bank [2019], Swiss National Bank [2019] and author's own creation)

adopted QE, such as former Federal Reserve chairman Ben Bernanke) who argue that this monetary policy tool has a strong impact on the real economy. On the other hand, those who embrace the concept of monetary neutrality disagree with QE, both in terms of its effective impact on the real economy and its contribution to the gradual push of long-term interest rates downwards.

Although the organic composition of QE theory remains controversial and, consequently, its method of operating in general, its effectiveness seems to be achieved through the restructuring of the asset portfolio, as the reduction in government bond yields motivates investors to shift their investments to private-corporate bonds and/or stocks, a step which reduces the cost of capital for businesses and also triggers more investments.

But beyond the controversial nature of QE, forward guidance also seems to have several flaws. More specifically, the hypothesis that financial actors, i.e., businesses, households, and investors, make decisions with their eye on the distant future, is rather defective, if not utopian. Furthermore, this view seems to be in conflict with credibility issues, as it assumes that financial actors have included in their expectations central bank promises that will be implemented over a long-term horizon. Perhaps, central banks should adopt more unconventional tools, without necessarily putting aside their two pillars of monetary policy (QE and forward guidance), in an effort to tackle the next recession and ease shocks resulting from it. Can such a thing be achieved? If yes, in what way?

One option seems to be sacrificing certain inflationary units above the highest limit, which may change the perception of investors who consider achieving the inflation target to be Heraklion achievement. The modern world is going through a large phase of demographic change. Given the impact of life-cycle patterns on a range of activities—such as savings, consumption, education, and retirement—it is particularly interesting to consider the impact demographic change will have on the effectiveness of policies being implemented. Characteristic of this is the work of Leahy and Thapar (2019), who examine whether the effects of monetary policy depend on the demographic structure of the population, which they divide into three different age groups. More specifically, in response to an increase in interest rates, the effects of private employment and personal income are weaker the greater the share of population under 35 years of age, are stronger the greater the share of population between 40 and 65 years of age, and are relatively unaffected by the share of population older than 65 years. They find that all age groups become more responsive to monetary policy shocks when the proportion of middle-aged increases.

Finally, there is the choice based on the fairly popular concept introduced by Milton Friedman in the 1970s, "helicopter money" (Friedman, 1969), which emphasizes that the central bank should distribute cash to economic actors with the hope that they will spend it, thus boosting inflation. This idea, although it reflects fiscal expansion, does not identify with it, since the financing of the helicopter is carried out by creating new money and not with public spending. It is easy to see that this policy is completely unconventional and, in addition to requiring reforms at a legal level, may create conditions that lead to hyperinflation. Consequently, "money from heaven" is the last solution, while it seems that it can only be applied in conditions of intense deflation—in a period of deep recession. The crisis of Covid-19 creates similar short-term situations.

If we accept and find that monetary policy—initially applied in the transnational (European) field—is effective in the short-term, and ultimately in the medium term, which over time organizes a much longer period of these policies being implemented, it is important to understand that in the end the Greek economy is also affected. The main channels are central bank interest rates and the banking system's liquidity. Through these channels, the liquidity and financing conditions of the Greek private sector are affected.

The role of the Phillips Curve is important, regarding the limits of monetary policy effectiveness. In the 1960s, low unemployment pushed prices higher. In the 1970s, high oil prices put upward pressure on general price levels. In the 1980s, the deep recession that was followed by rising unemployment, pushed prices down. On the contrary, in the last three decades, inflation (excluding food and energy) has remained low in Western countries, especially in the United States, despite the recovery after 2007–2009.

The reasons attributed to the low inflation are low expectations in combination with persistent slack in labor and product markets, monetary policy which is followed by forward guidance that cultivates quantitative expectations, labor market changes, the weakening power of worker groups, changes in the global economy, global production lines, technological changes (online pricing) that relate to low productivity, and finally shortcomings in measuring inflation.

11.3 Fiscal Policy

With limited opportunities for conventional monetary policy options, central banks and governments may need to turn to alternative approaches to combat slowing global development and tackle economic crises. Governments in advanced economies have limited room for interest rate cuts, but this tool has proved less effective in boosting development in recent years. This increases the need to look at alternatives such as negative interest rates, QE renewal, and fiscal incentives. While negative interest rates have helped reduce borrowing costs in some economies, the impact on banks has been ambiguous. Also, lowering interest rates to negative levels would have significant costs.

In the form that has been applied up until today, QE is likely to be less effective than in the past due to lower returns, narrower risk spreads, and higher asset valuations. Therefore, a deeper recession (like of Covid-19) requires more radical QE (buying corporate bonds, bank loans, and stocks), that present, however, significant disadvantages.

Some central bankers are beginning to recognize the limits of monetary action, and the next step is to consider fiscal action as a more effective alternative solution. Fiscal policy is likely to be particularly effective in a climate of weak development and low growth rates, with major multiplier effects. Advanced economies have more room for fiscal incentives than is often thought and could fund a large public investment program based on excessively cheap long-term debt.

The big central banks actively used both QE and forward looking guidance after the financial crisis. Although these tools have helped alleviate the economic impact of the crisis, their implementation has often been hampered by excessive concerns over their costs and risks and need for improved restructuring and implementation (Bernanke, 2020). Better execution of new policy tools, combined with increased public understanding and acceptance, should make them more effective in the future. New tools, in addition to QE and forward looking guidance, such as financing lending programs, negative policy interest rates and controlling the yield curve, could in some cases also be useful. For now, however, major changes seem premature. A logical intermediate approach may involve trying to increase the anti-cyclicality of fiscal policy, for example, through increased use of automated stabilizers. And of course, expectations should not be set below the inflation target, thus giving room to exercise policy. In a world where low nominal interest rates threaten the ability of central banks to respond to recession, excessively low inflation can be dangerous. According to the declared inflation targets, central banks will have to defend inflation that is particularly low.

The architecture of the euro area requires the completion of the banking union, the union of capital markets and a central fiscal capacity (Gaspar, 2020). The revision of the ECB's monetary policy strategy is timely. There is ample room for simplifying Eurozone fiscal rules using a single debt anchor that will be clear, taking into account the approved surplus target and a single operational (nominal) expenditure target. Additional complications associated with policy interest rate constraints, the temporal dimension of population dynamic, and green and digital transformations require:

- better information based on accrual accounting and
- strengthening of the role of an independent national tax advisory system centered on an independent European fiscal council.

The improvement of the fiscal framework concerns:

- the consolidation of preventive and corrective "weapons,"
- the shift to a single fiscal anchor and a single operational goal, and
- some central fiscal capability.

Fiscal space expresses the flexibility of a government to increase government spending and, more generally, to promote its financial well-being (Roy & Heuty, 2009). Heller (2005) defined fiscal space as, "the availability of budgetary room that allows a government to provide resources for a desired purpose without any prejudice to the sustainability of a government's financial position" (p. 3). However, there are different views on how to measure this as it is difficult to identify the current, future, and potential obligations of a country. An approach to measuring fiscal space can be taken by measuring the loss of access to capital markets or as a benefit of achieving long-term sustainability. Both approaches are interconnected. The difference between the current level of debt and the debt limit at which the government loses market access can be considered to be fiscal space. On the other hand, fiscal space can be defined in terms of long-term fiscal sustainability (Botev, Fournier, & Mourougane, 2016). Figure 11.2 summarizes the approaches to measuring fiscal space.

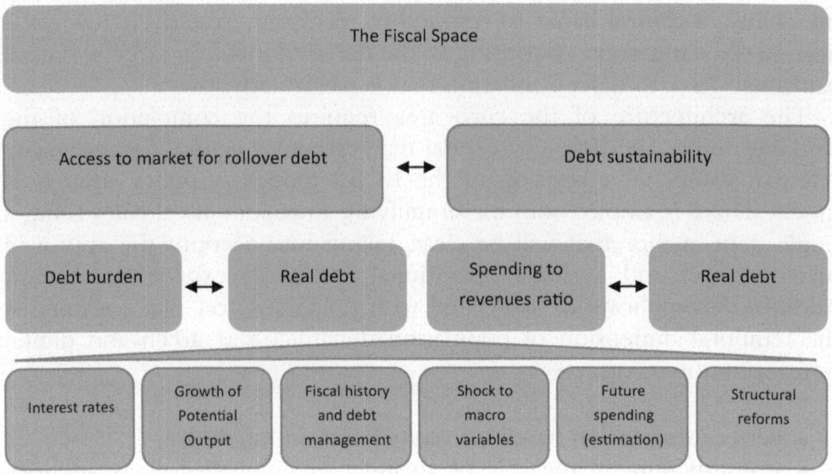

Fig. 11.2 Estimate of fiscal space (*Source* Botev et al. 2016 and author's own creation)

But why is fiscal space so important? The answer is simple. The higher it is, the less necessary it is for central banks to intervene through unconventional policies to tackle a recession. The ECB's QE program has helped, following the crisis, to reduce government bond yields and debt service costs. However, the use of fiscal space is the one that will be able to boost weak demand.

Table 11.1 shows the fiscal space of the Greek economy. It is typical that the structural surplus, i.e., the Greek primary surplus and the output gap, is the largest in the EU. But all these was valid before the outbreak of Covid-19.

A central concept of fiscal policy is that of the fiscal multiplier. It is the relationship that connects public spending to gross domestic product (GDP). The size of fiscal multipliers is particularly critical, as the effects on GDP caused by an exogenous change in the budget deficit depend on these multipliers. Therefore, the smaller the multipliers, the lower the cost of the fiscal suspension compared to the output. Thus, there is a large debate about whether the negative short-term effects of fiscal consolidation are more serious than expected because of the underestimation of fiscal multipliers, as was the case after the Great Recession of 2008 (Alesina & Ardagna, 2011).

Table 11.1 The fiscal space of the Greek economy: 2018–2020

(% of GDP)	*2018*	*2019*	*2020*
General government balance	1.0	1.5	−6.4
Primary balance	4.3	4.4	−3.4
Output gap	−6.5	−4.4	−13.0
Cyclically-adjusted balance	4.4	3.8	0.4
Structural balance	5.0	2.8	−0.1
Structural primary balance	8.3	5.7	2.9

Source European Commission (2020) and author's own calculations
Note Output gap (in % of potential GDP) and cyclically-adjusted balance as recalculated by European Commission. Structural (primary) balance corresponds to cyclically-adjusted (primary) balance excluding one-off and other temporary measures

The QUEST model used by the European Commission (Boussard, de Castro, & Salto, 2012) shows that under normal circumstances the short-term multiplier for the whole of the EU is about 0.4 and can increase to 0.5 through to 0.7, in times of crisis.

The debate concerning fiscal multipliers and their size should focus on the observation that different types of expenditures have different multipliers. What matters is not how multipliers were formed in the past, but the impact of a well-designed expansionary policy today (Stiglitz, 2014). If fiscal easing is the only option, it is important to understand through multipliers which countries can benefit from such a prospect. Countries with the highest multipliers are the ones that stand to benefit from fiscal expansion. Finally, it is of particular importance to note that the coordinated implementation of an expansionary fiscal policy becomes more effective, as many countries expand at the same time. Adversely, when only one economy is pursuing fiscal expansion, then its trading partners are very likely to benefit, and not the country itself.

Eurobank (2012) has estimated the size of the Greek economy's fiscal multipliers. This study uses two different methodologies to calculate Greece's multipliers, one of which is the classical estimation method introduced by Blanchard and Perotti (2002). Based on this methodology, Eurobank's (2012) estimates for public expenditure and revenue multipliers are not far from those previously used by the IMF in its estimates for the Greek economy, i.e., close to 0.5.

Despite this, estimates based on the second methodology, which is applied in times of great economic crisis, show that the multiplier of

Table 11.2 Investment, government consumption, and tax multipliers

	1 year	*2 year*	*3 year*	*4 year*	*5 year*	*6 year*
Investment multiplier	0.52	1.08	1.08	0.64	0.3	0.05
Government consumption multiplier	0.60	1.34	1.32	0.54	0.10	-0.22
Tax multiplier	−0.78	−1.08	−0.29	0.00	0.00	0.00

Source Oxford Economics (2017) and author's own calculations

public spending on wages, pensions, and benefits may be more than 2, while for other (current) expenditures it is calculated at being close to 1.4.

This does not seem to be fully confirmed by The Centre of Planning and Economic Research (KEPE) study (Papaioannou, 2015), which relates to the years 1995–2013 on the effects of government spending on GDP. The magnitude of the output response, after a government spending shock, is highly positive in Cyprus, Greece, and Italy, with the cumulative multiplier being higher than one. In Greece, a positive shock in government spending increases GDP, with the cumulative multiplier reaching 0.33 four quarters after the shock, 0.71 after eight quarters, and 1.08 after twelve quarters. Under conditions of economic crisis in Greece, the impact seems to be marginally lower, increasing by only 0.03 in three years.

Based on the Global Economic Model provided by Oxford Economics, the impact on GDP (multipliers) of three key macroeconomic data in the Greek economy is presented over a period of six year (Table 11.2).

The issue of the size of multipliers, combined with the available size of fiscal space, is very important, as it affects the ability to exercise fiscal policy aimed at the output gap. The issue is of particular value to the Greek economy, due to its size, which has been kept high for many years.

11.4 Structural Policy

The theoretical framework of supply-side economics argues that, when it is not possible and efficient in the long term to use macroeconomic tools to influence potential output (because there is no available fiscal space and state intervention should be kept to a minimum so as to not have a structural impact on the economy), the path opens for the introduction of structural changes.

Structural changes concern the process of intervening in product and labor markets, in a bid to create incentives that will improve the investment climate and productivity and reduce transaction costs. At the same time, they seek to reduce subsidies and social transfers as long as they claim that they create disincentives for labor and productivity.

Figure 11.3 shows the course of the Greek economy from 2003 until today, in terms of (net) external investment position, showing the consolidation of the country as a debtor country. As can be seen, the course of Portugal is similar. Adversely, Germany is the lender of the European economy, accumulating high surpluses from regional economies.

The implementation of a policy program on the supply-side requires the adoption of a series of structural reforms related to production and consumption, as well as consumer sensitivity to price changes.

Proponents of austerity and supply-side programs believe that troubled economies should be in a position to reliably increase their net external investment position or reduce the ratio of net external investment position to GDP. However, the size and speed of this should be large enough to accelerate the Adjustment Objective (AO). Obviously, achieving this goal depends (a) on the size of private and public debt levels (stocks)

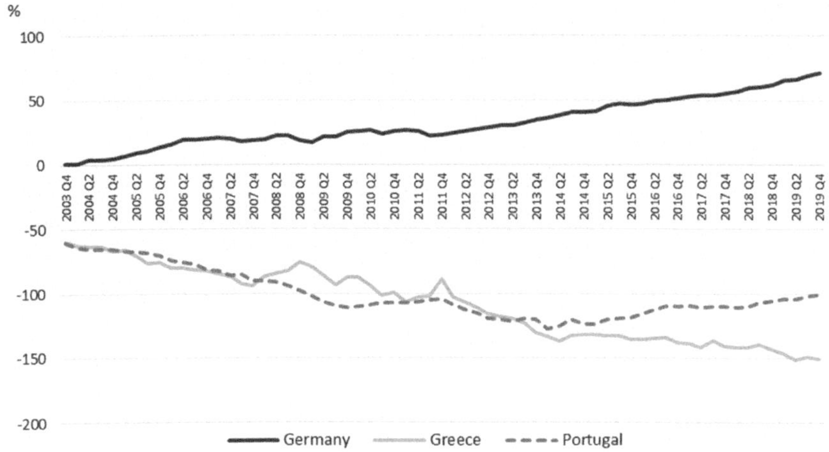

Fig. 11.3 Net External Investment Position (% of GDP) (*Note* Net positions at the end of period [partner: rest of the world]. *Source* Statistical Office of the European Communities [2020a] and author's own creation)

and (b) on the net result of the current account (flows) (Roubini, 2011), particularly the net result of current account of international marketable items. So, this last size (flow) should be positive, in order for it to also reduce the stock. If there were flexible exchange rates, an initial devaluation of the real exchange rate would be enough, with the other conditions being stable. If there is no possibility of a change in exchange rate, proponents of austerity policies argue that devaluation should be completed mainly by reducing labor costs (internal devaluation). This is true, if a fixed exchange rate system prevails.

Since 2010, the Greek economy has made very significant effort to address its fiscal problems and low competitiveness through structural reforms, as part of fiscal adjustment programs. During the period from 2011 to 2014, the Greek economy carried out the most structural reforms (Fig. 11.4), in comparison with other countries in the European Union (EU).

In fact, from Fig. 11.5 it is clear that the reform effort remains important and even above the OECD average for the years 2015–2018.

Ceteris paribus the intensity to which the economy should adapt, depends on five basic parameters: (a) the share of tradable goods and

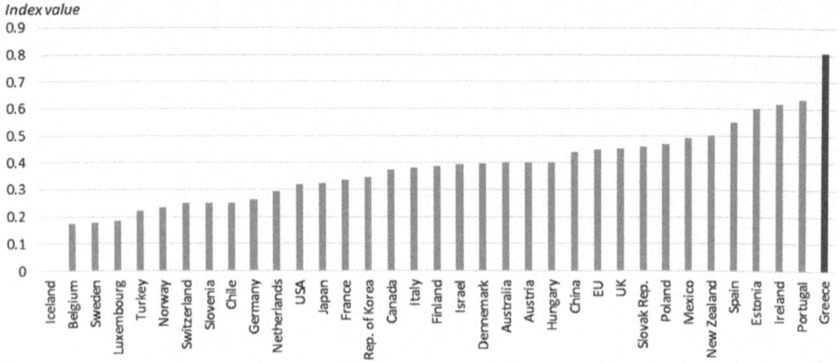

Fig. 11.4 Structural Reform Implementation Index (2011–2014 average) (*Note* The Structural Reform Implementation Index is based on a scoring system, according to which a country scores 1 if it has made significant effort to take into account the 2011 and 2013 Going for Growth recommendations and 0 if it has not. *Source* Organisation for Economic Co-operation and Development [OECD, 2015] and author's own calculations)

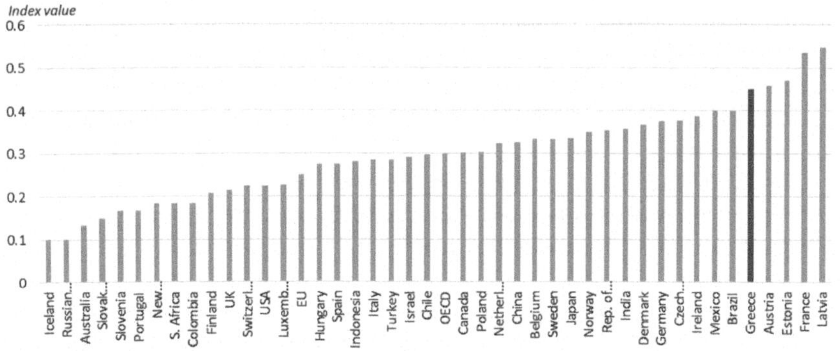

Fig. 11.5 Structural Reform Implementation Index (2015–2018 average) (*Note* The Structural Reform Implementation Index is based on a scoring system, according to which a country scores 1 if it has made significant effort to take into account the 2015 and 2017 Going for Growth recommendations and 0 if it has not. *Source* OECD [2019] and author's own calculations)

services in production; (b) the share of non-tradable goods in consumption; (c) the elasticity of demand for tradable versus non-tradable goods and services; (d) the share of domestic production in the total of tradable goods and services; and (e) the elasticity of demand for domestically produced tradable goods, versus tradable goods that produced abroad.

Essentially, in the transition period to achieving the adjustment target, the resulting restructuring produces signals (changes in relative prices, disasters in certain sectors and industries) that reactivate entrepreneurship, which will shape the new production model. It is clear that this interval period will not be less than 3–5 years. The reason is very simple: it takes 3–5 years for a new business endeavor to be organized and yield profits. If, during this period, we add one to two years of policy model implementation, we conclude that the period of returns cannot be shorter than two to six years. As long as, of course, there are no external slowing effects. These take various forms that are connected with the acceptance of reform programs by citizens, the rate of required change to institutions, and cultural backgrounds, etc.

Structural adjustment can be achieved through changes in demand between internationally tradable (commercial products) and internationally non-tradable goods (housing, land). For this reason, structural changes must be made, despite structural rigidities. However, these structural changes require and lead to resource shifts (between marketable and non-marketable sectors), while time is required for them to occur. Hence, this creates, at least temporarily, unemployment and underemployment of capital capacity.

Observed, therefore, in the economy will be (a) reduction of wages, (b) change in relative prices, (c) unemployment and underemployment of capital capacity. The above lead to decrease of demand in the economy and recession.

Thus, the reduction in demand is ultimately an expected result, which accompanies the process of restructuring economies in the short to medium term.

From the analysis of theories by supporters of austerity policies, it becomes clear that the general development of the relationship between NEIP and GDP, with the aim of reducing the size, requires a lot of time. This is mainly because the denominator, GDP, declines, making it very difficult for the NEIP/GDP ratio to stabilize on a downward trend.

Regarding the investigation of changes to real production capacity, it is interesting to consider whether the relative change in prices is effective in the productive restarting of the economy, through the improvement of competitiveness. This analysis is based on the Phillips curve. Shifting the Phillips curve down and to the right is the opposite to what is needed in order to reduce the cost of macroeconomic adjustment. Prices fall sharply, while the unemployment rate rises sharply, instead of falling. Ideally, the target is to move to the left—as has been the case since 2015 (Fig. 11.6)—in order to maintain reduced prices, but also to reduce unemployment.

The policy of internal devaluation in the Greek economy has gone through two phases: A "hard" one, which lasted from 2010 to 2015 and a "milder" one that lasts until today. This is reflected in the movement of the Phillips curve. The first period is characterized by movements along the length of the curve, as the decrease in inflation is associated with rising unemployment. However, in the second period, there is a shift in the curve, as for a given level of inflation the unemployment rate is lower, compared to the period 2010–2017. This is linked to the implementation of structural reforms that have eased the cost of internal devaluation in terms of employment.

In any case, the magnitude of the angle in the Greek Phillips Curve, which is not in line with the international findings (see Sect. 11.2) on

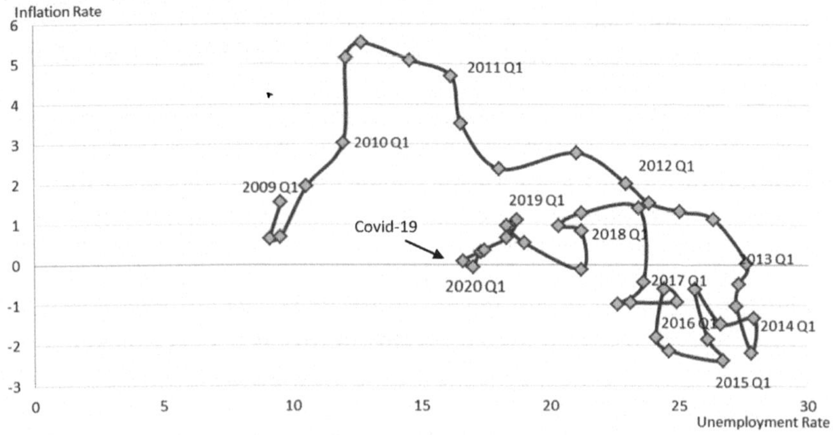

Fig. 11.6 The Phillips curve for the Greek economy (*Source* Oxford Economics [2020], Statistical Office of the European Communities [2020b], and author's own calculations and creation)

monetary policy, is impressive. According to this, a drop in unemployment rate will lead to a significant increase in inflation! It should be noted, however, that this angle has been created by increasing steps in unemployment (a phase of rising unemployment) and a structural change in the economy. When unemployment begins to fall sharply, the question that arises is whether we will have movements on the same curve so that inflation increases or will it be linked by continuous movements to the left?

11.5 Economic Policy in the Eurozone Until Covid-19

Buti (2020), in referring to lessons and policy implications for policymaking in EMU, found that the way the crisis unfolded altered the narrative in its nature. He believes that due to the crisis in the Greek economy, the problem of economies in other countries has been diagnosed insufficiently and/or incorrectly as fiscal. If, for example, the Irish economy had collapsed before the Greek one, crisis management in the Eurozone would probably have been different.

Financial crises, even in small countries, can have powerful implications and potential for spreading. As painfully seen in the case of Greece, a crisis in a relatively small corner of the Eurozone could have had devastating effects on a lack of monetary union, without the suitable use of emergency lending and risk-sharing mechanisms.

Financial markets do not put gradual pressure on borrowers. On the contrary, the stance of markets is rapidly changing toward the extremes, and due to this, risk is exacerbated, if there are no measures to share it. At the same time, any fiscal misconduct can be severely punished, in a warning to high-debt countries about the need to reliably maintain debt on a downward trajectory. The required risk sharing in the Eurozone can be achieved directly through the distribution of fiscal risks (through national budgets, a central fiscal capability in the euro area, or a common secure asset) or—in a less transparent way—through the ECB's balance sheet, a method which is selected.

As monetary policy faces increasing constraints, there is a growing consensus today that a more active role of fiscal policy is needed, especially from countries with fiscal space to do so. It is a fact that, unless countries pursue prudent fiscal policy, the independence of monetary policy can be challenged through pressure to monetize debt. Paradoxically, however, excessive fiscal prudence can also be a form of tax domination: when monetary policy is at the effective lower bound, fiscal inaction hinders Central Bank's attempts to meet its objectives (Buti, 2020).

With the world economy likely to be in recession in the future and the Eurozone still relying heavily on the ECB's monetary expansion (QE program), maybe should we turn to the opposite side of macroeconomic stabilization policy and fiscal policy in particular? At the same time, should member states, in this case, adopt structural policies to maintain supply opportunities? To what extent, however, a policy change is possible given the multifaceted structure of the Eurozone's economic policy framework?

In general, the reality of the Eurozone's economic policy framework seems to be a double-edged sword. On the one hand, interest rates tend to fluctuate negatively and the volume of bonds accumulated by the ECB on its balance sheet (2.6 trillion euros or 22% of Eurozone GDP) puts restrictions on further expansion of its asset purchase programs (APP). On the other hand, the fiscal finances of Eurozone countries, on average, are quite consolidated (government deficits below 1% of GDP in 2018, with a simultaneous reduction in gross debt since 2014) and ready to play a more vital role in the next recession, as it does happen during Covid-19, given the adequacy of the fiscal space. Furthermore, the low interest rates fluctuations in the near future are likely to be presented as the driving force behind the activation of fiscal policy, as they leave room for further debt accumulation, easing the Eurozone's fiscal constraints. Thus, forward looking has been materialized during the Covid-19 crisis of early 2020.

However, the Eurozone displays relative heterogeneity among its member states, while the absence of a common fiscal policy vehicle across the geographical area it covers leaves the Eurozone economy exposed to future adverse developments. The situation we have described often creates conflicts of interest between member states over the course of economic policy to be commonly adopted, as heterogeneity in the structure of member economies implies differentiated business cycle models and, therefore, separate and specialized (per country) economic policy needs.

In particular, the preparation should focus, in addition to the current monetary policy, on triggering fiscal policy, with the ECB playing a critical role in encouraging member states to pursue more intensive fiscal policy. Additionally, it should be noted here that fiscal policy is also characterized by internal time lag, as it takes time before it is drawn up as a plan and voted on by parliaments of member states.

Despite the fact that there should be an emphasis placed on fiscal policy, the way it is implemented is quite complex, due to the Eurozone's existing institutional constraints, while procedures for amending statute and governance contain political elements, making the transformation rather impossible in the short-term.

The establishment of an economic policy program with anti-cyclical fiscal aspects and structural policies is not new to the European Commission, given that in 2014 the Junker Package was set up, using public sector guarantees from the European Commission and the European Investment Bank. However, any plan attempts to rely financially on the European budget and the European Commission is rather doomed to suffer due to political nervousness felt across the Eurozone. Beyond this, because there is existential no risk of the Eurozone system collapsing economically, the euro area appears to be threatened by the possibility of being trapped for a prolonged period in a climate of persistent deflation, insufficient domestic demand, and weak, if not zero, growth as part of uncertainty in international trade that affects foreign demand.

Factors that are mainly short-term and have a demand side character at a pan-European level include four key elements: the global slowdown, the complexity of the US economy, technological changes in Asia, and the slowing of emerging economies. For the Greek economy we should add the output gap, which it inherited from the ten-year great recession following the 2008 global financial crisis.

Factors that are mainly short-term, but also have mainly supply-side characteristics, at a pan-European level, include the steady increase in trade restrictions and regulations changes in industrial products, such as cars. For the Greek economy, the regulatory backwardness in many sectors of the economy could be noted.

Factors that are mainly long term, but are classified as having demand side characteristics, include mainly two elements: the structural change in China, with the main feature being the slowdown in growth rate, and the rearrangement of supply changes around the world.

Finally, among the factors that have a medium term and mainly supply-side nature is ageing and the slowing down of Total Factor Productivity (TFP) that is associated with the slowdown in technology being introduced into the production process. On the Greek side, there are certain forces that maintain a high level of systemic risk, and finally, the long-term effect of certain behaviors (e.g., liquidity preference, high risk avoidance).

Of course, in the European and Greek economies, as in any economy, no issue is necessarily a demand side or supply-side problem alone. At the same time, none of the problems are easily classified as short-term or long term. Also, each of the issues concerning the European economy, to a different degree, are also of concern to the Greek economy, while the opposite is not the case.

Therefore, the policies that need to be developed to address the problems must belong to broad and complex portfolios of economic policies with a horizontal and long-term nature of implementation, such as demand and supply characteristics.

11.6 The Reflection of Covid-19 on Economic Theory and Policy

Covid-19 is creating new data on the macroeconomic figures of states. Fiscal deficits in developed economies are expected to reach historic highs in 2020, due to the need to support supply (business and employment) and demand (consumption) in economies, but also due to the expected reduction in tax revenues, which in fact can be extended to a period beyond 2020, in a scenario in which economic actors have formed negative expectations. At the same time, the country's debt-to-GDP ratio (and debt levels) will rise globally and, despite cheap borrowing, many vulnerable economies will be exposed to the prospect of fiscal constraint as of 2021 onwards.

As the economic impact of the pandemic increases, more emphasis is being placed on policies that address the immediate economic impact, at the cost of long-term estimates, such as government debt and fiscal deficits.

The Covid-19 pandemic crisis, however, has prompted governments to apply monetary and fiscal policies supporting and maintaining economic activity in order to prevent distortions in economies that could outweigh the effects of the virus itself.

In this context, policy-makers have taken steps on conventional economic policy standards, reactivating policies from the previous decade. Central banks are participating by continuing to use monetary instruments and interventions in financial markets, such as forward guidance, QE and low interest rate policies, and measures to boost liquidity in economies. At the same time, national governments have strengthened the role of fiscal policy through targeted tax measures and increased spending.

In the EU, however, the Covid-19 crisis has also highlighted positions, along with the leadership of regional member states, supporting the issue of a common European bond (Baldwin & di Mauro, 2020) guaranteed by the Community budget (corona bond) to finance support measures provided to states. This idea of debt mutualization is not new,[1] but has returned to the forefront in the midst of the Covid-19 pandemic, on the grounds that the health and consequent economic crisis from the lockdowns has been a symmetrical and exogenous threat to the economies of member states, the treatment of which now requires a type of joint fiscal policy at a European level.

The mutualization of debt at an EU level is capable of resulting in a low interest rate (without posing a risk to debt dynamics) needed to allow member states (particularly those with a high debt-to-GDP ratio) to secure their public finances at a healthy level, paving the way for a return to economic growth. At the same time, sharing the risk within the union—transferring it from high-debt to low-debt states—entails the moral risk of transforming individual into collective responsibility of member states in regards to their fiscal targets (free ride), making the acceptance of the corona bond politically impossible.

Extraordinary circumstances, however, demand extraordinary measures. The aftermath of the epidemiological crisis has challenged many stereotypes of economic thought, broadening consequential policy proposals. Special circumstances concerning Covid-19 come to reinforce views on non-conventional economic policy that had drawn interest in public debate in recent years.

Such is the case, for example, with Modern Money Theory (MMT) (Mankiw, 2020), which is a new approach to macroeconomics. In MMT (Wray, 2015) the public sector's critical role of determining economic stability and growth is decided by the sovereignty of states over national currency, balance between an economy's institutional sectors, and the achievement of full employment, which is the ultimate goal of economic policy.

The main points of the theory are the principles in which the budget deficit can be financed by the central bank, state expenditures do not burden the trade balance and the tax revenues do not affect the resources of the general government. This is because the amount of money is determined by the financial securities issued by the public sector, while inflation is a complex phenomenon that is primarily influenced by the institutional characteristics of an economy.

Money here consists of a legal relationship between citizens and the state, which operates via taxation—while losing control of the currency is the biggest obstacle to the smooth running of an economy (Wray, 2015). Thus, according to MMT, monetary unions and independent central banks contribute to the instability of the economy, preventing growth.

The alternatives for central banks proposed in public discourse for dealing with the financial implications of Covid-19 touch on the logic of a broader unified government and a single state balance sheet. Until the 2008 financial crisis, the distinction between monetary and fiscal policy and the independence of central banks was, in economic thought, an inviolable condition in exercising economic policy. However, in the midst of adverse economic conditions, finance ministries may have the appropriate policy tools without the necessary resources, which are held by central banks with a limited ability to make use of (Caballero, 2010).

So, according to MMT, the fact that there is no time limit on state budgets, the issuance of money and its direct, non-binding transfer to citizens' accounts is deemed to be a viable (and not just extraordinary) solution. This is "helicopter money"[2] and is a radical idea that has come to the fore academically over the last two decades[3] and, more recently, as an extraordinary policy proposal in the midst of the Covid-19 crisis (Gali, 2020; Sandbu, 2020; Yashiv, 2020). It is a fact that some governments (e.g., Japan, Singapore, and the United Kingdom), in order to deal with the epidemiological crisis, made direct transfers of state money. These, however, are not necessarily forms of "helicopter drops." For this to happen (Gali, 2020) there needs to be a fiscal transfer of money which, however, will weigh on the central bank's balance sheet without increasing public or private debt. So under certain extreme conditions, where traditional monetary policy has exhausted its scope for stimulating the economy (Caballero, 2010; Perrotti, 2014; Selgin, 2016; Turner, 2015) and while there is a reluctance or inability to support fiscal policies by increasing public debt, such a practice may be considered to be the best available alternative solution (Bernanke, 2016).

An equivalent economic policy tool emerging from the Covid-19 crisis is (Baldwin & di Mauro, 2020) the financing of government operations through debt monetization. The dominant position over time is that the purchase of government securities amounts to a risk for central banks because it can create the perception (Mishkin, 2011) that the central bank is willing to support "irresponsible" fiscal policies with debt monetization.

Large-scale government bond purchases have become part of the central banks' toolkit, including, in the context of "do whatever it takes" to support the economy amid the pandemic crisis, and now form direct funding (*Financial Times*, 2020) of government spending (direct debt monetization). Thus, concerns do not stem from this practice itself, as it may not necessarily be harmful to economies, but from its excessive use or exploitation for the wrong reasons (Blanchard & Pisani-Ferry, 2020).

The Covid-19 pandemic crisis has sharply increased the liquidity needs of states. The implementation of the support to mitigate unemployment risks in an emergency (SURE) program by Commission to support employment, the new pandemic credit line from the European Stability Mechanism (ESM), and the pandemic emergency purchase program (PEPP) by the ECB providing credit to member states contributed to meeting these needs. But the bottom line is that all of this increases the debt of excessively indebted countries.

Thus, it is now considered that the provision of necessary liquidity flows to EU countries (Vihriälä, 2020) must be combined with a drastic relief from the ECB on debt levels[4] of countries to meet the extraordinary fiscal needs, even if this raises expectations for a repeat of this (moral hazard) as a solution of last resort. This is because the given collapse in growth rate EU countries are projected to see in 2020, in combination with the increased uncertainty in markets and a refusal to share the burden (reduce the risk of borrowing) between member states, is sufficient in the medium to long term to threaten the sustainability of debt among fiscally vulnerable countries, some of which suffered a double disaster, in the economy and in health.

Additionally, this prospect raises concerns that Covid-19 will trigger the development of a Minsky Moment. According to Minsky (1981, 1983), the financial system is inherently unstable (Financial Instability Hypothesis), as periods of economic stability and prosperity cultivate conditions of economic instability on their own. This "paradox of stability" is due to the risky and speculative behavior of financially active people during periods of extended expansion (looser criteria for lending terms, low preference for liquidity among household and business, and high debt that boosts the price of real estate and securities). The Minsky Moment sets the peak where speculative activity reaches a point that is no longer sustainable, leading to rapid price deflation and an unhindered market collapse. Without the intervention of the state, the crisis in the financial system has a devastating effect on the real economy.

It is a fact that in most economies worldwide, public debt (as a percentage of GDP) was at high historical levels (Badia & Dudine, 2019) before the outbreak of the pandemic, while in advanced economies corporate debt gradually increased from 2010 to 2019 (Badia & Dudine, 2019) reaching 2008 levels—its maximum level.

Although the Covid-19 crisis did not start as a financial crisis, it could turn into one, acting as an accelerator of the underlying trend of rising asset prices, leverage, and debt (Lance, 2020). This could arise due to delays in the recovery of economic activity, as high debt levels make borrowers vulnerable to shocks that disrupt revenues and inflows of financing. As a result, banks are increasing lending criteria, while higher risk premiums are being added to government bonds, creating self-fulfilling negative expectations.

Covid-19's exogenous supply shock, which also evolved rapidly and into demand shock, can therefore be internalized by causing a financial collapse to the extent that many individuals (businesses and households) and public borrowers (governments) around the world are unable to repay debts due to the imminent global recession.

In general, in the new era after the outbreak of the second global crisis of the twenty-first century (Covid-19), the challenge of economic policy is twofold: aiming to support economies in the short-term, but also prevent permanent effects that the crisis may have. This necessity, therefore, has formed a broad consensus on overcoming the established rules of monetary and fiscal policy, with the implementation of innovative and distinct measures of economic policy, thus expanding the scope of the former and giving again a decisively active role in the latter decades later.

Notes

1. It was originally proposed by the Commission in 2011 (Eurobond) to address the European crisis of the three years 2009–2012.
2. The current use of the term differs as a concept from Friedman's (1969) imaginative parable of a helicopter from which money falls and is distributed to citizens. The aim was to describe the mechanism of quantitative theory, namely, that any increase in money supply automatically leads to a proportional increase in prices without any change in the product produced and that central banks can always avoid deflation by printing and putting money into circulation.
3. More specifically, it began to be seen as a serious policy proposal in the late 1990s, in the light of the fact that it could be a useful means of combating deflation in Japan.
4. Through the conversion of a part of the debt (debt conversion) into perpetuity with zero coupon.

References

Alesina, A., & Ardagna, S. (2011). *Fiscal Adjustments: Lessons from Recent History* (NBER Working Paper No. 15438).

Badia, M. M., & Dudine, P. (2019). New Data on World Debt: A Dive into Country Numbers. *International Monetary Fund* (IMF Blog). Retrieved from: https://blogs.imf.org/2019/12/17/new-data-on-world-debt-a-dive-into-country-numbers/.

Baldwin, R. & di Mauro B. W. (2020). *Mitigating the Covid Economic Crisis: Act Fast and Do Whatever It Takes* (a VoxEU.org eBook). London: CEPR Press.

Bank of England. (2019). *Effective Interest Rates*. Retrieved from: https://www.bankofengland.co.uk/news/statistics.

Bank of Japan. (2019). *Bank of Japan Statistics*. Retrieved from https://www.boj.or.jp/en/statistics/boj/index.htm/.

Bernanke, B. (2016). What Tools Does the Fed Have Left? Part 3: Helicopter money. *Brookings*. Retrieved from: https://www.brookings.edu/blog/ben-bernanke/2016/04/11/what-tools-does-the-fed-have-left-part-3-helicopter-money/.

Bernanke, B. S. (2020). The New Tools of Monetary Policy. *American Economic Association Presidential Address*. Retrieved from: https://www.brookings.edu/wp-content/uploads/2019/12/Bernanke_ASSA_lecture.pdf.

Blanchard, O., & Perotti, R. (2002). An Empirical Characterization of the Dynamic Effects of Changes in Government Spending and Taxes on Output. *The Quarterly Journal of Economics, 117*(4), 1329–1368.

Blanchard, O., & Pisani-Ferry, J. (2020). Monetisation: Do not Panic. *Vox CEPR Policy Portal*. Retrieved from: https://voxeu.org/article/monetisation-do-not-panic.

Board of Governors of the Federal Reserve System. (2019). *Federal Funds Effective Rate*. Retrieved from: https://www.federalreserve.gov/releases/h15/.

Botev, J., Fournier, J. M., & Mourougane, A. (2016). *A Re-Assessment of Fiscal Space in OECD Countries* (OECD Economics Department Working Paper No. 1352).

Boussard, J., de Castro, F. & Salto, M. (2012). *Fiscal Multipliers and Public Debt Dynamics in Consolidations* (European Economy - Economic Paper No. 460).

Buti, M. (2020). Riding Through the Storm: Lessons and Policy Implications for Policymaking in EMU. *Vox CEPR Policy Portal*. Retrieved from: https://voxeu.org/article/lessons-and-policyimplications-policymaking-emu.

Caballero, R. (2010). A Helicopter Drop for the U.S. Treasury. *Vox CEPR Policy Portal*. Retrieved from: https://voxeu.org/article/helicopter-drop-us-treasury.

Constancio, V. (2014). *Making Macro-Prudential Policy Work (Speech at High-Level Seminar organised by De Nederlandsche Bank)*. Retrieved from: http://www.ecb.europa.eu/press/key/date/2014/html/sp140610.en.html.

Eurobank. (2012). Fiscal Multipliers in Deep Economic Recessions and the Case for a 2-year Extension in Greece's Austerity Programme. *Economy & Markets, 8*(4), 1–44.

European Central Bank. (2019). *Key ECB Interest Rates*. Retrieved from: https://www.ecb.europa.eu/stats/policy_and_exchange_rates/key_ecb_interest_rates/html/index.en.html.

European Commission. (2020). *European Economic Forecast: Spring 2020* (Economic and Financial Affairs Institutional Paper No. 125). Retrieved from: https://ec.europa.eu/info/publications/economic-and-financial-affairs-publications_en.

Financial Times. (2020). Bank of England to Directly Finance UK Government's Extra Spending. Retrieved from: https://www.ft.com/content/664c575b-0f54-44e5-ab78-2fd30ef213cb.

Friedman, M. (1969). The Optimum Quantity of Money. In M. Friedman (Ed.), *The Optimum Quantity of Money and Other Essays* (pp. 1–50). Chicago: Adline Publishing Company.

Gali, J. (2020). Helicopter Money: The Time Is Now. *Vox CEPR Policy Portal*. Retrieved from: https://voxeu.org/article/helicopter-money-time-now.

Gaspar, V. (2020). Future of Fiscal Rules in the Euro Area (Workshop on "Fiscal rules in Europe: Design and Enforcement" [DG ECFIN]). *International Monetary Fund*. Retrieved from: https://www.imf.org/en/News/Articles/2020/01/28/sp012820-vitor-gaspar-fiscal-rules-in-europe.

Heller, P. S. (2005). *Understanding Fiscal Space* (IMF Policy Discussion Paper No. 05/4).

Lance, R. (2020). MacroView: The Next "Minsky Moment" Is Inevitable. *Seeking Alpha*. Retrieved from: https://seekingalpha.com/article/4322643-macroview-next-minsky-moment-is-inevitable.

Leahy, J. V., & Thapar, A. (2019). *Demographic Effects on the Impact of Monetary Policy* (NBER Working Paper No. 26324).

Mankiw, N. G. (2020). *A Skeptic's Guide to Modern Monetary Theory* (NBER Working Paper No. 26650).

Minsky, H. P. (1981). *Can "It" Happen Again? Essays on Instability and Finance*. New York: M.E. Sharpe.

Minsky, H. P. (1983). The Financial Instability Hypothesis: An Interpretation of Keynes and an Alternative to "Standard" Theory. In J. C. Wood (Ed.), *John Maynard Keynes. Critical Assessments* (pp. 282–292). London: Macmillan.

Mishkin, F. S. (2011). *Monetary Policy Strategy: Lessons from the Crisis* (NBER Working Paper No. 16755).

Obstfeld, M., & Rogoff, K. (2002). Global Implications of Self-Oriented National Monetary Rules. *The Quarterly Journal of Economics, 117*(2), 503–535.

Organisation for Economic Co-operation and Development. (2015). *Economic Policy Reforms 2015: Going for Growth*. Paris: OECD Publishing. Retrieved from: https://doi.org/10.1787/growth-2015-en and author's calculations.

Organisation for Economic Co-operation and Development. (2019). *Economic Policy Reforms 2019: Going for Growth*. Paris: OECD Publishing. Retrieved from: https://doi.org/10.1787/aec5b059-en and author's calculations.

Oxford Economics. (2017). *Oxford Economics Global Macro Model*.

Oxford Economics. (2020). *Oxford Economics Global Macro Model*.

Papaioannou, S. K. (2015). *Fiscal Multipliers in Euro Area Peripheral Countries: Empirical Evidence from a Structural VAR Model* (Centre of Planning and Economic Research (KEPE) Paper No. 141).

Perrotti, R. (2014). Eurozone Recovery: There Are No Shortcuts. *Vox CEPR Policy Portal*. Retrieved from: https://voxeu.org/article/eurozone-recovery-there-are-no-shortcuts.

Roubini, N. (2011). Four Options to Address the Eurozone's Stock and Flow Imbalances: The Rising Risk of a Disorderly Break-Up. *Roubini Global Economics*. Retrieved from: www.roubini.com/analysis/165338.

Roy, R., & Heuty, A. (2009). *Fiscal Space: Policy Options for Financing Human Development*. London: Earthscan.

Sandbu, M. (2020). Coronavirus: The Moment for Helicopter Money. *Financial Times*. Retrieved from: https://www.ft.com/content/abd6bbd0-6a9f-11ea-800d-da70cff6e4d3.

Selgin, G. (2016). Japan: The Way Out. *Alt-M*. Retrieved from: https://www.alt-m.org/2016/05/03/japan-way/.

Statistical Office of the European Communities. (2020a).*Eurostat: Net International Investment Position - Quarterly Data, % of GDP (TIPSII40)*.

Statistical Office of the European Communities. (2020b). *Eurostat: Unemployment by Sex and Age - Quarterly Average [une_rt_q]*.

Stiglitz, J. E. (2014). *Reconstructing Macroeconomic Theory to Manage Economic Policy* (NBER Working Paper No. 20517).

Swiss National Bank. (2019). *SNB Policy Rate*. Retrieved from https://www.snb.ch/en/iabout/stat.

Taylor, J. (2013). International Monetary Coordination and the Great Deviation. *Journal of Policy Modeling, 35*(3), 463–472.

Turner, A. (2015). *Between Debt and the Devil: Money, Credit, and Fixing Global Finance*. Princeton: Princeton University Press.

Vihriälä, V. (2020). Make Room for Fiscal Action Through Debt Conversion. *Vox CEPR Policy Portal*. Retrieved from: https://voxeu.org/article/make-room-fiscal-action-through-debt-conversion.

Wray, L. R. (2015). *Modern Money Theory: A Primer on Macroeconomics for Sovereign Monetary Systems* (2nd ed.). London: Springer.

Yashiv, E. (2020). Breaking the Taboo: The Political Economy of COVID-Motivated Helicopter Drops. *Vox CEPR Policy Portal*. Retrieved from: https://voxeu.org/article/political-economy.

CHAPTER 12

Economic and Development Policy in the Age of Low Growth Rates, Low Inflation, and Low Employment in the Greek Economy Until 2019

12.1 Introduction

Low growth rates, low investments, and low inflation rates form the new era of the global economy. In the second section of the chapter (Sect. 12.2) we focus on the case of the Greek economy, where these trends coexist along with high unemployment. These concepts interact with development and growth policy, both in theory and reality.

In this direction, especially at the heart of theoretical discussion on growth, there are a number of issues which are being analyzed in this chapter, such as the global recession and an investment-less recovery (Sect. 12.3) and the hyper cycle of debt and balance sheet recessions (Sect. 12.4). Section 12.5 discusses shortfalls and structural unemployment in the Greek economy. Finally, Sect. 12.6 presents economic growth under conditions of low development, low investments, low inflation, and also low employment in the Greek economy.

Note that the next chapter exclusively refers to Covid-19 crisis, that is in the short period from 2019 to September of 2020.

P. E. Petrakis, *The New Political Economy of Greece up to 2030*,
The Political Economy of Greek Growth up to 2030,
https://doi.org/10.1007/978-3-030-47075-3_12

12.2 Economic Policy with Low Growth, Low Inflation, and Low Employment

In early 2013, the European crisis had escalated into a low growth trap where four components played a central role. These were:

- the fiscal austerity and the risk of public debt;
- the vulnerability of financial systems;
- the high unemployment rates; and
- the deleveraging from the financial sector, businesses, and households.

A recession that has its roots in the financial system is deeper and recovery time is slower than in the case of a productive recession (Akerlof, 2013). Therefore, the question that arises is whether the fundamental assumptions of economic theory should be examined even more deeply, on the one hand by the quantitative theory of money, which attributes the collapse to the instability of money supply (housing mortgage crisis, etc.) causing an explosion in consumption and, on the other hand, by Keynesian theory, which emphasizes that the crisis arose from investments instability (Skidelsky, 2010).

The global economic crisis of 2008 has largely shown that unfavorable disruptions reduce inflation—even leading to deflationary conditions, shrinking economic activity—while central banks may be stuck in a situation with near-zero interest rates (Gerlach & Lewis, 2011).

In the liquidity trap there is a low interest rate area, which is mainly shaped by the central bank's interest rate, ranging from close from 0 to 1%, a level at which excessive risk-taking behaviors and speculation are developed in economic sectors. At the same time, there is always the possibility of new crises emerging, the treatment of which would subsequently require low interest rates.

Thus, a vicious circle of low interest rates is maintained with recovery dynamics being absent. More specifically, under conditions of low interest rates, the possibility of transferring liquidity from surplus to deficit portfolios is interrupted while, at the same time, monetary policy loses one of its main tools of implementation, managing interest rates. Therefore, only quantitative interventions remain, such as open market transactions or other non-conventional measures, in order to mobilize the economy.

Similar situations arise over fear whether short-term funds will not be available when required, because other participants in the interest rate system have the same goals, i.e., they expect to have access to funds whenever they wish (Giavazzi & Giovannini, 2010). For this reason, the demand for zero risk positions is being increased, something that only central banks can offer.

Deflationary conditions, moreover, lead to continually lower central bank interest rate targets (e.g., when targets follow Taylor's rule), resulting in a liquidity trap. This is particularly true if the central bank's goal is only price stability and not economic activity, as is the case for the European Central Bank (ECB), but not for the Federal Reserve (Fed)—Fed's Dual Mandate. When the second situation occurs, it is much more likely that the central bank will be involved in quantitative interventions in capital markets, increasing liquidity in quantity and duration, so that risk shaping depends on the provision of quantitative liquidity and not just from the capital price. At the same time, possible intervention through open market operations may not have the desired result, if central banks do not change the expectations of protagonists regarding future policy being implemented (Eggertsson & Woodford, 2003).

In the short-term, deflationary pressures sharpen, hitting already anemic economic growth and pushing the global economy closer and closer into decline. In short, low inflation rates, as well as low bond yields, exert deflationary pressure on the economy.

In regards to Eurozone, a possible patient of such an unfavorable deflationary situation on the verge of "Japanization," seems to primarily be Greece—with Italy coming next. This is due to persistent deflation, the demographic problem, high private debt, unattractive prices for assets and securities in international money and capital markets, the entrapment of the banking system due to a high level of non-performing loans in its portfolios, weak economic growth expected, and the excessive tendency of firms to save money. Note that the Covid-19 crisis intensified these tendencies (see next chapter).

Figure 12.1 shows the evolution of non-performing loans, with Greece presenting the biggest problem, in terms of excessive debt held by the private sector. Despite the fact that the phenomenon is in the process of de-escalation, non-performing loan levels are still high, compared to other European economies, with the exception of Cyprus.

The Greek banking system's non-performing loans crisis, the biggest crisis to occur in the world's developed system, arose in two phases.

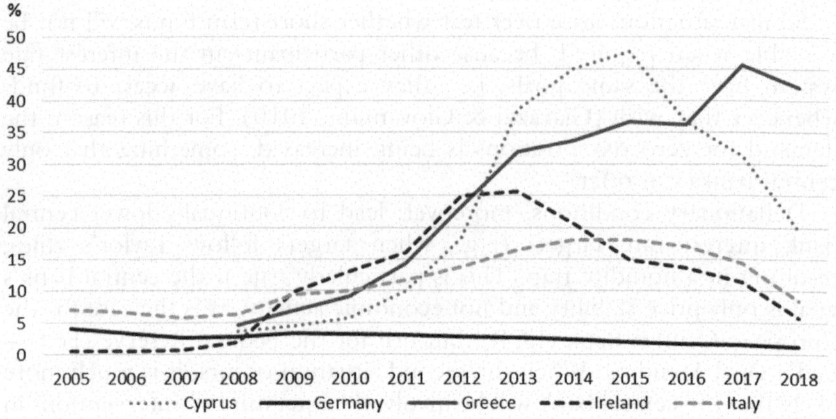

Fig. 12.1 Bank non-performing loans to total gross loans (%) (*Source* The World Bank [2020] and author's own calculations and creation)

The first phase related to the possession of Greek government bonds in Greek bank portfolios, included in the voluntary bond exchange program (Private Sector Investment [PSI]) in March 2012.

Banks were forced to record estimated losses of around 38 billion euros due to their participation in PSI and the (reduced) valuation of new government bonds, based on current values (Bank of Greece [BoG], 2012). This raised the need for the immediate recapitalization of the Greek banking system. Up until now, the Greek banking system has absorbed 64 billion euros from successive recapitalizations. The second phase is being related to the inclusion of loans that have stopped being serviced in bank portfolios (Fig. 12.1). These are essentially the effects of a typical "Minsky moment" created by market participants (borrowers) and bank executives (lenders).

The post-Keynesian theory of "financial expansion" is relevant to the Greek economy, not via the typical "Ponzi scheme" but in the form of continual expectations for higher returns, at a time (2001–2008) of high funding for the economy and the banking system. Essentially, self-fulfilling prophecies of increasing returns led to higher leverage, often without the necessary guarantees. The sudden drop in yields then led to the non-fulfilment of borrower obligations and increasing of non-performing loans. It should be noted that the inability of households to service debt was combined with the problem of unemployment, as a result of falling demand and production.

Risks to the domestic banking system remain, as non-financial enterprises retain high levels of leverage. After a significant decrease in the third and fourth quarters of 2013, they increased again in the first quarter of 2014 (Fig. 12.2). At the same time, household deleveraging seems to have started from the first quarter of 2012 and is continually progressing.

Greece's financial system still has a very large stockpile of non-performing loans, even when compared with Italy and Portugal. However, Greece is now a few steps away from tackling this structural challenge. The solution approved by the European Commission copies, up until a point, measures previously taken in Italy for non-performing loans. The government will provide guarantees to help banks deal with high levels of non-performing loans, but the time required to see the benefits is uncertain. The plan will accelerate the reduction of non-performing loans and boost banks' profitability. In this context, banks will be able to reduce non-performing loans worth up to 30 billion euros, with the Greek government providing guarantees for the higher levels of securitized loans, in exchange for a fee, subject to market conditions, and therefore, based on the risk it undertakes.

Indicative of the Greek economy's liquidity situation is the fact that total household disposable income from 2009 (Q4) to 2019 (Q2) decreased by 19%.

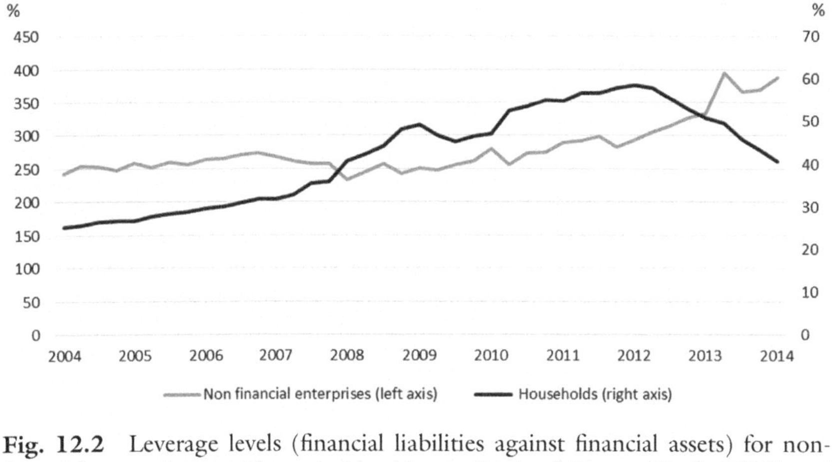

Fig. 12.2 Leverage levels (financial liabilities against financial assets) for non-financial enterprises and households (*Source* Bank of Greece [BoG, 2019] and author's own creation)

However, the situation seems to be gradually improving as of 2016, particularly in Eurozone, possibly due to higher prices and return on assets in money and capital markets, which were mainly the result of quantitative easing (QE) from central banks (Figs. 12.3 and 12.4). The

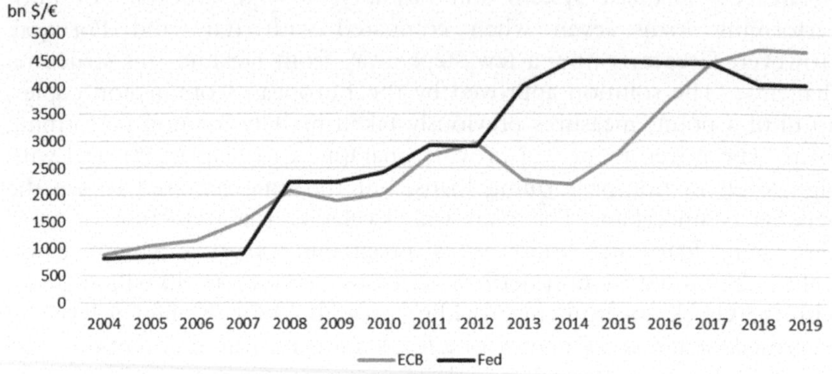

Fig. 12.3 Balance sheet FED and ECB (in bn USD or euros) (*Source* Board of Governors of the FED [2020], ECB [2020], and author's own creation)

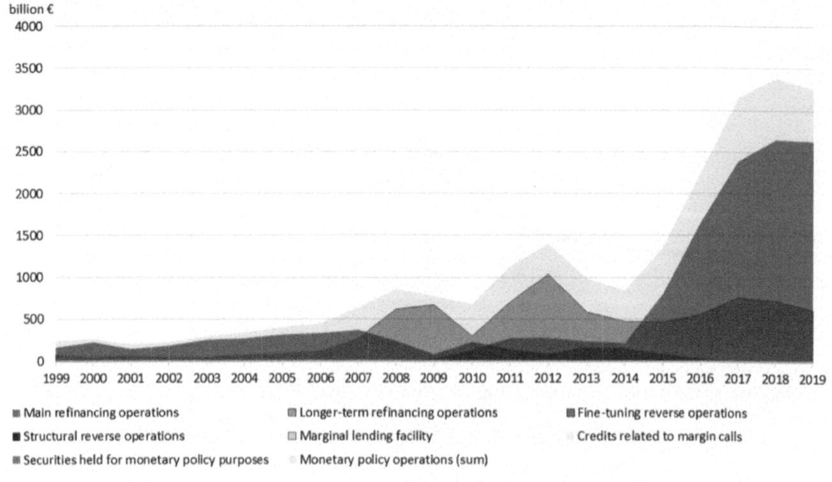

Fig. 12.4 ECB monetary policy operations (*Source* ECB [2020] and author's own creation)

Covid-19 crisis will decelerate the improvement process by two to three years.

More specifically, in Eurozone, the coordinated effort to stabilize the euro by implementing economic policies, according to the famous speech of Draghi (2012), which reassured pessimists about the euro course, the revised expansionary scope of policies (such as QE implementation) and the reduction of non-performing loans from bank portfolios contributed in helping European assets recover their attractiveness. These assets, from 1998 until 2012, presented a similar trend with assets in Japan during the period of deflation (1988–2002). Additionally, the global resurgence of economic growth, from 2014 onwards, has contributed to increasing expectations.

12.3 The Case of the Secular Stagnation and Investment-Less Recovery

The extended appearance of low growth rates has brought to the surface the possibility of a secular stagnation. The basic concern is that the global recession is making it very difficult to achieve full employment, given low inflation rates and zero-lower bound interest rates (Teulings & Baldwin, 2014).[1] It is argued that low interest rates, i.e., low returns, increased levels of uncertainty, and the slow adoption of new technologies in production create fertile ground for conditions that fuel a permanent recession, i.e., continual secular stagnation (Summers, 2017).

Similar conditions have emerged at global level after the outbreak of the Great Recession of 2008. Concerns relate to the possibility that developed economies, as a whole, will continue to be particularly vulnerable in the future to secular stagnation conditions (Rachel & Summers, 2019). In recent decades, neutral real interest rates have fallen by at least 300 basis points. These secular movements mainly reflect changes in the tendency toward savings and investments rather than the safety and liquidity properties of Treasury instruments.

In this regard, the predominant assumption is that, although negative real interest rates are required to equalize savings with investments securing full employment, this is, in fact, impossible. If the existence of secular recessionary conditions is confirmed, while real interest rates are low, or even negative for a long time, traditional monetary policy instruments become inadequate (Wolff, 2014). Consequently, on the one hand, extraordinary monetary and fiscal measures currently being applied may be ineffective in dealing with the next crisis (Teulings & Baldwin,

2014). On the other hand, these conditions may lead to the resumption of the role of fiscal policy strengthening and, consequently, the debt accumulation process (Blanchard, Furceri, & Pescatori, 2014), so that if we succeed, the growth rate will be higher than the cost of borrowing, possibly to justify the increase in public debt (Blanchard, 2019).

In the secular stagnation environment, a set of unusual features is observed in the structure of economies, which strengthen the conditions of constant economic stagnation (Krugman, 2014). In particular, the existence of extreme conditions in the money market, such as the zero interest rate threshold, has bigger effects than expected.

The secular stagnation has spread to different countries through two complementary channels (Eggertsson, Mehrotra, Singh, & Summers, 2016):

- the reduced demand from abroad and the binding zero limit, which led to an appreciation of the domestic exchange rate and pushed central banks to reduce interest rates; and
- capital flows being directed through current accounts to countries that do not face conditions of a secular stagnation.

However, this situation is pushing down real interest rates for those receiving capital inflows. However, it is argued that economic policy, in monetary terms, has exhausted the stockpiles of its arsenal, and this is something that traps central banks in their attempt to normalize the impact of economic volatility. Summers (2014) expressed the belief that low interest rates may encourage economic stagnation and create instability through three channels:

- the increased probability of taking a "sustainable" risk, which reflects the tendency of investors to seek additional returns;
- the promotion of "irresponsible" borrowing or non-repayable borrowing, as the degree of demand and weight of borrowing obligations softens, making it easier for borrowers to respond to them; and
- the increase of financial Ponzi schemes (or pyramids), given that interest rates seem low in relation to expected growth rates.

In conclusion, deflation and negative interest rates create disincentives for new investments due to low returns (see Figs. 12.1 and 12.16 below). Thus, investments in both physical (infrastructure and machinery) and human capital (education, technical training, competences, and experience) are limited. A lack of investments causes a drop in income; prolonged disinvestment conditions and pause of new investments; and, ultimately, a reduction in savings, thus creating conditions for long-term stagnation. The Covid-19 crisis amplifies and accelerates those tendencies (see next chapter).

12.4 The Debt Super-Cycle and Balance Sheet Recession

Debt management is one of the most critical determinants of growth conditions development. Two fundamental issues that arise concern both the relationship between public debt and budget deficits—with current and future economic activity, and, therefore, economic growth—and the long-term management and resolution of the debt problem.

The theoretical interpretation of Reinhart and Rogoff (2010) findings that relate to the effects of debt expansion on growth, is related to the principle of "Ricardian Parity." This principle argues that, if consumers have absolute predictability of the future and accessibility to capital markets, then any debt increase will lead to a reduction in their current consumption, because they will take into account the future burden of tax increase. In fact, the reduction in consumption will be so great that it will eliminate the benefits of expansionary fiscal policy. The rationale behind this thinking is that rational actors realize that tax substitution today is equivalent to taxes plus interest rates in the future, through government debt financing (Barro, 1974).

Adversely, Krugman (2011) stressed that the implementation of the assumption of full market efficiency is difficult to be applied in the real world, while, even in the event that assumptions for perfect links within a generation (non-distorting taxation, perfect rationality) are valid, increasing spending does not need to be permanent, as long as governments ensure that debt is increased at a rate lower than the tax base. This is how developed countries have come out of over-indebtedness in the past.

Research by Reinhart and Rogoff on the theoretical relationship between debt and growth includes a serious conceptual problem: it did not provide evidence of the causality between high debt and growth. The probability that debt will grow due to the recession, rather than being what causes it, is actually considered higher (Irons & Bivens, 2010). The same conclusion is reached by Krugman (2013), who, while looking at the link between high debt and slow growth, cites the example of Italy and Japan saying that, "both Italy and (especially) Japan ran up high debts as a consequence of their growth slowdowns, not the other way around."

In general, the debt problem has two sides. One concerns the formation of flows that reflect the outcome of economic policies. They are added to debt. The other relates to accumulated public debt (stocks). The debt to gross domestic product (GDP) ratio can be considered unusual, given that there are times when it is considered a crucial criterion for decision-making (small European peripheral countries) and other times when it is of negligible importance (Great Britain and Spain).

The ratio of deficit to GDP, which determines the possibility of repayment, significantly affects expectations. However, the deficit, the growth rate, and global borrowing create the so-called "snowball" effect, which changes a country's risk profile. In particular, it describes how the ratio of public debt to GDP may increase, even when the primary deficit (budget deficit minus interest) is zero, that is, even when there is no new borrowing from the public sector. Given that debt must be serviced each year, when a country pays interest to its creditors, the rate of change in the existing debt (when there is no new borrowing) may be the same as the interest rate. Therefore, when the nominal GDP rate is less than the interest rate, then the public debt-to-GDP ratio increases (the numerator increases at a faster rate than the denominator).

Table 12.1, based on the European Commission's (2020a) Spring forecasts, lists the debt decomposition for the Greek economy 2018– 2020 showing the impact of the "snowball" effect. It can be seen that the biggest factor in debt increase in 2020 is the primary surplus and the real growth effect (see also Fig. 12.5). More particularly, the contribution of the primary deficit to the change in the gross debt ratio is expected to reach 3.4% of GDP for 2020, compared with −4.3% for 2018 and −4.4% for 2019. Regarding the real growth effect, it is expected at 9.7% of GDP for 2020, versus −3.3% and −1.9% in 2018 and 2019, respectively.

Seven years after the Great Recession (2016), all major economies continued to have higher debt levels, as a percentage of GDP, than in 2007. The evolution of public debt, as a percentage of GDP, for the Greek economy and selected countries is presented in Fig. 12.6.

Rogoff (2015) argues that debt overhang and debt accumulation issues are the main causes of what happened after the Great Recession in 2008,

Table 12.1 Debt decomposition: Greece

(% of GDP)	*2018*	*2019*	*2020*
Gross debt ratio	181.2	176.6	196.4
Change in the ratio	5.0	−4.6	19.8
Contributions:			
1. Primary balance	−4.3	−4.4	3.4
2. "Snow-ball" effect	−1.0	0.5	13.3
Of which:			
Interest expenditure	3.3	2.9	3.0
Real growth effect	−3.3	−1.9	9.7
Inflation effect	−0.9	−0.5	0.6
3. Stock-flow adjustment	10.3	−0.7	3.1

Note The snow-ball effect captures the impact of interest expenditure on accumulated debt, as well as the impact of real GDP growth and inflation on the debt ratio (through the denominator). The stock-flow adjustment includes differences in cash and accrual accounting, accumulation of financial assets and valuation and other residual effects.
Source European Commission (2020a) and author's own creation

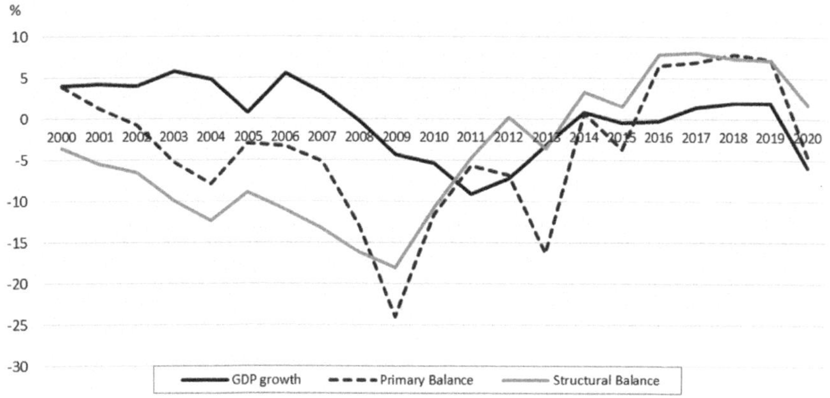

Fig. 12.5 GDP growth rate, primary balance, and structural balance for Greece (*Source* Oxford Economics [2020] and author's own creation)

and that the deleveraging process could keep the risk of over-indebtedness to a sustainable level. As he states "some argue that we live in a world of inadequate demand, doomed to decades of secular stagnation." However, the alternative possibility is that the global economy will be in the final stages of a debt super-cycle and will be crushed under the weight of a

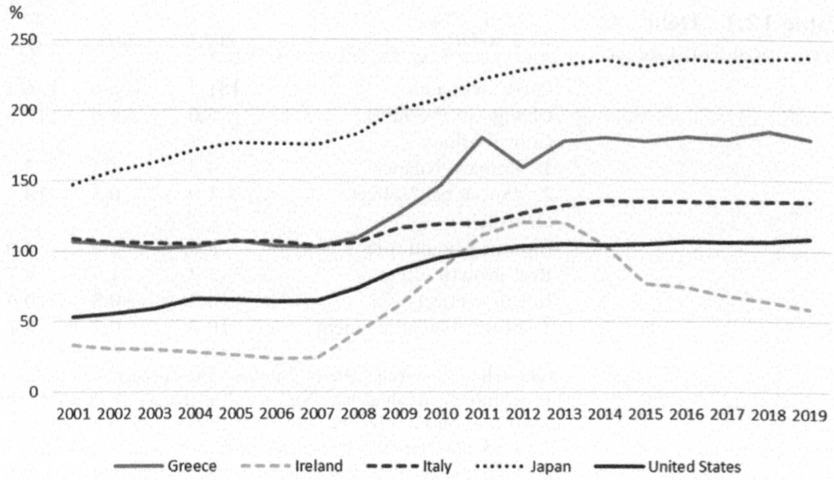

Fig. 12.6 General government gross debt (% GDP) (*Source* International Monetary Fund [IMF, 2020] and author's own creation)

burden that has accumulated over time through elastic regulations and financial exaggerations. When deleveraging process and over-indebtedness decline, expected growth trends may prove to be enough for economies to return to normality. But what has not been clarified is what will be the stage that will follow the phase of over-indebtedness. Will the problem "explode" with catastrophic consequences?

Beyond the amount of public debt as a percentage of GDP and its composition (Figs. 12.7 and 12.8), what is also important is that most of the debt after 2012 has been transferred to the official sector. In other words, it is proved that the amount of public debt to GDP does not play a decisive role in a mechanical way, despite the importance of who possesses the debt.

Figure 12.9 presents the evolution of public debt and the course of bond spreads (i.e., the cost of borrowing for the Greek economy) for the 2000s. Then, despite the de-escalation of borrowing rates (after 2015), debt remains at high levels.

The debt distribution and repayment path of the Greek economy show that the servicing of public debt service is covered by a cash buffer created by the primary surplus until 2022. This profile identifies two issues: The first is that under normal circumstances, debt issues can take

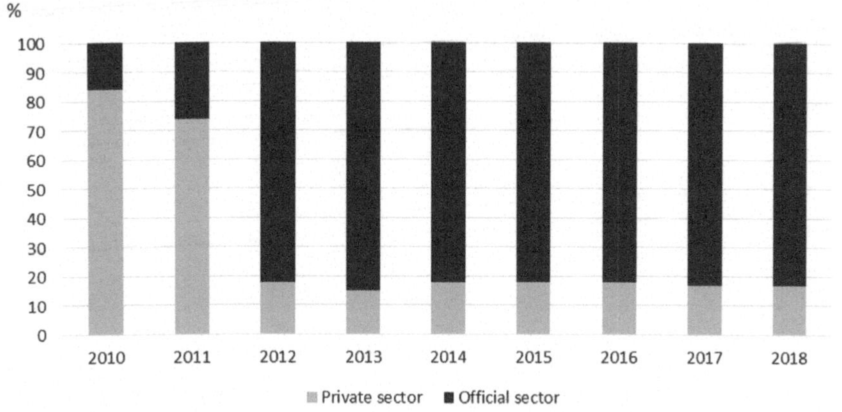

Fig. 12.7 The Structure of Greek public debt per creditor type as of 31-12-2018 (*Source* Hellenic Republic Ministry of Finance [2019] and author's own creation)

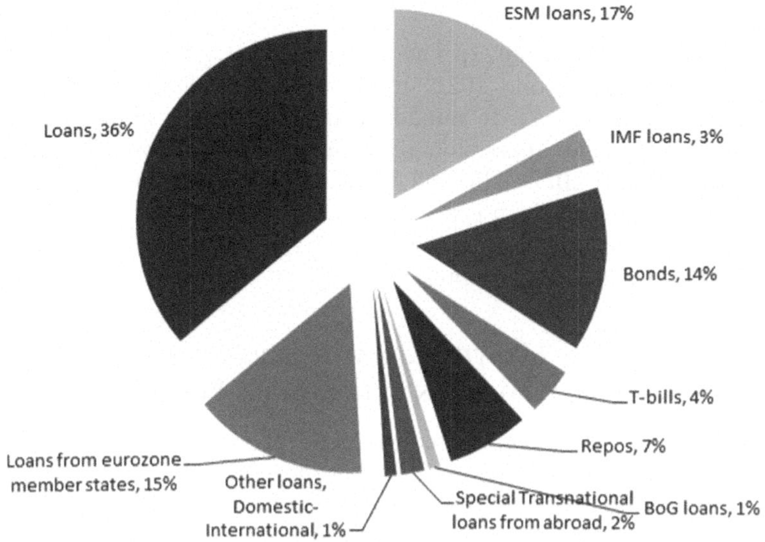

Fig. 12.8 The structure of the Greek public debt per lender as of 31-12-2018 (*Note* ESM = European Stability Mechanism and BoG = Bank of Greece. *Source* Hellenic Republic Ministry of Finance [2019] and author's own creation)

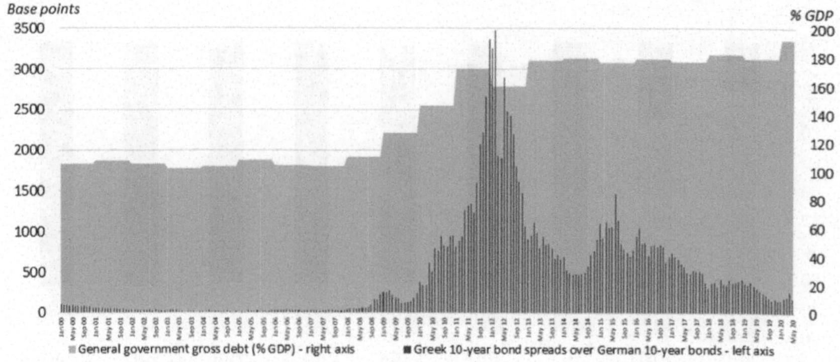

Fig. 12.9 General government gross debt and spread* of Greek 10 year bonds (*Note* Annual debt data and monthly data for the Greek 10-year spread. As for the first months of 2020, the debt data refers to the Oxford Economics forecast for the Greek debt in 2020 [as a percentage of GDP]. *Source* Invsting.com [2020]*, Oxford Economics [2020], and author's own calculations)

place if they expire by 2022. The second is that gross financial needs (GFNs), which go beyond 2022, appear to face funding difficulties (see Chapter 13, Fig. 13.14). It should be noted that this finding deviates from the widespread impression that the financing of public debt has been secured until 2030. This will be reconsidered when Greece regains an investment grade, which is placed around 2021.

The conclusions of debt sustainability have been changed under the Covid-19 effect (see next chapter).

12.5 Hysteresis and Structural Unemployment in the Greek Economy

One of the most important consequences of the Great Recession of 2008 was the change in GDP trend, in relation to the trend prior to the crisis. As a result, the debate over the issue of GDP hysteresis has begun.

The term hysteresis was first discussed in the labor market, where Blanchard and Summers (1986) argued that cyclical unemployment could become permanent, as unemployed lose part of their skills over time, resulting in a persistent cyclical shock, while high periods of high unemployment tend to increase unemployment to a rate that does not accelerate inflation (non-accelerating inflation rate of unemployment [NAIRU]).

On the one hand, in the downward phase of the economic cycle, where the economy is in a bust, companies hold the bargaining power in determining wage levels and usually asking for fewer employees due to reduced production caused by weak demand, even completing redundancies. On the other hand, in the upward phase of the economic cycle—where the economy is booming, expanding, or overproducing—it is employees, who have the bargaining power to affect wages, as firms try to meet higher demand and increase production, intending to create jobs by hiring new employees. In short, in times of recession, employees need firms more and are therefore willing to work for the equilibrium wage in the labor market, while in times of prosperity, companies are the ones who need more the employees, so they are willing to pay them higher wages. However, as one can see, there is a hysteresis, i.e., unemployment becomes permanently high after negative shocks (Blanchard & Summers, 1986).

The issue of hysteresis is directly linked to the prevalence of high levels of structural unemployment. The composition of unemployment in Greece shows that the problem of the economy is mainly structural. Of the 805,000 unemployed in 2019, the long-term unemployed (who have been looking for work for more than 12 months) amount to 570,000, or 71% of total unemployed, according to official data from the Hellenic Statistical Authority (ELSTAT, 2019a). The hysteresis is very likely to appear again as a Covid-19 consequence (see next chapter).

At the same time (ELSTAT, 2019a), the 279,900 unemployed are young people with no work experience, 101,800 come from wholesale and retail trade, 90,600 come from accommodation and catering services, and 41,500 from the construction sector.

The problem in the Greek labor market has two sides and is located in the mismatch of workforce skills and job vacancies: in terms of demand, vacancies require skills that are not provided to new employees by the education system. On the other hand, the labor supply is overqualified for the vacancies.

Beveridge curve (Fig. 12.10) relates unemployment rates with job vacancies and highlights the structural nature of unemployment in Greece. Vertical curve movements represent circular changes in job demand: more vacancies and lower unemployment are reflected in an upward movement and fewer vacancies and higher unemployment is reflected in a downward movement. In contrast, left and right curve

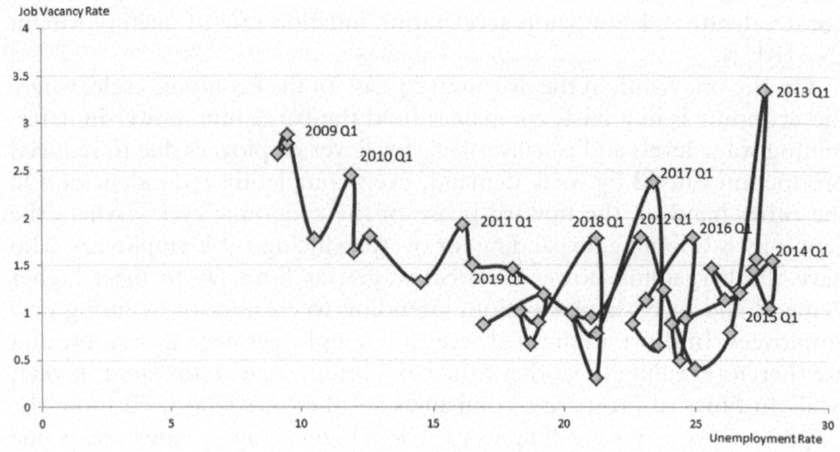

Fig. 12.10 Beveridge curve for the Greek economy (*Note* The job vacancy rate [JVR] measures the proportion of total posts that are vacant, expressed as a percentage: JVR = [number of job vacancies]/[number of occupied posts + number of job vacancies]. *Source* Statistical Office of the European Communities [2019a, 2019b] and author's own creation)

movements represent structural changes. The curve's mapping, as shown in Fig. 12.10, is complex, as there are simultaneous movements in length and shifts with different intensity. Thus, in 2009, unemployment in Greece can be characterized as circular, while from 2010 to 2013 it acquired a structural character. For the period 2013 –2017 it is characterized as circular, and acquires a structural character in the period 2017 until the first quarter of 2019.

The existence of hysteresis is at the same time the cause and effect of the reduced effectiveness of monetary and fiscal policy. Traditional analysis forecast that if there is no hysteresis in unemployment, central banks that want to reduce inflation can pursue contractionary monetary policy. If contractionary monetary policy is not fully expected, it will temporarily increase unemployment. But if this policy continues, theoretically, rising unemployment will be eventually disappeared and unemployment rates will return to normal.

The emergence of hysteresis in GDP contributes to the development of economic policies, which focuses on two key components:

- the implementation of low interest rate monetary policy (QE), the policy of front-loaded guidance, and the "money from heaven"; and
- the implementation of supply-side economics policies to boost capacity.

12.6 Economic Growth Under Conditions of Low Development, Low Investments, and Low Inflation in the Greek Economy

In recent decades, GDP growth, investments, and interest rates in developed economies have been declining at the same time. It can be argued that this situation does not come from the demand side, but from a reduction in supply, as in fact unemployment has fallen sharply in the last five years, while economic growth has been modest.

Low growth rates may be the result of a reduction in working age population (n) and labor-augmenting technological progress (g) that reduced potential output and shifted the Okun curve (a curve linking unemployment to GDP) to the left. The reduction in working age population and labor-augmenting technological progress also reduced investments in the economy. Essentially, companies are reducing their investments to prevent a sharp drop in return on capital. Central banks, from their part, ignored (Bakker, 2019) the slowdown in the growth of potential output. In Japan, in the 1990s, and in United Kingdom, Eurozone, and United States in the 2000s, they felt that the inability to grow was cyclical and that the potential growth of output remained strong.

However, it seems that expansionary monetary policy by central banks may stimulate gross investments, but not net investments or economic growth. Additionally, low interest rates will lead to an increase in the capital to output ratio (K/Y), low return on capital, and an increase in leverage.

This rejects the view that investments in developed economies are low relative to the state of the economy. Indeed, investments are lower than in the past, but this is due to the fact that the working age population and labor-augmenting technological progress have declined. A possible increase in investments, without a corresponding increase in total factor productivity (TFP) or working age population, may simply increase the K/Y ratio and further reduce return on investment. In reality, if a country with low $n + g$ has high gross investment, it will not be driven to high growth rates, but to high capital consumption, as proven in the case of Japan.

But let's see what happened in the case of Greece. Greek economy, after the outbreak of Great Recession in 2008 and debt crisis, showed declining GDP growth rates until 2016, with the recovery being low-flying.

The reasons for Greek economic growth, before 2008 as well as the reasons for the deeper recession prior to 2016 (−25% of GDP), have been analyzed (Chodorow-Reich, Karabarbounis, & Kekre, 2019). Low external demand for tradable goods and fiscal contraction are the main reasons for the recession. For the recovery, a mix of policies increasing supply and improving demand (Ioannides & Pissarides, 2015) is required, along with shifting the equilibrium weight from nominal internal devaluation and taxes on spending to cover long-term production and consumption gains. However, these analyzes, while in the right direction, do not seem to cover the deeper requirements to analyze exit conditions from the crisis. At the same time, we see (Fig. 12.11) a shift of Okun's curve to the left from 1991–2000 to 2008–2019.

At the same time, the gross fixed capital formation and interest rates have been declining over the last decade (Fig. 12.12).

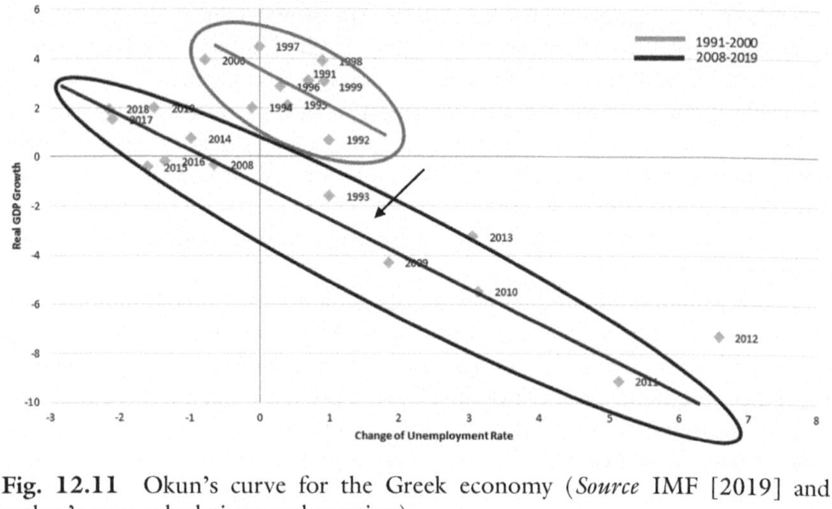

Fig. 12.11 Okun's curve for the Greek economy (*Source* IMF [2019] and author's own calculations and creation)

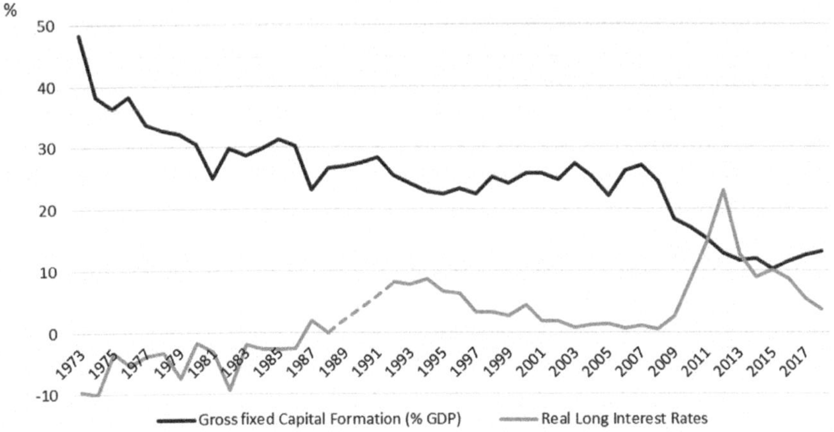

Fig. 12.12 Gross fixed capital formation* (% GDP) and real long-term interest rates (deflator GDP) (*Source* European Commission [2020b], The World Bank [2019a]*, and author's own creation

The high levels of unemployment that followed the debt crisis in the Greek economy are in a de-escalation phase without having reached pre-crisis levels (Fig. 12.13).

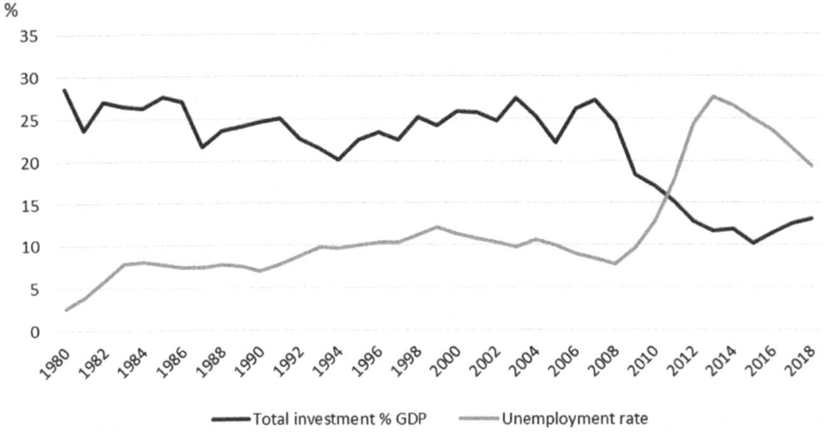

Fig. 12.13 Unemployment rate and total investments (*Source* IMF [2019] and author's own creation)

However, the decline in unemployment was not accompanied by a similar rate of economic growth and higher investment. But if we look at what is happening with the working age population and labor-augmenting technological progress, it is possible to relate them to the reduction of potential output. The workforce has been growing steadily for many decades until the 2000s. But then there has been a decline in the working age population (Fig. 12.14), and since 2008 the brain drain has been estimated at 425,000 people.

Productivity follows a similar trend as it declines after 2008, following years of steady growth, with signs of recovery after 2016. Thus, it has returned to levels seen in the 1970s.

Businesses, for their part, reduced investments to prevent a sharp fall or to stabilize return on capital (Fig. 12.15). This is obvious if we take into consideration the relationship between the real rate of returns and private investment business (Fig. 12.16).

Private investments, without housing, i.e., the productive investments of the Greek economy, seem to be synchronized with the evolution of real returns. In particular, we note that in the period 2007–2013, the reduction in returns was combined with a disproportionately high reduction in investment. Subsequently, the slightly upward trend in returns was followed by an increase in investment.

At the same time, the capital accumulation, beyond the reduction in return on capital, is also responsible for high capital consumption, as companies are called upon to invest in maintaining the functionality of existing investments. Consequently, there is no increase in net investment, but an increase in gross investment due to high depreciation (Fig. 12.17).

In summary, the output gap of the Greek economy, while it seems like it is declining, remains at a high level, with the main determining factors being reduced potential output, working age population, and labor-augmenting technological progress, contributing to the brain drain and associated with low population expansion. At the same time, the output gap is affected by low active demand, as the ten-year recession has left deep signs which are not covered by exports.

Essentially, the Greek economy has been declining in recent decades, both in terms of the number of capable people in the workforce and in terms of labor-augmenting technological progress (Fig. 12.18). These two factors, together with the fiscal contraction that followed the policy of internal devaluation, are capable of interpreting low growth rates and weak flight of the Greek economy's potential output after 2008. Under

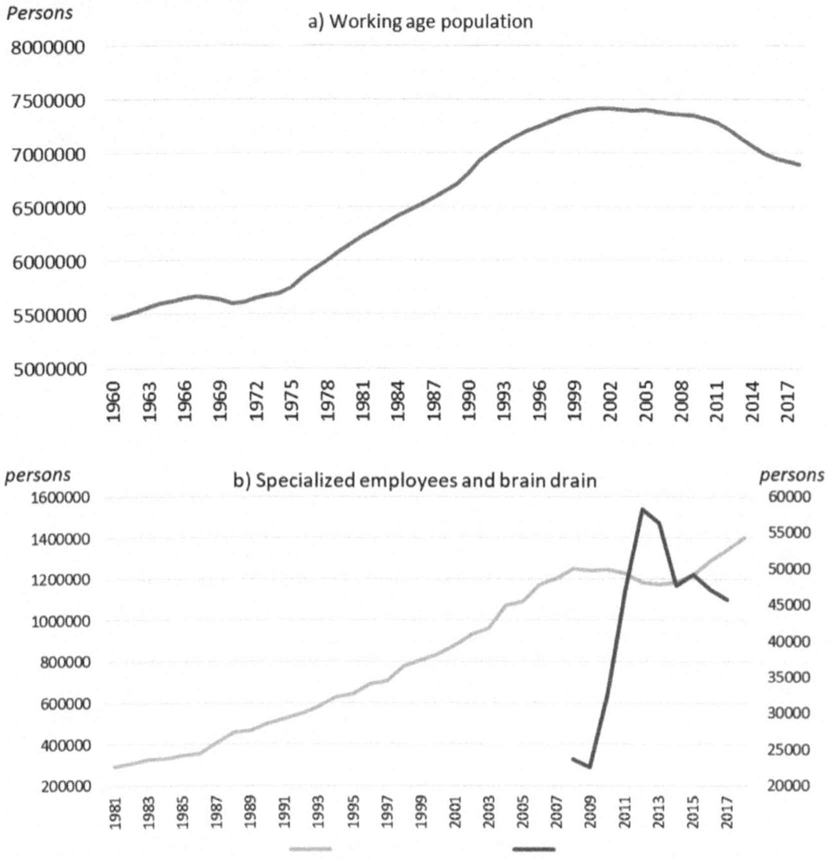

Fig. 12.14 Working age population, specialized employees*, and brain drain** (*Note* Specialized staff consists of the total of all employees that have graduated from tertiary education. The brain drain is an estimate of outgoing immigrants, aged 20–34. *Source* Hellenic Statistical Authority [ELSTAT, 2019b*, 2019c**], The World Bank [2019b], and author's own creation)

these circumstances, it is clear that policies that release supply-side factors are expected to play a stable role in recovery along with demand policies that will shrink the output gap.

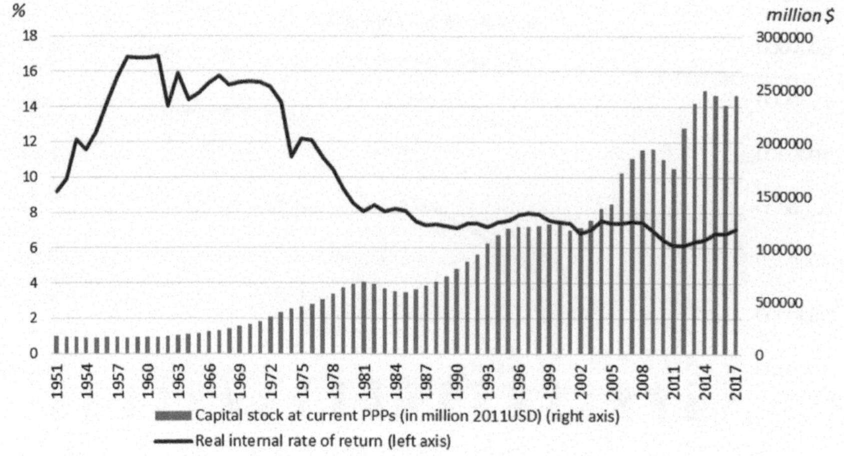

Fig. 12.15 Rate of return on capital and capital stock in the Greek economy (1950–2017) (*Note* Rate of return on capital is based on the variable "real interest rate of return on capital" [IRR]. Capital stock provide the accumulation of capital for 4 assets structures [including residential and non-residential], machinery [including computers, communication equipment and other machinery]. *Source* Feenstra, Inklaa, and Timmer [2015] and author's own creation)

Fig. 12.16 Rate of return on capital and private investments* in the Greek economy (*Note* Rate of return on capital is based on the variable "real interest rate of return on capital" [IRR]. *Source* Feenstra et al. [2015], Oxford Economics [2019], and author's own creation)

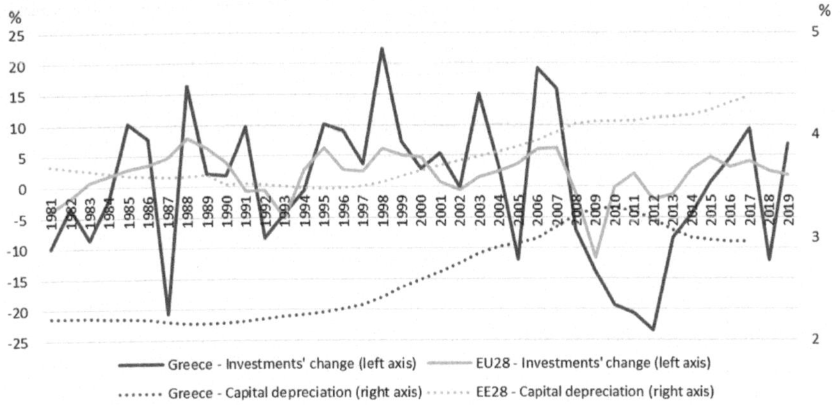

Fig. 12.17 Annual change in investment and rate of capital depreciation: 1981–2019 (*Source* Feenstra et al. [2015] and author's own creation)

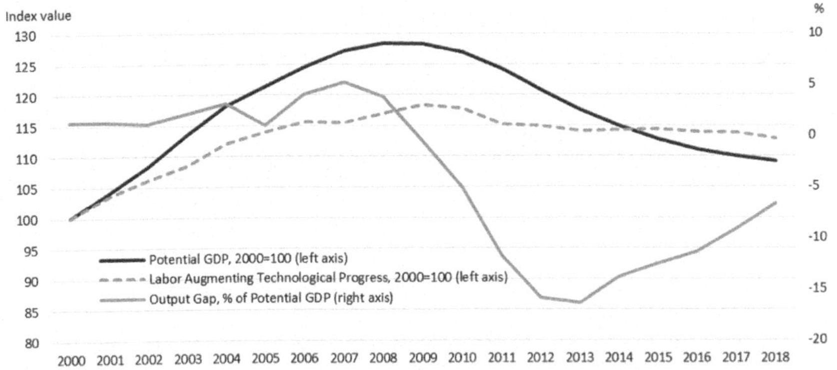

Fig. 12.18 Output gap, potential output, and labor augmenting technological progress* (*Note* Labor Augmenting Technological Progress is determined by the active population [15–64 years old] and the UN's Education Index. Potential gross domestic product at 2015 reference levels [euro]. Gap between actual and potential gross domestic product at 2015 reference levels [percentage of potential GDP]. *Source* European Commission [2020b], Statistical Office of the European Communities [2020]*, United Nations [UN] Development Programme [2020]*, and author's own calculations)

Note

1. According to Summers (2013), we may well need, in the years ahead, to think about how we manage an economy in which the zero nominal interest rate is a chronic and systemic inhibitor of economic activity holding our economies back below their potential.

References

Akerlof, G. A. (2013). The Cat in the Tree and Further Observations: Rethinking Macroeconomic Policy. *International Monetary Fund* (IMF Blog). Retrieved from: https://blogs.imf.org/2013/05/01/the-cat-in-the-tree-and-further-observations-rethinking-macroeconomic-policy/.

Bakker, B. B. (2019). *What Happens if Central Banks Misdiagnose a Slowdown in Potential Output* (IMF Working Paper No. 19/208).

Bank of Greece. (2012). *Report on the Recapitalisation and Restructuring of the Greek Banking Sector*. Retrieved from: https://www.bankofgreece.gr/Publications/Report_on_the_recapitalisation_and_restructuring.pdf.

Bank of Greece. (2019). *Statistics: Financial Accounts*. Retrieved from https://www.bankofgreece.gr/en/statistics/financial-accounts.

Barro, R. (1974). Are Government Bonds Net Wealth? *Journal of Political Economy, 82*(6), 1095–1117.

Blanchard, O. (2019). Public Debt and Low Interest Rates. *American Economic Review, 109*(4), 1197–1229. https://doi.org/10.1257/aer.109.4.1197.

Blanchard, O., Furceri, D., & Pescatori, A. (2014). A Prolonged Period of Low Real Interest Rates? In C. Teulings & R. Baldwin (Eds), *Secular Stagnation: Facts, Causes, and Cures* (A VoxEU.org eBook, pp. 101–110). London: Centre for Economic Policy Research.

Blanchard, O., & Summers, L. (1986). Hysteresis and the European Unemployment Problem. *NBER Macroeconomics Annual, 1*, 15–90.

Board of Governors of the Federal Reserve System. (2020). *Monetary Policy: Credit and Liquidity Programs and the Balance Sheet*. Retrieved from: https://www.federalreserve.gov/monetarypolicy/bst_recenttrends.htm.

Chodorow-Reich, G., Karabarbounis, L., & Kekre, R. (2019). *The Macroeconomics of the Greek Depression* (NBER Working Paper No. w25900).

Draghi, M. (2012). Verbatim of the Remarks Made by Mario Draghi: Speech by Mario Draghi, President of the European Central Bank at the Global Investment Conference in London 26 July 2012. *European Central Bank*. Retrieved from: https://www.ecb.europa.eu/press/key/date/2012/html/sp120726.en.html.

Eggertsson, G. B., Mehrotra, N. R., Singh S. R., & Summers, L. H. (2016). *A Contagious Malady? Open Economy Dimensions of Secular Stagnation* (NBER Working Papers No. 22299).

Eggertsson, G. B., & Woodford, M. (2003). The Zero Bound on Interest Rates and Optimal Monetary Policy. *Brookings Papers on Economic Activity, 34*(1), 139–235.

European Central Bank (2020). *Annual Consolidated Balance Sheet of the Eurosystem*. Retrieved from https://www.ecb.europa.eu/pub/annual/balance/html/index.en.html.

European Commission. (2020a). European Economic Forecast: Spring 2020. *Economic and Financial Affairs Institutional Paper No. 125*. Retrieved from: https://ec.europa.eu/info/publications/economic-and-financial-affairs-publications_en.

European Commission. (2020b). *AMECO Database* [online]. Retrieved from: https://ec.europa.eu/economy_finance/ameco/user/serie/SelectSerie.cfm.

Feenstra, R. C., Inklaa, R., &. Timmer M. P. (2015). The Next Generation of the Penn World Table. *American Economic Review*, *105*(10), 3150 – 3182. Retrieved from: at www.ggdc.net/pwt.

Gerlach, S., & Lewis, J. (2011). *ECB Reaction Functions and the Crisis of 2008* (CEPR Discussion Paper No. DP8472).

Giavazzi, F., & Giovannini, A. (2010). *Central Banks and the Financial System* (NBER Working Paper No. 16228).

Hellenic Republic Ministry of Finance. (2019). *Financial Data: Public Debt Bulletins*. Retrieved from: https://www.minfin.gr/web/guest/oikonomika-stoicheia.

Hellenic Statistical Authority. (2019a). *Statistics: Labour Force (Quarterly data)/2nd Quarter 2019, Unemployed persons 15 + (Age Groups, Duration of Unemployment, Sex)*. Retrieved from: https://www.statistics.gr/en/statistics/-/publication/SJO01/2019-Q2.

Hellenic Statistical Authority. (2019b). *Statistics: Labour Force Survey Yearly Time Series Since 1981/2018* (Labour Force Survey—Employed [1981–2018]). Retrieved from: https://www.statistics.gr/en/statistics/-/publication/SJO03/.

Hellenic Statistical Authority. (2019c). *Statistics: Migration flows/2018, Estimated Emigration by Sex, and Age Group (2008–2018)*. Retrieved from: https://www.statistics.gr/en/statistics/-/publication/SPO15/.

International Monetary Fund. (2019). *World Economic Outlook Database*: October 2019 Edition.

International Monetary Fund. (2020, April). *Fiscal Monitor Dataset*. Retrieved from: https://www.imf.org/external/datamapper/datasets.

Invsting.com. (2020). *Government Bonds*. Retrieving from: https://www.investing.com/.

Ioannides, Y. M., & Pissarides, C. (2015). Is the Greek Crisis One of Supply or Demand? *Brookings Papers on Economic Activity, 46*(2(Fall)), 349–373.

Irons, J., & Bivens, J. (2010). *Government Debt and Economic Growth*. Economic Policy Institute (Briefing Paper No. 271 (1–9)).

Krugman, P. (2011). Nobody Understands Debt. *The New York Times*. Retrieved from: https://www.nytimes.com/2012/01/02/opinion/krugman-nobody-understands-debt.html.

Krugman, P. (2013). Reinhart-Rogoff, Continued. *The New York Times*. Retrieved from: https://krugman.blogs.nytimes.com/2013/04/16/reinhart-rogoff-continued/?mtrref=www.google.com&gwh=B58C278A03752FA1A8BB99EAB712A1C8&gwt=pay&assetType=REGIWALL.

Krugman, P. (2014). Four Observations on Secular Stagnation. In C. Teulings & R. Baldwin (Eds.), *Secular Stagnation: Facts, Causes, and Cures* (A VoxEU.org eBook, pp. 61–68). London: Centre for Economic Policy Research.

Oxford Economics. (2019). *Oxford Economics Global Macro Model*.

Oxford Economics. (2020). *Oxford Economics Global Macro Model.*

Rachel, L., & Summers, L. (2019). On Falling Neutral Real Rates, Fiscal Policy, and the Risk of Secular Stagnation. *Brookings Papers on Economic Activity* (Spring 2019 Edition).

Reinhart, C. M., & Rogoff, K. S. (2010). Growth in a Time of Debt. *American Economic Review, 100*(2), 573–578. https://doi.org/10.1257/aer.100.2.573.

Rogoff, K. S. (2015). World's Economics Slowdown is a Hangover Not a Coma. *Financial Times*. Retrieve from: https://www.ft.com/content/c49e80c4-6d08-11e5-8171-ba1968cf791a.

Skidelsky, R. (2010). *Keynes: A Very Short Introduction*. Oxford: Oxford University Press.

Statistical Office of the European Communities. (2019a). *Eurostat: Job Vacancy Statistics by NACE Rev. 2 Activity—Quarterly Data* (from 2001 onwards) [jvs_q_nace2].

Statistical Office of the European Communities. (2019b). *Unemployment by Sex and Age—Quarterly Average* [une_rt_q].

Statistical Office of the European Communities (2020). *Eurostat: Employment and Activity by Sex and Age—Annual Data* [lfsi_emp_a].

Summers, L. (2013). *Speech at the IMF 14th Annual Research Conference.* IMF Economic Forum: Policy Responses to Crises. Retrieved from: http://larrysummers.com/imf-fourteenth-annual-research-conference-in-honor-of-stanley-fischer/.

Summers, L (2014). Reflections on the "New Secular Stagnation Hypothesis". In C. Teulings & R. Baldwin (Eds.), *Secular Stagnation: Facts, Causes, and*

Cures (A VoxEU.org eBook, pp. 27–38). London: Centre for Economic Policy Research.

Summers, L. (2017). Secular Stagnation Even Truer Today, Larry Summers Says. *The Wall Street Journal*. Retrieved from: https://blogs.wsj.com/economics/2017/05/25/secular-stagnation-even-truer-today-larry-summers-says/.

Teulings, C., & Baldwin, R. (2014). Introduction. In C. Teulings & R. Baldwin (Eds.), *Secular Stagnation: Facts, Causes, and Cures* (A VoxEU.org eBook, pp. 1–23). London: Centre for Economic Policy Research.

The World Bank. (2019a). *The World Bank Data* [ID: NE.GDI.FTOT.KN].

The World Bank. (2019b). *The World Bank Data* [ID: SP.POP.1564.TO].

The World Bank. (2020). *The World Bank Data* [ID: FB.AST.NPER.ZS].

Wolff, G. W. (2014). Monetary Policy cannot Solve Secular Stagnation Alone. In C. Teulings & R. Baldwin (Eds.), *Secular Stagnation: Facts, Causes, and Cures* (A VoxEU.org eBook, pp. 143–150). London: Centre for Economic Policy Research.

CHAPTER 13

The Vulnerability of the Greek Economy and the Recovery Requirements After Covid-19

13.1 Introduction

This chapter concludes the third part of the book where the emergence of Covid-19 crisis is analyzed. Based on the deep and rapid nature of the pandemic's impact on the economy, with accelerating and strengthening features of existing trends, a strong recessionary environment was created dominating 2020 with the weaknesses of the Greek economy deepening the recession.

The chapter addresses the main issues related to Covid-19 crisis and contains key short to medium-term forecasts reflecting the impact on the Greek economy.

Briefly, the channels diffusing the effects on the Greek economy (Sect. 13.2), the developments in the world economy (Sect. 13.3), the epidemiological and economic policy dealing with the crisis (Sect. 13.4), the vulnerability of the economy to Covid-19 (Sect. 13.5), and the evolution of the epidemiological and economic curve in Greece (Sect. 13.6) are described.

Section 13.7 presents the main forecasts for the Greek economy in Eurozone, including a Debt Sustainability Analysis, while in Sect. 13.8 the recovery requirements by 2030 are shown. Finally, in Sect. 13.9 the main points of the political economy in the Greek economy after Covid-19 are commented on.

P. E. Petrakis, *The New Political Economy of Greece up to 2030*,
The Political Economy of Greek Growth up to 2030,
https://doi.org/10.1007/978-3-030-47075-3_13

13.2 The Diffusion Channels of the Economic Impact

Covid-19's effects can be felt through four main channels: supply, demand, uncertainty, and international financial markets.

One way in which the virus harms the economy is to stop the supply of labor, goods, and services. People get sick, schools close, and parents stop working, staying home to take care of their children. Thus, quarantine can force people to work from home or even entire factories to suspend operations. Strict social distancing measures introduced in China and Italy exacerbated this effect through the supply channel.

Restrictions on people's movements create a negative shock on labor supply (in essence, they create an increase in unemployment). It is estimated that these conditions will last for at least one or two quarters in China as well as in other countries with large outbreaks (Italy, Germany, France, and Spain) depending on the conditions that arise.

An additional channel transmitting coronavirus's effects in the Greek economy is the disruption in global value chains. Although the participation of Greek companies in global value chains is still limited, the reduction, or even cessation in some cases, of the disposal of intermediate and capital goods is estimated to have negative effects on their production capacity. Additionally, the production of goods and particularly services may be adversely affected by the extended absence of workers from their duties as part of precautionary measures to prevent coronavirus spread.

On the demand side, people generally buy fewer goods, while also changing their consumer behavior, postponing the purchase of specific goods (such as durable goods) and immediately minimizing the consumption of others (such as restaurants). As a result, travel and transport also decline, while public health measures further restrict economic activity.

An important channel is the decline in external demand for Greek goods and services, due to the reduction in world trade and the deterioration of international economic climate. In fact, the effects on shipping will probably be particularly negative, where revenue momentum is mainly determined by the evolution of fares, largely reflecting fluctuations in world trade.

It is estimated, however, that the impact on travel revenues will be greater, given travel restrictions imposed and the general climate of vulnerability in the tourism industry.

Apart from external demand, the spread of coronavirus is expected to affect domestic demand as well. Private consumption is expected to decline due to deteriorating consumer confidence, precautionary measures to prevent the spread of coronavirus, and the pressure on disposable household income resulting from declining economic activity in general.

In particular, it is estimated that the sectors of transport, trade, catering, and services related to tourism, arts, entertainment, and leisure will suffer the most. Also, the rise in uncertainty and the deterioration of investment environment are expected to deter new investment plans and business risks.

Enterprises are subject to higher risks due to weak cumulative demand and the pandemic creates adverse effects. Uncertainty is likely to remain and fuel the slowdown in productivity growth with the delayed investment decisions of enterprises.

Finally, another important transmission channel is the deterioration in international and domestic financial conditions. In particular, rising uncertainty is fueling major turmoil in international financial markets, worsening the financing conditions of economies, and leading to a re-examination of investment positions around the world, with potentially negative consequences for ongoing investment plans and liquidity in the Greek economy generally. Additionally, the increase in financing costs due to the revaluation of risks internationally leads to a deterioration in terms and costs of raising new funding for banks, businesses, and households, as well as the Greek government.

In conclusion, the Greek economy is expected to be affected by declines in: exports, travel and shipping revenues, consumer and business confidence, international oil prices, production and employment due to precautionary measures taken to limit the spread of coronavirus.

13.3 Developments in the World Economy (May 2020)

Both in European and global level, the initial effects of Covid-19 on economies were determined by the type and severity of the social distance measures taken to safeguard public health, in combination with the individual economic policies implemented by national governments to address the economic crisis caused by the pandemic. Further consequences will be determined by pandemic's development scenarios and the structural economic vulnerability of each country to Covid-19, which widely varies. In Europe, the Eurozone's southern economies are more vulnerable to Covid-19 crisis, as they have less political and fiscal space, in comparison with economies in the north. This reinforces the need for coordinated European economic policy.

Within a short period of time, economic activity in most countries was severely hurt, showing the magnitude of the economic shock from Covid-19, while initial negative forecasts on the macroeconomic data of economies for 2020 were dramatically revised due to the rapid spread of the virus and continue to be revised downward as clarity emerges on the first quarter of the year.

Global economic data generally show large and broad shrinking economic activity for the first and second quarters of 2020, with global gross domestic product (GDP) estimated to fall by more than 3%. This decline is almost equal to the global downturn seen during the 2008 financial crisis (global GDP in 2009 fell by 1.1%). This was mainly due to the change in economic behavior of individuals; the change (reduction) in domestic expenditure by households was much higher than GDP change—despite the spill over effects on global economy from the health crisis in China. Most worrying, however, is the fact that most economies implemented lockdowns around mid-March, while the restrictive measures were gradually tightened until April, indicating a deterioration of the global recession in the second quarter.

As expected from the spread of Covid-19, China's economy experienced a major recession in the first quarter of 2020 (Fig. 13.1), with GDP contracting by 6.8% compared to the corresponding quarter of 2019 (13.3% points difference compared to the 2019 Q1 growth rate). At the same time, however, growth in Chinese economy is expected to recover in the second quarter of 2020, in contrast to economies in Europe (Fig. 13.1) and United States, where the recession due to the time lag of virus spread is seen continuing into the second quarter and be deeper—in Eurozone GDP decline in the second quarter of 2020 is expected to reach 13.9% (15.15 points difference compared to the 2019 Q1 growth rate).

Although economic growth rates in the second semester of 2020 are generally expected, at a global level, to recover and forecasts for countries' annual GDP in 2020 deviate significantly (Consensus Forecasts, 2020), a deep recession for 2020 in all economies is inevitable, driven by plunging consumption and investment, with developed economies expected to be

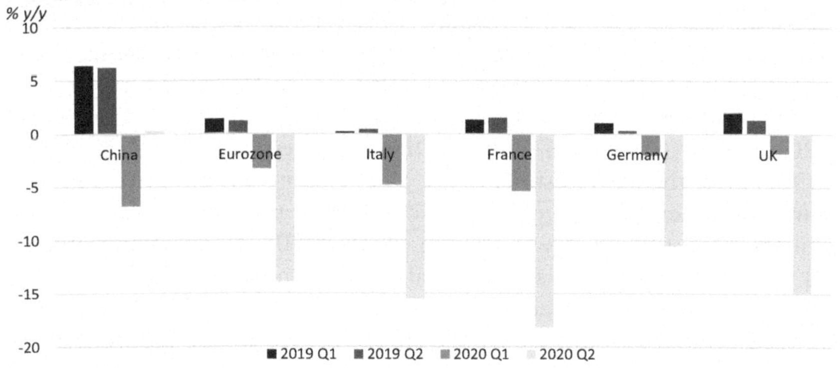

Fig. 13.1 Real GDP Growth in the first half of 2020 (Q1 and Q2, y/y percentage change) (*Note* The data for 2020 Q2 are forecasts. *Source* Oxford Economics [2020a] and author's own calculations)

hurt more. In global economy, the recession is expected to be −4.8%, when in 2019 the increase in global GDP was 2.5%. At the same time, however, significant recovery is expected worldwide in 2021.

Consequently, global trade is estimated (World Trade Organization [WTO], 2020) to fall between 13% (optimistic scenario) and 32% (pessimistic scenario) in 2020 (more than the Great Recession), reflecting the extent of damage to value chains but also the fact that, in general, changes in trade levels are more volatile than GDP growth globally, although both figures tend to move in the same direction. At the same time, inflation is globally projected (Oxford Economics, 2020a) to fall to 2.6% in 2020 from 3.2% in 2019, but in Eurozone and United States it will be stagnant (0.1% and 0.2%, respectively). The magnitude of the shock in demand dominates rising prices due to the shutdown of the supply chain to such an extent that inflation has become negative this year. Its levels were, even prior to the Covid-19 era, under the targets of most economies, but falling commodity prices are also driving down inflation expectations.

High debt and rising service costs are making it more difficult to pursue anti-cyclical fiscal policies. During the first wave of Covid-19, many governments could borrow at historically low-cost levels, while low interest rates in core developed economies are expected to continue after lockdowns' removal. On the contrary, borrowing costs have risen sharply for many emerging economies (International Monetary Fund [IMF],

2020) amid the pandemic, making them more vulnerable. Another common factor in all economies is the significant increase in fiscal deficits and public debt (as a percentage of GDP), due to the need for increased public spending, resulting in an expected increase in global debt (IMF, 2020) to 96% (in terms of global GDP) compared with 83.3% in 2019.

Of course, the above estimates are a basic approach on how economic figures may develop based on the conditions that have been formed until the time this book was written (May 2020). Control, monitoring and detection of the virus and social distance measures are preventing a major second wave, keeping new cases at manageable levels, thus allowing production and consumption to recover in the second half of 2020. At an economic policy level, governments and central banks will continue to support economies to the extent necessary by mitigating the short-term effects of Covid-19; this mainly requires that monetary policy will continue to finance fiscal needs of state, preventing anti-inflationary pressure, while at a political level, the basic scenario translates into international cooperation, and not international competition, to tackle the health and economic crisis.

However, uncertainty about the existence and magnitude of a possible second wave (or more) of Covid-19, the scale of restrictive measures, political developments and progress on pharmaceutical and medical research can change the existing prospects.

In a pessimistic scenario, the discovery of a vaccine would take longer time than expected, while other major waves of the pandemic is going to emerge after the early termination of the first lockdowns, allowing for transmission of the virus from country to country and seriously undermining trust among consumers, businesses, and markets. Such a development would completely change the figures of countries' economies.

Another danger exists in economic policy being unable to cope with the demands of the recession and pressure from increased debt levels among states, developments that would be worsened by the impossibility of international cooperation. Especially at the regional level of Eurozone, a combination of the above would put pressure on the European Union (EU) structure.

On the contrary, the optimistic scenario would include the effective treatment of the virus by health systems and competent bodies (minimizing contagion of the virus) at the beginning of the third quarter of 2020 and a treatment being found before 2021, while the fiscal measures to strengthen economic activity would further expand, helping offset the recession in 2020 and leading to a strong recovery in 2021.

13.4 The Greek Economy's Epidemiological and Economic Policy in Covid-19 Crisis

Globally, the management of the Covid-19 crisis has developed into a trade-off between the operating of economies and the value of human life. Some leaders gave more weight to the former, rather than the latter. In Greece, a choice was made to protect society, in the second option. This proved to be an excellent policy as the other choice (of favoring the functioning of the economy) had seriously back fired effects, causing nearly the speedy collapse of economies, along with considerable social pain associated with the choice of not protecting human life (elderly [Sweden]).

The political choice therefore made in the case of Greece was based on two points. The choice between the value of human life and the operating of the economy (where the former was chosen) and the choice of gradual development, as a response from economic policy. Thus, there was no one-off response program in the broader picture of the problem, but a wait-and-see attitude was adopted, which implied the formation of economic policy in parts.

The gradual development of economic policy as a defence was at first preferable, for a number of reasons:

- Until the start of April 2020, there was a low amount of epidemiological and economic information, making it difficult to see the immediate future. So, we knew very little about epidemiological characteristics (behaviors, drugs, tests, etc.). As time goes by there is more complete information, allowing an exit road map to be drawn from restrictive social policies.
- There were not enough analyzes on the cost of the "sudden stop" of economies, given that this was almost surprisingly implemented for epidemiological reasons.
- There was no clear the international, and particularly the European, economic reaction to the crisis, but at that time only national efforts had taken place.

But as time moves on, all of the above information has accumulated and the choices available are more visible. Therefore, it can be seen that the wait-and-see tactic should be replaced by an approach adopting specific future scenarios, one of which will be the most likely and one of which will be the worst.

If, for any reason, conditions change (extension of closed enterprises, discovery of tests, drugs, vaccines, etc.), the prevailing scenario will be replaced by a better or worse one.

As this is being written, we assume that in the Greek economy (as seen below) the recession will be around −6% and in Eurozone around −5%.[1]

These estimates suggest (critical assumption) that the measure of closing down businesses will last for 6–12 weeks.[2] With this recession and forecasts below, it can be seen that the crisis maintains a manageable nature, allowing for a worse scenario, if required. Certainly, the worst-case scenario will prompt a wider European reaction, that is an important determining factor of national policies.

Epidemiological policies have evolved in Greek society as shown in Fig. 13.2, initially with the first set of government measures and then with the gradual implementation of social distancing measures and the cessation of economic activity (restaurants, shopping malls, shops, hotels).

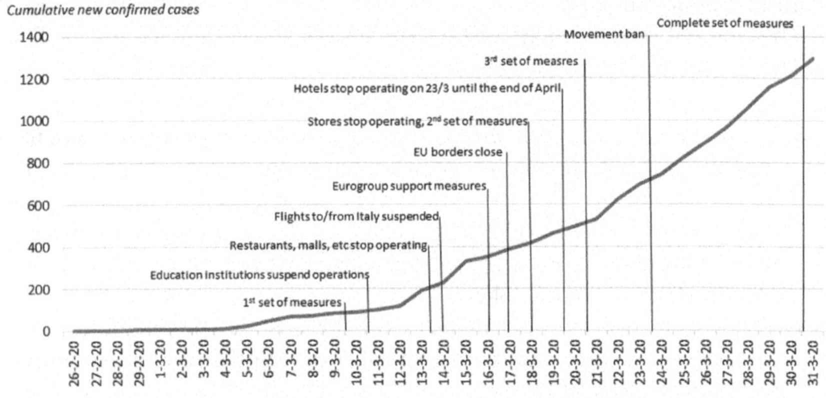

Fig. 13.2 Greek government's actions to reduce the impact of the pandemic in Greece and fiscal measures announced to strengthen businesses and employees (*Source* Our World in Data [2020] and author's own calculations)

The epidemiological policies implemented resulted (see Sect. 13.6 below) in the significant levelling of the epidemiological curve. Then all the economic policies implemented in the Greek economy are presented (IMF, 2020). These are a combination of national and European response measures until early April 2020. The 9th of April 2020 Eurogroup decisions were added to these.

I. Fiscal Policy

The government announced a package of measures totalling 7.5% of GDP (2019) (15 billion euros)[3] financed by national and European resources (and via the redirecting of European resources). The basic measures include: (a) increasing health spending to hire 2000 doctors and nurses; provision of medical supplies and benefit payments to health care employees; (b) transfers to vulnerable individuals, including cash payment by the end of April and full coverage of pensions and health benefits to workers and self-employed professionals hit hard, extension of unemployment benefits by two months, and provision of special leave to parents to care for children and students who are forced to stay away from school; and (c) support the liquidity of businesses that are severely affected through subsidized loans, loan guarantees, interest payments subsidies and deferred tax payments and social security contributions.

II. Monetary and Macro-Financial Measures

European Central Bank (ECB), in addition to initial monetary policy measures taken in March 2020 (see Chapter 3, Sect. 3.7) to support member states' economies, announced around late April 2020 additional long-term refinancing operations to ensure adequate liquidity and smooth money market conditions during the pandemic period.

Thus, after the expansion of the asset purchase program (APP), the implementation of the pandemic emergency purchase programs (PEPP), the expansion of the corporate sector purchase program (CSPP), the easing of collateral for Eurosystem refinancing operations (main refinancing operations [MROs], long-term refinancing operations [LTROs], targeted longer-term refinancing operations [TLTROs]), the temporary easing of fixed interest rate liquidity and more favorable terms for long-term financing of credit institutions (TLTRO-III), ECB decided to carry out a new series of seven more long-term refinancing operations, the pandemic emergency longer-term refinancing operations (PELTROs).

The PELTROs will be conducted as fixed rate tender procedures with full allotment, consisting of a series of non-targeted Pandemic Emergency Longer-Term Refinancing Operations carried out with exceptionally favorable terms, with the interest rate being 25 basis points below the average interest rate applied in Eurosystem's main refinancing operations, during its application. Their goal is to support liquidity in the euro area's financial system and to contribute to the smooth operating of financial markets by providing an effective backstop after the end of the LTROs that were held as of March 2020 and long-term financing of parties.

To mitigate rating downgrades, ECB announced that by 2021 it would exempt the eligibility of marketable assets used as collateral in Eurosystem credit operations falling below current minimum credit quality requirements of "BBB-," as long as their rating remains at or above "BB" and "BB +," while assets falling below the minimum credit quality requirements (below "BB") will be subject to a haircut based on their actual score.

At the same time, major institutions will be able to operate temporarily under the Pillar 2 Guidance, the capital conservation buffer, and the liquidity coverage ratio (LCR), while new rules on the composition of capital meet the Pillar 2 Requirement (P2R) front-loaded to release additional capital.

The ECB also recommended that financial institutions cover losses from non-performing loans backed by public guarantees related to Covid-19 and select IFRS9 transferable rules to avoid procyclical assumptions on foreseeing losses, while seeking that dividends not be paid for the 2019 and 2020 financial years, but instead use the available capital to support households, small businesses, and corporate borrowers.

It is difficult to accurately calculate the liquidity injections provided to the Greek economy by the ECB's decisions. If we accept that there is a participation rate similar to that of the EU budget (1.4%), then we would expect an amount of around 10–12 billion euros in available liquidity. This liquidity may be injected into the private or (most likely) public sector.

III. The Decisions of the April 9, 2020 Eurogroup[4]

The importance of the 9th of April 2020 Eurogroup decisions is fourfold:

- They stabilized within the European reaction framework to Covid-19 crisis, allowing for the stabilization of the entire political functioning of Eurozone and EU.
- In the context of stabilizing Europe's reactionary framework, ECB can implement its decisions in a more stable environment.
- Conditions are created for a second round of large-scale measures with the main feature being the monetization of debt with the ECB's Outright Money Transactions (OMT) and the France-inspired recovery fund.
- They activated (together with the ECB's decisions) the ability of the Greek state to turn to the markets at a sustainable cost (Fig. 13.3). While the spreads of Greek and Italian bonds, versus the yield of the German 10-year bond, peaked on March 18, there was then a de-escalation, with borrowing costs remaining at satisfactory levels.

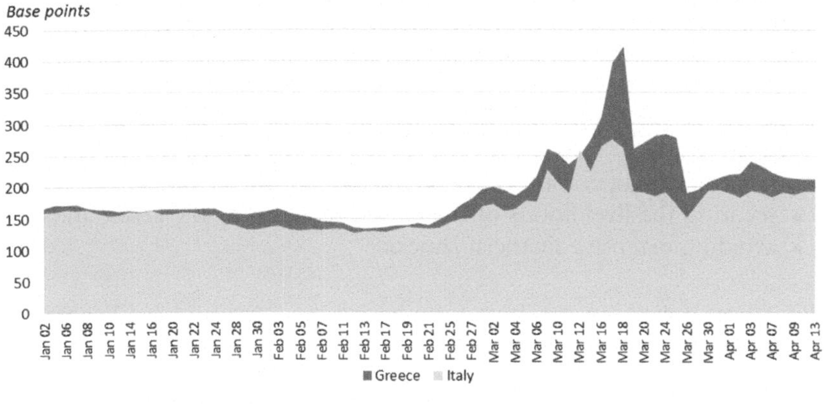

Fig. 13.3 Greek and Italian 10-year bond spreads against German 10-year bonds (January 2020–April 2020, in base points) (*Source* Invsting.com [2020] and author's own calculations and creation)

In assessing the immediate impact of the Eurogroup's decisions on the Greek economy, it is estimated that the benefit could reach 6–7 billion euros. Essentially, via the European Commission's SURE packages, it is estimated that the inflow could amount to around 1.5–2 billion euros.

As far as the European Stability Mechanism (ESM) is concerned, Greece is entitled to 2% of its GDP so it could ask for an amount of 4 billion euros for support. However, the use of the ESM's enhanced conditions credit line (ECCL) by any country bears the stigma of its use and therefore makes it problematic. It is also unlikely that there will be any amounts drawn from the so-called public liquidity buffer.

Finally, the activation of the European Investment Bank's financial program that will be based on guarantees from the European budget creates additional funding opportunities, mainly for small and medium-sized enterprises (SMEs).

The Eurogroup's decisions are not in addition to those described in parts I and II, with the exception of the ECB's TLTRO actions, which create additional liquidity opportunities for banks, the size of which cannot be estimated.

An important question that arises in relation to the economic policy being followed is whether the primary issue of the economy is the fall in total demand or the disruption to the supply of products. It is clear that supply problems were the first to appear in the economic system which were then followed by problems to total demand.

Consequently, policies to be implemented at the mature stage of the crisis must be based on the following three points (IMF, 2020):

- securing the operation of the key sectors of the economy,
- securing the livelihoods of the people affected by the crisis, and
- avoiding extensive financial shocks.

Thus, these policies in the short-term have a monetary and fiscal character and in the medium term a restructuring nature. The difference with 2008 crisis policies lies in the fact that fiscal policy now plays a more serious role as, firstly, monetary policy has been almost exhausted (with the exception of debt monetization) due to approaching zero-lower bound interest rate and, secondly, because fiscal policy can better address supply distortions.

The Merkel-Macron agreement proposing the introduction[5] of a recovery fund to restart the European economy that will include 750 billion euros of aid for member states hurt by the crisis, is a step in this direction.

This amount will be raised from international markets and guaranteed by the EU's seven-year budget and the annual contributions of states. It will be provided in the form of grants under the EU's multi-year financial framework. This will ease the ECB's burden of dealing with the crisis, providing room for a common form of European fiscal policy. It has been proposed that European Commission will be authorized to borrow the money, with resources being directed particularly to heavily affected countries and sectors facing the risk of collapse due to generalized restrictive measures.

For a long time, Germany was wary of providing money as grants that would come from loans as this way European debts would not have to be repaid by the state receiving the funds, but jointly and probably through the European budget or the EU's own revenues The Merkel-Macron agreement is not about the issuance of a corona bond, but of a relative solution to common European lending, and under this plan, the rules of the European budget apply and only programs will be funded and not the state budget of individual member states. An important difference from the corona bonds is that the common risk related to these debts is limited to guarantees member states have provided to the EU budget.

However, this plan is the first step in the mutualization of European debt, in what could be a possible starting point for the establishment of a European fiscal union—an important step toward European integration. With this proposed solution, the foundations for overcoming the pandemic crisis have been laid for Greece (as well as for other regional countries).

13.5 The Vulnerability of the Economy

To examine the vulnerability of the Greek economy, we focus on specific sectors of the economy and mainly sectors that cover the shock to labor supply and production lines, the capacity of health systems, and the production structure.

Then we combine the results of the last column from Table 13.1 (structural pandemic vulnerability score) with Covid-19 related deaths (data from the 25th day of the crisis, i.e., the 9th of April, when this is being written), with April 2020 forecasts for GDP growth in 2020 and with changes in forecasts (April 2020 compared with January 2020). In other words, we look at the projected change in GDP for Greece in

Table 13.1 Oxford economics structural pandemic vulnerability score

	Supply chain exposure	*Share of population*	*Share of hospitality & tourism*	*Share of manufacturing*	*Internet speed*	*Share of self-employed*	*Share of small firms*	*Hospital beds for acute care*	*Total score*
Greece	−0.8	1.4	2.1	−1.2	1.8	3.0	2.3	0.1	1.0
Italy	−0.9	1.7	0.4	0.1	0.9	1.3	1.7	1.0	0.7
Czech Republic	1.7	0.2	−0.6	1.6	1.0	0.1	0.0	−0.4	0.4
Netherlands	1.3	0.0	−0.5	−0.5	−0.5	0.8	−0.3	0.7	0.1
Belgium	2.0	0.0	−0.6	−0.4	0.2	0.4	0.5	−1.2	0.1
Spain	−0.9	0.2	1.5	−0.6	−1.0	−0.4	0.9	1.2	0.1
Hungary	1.7	0.1	−0.5	0.8	−1.0	−1.1	0.3	−0.5	0.0
Austria	−0.1	0.0	1.0	0.6	1.1	−0.4	−0.7	−1.6	0.0
Sweden	−0.8	0.5	−0.7	−0.1	−1.1	−0.7	−0.9	1.5	−0.2
Germany	−0.4	1.2	−0.7	1.1	0.1	−0.8	−1.5	−2.1	−0.4
Denmark	−0.9	0.2	−0.8	−0.3	−1.0	−1.2	n/a	1.1	−0.4
France	−1.0	0.4	−0.2	−0.8	−1.2	−0.6	−0.7	0.6	−0.4

Source Oxford Economics (2020b) and author's own calculations

2020 under normal circumstances— in January 2020—compared with the predicted GDP rate change in 2020 during crisis conditions, April 2020.

From Table 13.2 it can be seen that despite all indicators showing that Greece would be hit hardest by Covid-19, it showed strong resilience. Thus, while it is in first place among 13 countries in the column of the structural pandemic vulnerability score, it is 10th place in terms of deaths from Covid-19 per 10,000 inhabitants on the 25th day of the crisis (i.e., on the 9th of April when this was written), and occupies 2nd place in terms of weakest GDP forecast for 2020 and top position regarding the worsening of the GDP forecast within 2020.

The above leads to the conclusion that, in terms of institutional conditions of health policy and economic policy, the Greek economy's performance was satisfactory. Noted that the better performance of the Greek economy, in comparison with other European countries presented in the table, should be primarily attributed to policies pursued and also to the institutional and cultural organization that existed or developed during the crisis (social discipline, functioning of the NHS, and scientific community, etc.).

13.6 The Epidemiological and Economic Curve in Greece

The aim of the epidemiological measures is to level the curve of cases and minimize the recession related mainly to the lockdown measures.

At this point, we present the flattening of the epidemiologic and recession curves, to get a sense of the relationship between these two policy objectives.

It is very difficult to imagine what the Greek case would look like if epidemiological and economic measures had not been taken, at least in terms of the epidemiological curve, so that we could reproduce Fig. 13.4 on a theoretical basis.

That is why we produced Fig. 13.5 that approaches the logic of Fig. 13.4. At the top graph of Fig. 13.5, there are presented the two epidemiological curves: what could happen "if Greece was Italy" and the second is Greece's actual curve.

For this reason, we assume that Italy's curves are characteristic of the uncontrolled epidemic case, i.e., without public health measures, although this is not accurate. However, delayed health care (political

Table 13.2 Pandemic vulnerability score and GDP growth

		Structural pandemic vulnerability score[a]		*Deaths from Covid-19 per 10,000 inhabitants on the 25th day of the crisis*[b]		*GDP (% change) April 2020 for 2020*		*Difference of predictions April–January 2020*
1	Greece	1	Spain	1.03	Italy	−7.62	Greece	−8.19
2	Italy	0.7	Italy	0.57	Greece	−5.94	Italy	−7.91
3	Czech Rep.	0.4	Netherlands	0.32	Portugal	−5.79	Portugal	−7.13
4	Portugal	0.3	Belgium	0.3	Spain	−5.61	Spain	−6.83
5	Netherlands	0.1	France	0.3	Austria	−5.58	Austria	−6.56
6	Belgium	0.1	UK	0.21	France	−5.32	France	−6.55
7	Spain	0.1	Portugal	0.16	Belgium	−5.31	Belgium	−6.52
8	Hungary	0	Sweden	0.09	UK	−5.12	Hungary	−6.33
9	Austria	0	Austria	0.06	Sweden	−4.70	UK	−6.16
10	UK	−0.2	Greece	0.04	Germany	−3.88	Sweden	−5.94
11	Sweden	−0.2	Hungary	0.04	Netherlands	−3.59	Germany	−5.12
12	Germany	−0.4	Germany	0.04	Hungary	−3.05	Netherlands	−4.92
13	France	−0.4	Czech Rep.	0.02	Czech Rep.	−1.75	Czech Rep.	−2.04

Note The death toll per 10,000 people as estimated on the 25th day of the Covid-19 crisis for each country, with the first day of the crisis being the day with 100 Covid-19 cases per 60 million people. So for Greece, day 1 is March 5, 2020, for Italy it is February 22, for France, Germany, Austria and Spain it is March 3, for the Netherlands and Sweden it is March 4, for Belgium it is March 5, for the United Kingdom March 6, for the Czech Republic March 7, for Portugal March 8, and for Hungary March 13. "GDP (% change) April 2020 for 2020" is the difference between the forecast in April and January when the crisis that has not yet been integrated. The April forecasts taken into account the negative conditions as known in March. They therefore include a large part of the negative effects from Covid-19

Source [a]Our world in data (2020), [b]Oxford Economics (2020b), Oxford Economics (2020c), and author's own calculations

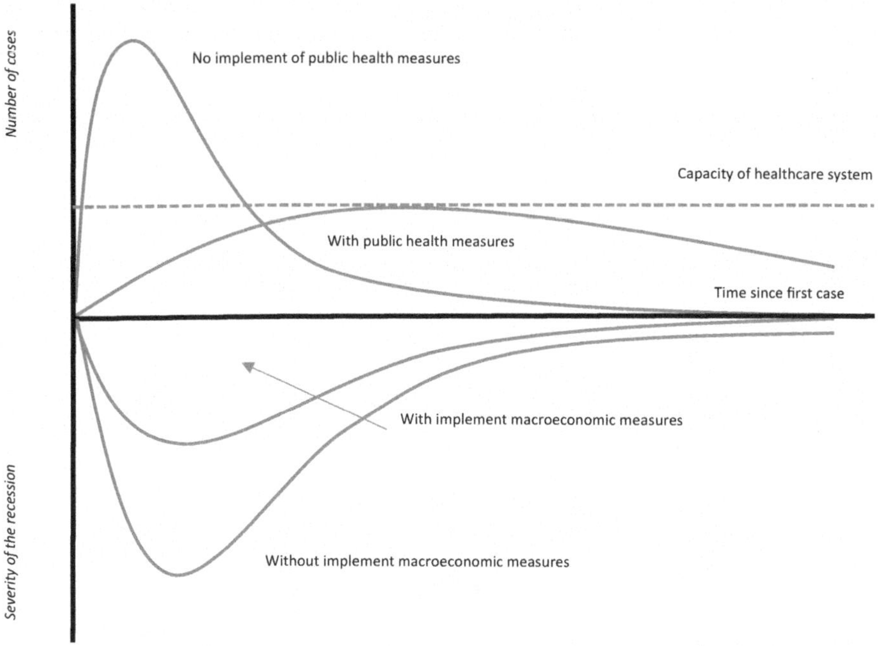

Fig. 13.4 The pandemic and recession curves (*Source* Gourinchas [2020] and author's own creation)

choice?) create a worst-case scenario and this can be compared with any other country case.

While the upper part of Fig. 13.5 is easier to be understood, the lower part needs further explanation. The question we are called upon to answer concerns not so much a projection of the future based on the current situation ("Greece with economic measures" curve) but the economy's state in case economic policy had not been activated to mitigate the effects of the crisis, including the decision to shutdown the economy.[6]

So, what would economic policy in 2020 have been like if it had not been adapted to developments? In other words, if policy "insist and succeed" in increasing state's revenue and did not increase its public expenditures, or if the situation evolved like it did in January 2020.

We get the answer by looking at Fig. 13.5. At the bottom of the chart there are two GDP growth curves. The first one is how Greek

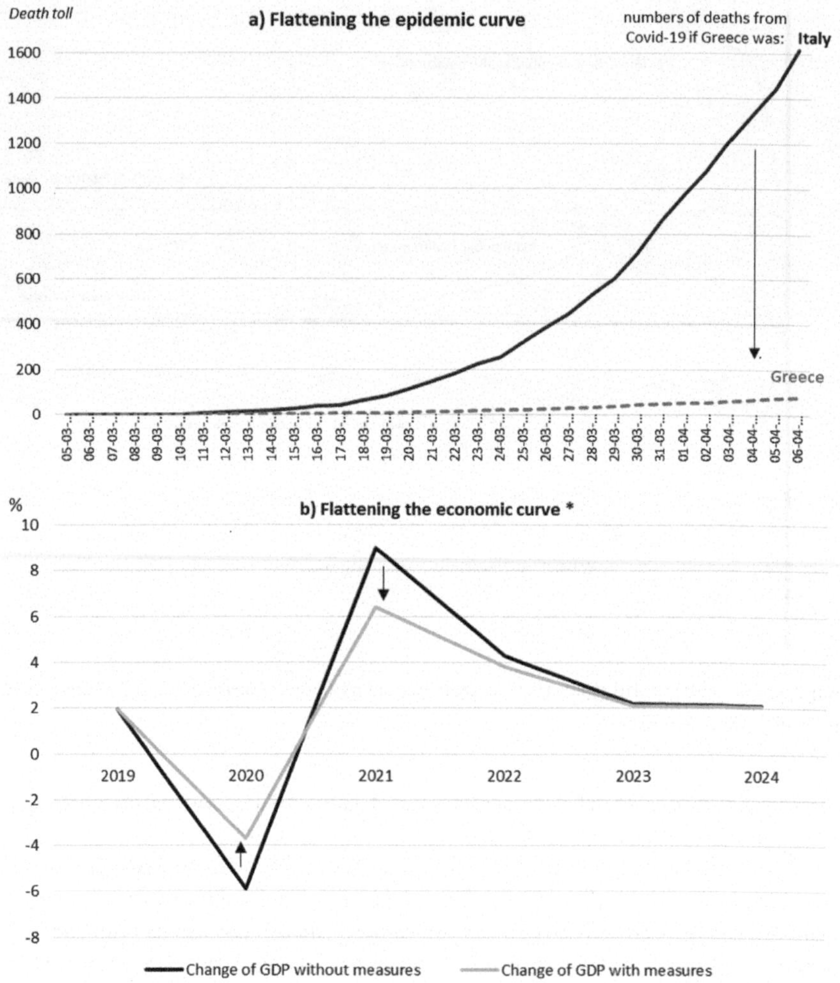

Fig. 13.5 The evolution of Covid-19 in Greece and the effectiveness of measures (*Source* Our World in Data [2020], Oxford Economics [2020c], and author's own creation)

GDP is forecast to evolve after incorporating (a) negatively events triggered (closing down for 6–12 weeks starting as of early March) and (b) the increase in public spending, deficits, and debt due to interventionary macroeconomic measures. The second one contains the first factor (the 6–12 week close down starting from the beginning of March) but not the second factor, as the January 2020 forecasts are used for public expenditures, deficits, and debt; as things would be if new macroeconomic requirements created by the recession had not begun to emerge.

Essentially, we find that both curves "flatten," but the epidemiological one much more.

13.7 Predictions for the Eurozone and Greek Economy

Up until now, while we were at the start of the crisis, we realized that it is very difficult to assess the impact of Covid-19 on the Greek and global economy.

We know with enough uncertainty that a month of closing down the Greek economy (Organisation for Economic Co-operation and Development [OECD], 2020) costs about 35% of annual GDP.

Today we are able to make relatively accurate predictions after having already the experience of March and April 2020, which was a period that fully reflected the negative effects and based on the critical hypothesis that the activity's closure in basic economies will be maintained for 6–12 months.[7]

These predictions (Consensus Economics, 2020) lead to the following picture for the Greek economy (Table 13.3).

Consensus Forecasts predicts a recession of −7.9% for Greece in 2020. We are adopting here a slightly smaller recession for the Greek economy

Table 13.3 Forecasts for the Greek economy

	2016	*2017*	*2018*	*2019*	*2020*	*2021*
Gross Domestic Product (% change on previous year)	−0.2	1.5	1.9	1.9	−7.6	5.3
Industrial production (% change on previous year)	2.6	3.9	1.6	−0.6	−8.1	4.9
Consumer prices (% change on previous year)	−0.8	1.1	0.6	0.3	−0.4	0.6
Current account (Bn USD)	−3.4	−3.8	−6.2	−2.9	−6.1	−5.7

Note Nominal GDP, USD 2018. Forecasts have been made in May, 2020
Source Consensus Economics (2020) and author's own calculations

(−6%), because the model we use comes from the partnership of National and Kapodistrian University of Athens (NKUA) with Oxford Economics (April 2020) and this is the exact recession rate given by the relevant model. For Eurozone, the model predicts a recession of −5%.

These estimates are comparable to what the largest companies predict, with the GDP change rate in 2020 for the Eurozone to the order of –7.9%. In comparing Oxford Economics' forecast with the other projections, the forecast we follow is at 60–80% of the Consensus Economics mean.

13.8 The Recovery Requirements up to 2030

As this book was written in May 2020, we were already in the midst of the Covid-19 financial crisis and we had already realized how serious it would be but it was difficult to get an accurate picture of the extent of the crisis.

The IMF in its spring report in April 2020 came out with some forecasts on the depth of the recession, which in some cases were surprisingly bad. More particularly for the world, it predicted a recession of 3% as its base line scenario, for Eurozone –7.5 and –10% for the Greek economy.

We here accept the assessment of Oxford Economics at the end of April 2020, which foresees a global recession of –3%, –5% for Eurozone, and –6% for the Greek economy as its base line scenario.

The Covid-19 recession, when compared to previous recessions, has one particularly important feature. It mainly reflects the economies' lockdown due to the social distancing policies since the most important assumed factor forecasts number of weeks the economy will remain closed. In this sense, most of the recession will be concentrated in the first half of 2020 for most of the world economies, including Greece.

Of course, there are many concerns relating to the concept of lockdown, how extensive it can be, and so on. Therefore, forecasts, even if they have an agreed technical horizon, can differ significantly from each other.

However, in the case of Covid-19, there is a special feature regarding the recession. They are only referred to as predictions. In fact, they incorporate the recession that has already been caused by the lockdown. Forecasts of economic activity are of particular value when they are able to assess how future economic activity will evolve and not when they are assessing the damage that has already been done. This is especially

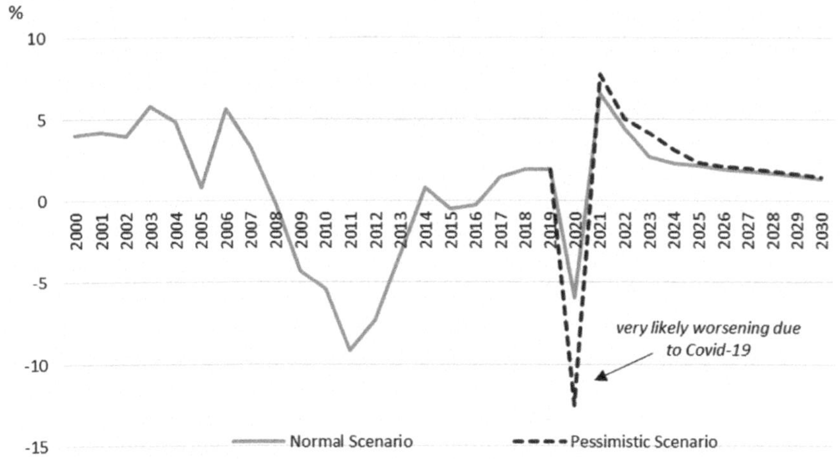

Fig. 13.6 Real GDP Growth: 2000–2030 (*Source* Oxford Economics [2020c] and author's own calculations)

true when most of the expected recession comes from lockdown. This is essentially the difference between an endogenous and exogenous black swan-type crisis.

Of course, previous losses leave significant marks on the economy that produces losses in the near future (public revenues, bankruptcies, etc.). Particularly on the Greek economy, when there was a similar recession in 2011, we knew that this was because a large part of the production network had been destroyed, such as business activity related to the public sector, construction, etc. Now the same is not the case as a significant part of economic activity has been instructed to close down.

Figure 13.6 shows the annual change in GDP growth rate at real prices in the Greek economy. The reduction of 6% is a very big recession, which of course for Greece, is being compared with that of 2011.

There are respective developments in debt growth, while the current account balance (as a percentage of GDP) is at a much better level than in 2011 (Fig. 13.7). However, due to the short-term and exogenous nature of the crisis the impact on other figures is not in line with that seen in 2011 despite the very large decline in GDP for 2020.

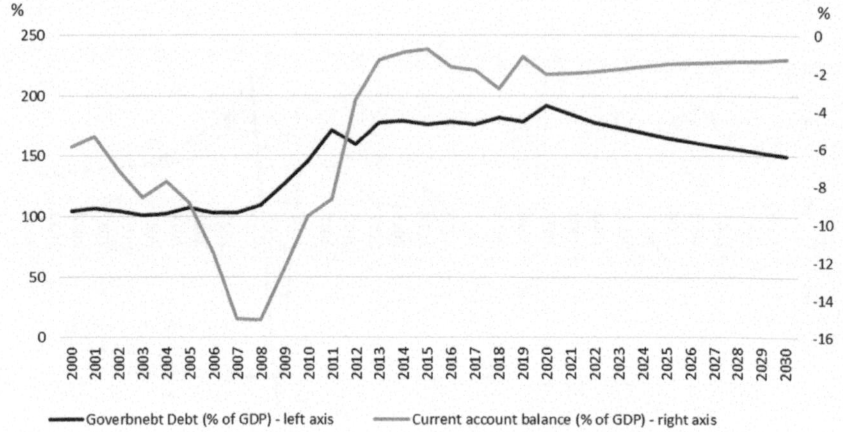

Fig. 13.7 Government debt and current account balance as a percentage of GDP: 2000–2030 (*Source* Oxford Economics [2020c] and author's own calculations)

The interesting thing is that in the next year GDP will increase significantly, while debt and unemployment appear to be significantly reduced. Developments in unemployment and investment are shown in Fig. 13.8.

At the same time, in analyzing the changes in the impact of GDP determinants, it can be seen that the main declining effects primarily come from consumer spending which is reduced by 7.7 billion euros in 2020 and, secondarily, by a decrease in investments in 2020 by 0.7 billion euros. Only government consumption saves the day in 2020 (Fig. 13.9).

The implementation of an economic recovery program after Covid-19 can be carried out in two phases: In the first, which will cover the two years 2020–2021, the main emphasis will be on policies to address supply problems and demand enhancement, and consequently to reduce the enlarged production gap, while the second period (2022–2030) will be a period of implementing a broader program of structural changes, expansion, and diversification of supply opportunities.

These structural changes should be focused on changing the economy's productive prototype, as the fact that the production focuses on only a few sectors (tourism, shipping, agriculture) makes the economy particularly vulnerable to external shocks. Also, a critical element of the implementation of the structural change program is to focus simultaneously

Fig. 13.8 Investments in real prices (bn euros) and unemployment rate: 2000–2030 (*Source* Oxford Economics [2020c] and author's own calculations)

on five factors: sustainable development, sustainable governance, inclusive growth, social behavior friendly toward development, and dynamic growth.

It is noted that this will create favorable conditions for the implementation of a development structural program, even if there are epidemiological disturbances (however, assuming of lesser importance). This point is particularly emphasized because the implementation of structural change programs is greatly facilitated particularly when it is based on a strong recovery of demand and growth as expected after the end of epidemiological phenomena.

It is also emphasized that the experience of implementing and economic restructuring for ten years, along with the coordinated social response of citizens on the effects of the crisis, have created a favorable background for social behavior, allowing for the stable and systematic implementation of a structural change program that will include decisions on productive reconstruction and institutional effectiveness.

After all, the messages gathered about the recessionary need to transform the economy are now very difficult to ignore by both society and political power. Thus, two scenarios for the Greek economy can be specified until 2030.

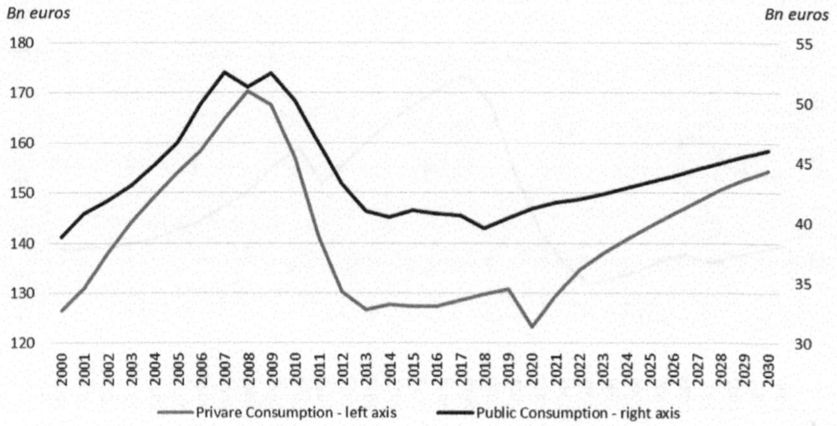

Fig. 13.9 Private and government consumption (bn euros): 2000–2030 (*Source* Oxford Economics [2020c] and author's own calculations)

The Normal Scenario which includes the developments on the recession from Covid-19 and the Optimal Scenario which incorporates the conditions of an economic recovery. The Optimal Scenario differs from the Normal (Crisis) Scenario because:

- It includes additional fiscal interventions for 2020–2021 amounting to 3 billion euros (in addition to those that have already been integrated into the normal scenario).
- It includes the impact on GDP of a comprehensive structural intervention program that takes place from 2021 onwards. This program specifically affects total factor productivity (TFP), which in turn affects GDP growth and a series of key economic variables. This analysis, which examines how TFP is affected in order to influence GDP growth, is the subject of the next book in the series entitled *The Evolution of the Greek Economy: Past Challenges and Future Approaches* (Petrakis & Kostis, in press).

Figure 13.10 compares the Normal (Crisis) Scenario (Crisis Model) with the Optimal Scenario (Optimal Model).

The difference between the potential and the actual product produced is the reason that the exit gap for the Greek economy has been negative

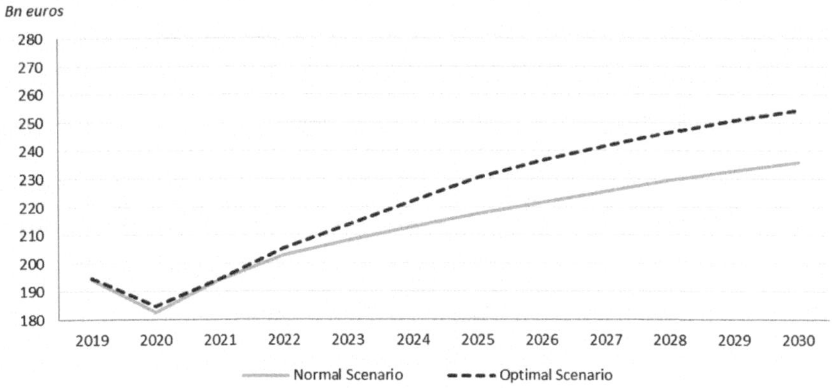

Fig. 13.10 Development of real GDP in Normal and Optimal Scenario (bn euros) (*Source* Oxford Economics [2020c] and author's own calculations)

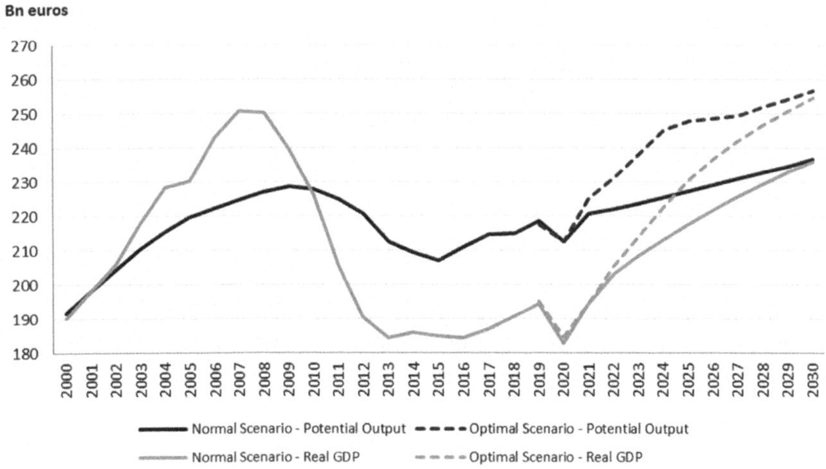

Fig. 13.11 GDP and potential output (bn euros) (*Source* Oxford Economics [2020c] and author's own calculations)

since the beginning of the 2008 crisis and is expected to remain negative (Fig. 13.11). Additionally, the level of the output gap is crucial for determining inflationary pressures in the economy. A large negative output gap suggests inflation should be low. It is a situation where monetary policy

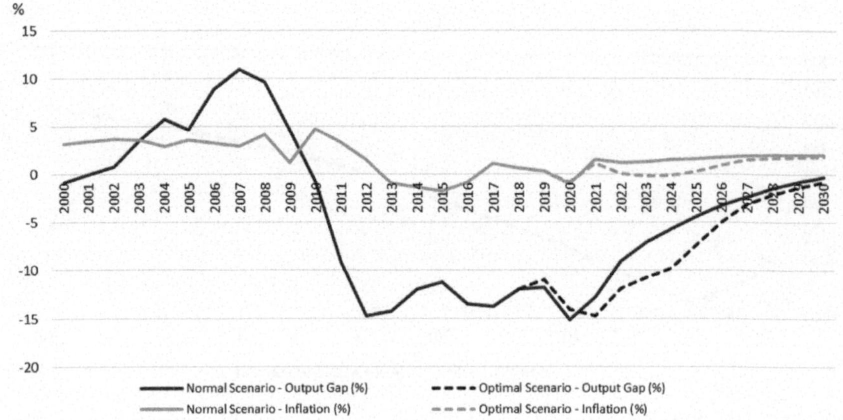

Fig. 13.12 Output gap and inflation (*Source* Oxford Economics [2020c] and author's own calculations)

will be lax (low interest rates to stimulate growth and reduce negative output gap). A positive output gap, where growth is above the trend rate of growth, should lead to inflationary pressures (Figs. 13.12 and 13.13).

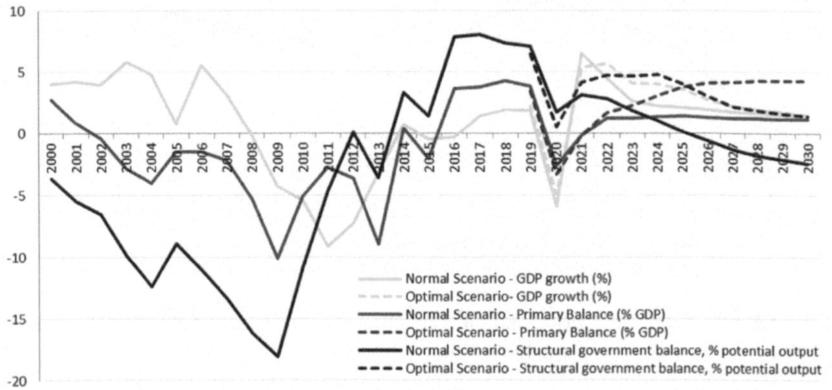

Fig. 13.13 GDP growth rate, primary balance, and structural balance for Greece (*Source* Oxford Economics [2020c] and author's own calculations)

After Covid-19, a risk to the sustainability of Greek debt will appear, if debt sustainability assessments are held with 2020 and 2021 data and pessimistic medium-term forecasts on development and primary surpluses.

Of course, due to the peculiarities of the debt structure, the real risk of debt sustainability is very small, given that the bonds traded on the international market (50–60 billion euros) should be taken into account and not the total debt!

In general, however, as the growth rate of a country is less than the funding cost, there is a question of sustainability and fiscal discipline. That is why (a) it is imperative to increase the growth rate and (b) it is useful to consider the proposal of debt forgiveness.

To examine debt sustainability, two criteria are used that correspond to two different approaches without, of course, changing the essence of the issue:

- Sustainability criterion is the debt to GDP ratio taking into account the rate of growth of nominal GDP, primary balance, and financing cost within the same criterion. Usually this is a multidisciplinary methodology used by rating agencies.
- Sustainability criterion based on 1.5% in financing needs in relation to GDP.

Table 13.4 shows the level of debt as a percentage of GDP and the level of gross financing needs (GFNs) based on the IMF's (2019) Article IV Consultation in November 2019 and Normal and Optimal Scenario (which include the appearance and effects of the Covid-19 pandemic) until 2028.

Debt sustainability check with 2020 data is based on the following assumptions (Table 13.5):

- debt to GDP ratio at 189.6%,
- financing costs at 2.5%, and
- medium—to long-term nominal growth 1.5%.[8]

Under these conditions (2.5% funding cost) a primary balance of more than 2% is required to start reducing the debt to GDP ratio. Depending on the scenario used, different conclusions can be drawn. That is why it is imperative to implement a scenario that will give high (nominal) growth rates.

Table 13.4 Debt and gross financial needs in IMF and the normal and optimal scenario

	IMF		*Normal*		*Optimal*	
	Debt % GDP	*GFN % GDP*	*Debt % GDP*	*GFN % GDP*	*Debt % GDP*	*GFN % GDP*
2020	171.4	5.8	189.6	12.0	190.7	12.8
2021	166.3	5.6	182.3	9.4	186.0	9.6
2022	161.0	6.5	175.2	9.0	179.1	8.8
2023	155.6	6.6	170.1	9.2	174.1	8.4
2024	152.0	6.9	165.8	9.5	168.2	7.9
2025	150.0	8.5	162.1	11.2	161.9	8.8
2026	148.1	8.9	158.6	11.7	155.7	8.7
2027	146.5	7.7	155.5	10.6	149.5	7.1
2028	145.1	10.1	152.6	13.1	143.5	9.1

Source IMF (2019), Oxford Economics (2020c) and author's own calculations

Table 13.5 Multi-criteria debt sustainability analysis: the Greek case

Public debt ratio of 189.6% of GDP (2020) and a cost of 2.5%

Nominal GDP growth (%Y)

Primary balance growth (%GDP)	0.0	0.5	1.0	1.5	2.0	2.5	3.0	3.5	4.0
3.0	1.7	0.6	-0.5	-1.5	-2.6	-3.6	-4.6	-5.6	-6.5
2.5	2.2	1.1	0.0	-1.0	-2.1	-3.1	-4.1	-5.1	-6.0
2.0	2.7	1.6	0.5	-0.5	-1.6	-2.6	-3.6	-4.6	-5.5
1.5	3.2	2.1	1.0	0.0	-1.1	-2.1	-3.1	-4.1	-5.0
1.0	3.7	2.6	1.5	0.5	-0.6	-1.6	-2.6	-3.6	-4.5
0.5	4.2	3.1	2.0	1.0	-0.1	-1.1	-2.1	-3.1	-4.0
0.0	4.7	3.6	2.5	1.5	0.4	-0.6	-1.6	-2.6	-3.5
-0.5	5.2	4.1	3.0	2.0	0.9	-0.1	-1.1	-2.1	-3.0
-1.0	5.7	4.6	3.5	2.5	1.4	0.4	-0.6	-1.6	-2.5
-1.5	6.2	5.1	4.0	3.0	1.9	0.9	-0.1	-1.1	-2.0
-2.0	6.7	5.6	4.5	3.5	2.4	1.4	0.4	-0.6	-1.5
-2.5	7.2	6.1	5.0	4.0	2.9	1.9	0.9	-0.1	-1.0
-3.0	7.7	6.6	5.5	4.5	3.4	2.4	1.4	0.4	-0.5

Note The calculations are based on the following formula: $\Delta bt = (it - gt1 + gt)bt - 1 - pbt + ddat$ (eq. 1). Equation 1 (the typical debt accumulation equation) provides a simple accounting framework to decompose the change in the government gross debt-to-GDP ratio ($\Delta bt \Delta bt$) into its key drivers, consisting of: (i) the "snowball effect", i.e. the impact of the difference between the average nominal interest rate charged on government debt (it) and the nominal GDP growth rate (gt) multiplied by the debt-to-GDP ratio in the previous period (bt − 1); (ii) the primary budget balance (surplus) ratio (pbt); and (iii) the deficit-debt adjustment as a share of GDP (ddat) or the stock-flow adjustment, comprising factors that affect debt but are not included in the budget balance (such as acquisitions or sales of financial assets).

Source Oxford Economics (2020c) and author's own calculations

A debt sustainability check with 2020 data is based on the following assumptions:

- debt to GDP ratio of 189.6%,
- financing costs at 2.5%, and
- medium—to long-term nominal growth 4%.

Under these conditions, debt is sustainable (in both scenarios) as a primary balance from −3 to 3% of GDP results in a decrease in the debt to GDP ratio.

The lower the funding cost and the higher the nominal rate of growth, the higher the debt feasibility and therefore the sustainability of growth as the degree of freedom on economic policy increases.

A second sustainability criterion is usually used, that GFNs, in the medium term (until 2030), should not exceed, 15% of GDP (3rd Economic Adjustment Program [EAP] and the European Semester [ES]).

Figure 13.14 shows the evolution of GFN (as a percentage of GDP) in combination with the 15% threshold.

Based on the second sustainability criterion, for all scenarios, the debt is characterized as being sustainable as GFN are below the 15%[9] threshold.

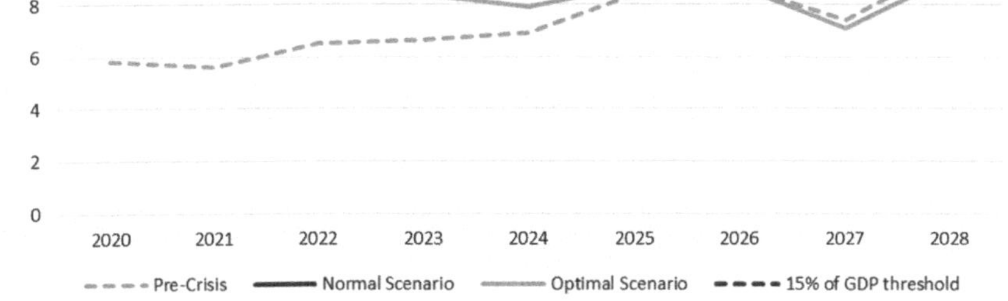

Fig. 13.14 Gross Financing Needs (%GDP) and the threshold of 15% (*Source* Oxford Economics [2020c] and author's own calculations)

However, it should be noted that since funds available to the economy are to the order of 36.6 billion euros, based on the relevant presentation by the Ministry of Finance in Parliament on April 24, 2020,[10] the cash buffer combined with the primary surpluses, seem to be enough just to cover the GFNs that are being created at some stage in the year.

Thus, for the pre-crisis scenario, GFNs could be funded by the cash buffer and the primary results until 2024 as from 2020 to 2024 in total GFNs were expected to be in the range of 65.8 billion euros while the cash buffer combined with the primary surpluses to the order of 66.4 billion euros.

However, the effects of the Covid-19 pandemic have caused significant problems resulting in both the Normal and the Optimal Scenario, the cash buffer, combined with the fact that a primary deficit is expected for 2020 and 2021, is not enough to fund GFN after 2020.

Table 13.6 presents the course of GFN and the government primary surplus for these three scenarios. The pre-crisis scenario (based on the end of April 2020 estimates) and the Optimal Scenario. Figure 13.15 depicts this.

Table 13.6 Gross financing needs and government primary surplus (bn euros)

	Pro-crisis		*Normal*		*Optimal*	
	GFN	*Government Primary surplus*	*GFN*	*Government Primary surplus*	*GFN*	*Government Primary surplus*
2020	11.6	6.8	22.1	−5.5	23.4	−5.9
2021	11.4	6.2	18.3	−1.4	18.6	−0.2
2022	13.6	6.2	18.5	1.6	17.8	3.4
2023	14,2	5.7	19.7	2.2	17.5	4.7
2024	15.0	4.9	21.1	2.6	16.8	6.6
2025	18.6	4.5	25.8	2.8	19.1	8.4
2026	19.6	4.3	27.8	2.7	19.2	9.4
2027	17.0	4.3	25.6	2.6	16.0	10.0
2028	22.3	4.4	32.4	2.7	20.8	10.5

Note It should be noted that the government primary surplus, as calculated here, is not identical to the Enchained Surveillance criterion which also contains certain data (e.g. privatizations, etc.)
Source IMF (2019), Oxford Economics (2020c), and author's own calculations

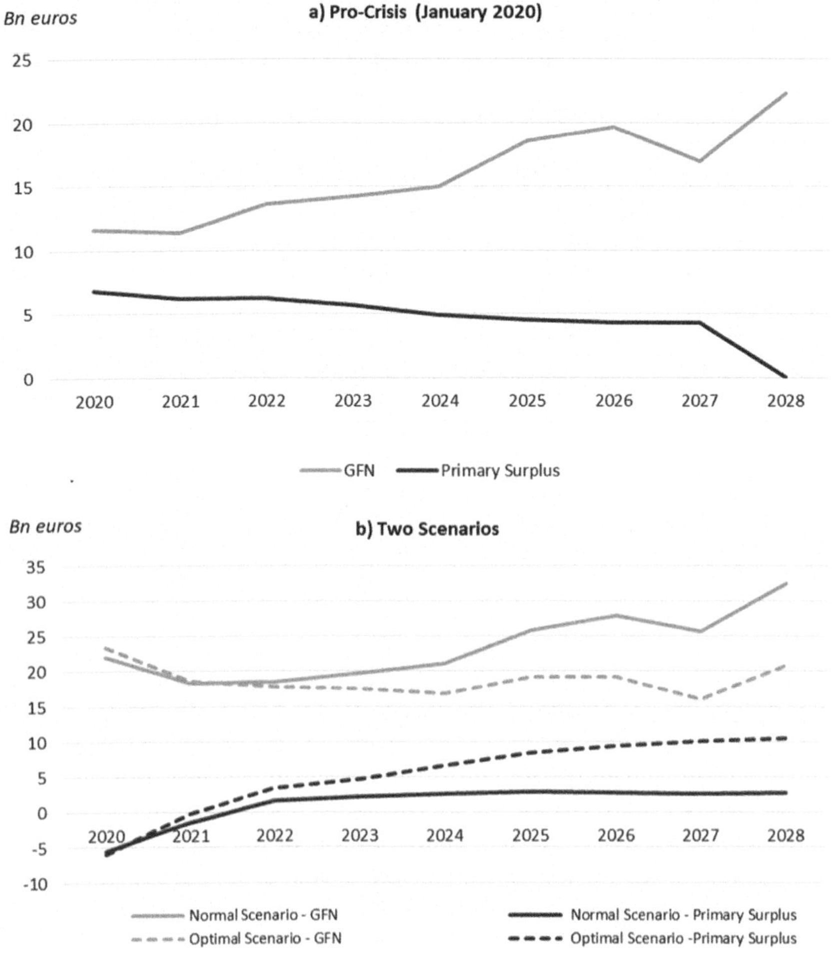

Fig. 13.15 Primary Surplus and Gross Financing Needs (bn euros) (*Note* Gross Financing Needs [GFN] is derived from the Debt Sustainability Analysis presented in the IMF's [2019] Article IV Consultation of November 2019 and has been adapted to three scenarios based on the development of debt in each of them. *Source* IMF [2019], Oxford Economics [2020c], and author's own calculations)

13.9 The Political Economy in Greece After Covid-19

From the previous analysis it can be seen that Covid-19 brings about significant changes to the ideological and theoretical level of economic policy management, which can be summarized in the strengthened role of fiscal policy. This can be done through deficient fiscal management and higher debt to the point where their sharp increase is acceptable, raising issues of mass monetization of debt and risk sharing in terms of state unity, but also at a global level between economically strong and weak countries, bringing to the surface issues of forgiveness of debt.

In the monetary and financial sector, the risk of financial imbalance at corporate and national levels is emerging. Here the similarities in reports are more pronounced than in 2008, which requires a higher information load.

However, what has become quite clear is that the production model of the Greek economy involves a high level of systemic risk, mainly due to the high participation of one sector, tourism, in producing GDP and other labor-intensive sectors or industries that are particularly affected by rising uncertainty, such as real estate management. A consequent problem is the high participation of SMEs (which, based on international standards, are very small businesses) and the performance of the economy. On the positive side is the fact that the Greek economy has a small degree of integration in the international production system, has displayed a high-quality epidemiological policy and disciplined social behavior.

The severity of the Covid-19 crisis thus leads economic policy to unprecedented areas (e.g., high monetization of debt). These areas can very easily be occupied by political forces that often do not recognize the cost of their proposals. This is because we will be in policy-making areas where the cost of capital will not be as important as a criterion for selecting and allocating resources, as it will be zero or close to zero. Therefore, their distribution priorities can be changed and keep doing so in an almost anarchic way. Consequently, the concept of taking careful strides in shaping economic policy will be deemed as having less value than it does today, as it will be easy to make big steps in the short-term.

But because today the epidemiological and economic crisis is very serious and the answers to economic policy in Japan, the United States, and Europe include—and have already included, for example, monetization of debt and mutualization—the collection of huge sums of capital

as a defense, there are elements of "changing examples" in the economic and social system.

The "paradigm shift" leads to "whatever it takes for the European and the Greek Economy" and consequently to "going big for the recovery."

In the current crisis, there are two levels and two fronts, each of which is confronted by politics. One field consists of expectations and the other reality. In each of them there are the health and economy fronts.

The Covid-19 crisis has affected the Greek economy and society in all six areas studied in this book as the "New Political Economy of Greece." Specifically, it has affected foreign economies and political relations, sustainable development, sustainable governance, inclusivity, pro-growth behaviour of the population, and, of course, above all, as we have already commented, the dynamism of the Greek economy.

In external economic relations, it took steps in strengthening Greece's objective relationship with the Eurozone, as it provided more or less effectively a safety net. At the same time, it weakened the economic strength of the Turkish economy (a geostrategic factor and an important Greek trading partner) but it remains unknown whether this will work for or against foreign relations with the country. It is certain, however, that it reduced the value of the south eastern Mediterranean's energy reserves and consequently weakened a serious source of tension with Turkey.

In the area of sustainable development, it is obvious that it created increasing pressures on poverty after depriving workers of income and negatively affecting the health of the population in terms of this disease, because at the same time there is a reduction in other serious diseases, etc. The educational systems of countries were negatively affected, creating negative images in the memory of children at a younger age, mainly due to the change in their daily life and removal from the structured educational processes. At the same time, however, it has had a positive but violent effect on the introduction of distance learning methodologies at all levels.

Industry and infrastructure have undergone major changes, mainly due to the introduction of digital activities and remote work.

Two areas also seem to be significantly affected: climate change, which should have been significantly affected by declining economic activity, and justice procedures, which have been significantly affected, mainly leading to the forgiveness of minor offenses.

There have been more complex effects on the area of sustainable governance in Greece for two main reasons: the first is that the relatively successful management of the epidemiological crisis corresponded to highly organized management mechanisms, which led to the introduction of a series of digital administrative innovations (automatically issuing birth certificates, sending certificates to homes, etc.) that upgraded their level. The second is related to the fact that the political leadership has shown rapid reflexes in dealing with the crisis, increasing the country's political and administrative resilience by improving governance sustainability.

Another serious crisis in ten years was a very serious problem in the issue of inclusivity. The ones mainly affected could only be the middle class again, a fact that boost income and wealth inequality indicators in the Greek economy. Remote work is not a situation that favors less skilled workers and Greece has a high employment rate in this category, further burdening income inequality.

However, pressures on income inequality are not only increased by recessionary pressures. On an international level, recessionary pressures will create issues of an unequal distribution of productive power and wealth, as some countries will be able to better support their production than others, mainly due to differences in fiscal space available. This will lead to explosions in social unrest and questions about the legitimacy of governments. It will also change the relevant position in international competition rankings, worsening, based on these criteria, the special position of employees in less favored economies, such as Greece. This will further aggravate the domestic situation.

At the same time, however, the redefining of public resources in favor of public health systems will stimulate the health situation of the population in the medium to long term. As conditions of poverty have been found to be the most vulnerable in pandemic conditions, tackling them seems to have higher support than in the past. Vulnerable parts of the population, such as immigrants, refugees, and minorities, can easily become epidemic targets and this can have consequences for the entire population.

People's behaviors are of particular importance to the growth process. Concepts such as trust, uncertainty, and savings behavior are significantly affected in times of crisis. Of course, these behaviors have picked up significantly, mainly during financial crises (which last and have a long duration period for treatment) and much less after epidemiological crises, which are theoretically short-term. At the same time, around the world, and especially in the Greek economy, there has been an extraordinary accumulation of instructions from the central government and team of experts in charge, which has been used as a sign of confidence in making rational decisions and implementing social discipline. Both characteristics were not at their highest point of acceptance until recently in the Greek economy. An effective and successful social experience respecting specific goals can have long-term consequences on pro-growth social behaviors.

Returning to the field of dynamic growth, we note that in the Greek economy, but also around the world, Covid-19 acquired a role of accelerator and enhancer of developments and trends that already existed in economies, while it did not acquire at least one role (while this book was written) of being a game changer in terms of prevailing examples in the economy.

In essence, if we ignore the acute epidemiological phase of the 2020 crisis internationally, the estimated medium—to long-term effects of Covid-19 are summed up by the fact that they accelerated the emergence of a long-awaited recession, enhancing the characteristics of the economy, that is low development rates, high debts and deficits, low inflation, reduced investment and low interest rates, but adding higher unemployment, something that existed in the Greek economy anyway.

An area where Covid-19 may turn into a game changer relates to economic policy being followed. It will obviously boost policy on debt monetization and risk sharing in Europe far more than what was the case prior to the Covid-19 crisis.

The two situations preceded the Covid-19 crisis. Both the European Financial Stability Fund (EFSF) and the European Commission had issued bonds to strengthen national governments during the 2008 crisis, and Draghi had developed the OMT program to support "whatever it takes," but the use of these tools was limited (Blanchard & Pisani-Ferry, 2020). Covid-19 will change the intensity that the eurozone uses monetization and adopts risk sharing.

When the crisis was in its infancy, a question that arose was whether the outbreak posed a matter of superiority in the way some social systems handle large crises in comparison to others (China vs Western liberal democracies). There is the impression that the nature of China's actions allows for a more effective responses to major crises, such as the Covid-19 pandemic. Obviously, this position has a high degree of truth in it, but it soon became clear that experiences from previous similar crises (SARS) played a major role in China. Moreover, many Western liberal democracies (Germany, Greece, etc.) proved to react in a satisfactory fashion. At the same time, the Covid-19 crisis gave leaders, who were already leaning toward autocracy, a chance to boost powers (e.g., V. Orban in Hungary and J. Kaczynski in Poland) that were supposedly necessary in effectively tackling the pandemic. However, it seems that an excessive concentration of power and violation of democratic freedoms are not necessarily linked to effective treatment, although there is a need around the world, as in all major crises, to strengthen the structures of executive power.

But then concerns entered deeper political fields. The question, then, is whether liberalism of confidence in market efficiency has been dealt a decisive blow since everyone's eyes turned to the land of the last resort, which was the state and the central banks.

In this sense, political forces in liberal democracies gather around the center will strengthen, since traditionally they have much better relations with the regulatory role of the state. In fact, it seemed that populist political regimes (such as Italy, the United States, and Great Britain) showed a characteristic inability to control the phenomenon. However, non-populist regimes, such as France and Switzerland, were also unable to respond in an effective manner.

It is certain that a pandemic is beyond the operation of markets that cannot manage it. Moreover, the theoretical infrastructures based on the ideology of market supremacy allow for the existence of the state's regulatory factor in the presence of Hobbes' Leviathan.

Consequently, the question of "how much and where the state" is not posed anew by Covid-19. It existed before and will always exist. What appears to be a new dimension, however, is an emphasis on supporting health systems. Let's not forget that deaths from Covid-19 are not caused by the virus itself, but by the combination of its presence, along with the absence of medical facilities.

So, what is it that shapes the reactions of political systems to the crisis? It is too early to have similar answers, while research in political science will help us in the future.

Now, however, it is certain that the timely mobility of experts and their good cooperation with policy are key to a satisfactory response. Experts include epidemiologists and doctors of all specialties, economists, communications experts, etc. It is also a given that from the moment the crisis hits, there is an initial focus on leadership and then later policy concerning crisis management develop.

However, the effects of the crisis trigger changes in social behavior, which are important and noteworthy. We knew that this occurs from other crises of the past (1929, 2008, etc.). Children living in these crisis conditions adopt more permanent attitudes and behaviors, especially after the closure of educational systems.

At the same time, it is certain that higher uncertainty levels to the point where "we do not know what we don't know" has a profound effect on all aspects of economic activity, mainly on consumption, savings, and investment.

The question, however, is whether and to what extent damages is done or whether there is a mild boost in confidence to the institutional framework in which the economy and society operate.

If a society successfully copes with the crisis then it will come out of it with a much better chance of implementing policies with social costs for the broader community, or to groups of it. This brings it closer to the possibility of implementing structural policies, a possibility that newer societies normally have. If the need to tackle the pandemic leads to very large horizontal programs aimed at improving overall demand, then again, conditions to implement reform programs are created, as it is known that under austerity conditions, they are less likely to succeed.

At the same time, communities that experience the fortunate management of a similar crisis with the help of the scientific community seem to increase their confidence in research and expertise of experts.

The opposite is true in societies that experience the failed management of the crisis. They become much more vulnerable to the spread of random ill-intentioned news, creating representations of injustice, racial and nationalist segregation, illusions of national isolation, etc. In practice, this means that they support political forces that ignore the cost that burden future generations, something which is politically easy.

A crisis of this dimension may, however, affect much deeper attitudes, as is the case of Inglehart's "insecurity hypothesis" and the "economic have not hypothesis" (see Chapter 4, Sect. 4.6).

We know very well that in the 2008 crisis, where societies were particularly affected, the feeling of insecurity increased and led to social behaviors being driven by pressure to improve people's finances, leaving behind post materialistic concerns.

If the current economic crisis maintains its character as being deep-fast-short, it may not reach the point of activating these behavioral issues, as opposed to the 2008 financial crisis which was deep-slow coming and long lasting. But there is now skepticism as to whether the Covid-19 crisis will be short-lived. It is very likely that the 2020 health crisis will create broader turbulence, creating Covid-moment situations (as in Minsky Moments) that are accompanied by financial imbalances.

In the end it is possible that classic "insecurity hypothesis" and "not-have hypothesis" behaviors are activated, if the economic crisis lasts much longer.

In addition, if we live in a world where money has a zero cost (zero interest rates), then social demands are likely to lose their rationality and take on an anarchic formulation. This, however, creates an environment that is much more difficult to control, where policy implementation becomes more difficult. At the same time, however, the forces created by these behaviors remove heavily anchored recipes, which are likely to act as inhibitory variants of development. Political changes, then, can have both positive and negative dimensions.

In concluding, the previous formulation leads to the formation of a perspective with characteristics of the Great Potential Change for Greek society that include the following elements:

- Short-term intervention that is in progress to address the effects of the Covid-19 crisis.
- Changes to the production model that will increase the "risk dispersion of the production standard," reducing the possibility of systemic crises causing steep recessions or, if this is not possible, leading to rapid recovery.
- Broad fiscal intervention that will improve the potential for recovery and will also allow for the better implementation of a strong economic structural package. It should be noted that this point has a pan-European application.
- Political stability which is necessary for the implementation of a long-term development plan and enhanced public administrative supervision to guide a reform plan.
- Maintain social cohesion and improve the possibility of increased participation in development, especially among the middle class.
- Implementation of a broad reforms program that the Greek economy has always needed, emphasizing support to health systems and the existence of distance learning processes.

- Utilization of positive changes to the cultural model of political behavior. Changes that would take decades to occur, creating the conditions for them to be strengthened in a few months.

In concluding, the coexistence in Greece of social discipline and appetite for security and progress of a reformist logic and softening of fiscal and monetary policy, create a positive combination that is unique for the last 200 years of modern Greek state's existence. This opens a rare window of opportunity for the Greek economy.

Notes

1. It is estimated that the final numbers of the recession will be higher than these figures, but the direction of the analysis will be approximately the same.
2. That is why May 15th was chosen as a landmark date for Greece.
3. The measures are not converted into equal financial flows for different reasons.
4. The decisions are taken unanimously.
5. This agreement between the two parties must be approved by all 27 EU member states.
6. It should be noted that this decision is classified with epidemiological decisions, although it certainly has the most serious economic impact.
7. This means that in Greece the economy will open in the first ten days of May. Here it seems that the accuracy of the estimates depends much more on the epidemiological issue rather than the accuracy of the model used.
8. Note that this assessment is very strict.
9. This is confirmed by the relevant conclusion from Eurobank Research titled The Greek Economy in 2020. Impact from the Covid-19 crisis and Outlook.
10. The 15.7 billion euros of these are the last disbursement from the stability mechanism (ESM) toward the economy and from the surpluses of that period (of these 9 billion euros come from installments of the European support mechanism, 3 billion euros from debt issues, and 3.7 billion euros from surpluses). The 10.7 billion euros are available to government agencies in commercial banks and the Bank of Greece (BoG). The 10.2 billion euros relate to the central government's cash reserves.

References

Blanchard, O., & Pisani-Ferry, J. (2020). Monetisation: Do Not Panic. *Vox CEPR Policy Portal*. Retrieved from: https://voxeu.org/article/monetisation-do-not-panic.

Consensus Economics. (2020, May 11). Survey of International Economic Forecasts. *Consensus Forecasts*.

Gourinchas, P. O. (2020). Flattening the Pandemic and Recession Curves. *Vox CEPR Policy Portal*. Retrieved from: https://voxeu.org/article/flattening-pandemic-and-recession-curves.

International Monetary Fund. (2019). Greece: 2019 Article IV Consultation-Press Release, Staff Report, and Statement by the Executive Director for Greece. *IMF Country Report* No. 19/340.

International Monetary Fund. (2020, April). Chapter 1: Policies to Support People During the Covid-19 Pandemic. *IMF Fiscal Monitor*.

Invsting.com. (2020). Government Bonds. Retrieving from: https://www.investing.com/.

OECD. (2020, June 10). *OECD Policy Responses to Coronavirus (COVID-19): Evaluating the Initial Impact of COVID-19 Containment Measures on Economic Activity*.

Our World in Data. (2020). *Data on COVID-19* (*Coronavirus*). Retrieved from: https://github.com/owid/covid-19-data/tree/master/public/data.

Oxford Economics. (2020a, May 6). Coronavirus Watch: A Slow Revival as Restrictions Ease. *Oxford Economics Research Briefing*.

Oxford Economics. (2020b, May). *Research Briefing*.

Oxford Economics. (2020c). *Oxford Economics Global Macro Model*.

Petrakis, P. E., & Kostis P. C. (in press). *The Evolution of the Greek Economy: Past Challenges and Future Approaches*. New York: Palgrave MacMillan.

World Trade Organization. (2020). *Trade Set to Plunge as COVID-19 Pandemic Upends Global Economy* (press release). Retrieved from: https://www.wto.org/english/news_e/pres20_e/pr855_e.htm.

Index

P. E. Petrakis, *The New Political Economy of Greece up to 2030*, The Political Economy of Greek Growth up to 2030,
https://doi.org/10.1007/978-3-030-47075-3

The manufacturer's authorised representative in the EU is Springer Nature Customer Service Centre GmbH, Europaplatz 3, 69115 Heidelberg, Germany. If you have any concerns regarding our products, please contact ProductSafety@springernature.com

Printed and bound by CPI Group (UK) Ltd, Croydon, CR0 4YY
30/09/2026
02225704-0007